The Bible as Story
An Introduction to Biblical Literature

First Edition published by Workplay Publishing, August 2016
Newton, KS 67114
workplaypublishing.com

In cooperation with Hesston College

START HERE, GO EVERYWHERE

Additional research and scholarship by Justin Heinzekehr, PhD

ISBN 978-0-9905545-4-7

Cover design and interior layout by André Swartley
Cover artwork "Supper at Emmaus" (1648) by Rembrandt van Rijn (1606-1669)

PRINTED IN THE UNITED STATES OF AMERICA

Contents

Preface by Marion Bontrager   7

Introduction by Marion Bontrager   9

Part I: The Biblical Story   15

Is the Bible Relevant Today?   17

The Bible as Story   23

Narrative Genre   32

Primeval *Geschichte*   41

Matriarchs and Patriarchs   50

Exodus-Sinai: Liberation   56

Exodus-Sinai: Covenant   67

Wilderness Wanderings   75

Entering Canaan   83

Judges and Tribal Confederacy   92

Toward a United Monarchy   101

The Role of the Prophet   113

Oracle Genre   122

The Kingdom Divides   128

Israel and its Fall to Assyria   136

Judah and its Fall to Babylonia   143

Exile Adaptations   150

Return and Attempted Renewal   157

Psalm Genre   164

Wisdom Genre   174
Intertestamental Times   183
The Historic Jesus   189
The *Geschichte* of Jesus   202
Pentecost and the Jerusalem Council   218
History of the Church   227
Gospel Genre   238
Parable Genre   248
Epistle Genre   258
Apocalyptic Genre   266
Part II: Study Methods   281
Bible Study Types and Tools   283
Inductive Bible Study   292
The Impact of Worldview on Bible Study   304
Part III: Hermeneutics   313
Formation of the Canon   315
The Unity and Disunity of the Biblical Library   320
Model *Heilsgeschichte* by Marion Bontrager   334
Bibliography   353
Acknowledgments   361

Preface

By Marion Bontrager

My approach to the Bible as story has its origin in my father reading *Egermeier's Bible Story* book to me, often for more than an hour at a time. My Amish grandfather's ten children each received that Bible Story book when they married. In the Amish church marriage is about children and parenting is about teaching the Bible story at home. Hearing stories read one after the other connected them into a Grand or Big Story that started and went somewhere. Though I could have read the stories myself, hearing the Bible stories read to me is one of the best memories of my father. They were oral stories first for me!

Hearing Bible Stories read by the hour was supplemented by hearing Salvation History (*Heilsgeschichte*) told by ministers in relay fashion in two preparatory 4-5 hour services two times a year in the Amish church in preparation for the coming communion service. That practice continues today. They skip parts but they do it. When I began attending a Mennonite church, I discovered that I knew the Bible stories better than my Sunday school classmates even though I had never attended Sunday school. They had only single Bible stories read to them.

Amish way

In college and graduate courses the Old (First) and New (Second) Testaments were separated by disconnected semesters. In addition, the Bible was approached more as a library of separate literature books rather than first a Grand Story of the missionary God's acts behind the documents throughout biblical history.

Then a small textbook in a missions class in graduate school opened the Bible to me as the overarching story of God choosing a missionary people to reveal God to the whole world by life and word. It was called *The Kingdom Without Frontiers* by Hugh Martin (Friendship Press, 1946), and it reconnected me back to the Bible as story.

The opportunity came to create a new Introduction to the Bible course at Hesston College in 1986. Should the semester course be about the Bible and the books of the Bible as in most colleges or the story behind the books? If so, then which stories are included and excluded? The course evolved over a period of years for primarily first or second year college students who were increasingly biblically illiterate. As a required course, over five thousand students have taken it over the last thirty years. It has been immensely rewarding to see the Bible become an accessible and alive book to the students. At the end of the course and using a unique Salvation History timeline, students write or speak the salvation metanarrative (*Heilsgeschichte*) with several stops in church history and then connect it to their own life faith story if they are Christian. A short version of *Heilsgeschichte* or salvation history has been presented in over 40 churches, pastor retreats and convention seminars.

With large sections the course has been team taught along with study group leaders. Keith Harder teamed with me the first year. Duane Yoder who team taught the course for ten years, helped condense and refine the course and wrote parts of the course notebook that has evolved into this book. Howard Keim, Palmer Becker, and David B. Miller also helped teach for several years. Kevin Wilder creatively adapted the course for nursing students. Michele Hershberger began team teaching the course in 2000 and has contributed significantly in refining the course's content and pedagogy. John Sharp now adds his contributions team teaching the course with Michele. I am indebted to all of them and the many faculty study group leaders and students for suggestions, inspiration and support as the written word became a living word.

Thanks also to Susie Swartley, Department Secretary in the early, less organized days of the course. Thanks also to Elaine Schmidt, Academic Assistant, for invaluable contributions to the teaching of the course. And lastly, thanks to André Swartley and Justin Heinzekehr for their helpful critique and editing to make this book's publication possible.

Sola Deo Gloria.

Marion Bontrager, June 2016

Introduction

By Marion Bontrager

The Introduction to Biblical Literature course consists of three parts: Story, Method (inductive study), and Hermeneutics (interpretation).

The biblical story can be seen as a divine drama with a problem, development and resolution. Three orientation questions constantly asked while reading the biblical story are: "What is the problem?" "What is God doing to solve the sin problem?" and "How faithfully are God's people cooperating?"

The overarching scheme of the Salvation History timeline in the book is: Creation, Problem Defined, Solution Begun, Attempted Solution Continued, Solution Accomplished, and Solution Being Realized. The story moves from the good creation to the resulting problems human sin created to the climax of Jesus Christ, Pentecost and the New Creation (church). Church history continues the salvation story. God's future salvation story ends in recreation and restoration of the whole creation, not in escape and destruction. The Jewish faith story continues the Old Testament story to today.

Heilsgeschichte is not mere history as we would know it today, but a kind of confession of faith and proclamation of Yahweh and salvation. Versions and summaries of the salvation story appear in a number of literary forms in the Old Testament. The Covenant Recital in Deuteronomy 26:5-10 is considered one of the oldest documents. It is to be recited as a liturgy, remembering and giving thanks in a worship ceremony. The salvation

* Hx of Salvation (German)   9

history Psalms are 78, 105, 106, 135, 136. Joshua recites an abbreviated version at the Shechem covenant ceremony in Joshua 24. Ezra's prayer in Nehemiah 9:6-37 is another version. And finally Stephen connects Jesus to salvation history as he recites the story in Acts 7 before he is stoned to death. The Apostle Paul also connects Jesus to the salvation history story at Antioch in Acts 13. Story creates identity so it needs to be repeated often. We choose our stories then our stories shape us.

In four stories in Genesis 1-11, sin breaks four relationships: with God, self, others, and all creation. God is a missionary God throughout the salvation history story seeking to re-establish holistic relationships. Graciously and ironically, God chooses a human people to help solve the problem. They are to be the missionary people to reveal God to all people groups in the world so they may share this restored holistic salvation. Two important theme words throughout *Heilsgeschichte* in Genesis 12 are chosen for a mission (not as God's favorite), and as a "nation" rather than a nation-state.

How sin is defined determines how salvation is defined. The Adam and Eve fall story shows sin breaking four relationships: with God, self, others and the whole creation. So salvation is the healing or restoring of all four relationships. Sin's biblical definition is broad and deep, so salvation must also be broad and deep. God's goal is not merely the salvation of individuals for a future heaven but transforming people into a restored missionary community here and now. That is most fully realized in the loving radical new creation (church) where Jesus is Lord and all barriers like race, nationality, gender, and social status are overcome. The approach in this book keeps Exodus and Sinai integrally connected. Salvation is deliverance from slavery to freedom and mission. In the New Testament Christ, Pentecost and the Jerusalem Council are also integrally connected.

The biblical salvation story is the dynamic story of the interaction between a living God and the People of God who have freedom of choice. It is an up and down story of a faithful God and a sometimes faithful and unfaithful people. Understanding the salvation history historical context is also important in interpreting the Bible.

The sovereign God of the Bible is not a static God, but a dynamic active God whose actions change in response to the people's faithfulness and unfaithfulness. God responds to Abraham's intercession for Lot (Genesis 18), and to Moses' challenge, "And the Lord changed his mind about the disaster that he planned to bring upon his people" (Exodus 32:15), God responds to Jeremiah "but if that nation turns from its evil, I will change my mind" (18: 5-11). God's response is both judgment and grace, which are often pitted against each other by surface readers of the Bible. God's grace and judgment are like two sides of a coin. God's acts of judgment are disciplines revealing a God who cares and seeks to bring about awareness of sin, repentance and restored relationships. But God graciously never makes a complete end of the people in judgment. God is a tenacious loving missionary God. His "steadfast love endures forever" (Psalm 136).

Some people read the Bible like a puppet show with God pulling the strings of wooden-like human puppet actors who don't have a will. That approach says God has a static "plan of salvation" and makes everything happen according to that static plan of salvation. The approach of this book is that the sovereign God has a "purpose" to restore or heal all the broken relationships of the good but fallen creation. God graciously and ironically chooses and works with fallen humans with minds and wills to accomplish his mission.

Similar to the "puppet" reading of the biblical story above, some see only isolated events of the acts of God like so many disconnected lightning strikes. The ultimate lightning strike is Jesus, who seems to come out of nowhere, as this view fails to put Jesus into his historical, 2000-year-old context. And while it is true that the life, teachings, death and resurrection of Jesus are clearly the high point of the biblical narrative and God's way of healing all relationships, God's solution to the sin problem continues. We still have sin and evil today. We still have the church, that alternative community of persons, open to all and attractive because of their love for all.

Jesus is deeply connected to the Old Testament. It is within the context of an unfaithful people that Isaiah claims that "God will do a new thing" (Isaiah 42:9, 43:19). Jesus re-reveals God's ultimate will which was partially hidden by the Old People of God's unfaithfulness. The apostle Paul refers to that hiddenness as a mystery (Ephesians 3:3-6 and Colossians 1:25-27). The biblical story begins somewhere and has a trajectory that is read with the ultimate relationship through Jesus Christ in view (Hebrews 1:1-3a). Jesus reveals what God was trying to accomplish throughout the Old Testament story. So reading the Bible in a Christ-centered way doesn't diminish the value of the Old Testament. The writer of Hebrews says that God spoke through the prophets. The Hebrew/Jewish story is indispensable for fully understanding the New Testament.

Some scholars argue against any unity in the Bible. The unfaithfulness of God's people may obscure our seeing God's constant purpose of creating a chosen, covenant, shalom community to restore the whole creation. The often unfaithfulness of God's people does argue against a positive upward "progressive" view of salvation history. Nevertheless, there is a faithfulness trajectory and an unfolding of God's revelation that moves forward. For example, the view of God moves from henotheism (one god among the many gods) to monotheism in the exile where "there is no other god" (Isaiah 45:5).

God's purpose was not fully revealed in the Old Testament because of the people's unfaithfulness, not because God wanted to keep it hidden. In the radical new creation church (II Corinthians 5) where Jesus rules there is neither Jew or Gentile, all barriers are broken down and all relationships restored. This was God's purpose or goal throughout salvation history. But it was hidden because of the people's unfaithfulness. The Apostle Paul calls it the "mystery" that is now revealed through Jesus Christ and the radical new creation church (Romans 16, Ephesians 3).

The *Heilsgeschichte* timeline seeks to reflect some of both the faithfulness and unfaithfulness of God's people to their mission. Monarchy placed geographic and political boundaries around God's people, keeping them from being a faithful missionary people. On the *Heilsgeschichte* timeline the monarchy line drops below the horizontal line of dashes that represent the prophetic vision. Monarchy is the most significant crisis before the exile. Ever after the monarchy's beginning the reader needs to remember that God is dealing with an unfaithful people with a remedial will. They make Yahweh faith into a national and geographic civil religion that continues until the fall and exile of Judah, when Yahweh smashes the civil religion of the nation state and geographic boundaries. The exile offers the people a new opportunity to be faithful to their missionary chosenness. Nevertheless, the Hebrew Yahweh faith and people endure through the monarchy, exile and return.

With the rise of kings and centralized power comes the rise of prophets. It is primarily the prophets who carry the vision of theocracy and God's people called to be a missionary people. The prophets Moses and Elijah, not two kings, appear to Jesus on the Mountain of Transfiguration. Our view of Jesus and the kind of kingdom he establishes is changed dramatically by whether we connect Jesus with the prophets or with the kings and the monarchy. Jesus' style, kingdom and teachings fit the prophets, not the kings. Monarchy is God's remedial, not ultimate will. The tenacious God keeps working with the unfaithful people. Jesus continues God's revelation and is the fullest revelation of God's will and purpose because he was completely faithful (Hebrews 1:1-3).

Misunderstanding two crucial words leads to a misreading of the entire *Heilsgeschichte* and even world politics today. "Chosen" is the first word which we find in God calling Abraham in Genesis 12. It means chosen for a mission to bless the whole world, to be a missionary people to help bring God's restoration of all the broken relationships. The second word is "nation," which means a "people group," not a nation-state or empire. They were to be a theocratic peaceful people ruled by God, a unique people whose existence depended on God not on king and army. This missionary people were to have no geographic, political, economic and ethnic boundaries. In spite of times of unfaithfulness there were also times of faithfulness when some individuals, families, and groups not ethnically Jewish joined the people of God. Some are included in the genealogy of Jesus.

It is critical whether one begins the story with the good creation rather than with the fall of humans into sin and its results. God loved his good creation and continues to love the fallen people who still have some image of God in them. The missionary approach should begin as the biblical story begins, with the good creation not with sin. So the salvation story is about the recreation of God's original good creation.

(3) The third part of the book deals with biblical interpretation, called hermeneutics. Two equally sincere persons can read the Bible and come away with radically different views about what God's will is today. Why? These different interpretations emerge out of different assumptions about the Bible and Jesus within it. How do the Old and New Testaments relate to each other? How does one deal with the differences and disunity in the the two testaments? That Jesus was a good Jew and affirmed parts of the Old Testament is often missed because readers of the Gospels do not see how much comes from the Old Testament. But Jesus also disagrees with previous teachings. Jesus identifies his teachings as the higher truth and revelation as in Matthew 5, "You have heard, but I say to you."

Many Christians interpret Jesus and his teachings as something other than the norm for today and for all of life. How do they arrive at that? First, they interpret the Bible Christ-centered spiritually but not ethically. Jesus is superior to the old law and replaces the temple and sacrifices and he came to die for sin so his teachings are secondary. A second way Jesus is not the norm for many Christians is that they divide life between the personal and the corporate with different ethics for each one. Jesus' teachings are only for one's personal life, not for all of life. In corporate life one has to find ethics from the Old Testament or from rational philosophical sources other than Jesus. The assumptions one brings to interpreting the Bible greatly determine what the Bible says to them about God's will and truth. A third way Jesus' teachings are not the norm for today is that his teachings were only for his disciples and the future Kingdom when Jesus returns.

This book views Jesus as God's fullest revelation (Hebrews 1:1-3). Jesus' life, example, decisions, and teachings are the "rule of truth and ethics" when the Bible does not agree. This is a Christocentric biblical hermeneutic both ethically and spiritually and for all time and all of life. One finds this in most denominations, but nearly universally in Anabaptist churches.

The third part of the Biblical Literature course is the unique Hesston College Inductive Bible Study template that guides students through four study steps: Observation, Analysis, Interpretation, and Application. Learning the Inductive study method is crucial for understanding the biblical story.

The biblical story takes place in a given culture with vocabulary from a given time. The time between an act of God and when it was further interpreted and/or written by the biblical writers may be hundreds of years and in a different historical context. The biblical story needs to be read in contexts, both historical-cultural and literary. If we don't know the biblical worldview, we misinterpret. If we don't understand our own worldview, we misapply.

There are two extremes in dealing with context. Without considering the historic cultural context, we often misinterpret the Bible, but if we overemphasize the gap or differences between the biblical and today's worldviews and cultural contexts, the Bible becomes irrelevant.

May *Heilsgeschichte* continue as God's Kingdom comes and his will is done on earth as it is in heaven.

Part I
The Biblical Story

Is the Bible Relevant Today?

Bible Passages: John 20:30-31, II Timothy 3:16-17, Hebrews 4:12-13

How can a book composed by many different writers over a period of a thousand years in another culture be relevant in our time and culture today? How can a book that comes from one area of the world be relevant for the entire world? How can books written more than two thousand years ago be authoritative today? These and other questions challenge the Bible's relevance.

Some Christian and public leaders in the United States argue and debate public policy from values and teachings that can have Judeo-Christian biblical foundations. But increasing numbers in the post-Christendom culture simply ignore the Bible as a quaint, out of date, ancient Near Eastern book. The Bible is considered largely irrelevant and not read even by many professing Christians. Arguably, the biblical illiteracy among U.S. Christians today provides ample evidence. What we don't know can't be relevant to us.

Finally, the Bible's relevance is not in what we say we believe about the Bible's inspiration and authority. We believe it is relevant only if we read, study and then live it.

Before dismissing the Bible's relevance we need to "hear" what the Bible says. We have to come to grips with what the Bible teaches on its own terms before we can decide on its relevance. It is another matter if after seriously studying the Bible, we decide that the Bible is irrelevant.

If we reject the Bible as irrelevant today then it follows that we have to give preference to some other option, explanation of life or worldview. Also we need to critique the alternatives to the Bible with the same rigor we do the Bible.

Doctrinal statements can't prove the Bible's relevance. Each person must study the biblical documents before coming to a conclusion. Dismissing the Bible as irrelevant without serious reading and study is hardly logical or honest, much less academic. We can come to an honest conclusion about the relevance of the Bible only after serious reading and study. An example would be that the biblical writers assume a living God who is active in the world today.

Ultimately the relevance of the Bible hinges on to the relevance of Jesus of Nazareth. Is Jesus who the Gospels say he is, the Messiah, the Son of God?

It is impossible to prove the relevance of the Bible. Each person must discover it for themselves. The Bible presents itself as "Good News" and a witness to God, not as an argument. So you won't find this book trying to prove God or the Bible. *The Bible doesn't need to be defended, simply presented.* It simply attempts to provide ways to study and understand the Bible. It seeks to let the Bible speak for itself to the reader in its historical and literary contexts.[1]

Many witnesses testify to the relevance of the Bible. Emilie Calliet is one such witness. Born in France in the early years of the 20th century, he didn't grow up with the Bible. Like many his age, he went to the front lines in World War I. His schooling in liberal humanism didn't suffice in the face of the violence of that war. Disillusioned, he returned home, married and kept on a search for truth. He longed for a book "that would understand me."[2] He even wrote his own anthology, but it too fell short. One day his wife gave Emilie a Bible. He opened it to Matthew 5 and was so enthralled, he read all night long. Jesus came alive to him through the scriptures and he knelt in surrender. He became a professor at Princeton Theological Seminary. He discovered the Bible's relevance, the Living Word to which the printed words pointed.

What the Bible says about its inspiration and relevance carries little

---

1   Howard H. Charles, "Why Study the New Testament," Lecture from Introduction to the New Testament course at Associated Mennonite Biblical Seminaries, Elkhart, IN. 1962.

2   James Montgomery Boice, *Foundations of the Christian Faith* (Downers Grove, IL: InterVarsity Press, 1986), 50-51.

weight for those who do not accept its authority. People have difficulty with the authority of the Bible when they attempt to make the Bible into a science or exact history book. Nowhere does the Bible claim to be a science or exact history book. Its purpose is different. The final editors of the biblical documents didn't make all the dates agree. They treated the documents they received as sacred and did not change them to make everything agree in the books of Kings and Chronicles for example. The attitude of the biblical editors who put the Bible together should give us more, not less, confidence in the Scriptures.

The writer of II Timothy 3:16-17 says, "All scripture is inspired by God and is useful for teaching, for reproof, for correction and for training in righteousness so that everyone who belongs to God may be proficient, equipped for every good work." The *New International Version* says it makes us "wise for salvation." The writers of this textbook make every claim the Bible makes for itself, no more and no less.

What do the biblical writers mean when they say that it is inspired? When used in the Bible, "inspired" indicates the belief that God's influence and the Holy Spirit's presence makes the Bible alive, "truthful," and powerful to change lives. The writer of the Book of Hebrews says, "Indeed, the word of God is living and active, sharper than any two-edged sword, piercing until it divides soul from spirit, joints from marrow; it is able to judge the thoughts and intentions of the heart. And before him no creature is hidden, but all are naked and laid bare to the eyes of the one to whom we must render an account" (Hebrews 4:12-13) "Inspired" includes the power of the Bible to help us know ourselves so we can repent, be transformed and become more Christlike.

Ways We Experience the Bible

Those who grow up with the Bible experience it in different ways in their development from childhood to adulthood. The chart below suggests the following ways:

Age	The Bible is...
Preschool	Mystery: Parents and others give the book special treatment. Some never put another book on top of the Bible.
Childhood	Heroics: Characters become inspiring heroes to imitate.
High School	Ethics: A lengthy list of dos and don'ts!

College	Theology: It is full of ideas about God, the world, the meaning of life.
Adulthood	Miracle Encounter: A way to encounter God (like Emile Calliet did) The Bible reveals the God who comes into the world to solve the problems of sin and evil, to convey God's forgiveness and give meaning and purpose to life.

How to View and Approach the Bible

Some describe the Bible as "God's word in human language." Christians say that the Bible is inspired and authoritative. Christians also recognize that the Bible is composed of different literary genres that communicate truth in different ways. First, each genre has unique characteristics that call for specific principles of interpretation. Second, language and vocabularies change in different times and places. Third, anyone who knows different languages knows that translating is not an exact science. So the Bible must be read in its original context before applying it to contemporary life. If we do not consider the historical-cultural context of the Bible we tend to misinterpret. On the other hand, if we overemphasize the difference between the biblical and today's cultural contexts we risk making the Bible irrelevant.

Games People Play

Old Testament scholar Perry B. Yoder helps us think about how we approach the Bible. Sometimes we play games with the Bible though we may be unaware of it. The games we may play may look like these:

1. Interpretational game. We may think we are not interpreting the Bible when we read it, that we take it as it is. We are tempted to think that our understanding is the only valid interpretation.
2. The Author game. In this game, the text is a passive "it" and we the readers breathe into the text our meaning. We call this eisegesis. When we do this, we become the authors and we use the Bible to support our views.
3. The Opinion game. Ours is the only right opinion. We may think that if I'm really spiritual, I'll understand the text. The Holy Spirit will surely show me the truth. We are not open to someone else's views.

4. The Caveman game. We're good at this one! We use verses as a club against anyone who disagrees with us. We never learn because we are too busy defending our views against everyone else's opinion.

5. The Born Again game. We mistake the beginning of faith for the goal. I'm born again, so I will automatically understand what I read. I don't need to use Bible study methods. I'll get it on my own. Study methods spoil what I know.

6. The Literal game. Oh this is a good one. I may claim to take the Bible literally. No one does this. We pick and choose. We become the authors again and we miss the original meaning of the text.[3]

Our goal is game-free Bible study, where we take the words and meanings of the authors seriously and seek to understand the passage as the first readers or hearers understood it.

Honoring the Bible by Asking Deep Questions

It is easy to become confused about the purpose, meaning, and significance of questions about the Bible. However, some readers may feel uncomfortable questioning or having doubts about a book they believe is inspired by God. Asking questions is not heresy. Expressing doubts is not a rejection of faith. Asking questions is a part of good inductive Bible Study. We worship the God of the Bible, not the Bible itself. We can ask serious questions about the Bible without being threatened especially if we have had an encounter with the God the Bible points us toward.

The following questions are NOT about undermining the inspiration or authority, but about the nature of the documents. These questions can help us understand the meaning of a passage in its original context. They can help us do critical, meaningful, and careful study in order to understand the Bible and the God of the Bible. Asking these and other questions can enhance the Bible's authority in our lives.

1. Who wrote a specific book or parts of a book in the Bible?
2. What is the historical-cultural context of a book or passage?
3. Where does a passage belong in the text (particularly when different manuscripts have the same story at different places, like the gospel story of the woman taken in adultery)?

---

3   Perry B. Yoder, *Toward Understanding the Bible: Hermeneutics for Lay People* (Eugene, OR.: Wipf and Stock Publishers, 2006), 2-6.

4. What type of literary genre is a given passage?
5. Did a passage or story exist before a biblical writer put it into the Bible?
6. What other documents did biblical writers use for reference or inspiration?

While the Bible doesn't answer all questions we can ask, we can trust the Bible to be adequate to reveal God to us, to point and lead us to God, and teach us how to live. The message of the Bible or the "Living Word" makes God real to us as it did to Emilie Calliet. We trust the Bible to point us to God.

A 16th century Anabaptist leader, Hans Denck said, "He who honors scripture but lacks divine love must take heed not to turn scripture into an idol as do all scribes who are not learned (taught) for the kingdom of God."[4]

Ulrich Stadler, another Anabaptist leader, emphasized the "living word" that is beyond and within the written word. Using a European analogy he said that the outer word (written) is like a sign on an inn which witnesses to the wine (living or inner word) in the cellar. But the sign is not the wine.[5] The songwriter of the hymn "Break Thou the Bread of Life" echoes the same thought: "Beyond the sacred page I seek thee Lord, my spirit pants for thee O living Word."

---

4   Edward J. Furcha and Ford Lewis Battles, *Selected Writings of Hans Denck: Edited and Translated from the text as established by Walter Fellmann* (Eugene, OR: Wipf and Stock Publishers, 1976), 63.

5   Walter Klassen, ed. *Anabaptism in Outline* (Scottdale, PA: Herald Press, 1981), 141.

The Bible as Story

Bible Passages: Deuteronomy 26:1-10a; Joshua 24:1-28; Psalms 78, 136; Nehemiah 9:9-27; Acts 7, 13:16-41

Stories existed before there were any biblical documents. Stories were central and still are in oral pre-modern cultures. The modern scientific culture replaced stories with written propositions and abstractions. The postmodern culture into which the western world has been moving is rediscovering story. God's acts were told before they were written down.

Biblical illiteracy in the church today is a critical issue, even for youth and adults who have grown up in a church. At best people know bits and pieces of the Bible—verses and chapters. But they have little sense of where verses and chapters fit into the overall Bible or salvation history. For most people the Bible is formidable, not user friendly. So they give up or live with a book of disconnected stories and truth fragments. They have not been taught to see the overarching Big Salvation Story or metanarrative. They may even read individual books of the Bible but don't see the grand story. This book seeks to help you see that overall salvation history story, in German called *Heilsgeschichte*.

Various theological traditions view the Bible in different ways:

- A collection containing a variety of different books.
- A book of prophecies, propositions, ideas, theology and laws.
- A book of scattered disconnected stories.
- A book of a God-scripted wooden puppet show of God preparing for and solving the sin problem. The scripted "plan of salvation"

makes the Old Testament largely about promising the solution and biding time until Jesus arrives. The decisions of the human puppets, both good and evil, are part of the divinely scripted drama where all human decisions are divinely initiated.

- A dynamic story of God's interaction with a perfectly created people with free will who have fallen into sin. God chooses good and fallen humans to be the missionary community through whom God will seek to be revealed to the whole world. The people fail in their calling and mission. So Jesus comes and fulfills God's mission.

The last view is the approach of this book. The reader can test that approach by the study of *Heilsgeschichte* or salvation history to see if it fits the nature of God, the people, their purpose and God's interaction with them.

Edward Hayes tells the story of a poor honest jeweler who was arrested and imprisoned for a crime he didn't commit. His wife was able to get the drawings of the prison and locks. She wove the design of his cell lock into a prayer rug. She brought the rug to the prison explaining that her husband needed the rug to say his prayers. The guards let the prisoner have the rug. Each day he unrolled it, knelt and prayed with his face near the rug. Some time later the jeweler suggested to the guards that if they brought him some metal and tools he could make jewelry they could sell and add to their low wages. So they agreed and he made jewelry they sold. Each day the guards brought him some silver, metals and tools. Each night they took the metal, jewelry and tools home. Some days later the guards found the jeweler's cell empty. They found no clues how he escaped.

The real criminal was eventually arrested for the crime. Later one of the guards spotted the jeweler selling jewelry in the city's market. The guard explained that the real criminal had been arrested and asked how he had managed to escape. The jeweler said his wife had woven the design of the prison and locks into the rug. Each day as he bowed his head to the rug in prayer, he began to see a design. He saw designs within designs and finally saw his prison door lock design, from which he made a key.[1]

Hopefully this book will be like the prayer rug to help you see and learn the overarching salvation story. In this book you will see the biblical story as the ongoing dynamic relationship between a creative God and

---

1   Edward Hayes, "A Prayer Rug Introduction," in *Twelve and One-Half Keys* (Leavenworth, KS: Forest of Peace Books, Inc., 1981), 9-10.

God's people. Other literature in the Bible, like Psalms, laws, and prophetic oracles all grow out of this interactive story between a dynamic responsive God and God's people who were sometimes faithful and unfaithful.

A Glimpse of the Salvation History Story: *Heilsgeschichte*

God creates a good creation but then sin enters the world, as described in four stories (in this book called "fall stories"). Then the missionary God chooses Abraham and Sarah and their family to be a missionary community for the whole world. This missional community is created in the Exodus-Sinai event when God delivers them from Egyptian slavery to become a free "priestly" missionary people (Exodus 19:6). God becomes their king at Sinai.

The Exodus-Sinai event is the Old Testament salvation event to which God's chosen people look back. But they often forget to tell the story and end up being unfaithful to God's mission and their chosenness. But the steadfast loving God continues to work with this faithful and unfaithful people through the generations-long sequence of the Exodus-Sinai, wilderness, conquest, tribal confederacy, nation state kingdom, the division, fall of Israel and Judah, Judah's captivity in Babylon, and the return from exile.

God gives them a second chance at being a faithful missionary community when some of them return to Judah from Babylon. Their leaders Ezra and Nehemiah lead in telling the salvation story up to date. The people re-covenant with God but still don't get it right. Now rather than adopting a national identity, they define the Old People of God as those who have pure Jewish blood! So they have to get rid of their non-Jewish wives and children. In this time, the leaders asked the wrong question— the ethnic question rather than the missional question of whether they would become believers in God. Their failure means God must yet again try something new in working with the chosen for mission people.

Jesus is born and has a three-year ministry of teaching, healing, and establishing a following. He is killed by the political and religious leaders who feel threatened by his message. But God raised Jesus from the dead. Jesus ascends and his spirit appears to the disciples at Pentecost. Peter preaches about salvation history and Jesus, and thousands become believers in Jesus. The New People of God are born. The Gospel spreads and churches spring up, composed of all kinds of people. The Jerusalem Conference decides that nothing other than Jesus is Lord or rules in the church. In this radical new creation missionary church, all barriers with God and in society are overcome: race, gender, wealth, slave, free, and nationality don't matter. The solution to the sin problem is accomplished and is still being realized today.

The Re-emergence of Storytelling/Narrative

In the oral culture of premodern times, storytelling was the way in which truth and wisdom were communicated. After the printing press and increased literacy, truth became more abstract with propositions. Propositional truths and scientific facts and worldview can be fairly lifeless to many people. Their limits have contributed to a recovery of storytelling in our postmodern era. Attention to the right brain's contribution to which story appeals has also contributed to story's reemergence. One national storytelling organization lists over 200 professional storytellers. Besides those there are many amateurs. Increasingly, pastors are moving to more narrative preaching and teaching.

Long before contemporary theologians got excited about narrative theology, the Old Order Amish were doing it. Two times a year the ministers in Old Order Amish churches tell the biblical Salvation History story in relay fashion in a service that can last 4-5 hours. They have done it for over two centuries. How much does it contribute to their identity, cohesion and growth? They are now doubling every 25 years in a culture where most churches are declining.

The emphasis on the Bible as story does not in any way mean to imply that the Bible isn't true. Story doesn't equal myth. The biblical narrative gives us real history and the interpretation of what that history means. God worked with real people and still works today. The story is still unfolding.

Story and the Old People of God

The religion of Israel was concrete and rooted to the earth and life now. Stories are the stuff of life.

When faithful Israelites were asked who they were
    they told a story.
When asked who God is and what God is like
    they told a story
When asked why things are the way they are
    they told a story.

26

When asked where they came from
they told a story.
When asked their purpose in life
they told a story.

We choose our stories, then our stories shape us.

Ways Stories Function

Stories are powerful. They shape lives, communities, nations and history. They make people do great good and evil things. Some even die for them. We choose the stories we live by consciously or unconsciously. One task of older persons is to tell their stories. Listen to the stories they select and you discover their faith, how they see the world, other people, happenings in their lives and themselves. We create our life story by the stories we select and how we interpret events and people in our lives.

If you want to observe the power of story go to a War Veterans, Alcoholics Anonymous or similar group meeting. Their stories plumb the depths and heights of human darkness and light.

When a person chooses to become a Christian, the first decision they actually make is, "What story or stories will I choose as my own?" All major religions have a story of their gods or human leaders. Nation-states, tribes, and biological families have stories. Every individual has a life story. Whichever story one chooses as their primary story determines their identity and who their god is. If one chooses their national story as primary, then the nation-state becomes their god, their ultimate authority and identity.

William Bausch identifies some ways stories function:

1. Stories nurture curiosity. They catch us, our whole being, head, heart and emotions. Like parables they hook us when we hear them. We can't avoid identifying with a person or event. If stories are anything they are powerful. Different kinds of stories evoke different responses. Some make us reflect or think. Others make us cry and some send us into gales of laughter.

2. Stories create community. Shared stories bond us together even to past generations. Retelling stories keeps families meeting year after year. They are called re-unions! The stories reunite them! God

created the Old People of God through the common experience of Exodus-Sinai. God delivering them from slavery to freedom was their salvation story. "The Lord brought us out of Egypt." When people don't know the salvation history story the very life of the church is threatened. When the story was not told in salvation history the people strayed away to worshiping other gods. Is it any different today? The prophet Jeremiah lamented that even the priests and prophets did not say "Where is the Lord…who brought us out of Egypt?" (Jeremiah 2:8).

3. Stories create our identity and connect us to our roots. The television series *Roots* based on Alex Haley's celebrated novel was the most watched TV program up to that time. While it traced an African American person seeking to find his roots, the story resonated with all people because everyone needs roots to know who they are. The U.S. slavery system sought to dehumanize slaves by cutting them off from their African memory, roots and culture. Then they wouldn't have any human identity beyond their slave owner. Why do governments require all students to study their country's history or stories? Because they create loyalty, a common identity and community.

4. Stories help us preserve our history. Facts are best remembered when attached to stories. We remember stories because they connect with us on so many levels. One definition of worship is "Remember and give thanks." Christian hymns refer and allude to many biblical stories. Consequently when people don't know the biblical stories, the hymns are like a foreign language with little meaning.

5. Stories can teach morality both positively and negatively, be they biblical or not. Many biblical stories of unfaithfulness teach what not to do. The Apostle Paul writes about the people's sin long ago, "These things happened to them to serve as an example" (I Corinthians 10:11). The children's story "Peter Rabbit and Mr McGregor's Garden" teaches children to obey their mother because Peter did not.

6. Stories inspire and renew us. Bible stories like Joseph, Daniel, and Esther inspire us to be faithful and courageous.

7. Stories entertain, develop imagination and provide healing and escape when life gets too hard. Therapy and healing exercises involve persons delving deep into their memories and tell stories that have been denied or repressed.[2]

The Covenant Recital

Scholars believe that one of the oldest pieces of literature in the Bible is the recital of the Exodus-Sinai to Canaan story found in Deuteronomy 26:5b-11a. Each year at harvest time the Israelite father was to take the first ripe fruits, go to the priest and recite his short salvation story as follows:

A wandering Aramean was my ancestor; he went down into Egypt and lived there as an alien, few in number and there he became a great nation, mighty and populous. When the Egyptians treated us harshly and afflicted us, by imposing hard labor on us we cried to the Lord, the God of our ancestors; the Lord heard our voice and saw our affliction, our toil and our oppression. The Lord brought us out of Egypt with a mighty hand and an outstretched arm, with a terrifying display of power, and with signs and wonders; and he brought us into this place and gave us this land, a land flowing with milk and honey. So now I bring the first of the fruit of the ground that you O Lord have given me.

This recital of God's action and the response of gratitude is fascinating. The story moves from third person—he—to first person—we—and eventually to *I*. Even though the people reciting this story were not part of the original slaves who were rescued out of Egypt, the story was so important to them, they acted as if they were. When a story is told well, the past becomes the present. The old African-American spiritual holds the same principle: "Were you there when they crucified my Lord?" Obviously we weren't there, but the cross means so much to us it's as if we were there.

The Covenant Recital also illustrates a common pattern in the Bible, the pattern of God's grace followed by a grateful response. God acts first to free the slaves, then they respond with gratitude, giving their first fruits. Before the Ten Commandments in Exodus 20, we find the story, the word of grace: "I am the LORD your God, who brought you out of the land of Egypt, out of the house of slavery." Joshua begins his *Heilsgeschichte* at

---

2   William J. Bausch, *Storytelling: Imagination and Faith* (Princeton, NJ: Clear Face Publishing, LLC, 2015), 23-64.

Shechem by reciting all the wonderful things Yahweh had done for them. After this recital, he asks them to choose which god they would serve. Romans 5:8 says, "While we were yet sinners, Christ died for us."

Over time the salvation story grew longer and longer, but repeating the story remained critical in the People of God biblical story. When God's people told the story, they stayed connected to what God had done for them (grace) in the past. The Covenant Recital or condensed story is repeated throughout the Bible Salvation Story in various literary forms. The story is adapted for worship in the Salvation Psalms 78, 105, 106, 135, with 136 being the most familiar. When the story was not told, the people strayed away from the Exodus-Sinai God and fell into all kinds of sin. Next to loving God and neighbor, the third command is to tell the story to your children (Deuteronomy 4:4-6, 11:18-20).

Joshua repeats the salvation story at the Shechem Covenant ceremony (Joshua 24). Ezra repeats the story up to date when the returned exile Jews re-covenant with God (Nehemiah 9:9-27). Then in the New Testament Stephen tells the extended Covenant Recital and connects Jesus to the story (Acts 7) before he was stoned to death. The Apostle Paul at the city of Antioch also repeats parts of the story and connects Jesus to it (Acts 13:16-41). Repeating the salvation story was a central part of the lives of God's people.

One of the reasons people do not know the salvation history story is because they were not given a way to organize or remember it in a meaningful way. They do not have "hooks" on which to hang their knowledge. So the unorganized bits and pieces of information fall to the floor. This course's approach to the Bible includes a unique *Heilsgeschichte* Timeline and theme that provides hooks on which to hang and organize the stories. Even students without any Christian background can tell or write *Heilsgeschichte* at the end of the study!

Welcome to learning the salvation history—the *Heilsgeschichte*—with a unique timeline so you can decide whether or not to choose it as your story and to repeat it with thanksgiving!

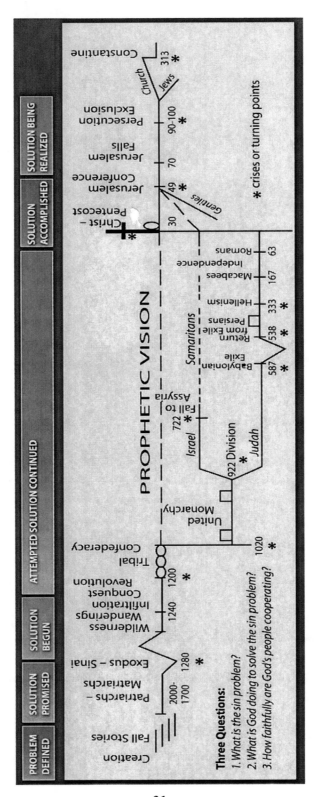

PROPHETIC VISION

| PROBLEM DEFINED | SOLUTION PROMISED | SOLUTION BEGUN | ATTEMPTED SOLUTION CONTINUED | SOLUTION ACCOMPLISHED | SOLUTION BEING REALIZED |

Creation
Fall Stories

Patriarchs – Matriarchs
2000-1700

Exodus – Sinai
1280 *

Wilderness
Wanderings
Infiltration
Conquest
Revolution
1240   1200 *

Tribal
Confederacy

United Monarchy

1020 *

922 Division *
Israel   Judah

Fall to Assyria
722 *

Samaritans

Babylonian Exile
587 *

Return from Exile
538 *

Persians

Hellenism
333 *

Macabees Independence
167

Romans
63

Christ – Pentecost
30   *

Gentiles

Jerusalem Conference
49 *

Jerusalem Falls
70

Persecution Exclusion
90-100 *

Church
Jews

Constantine
313 *

* crises or turning points

Three Questions:

1. What is the sin problem?
2. What is God doing to solve the sin problem?
3. How faithfully are God's people cooperating?

Narrative Genre

If you needed information on how to build a picket fence, would you turn to a novel? If you longed to vicariously transport yourself to a distant land via a good book, would you choose a telephone directory? Would you try to decipher how atoms work by reading a book of poetry?

Although each of the texts listed above is a type of literature with a meaningful purpose, we don't use them in the same way nor do we discern their truth in the same way. The cornerstone of literary analysis is discerning the kind or type of literature we are interpreting. In other words, when we think about the different ways we use literature, we are studying genre.

The Importance of Genres

Part of understanding the Bible, as well as any work of literature, is to think about how a certain piece of writing compares to other writings of its time and place. If many of these writings share certain characteristics, a particular type of audience, and a common overall purpose, perhaps even similar content, we lump them together in a common category of literature. These categories become genres, and because different genres have different rules of interpretation and different ways they communicate their truth, it's important for readers of the Bible to be familiar with the various biblical genres. The Bible has a variety of genres, which include psalm or poetry, prophetic oracle, wisdom, epistle, apocalyptic and narrative genre. Each of these types of literature has a common set of characteristics, a stated or implied purpose and they each illuminate truth in different ways.

Narrative and Story

Literature that sounds like a story belongs to the category of narrative genre. Narratives have all the elements of story: characters, a setting in time and place, a plot complete with conflict and tension and interaction between all these elements. Narratives are written in such a way that they seem plausible in real life. Either the author believed the story really happened or believed that the story could have happened. Therefore, we as readers of narratives are to take the stories in their plain, literal sense. There is no figurative or hidden meaning. The narrative is simply stating the facts as they happened. On the other hand, we must also remember that the Bible does not purport itself to be a history book. The ancient writers weren't as concerned about historical accuracy as we are today. The history illustrated in a narrative serves as a vehicle to explain God and God's actions in the world to create a People of God.

History and *Geschichte*

These two words are used to distinguish between uninterpreted facts (if there are such things) and facts plus interpretation. Uninterpreted facts or a section of literature that seems relatively neutral and unbiased is called history. Other literature or even parts of the same literature contain interpretations or in other words, give meaning to the stated facts and these sections of literature are called *Geschichte*. To say that Jesus died on a Roman cross in the First Century is a history statement. To say that Jesus Christ was killed to bring salvation is a *Geschichte* statement.[1]

Salvation History and *Heilsgeschichte*

Much of the Bible is written as narrative. And while there is profound truth in all the different genres of the Bible, it's particularly beautiful that the primary way the Bible works to present truth about God is through story. Why is this so wonderful? Because story implies interaction and relationship. In the Bible we learn about the most important questions of life and meaning through character-driven stories, not through a set of

---

1   Karl Barth, Table Talk, ed. John Godsey (Richmond: John Knox Press, 1962), 45. "'Historie' is something that can be proved by general historical science, whereas 'Geschichte' is something that really takes place in time and space, but may or may not be proved. The Creation story has to do with 'Geschichte,' for instance. It has to do with something that happened and therefore something historical, but something that is not open to historiographical investigation." See also Richard E. Burnett, Karl Barth's Theological Exegesis (Grand Rapids: Eerdmans, 2004), 105n31.

rules or a list of propositional truth statements or a how-to manual. The stories are dynamic and subtle, sometimes confusing and other times quite clear—and always alive. More than any other way, God chose to reveal truth through the living, breathing Jesus. Narrative, more than any other genre, best helps us understand Jesus, and thus God.

All of the narratives of the Bible, in one way or another, work to tell the BIG story of God creating a community of people that functions in a vastly different way than other people groups. This unique community, made up of individuals from every nation and tribe (Rev. 5:9-10) is the People of God, a community reconciled to God and to each other so that they in turn can reveal God to the rest of the world. And it is through this community—a community that seeks to obey God, love their enemies, and care for the physical earth—that God works to solve the problem of sin. We call this part of the Bible salvation history, or *Heilsgeschichte*.

In salvation history or *Heilsgeschichte*, there are three levels of story. The first level is a single narrative that can stand alone as a story with a beginning, middle and ending.

The second level is a cluster of stories. A cluster is composed of several individual stories, but they all have the same central characters or the same geographic location. When a number of stories are grouped together in a cluster, the reader must ask how the stories relate to each other and what the cluster contributes to the ongoing purpose of creating a People of God.

The third level is the BIG story, which encompasses the entire salvation history. The BIG story includes all the narratives in the Bible. Each one of them works in some way to create or nurture the People of God. Each narrative also answers these three questions:

- What is the sin problem?
- What is God doing to solve the sin problem?
- How faithfully are God's people cooperating?

One example of these three levels happens in the book of Genesis. There are single stories of Joseph, such as the story in Genesis 37. Genesis 37-50 is the Joseph cluster. This cluster has an important role in the BIG story in that, as the fourth patriarch, Joseph helps set the stage for the People of God to be "birthed" in the next part of the story. And both single stories about Joseph and the Joseph cluster itself fit into *Heilsgeschichte*. They are part of the Matriarchs and Patriarchs part of *Heilsgeschichte*, the part of the Bible that illustrates the themes of chosen, covenant and providence and shows God getting a certain group of people ready for the birth of the Old People of God in the Old Testament.

Because narratives show what happened instead of simply trying to tell their audiences how to interpret what happened, sometimes the narrative shows the People of God failing to cooperate with God without explicitly telling the reader that they're being unfaithful. So how do we know whether or not the People of God are cooperating and being faithful? We place individual stories into the context of the whole biblical narrative, the overall *Heilsgeschichte*. We evaluate the actions of a single story by correlating it with *Heilsgeschichte*. This style of interpretation makes reading the Bible an even more enormous undertaking than it already is, at least at first. But the payoff is the deepest and most complete understanding possible, in which every story in the Bible provides a type of enlightenment. If a narrative shows the People of God being unfaithful, we can learn implicitly what not to do. And these narratives can give us hope that God can and does work despite a sometimes rebellious group of people.

Two Contexts

Every biblical narrative has two contexts and we must investigate both contexts when interpreting this genre. The first context is the literary context. By literary context, we mean what comes immediately before the story in question and what immediately follows. We must ask why the author placed a particular story at one point in the book instead of a different point. We must also consider an individual story's inclusion in its cluster and the context of the entire book, as well as how this individual story adds to salvation history, the BIG story. These elements of literary construction represent deliberate and meaningful choices made by the stories' authors, and so deserve our consideration.

The second context is the historical and cultural context. Here we pay special attention to the social customs of the day. How is such a concept of marriage viewed in this time period? What did the author mean when he used the terms "firstborn" or "inheritance"? We look at what was going on historically, politically, and socially because we realize that the meaning of the story hinges on a proper understanding of these important concepts. We as modern readers cannot simply make a story mean something to us that it didn't mean to the original audience. If we do, then we are misinterpreting the story.[2]

---

2   Gordon Fee and Douglas Stuart, *How to Read the Bible for All Its Worth* (Grand Rapids: Zondervan, 2003), 23.

The story of Abimelech in Judges chapter 9 is a good example on the importance of understanding the literary and historical-cultural contexts. At first glance, it's a strange story. Abimelech is asked to be king in Shechem. He has his seventy brothers killed, but the youngest brother escapes and condemns Abimelech. Then the very leaders of Shechem who wanted him to be the ruler turn against him, so he fights a battle against them and burns all the people of Shechem as they are held captive in a tower. Abimelech proceeds to the next town, only to be defeated by a woman who throws a millstone from the top of that town's tower and crushes his skull.

The narrative is full of strange details like salting a field, the assassination of the brothers on a single stone, and Abimelech asking one of his soldiers to run him through with a sword so that no one could say he was killed by a woman. Historical-cultural context helps us see that scattering salt over devastated cities was a curse, commonly practiced among several ancient cultures. The single stone suggests a ritual execution that was sometimes done for all persons who might be competitors for the throne. Historical-cultural research also reveals that it is great shame for a man to be killed by a woman.

Uncovering the literary context helps clarify the story even more. In Judges 8:22-23, Abimelech's father Gideon was asked to be king and he refused, reminding the people that only the LORD was to be their king. This sits in creative tension with Abimelech who was also asked to be king and who gladly accepted that role. The biblical narratives paint Gideon as a man of God, but with Abimelech, especially with his dishonorable death, it implies that human kingship is against God's will. When we put both the historical-cultural context and the literary context evidence together, we can see that Abimelech's narrative warns of the danger of the monarchy. In the larger salvation history story, this theme of whether or not to have a human king becomes a major focus.

Crossing the Hermeneutical Bridge

Every story has a unique context, a cultural and historical setting that brings meaning to the story. This is true for biblical narratives and for all the other genres as well. To really understand any passage of scripture, we must research this history and culture. We must "cross the Hermeneutical Bridge!"

Hermeneutics is a fancy word for interpretation. The imaginary Hermeneutical Bridge is simply an interesting way to describe how we must put aside our assumptions and enter into the worldview of the biblical passage we are studying. This happens in a series of steps:

- We take off our modern worldview "glasses" or way of seeing the world.
- We put on the biblical worldview glasses by researching what words meant in their original time period. We study both the cultural and historical context and the literary context.
- We analyze the story, taking it apart to see how the story itself functions.
- We discover the meaning of the story for the original audience.
- We take the eternal truth of the story, the part of the story that's the same regardless of changes in context, and apply that to our society today.

It's a lot of work, but it's worth it. Contexts change, but eternal truth doesn't. And if we don't "cross the bridge," we are likely to misinterpret the story.

Principles for interpreting Narrative Genre

Narratives record what happened, not necessarily what should have happened.[3] The most important rule of interpretation for narrative genre is to remember that **narratives are descriptive and not prescriptive.** Narratives are descriptive in that they describe or retell what happened. They don't directly tell the reading audience what should be done or understood as truth, which would be what prescriptive genres, like Epistles, do.

Put another way, narratives usually don't teach a doctrine in a direct way. The reader must "read between the lines." For example, in Judges 11:29-40, Jepthah sacrifices his daughter because earlier he made a vow to God that he would sacrifice the first thing that comes out of his house (Judges 11:30). When we carefully read the story, look at the literary context of the book of Judges and remember the overall thrust of *Heilsgeschichte*, we can easily deduce that Jepthah's vow was hasty, his actions wrong and that we should not follow his example in our own lives. It's important to remember that what people do in narrative is not necessarily a good example for us to follow.

Narratives can just as easily teach from a negative example as from a

---

3   Ibid., 106.

positive one, and they may teach explicitly or implicitly. The moral of the story is not always immediately identifiable. As Stuart and Fee say, "Do not be a monkey-see-monkey-do reader of the Bible. No biblical narrative was written specifically about you...you can always learn a great deal from these narratives,...but you can never assume that God expects you to do exactly the same things that Bible characters do."[4]

Ask the question, "Why this story?" We can only imagine how many things happened to God's people that did not make it into the Bible. The gospel of John gives a nod to this idea in John 20:31 where the writer says, "Now Jesus did many other signs in the presence of his disciples, which are not written in this book." So a good interpretation rule to follow is to always think about why a particular story "made the cut" when so many others did not. What is it about this story that was so important, so crucial to *Heilsgeschichte*, that it was included, while hundreds of other stories were not included? Trying to answer these questions helps unlock the meaning of the story.

Remember that biblical narratives are incomplete in detail. Many stories in the Bible suffer from what scholars call "narrative gaps." The original authors wrote for people who already knew certain details and so they didn't need those details repeated in the story. But now, two thousand years later, most of us lack those details. And in the same way that we must remember that not every story made it into the Bible, we must also ask why the author chose the details he or she did. Given the limited space on the papyrus or the animal skin, why does the story slow down and give lots of detail in some places, and give scant detail in other places?

The writers of Matthew, Mark and Luke all included the narrative of Jesus preaching in the synagogue of his hometown in Nazareth (Matthew 13:53-58, Mark 6:1-6a and Luke 4:16-30). Reading the three narratives, it's clear they are relating the same story, but Luke gives much more detail about what happened. So as readers we logically ask why. The larger context of the book of Luke gives us one possibility. Luke, more than the other gospel writers, wants to emphasize Jesus' care for Gentiles and other marginalized people. His added details in the Nazareth synagogue story help highlight this emphasis and bring added meaning to the story.

Remember that narratives don't answer all our theological questions. Not only do narrative not teach doctrine directly, but even if they

---

4   Gordon Fee and Douglas Stuart, *How to Read the Bible for All Its Worth*, Grand Rapids, MI: Zondervan, 2003, page 105.

did, they can't address several theological questions in just one story. At best a single narrative hints at one important theological point. They are not meant to teach systematic theology: the primary purpose of narratives is to relay the events that happened and help the reading audience put meaning to those events. A single narrative cannot answer all our important questions about God, and when we try to make a certain narrative answer deep questions it never intended to address, we will almost certainly misinterpret the story.

Do not allegorize narratives. Instead of concentrating on the clear meaning of a story, some readers seem eager to make the story to mean something beyond itself. They put a symbolic meaning to every detail in the story, which is a literary technique called allegory. Some parts of the Bible can legitimately be interpreted allegorically, but narratives never function this way. If we allow ourselves to allegorize narratives or other parts of Scripture not meant to be used in this way, we can make the Bible say whatever we want.

Read the entire narrative as a whole, and read the surrounding narratives for literary context. We may be tempted to select specific phrases or parts of the story to focus on, while ignoring other parts. This practice leads us to miss the grand sweep of the story. The writers intended for the story to function as a whole; they also were intentional when they organized the single stories into the whole narrative of their book. None of us appreciate being "taken out of context." We want to people to listen to our complete message, to get the whole story before they make evaluations. The biblical writers are no different.

Pay attention to dialog, repetitions, and foreshadowing. All good narratives use literary techniques such as repetition and foreshadowing, and biblical narratives are no exception. For the Old Testament narratives in particular, repetition was key because these stories were passed down over many generations by oral recitation; they were not written down until hundreds of years later. So the narratives have an oral quality to them; there is a rhythm and a stylized repetition that helped the original storytellers to remember every detail.[5]

---

5   James Bailey and Lyle Vander Broek, *Literary Forms in the New Testament: A Handbook* (Louisville: Westminster/John Knox, 1992), 178. "One of the most common types of repetition in the Bible, "chiasm," occurs when one set of words or ideas are repeated in an inverted order (A B B' A'). "A chiastic form can appear in poetry or prose and can include a single verse, an entire passage, or a more extended section...Mark 2:27 is one example: 'The sabbath (A) was made for humankind (B), and not humankind (B') for the sabbath (A').'"

When reading a biblical narrative, **take note if a word is repeated throughout a narrative,** because the writer was intentional and this is a key to the interpretation. If an element in the story appeared in an earlier narrative, this is another hint about what is truly important. Finally, look to the dialog for interpretation clues. Dialog can help us understand the characters. Repeated content in the dialog, which can seem a bit annoying to the modern reader, is another clue that something important is going on.

Study the literary and historical-cultural contexts. Finally, don't forget to do careful study of any biblical narratives that researches the historical and cultural background (see the chapter on Inductive Bible Study). Study the historical and cultural background. Look for clues in the surrounding scripture texts. Do your contextual work.

All these interpretation rules are important for modern readers to use so that we don't make the Bible stories mean something they were never intended to mean. Using these principles, as well as doing careful study of both the literary and the historical-cultural context, will go a long way to insure that we understand what the ancient audience understood. We are invited into a world very different from ours, but the story becomes real.

Remember that God is the hero of biblical narratives. Biblical narratives were written down for a clear purpose. In their telling, they mean to draw persons toward Yahweh, the God of the Bible, and into God's people. Whether God is an active player in a single narrative or the Narrator behind the narrator, God is the main actor. That's part of the wonderful gift narratives give to us. Because they don't give us exact statements on how to behave and what to believe, but rather intrigue us with stories that can be interpreted in a variety of ways, narratives encourage our analytical thinking and our emotions. Stories help us interact with truth in a different way than other genres; as we immerse ourselves in the biblical narratives, we are invited to interact with God.

Primeval *Geschichte*

Bible passages: Genesis 1-9, 11

Creation and Fall Stories: The Problem Defined

In the beginning is a logical place to begin. This phrase, translated from the Greek *Septuagint* as Genesis (source, origin) introduces us to the dramatic story of God's acts of creation. The story is universal in scope (it's about the entire universe) and philosophical in nature (addresses the big questions of the nature of God, of humans, of sin, of judgment and grace).

We ask, what kind of a God is this? What kind of world did God create? Why did God create the world? Does God have a purpose for humans? What happens when sin destroys the harmony and perfection of creation—is that the end of the story or does God have a fix, a solution?

To answer these questions, we enter the biblical world, far removed from our modern world—in time, language, and cosmology or worldview. We put aside our modern assumptions in order to comprehend the Hebrew worldview. An adventure awaits! But first a word about the literary structure of Genesis.

The book falls into two obvious but unequal divisions: the first eleven chapters are prologue to the story of God's call to Abraham and Sarah to bless all the peoples of the earth. Both parts, the prologue and God's call to Abraham and Sarah's family, have a universal scope. The second part, however, moves from universal to a particular people. We follow the patriarchs and matriarchs from Haran to Egypt, from Abraham and Sarah to Joseph and Asenath. (Now the story is focused on a particular people.) To use a theater analogy, the early chapters set the stage for the greatest drama of the Old Testament, the Exodus-Sinai event, played out in the second book, Exodus.

GENESIS 1-11
Creation & Fall: The Sin Problem Defined
• Creation Liturgy: 1-2:4a Story: 2:4b • Fall Stories: Garden, **Cain-Abel**, Flood, **Tower of Babel** • Sin results in loss of shalom community & relationship **with God, others, self, and creation**

GENESIS 12-50
Patriarchs & Matriarchs: The Solution Promised
• **Abraham & Sarah (12-20)** • **Isaac & Rebekah (21-26)** • **Jacob & Leah/Rachel (27-37)** • **Joseph & Asenath (37-50)**

Prologue: Setting the Stage

We refer to the stories of the first eleven chapters of Genesis in two ways. First, we describe the stories as *Geschichte*—borrowed from the German word for "story." The stories in Genesis are not straight history, but highly interpreted accounts. The Genesis writers wrote with spin, angles, intention, and bias.

Second, we call the stories in Genesis primeval, meaning that they refer to earliest ages of time. Primeval narratives are etiologies. In other words, they are stories about the origin of things, stories that explain why things, including the universe itself, are as they are. We make no effort to assign calendar dates to these primeval stories, even though they are connected by human genealogies.

These genealogies are not complete records of humanity. They cannot be used to calculate the age of the earth with any accuracy. Genesis is not a mathematics textbook, nor is it a book of science. Inspired? Absolutely. Science? No. Insisting on scientific inquiry misses the point of the narratives. Remember, our task is to understand the biblical cosmology and to resist imposing our current worldview onto the biblical world.

Literary Forms and Meanings in Genesis

First, notice that there are *two* creation accounts, not just one. Biblical scholars have noted that the first story (Genesis 1) seems to be a worship liturgy, a form of poetry, similar to Psalms 8 and 19. The second story (Genesis 2:4b-24) is a narrative.

Why two? Often our temptation is to argue about which is right which is wrong. But once again, if we free ourselves from the view that the Bible is verifiable science, we can see that both stories are "right," in that they both tell us something different and essential about God and creation.

In the first story, God is *transcendent*, powerful, lofty, removed—an entity who creates by proclamation. God speaks: "Let there be" and it happens! The second creation story shows us an *intimate* God who kneels on the earth, scoops up clay, artfully shapes human forms, and then breathes life into them. The breath of God! It doesn't get more intimate than this!

The editors of Genesis could have deleted one of the stories to keep things neat and tidy, thankfully they did not. They valued both accounts enough to stitch them together (as they did with dual flood stories) to give us a richer understanding of a God both transcendent and intimate who created all things.

Dabar, Words with Power

In the Hebrew world, speaking creates reality. In the first Genesis account of creation in Genesis 1, God creates order out of chaos with *dabar,* the Hebrew term that means "spoken word." In Genesis, the spoken word is a powerful force, like a missile blasting from the mouth of God, exploding in nothingness to create light, life, the universe. *Dabar* in the form of blessing was **"life-changing" and "world-transforming."**[1] Kings of Israel and Judah, when confronted by the prophets speaking *dabar,* trembled. Consider the following examples of *dabar* in the Old Testament:

- *So shall my word be that goes out from my mouth; it shall not return to me empty, but it shall accomplish that which I purpose and succeed in the thing for which I sent it* (Is. 55:11).
- *[God] sends out his word, and melts [snow and hail]; he makes his wind blow, and the waters flow* (Ps 147:18).
- *Then the LORD put out his hand and touched my mouth; and the LORD said to me, "Now I have put my words in your mouth. See, today I*

---

1   Walter Breuggemann, *Prophetic Imagination* (Minneapolis: Augsburg Fortress, 1982), 227.

appoint you over nations and over kingdoms, to pluck up and to pull down, to destroy and to overthrow, to build and to plant" (Jeremiah 1:9-10).

- *As Samuel grew up, the* LORD *was with him and let none of his words fall to the ground. And all Israel . . . knew that Samuel was a trustworthy prophet of the* LORD (I Samuel 3:19-20).

- The priest Amaziah told king Jeroboam of Israel that "the land is not able to bear all [the prophet's] words" (Amos 7:10).

- Spoken words could not be taken back; the shocked Isaac says to Esau that he has already blessed Jacob. He could not take them back and transfer them to the oldest son Esau (Genesis 27).

The concept of *dabar* doesn't fit our modern concept of verbal communication. Our words are not little missiles going through the air and entering people. But words still have power. Consider the psychological effects of words. Do you remember compliments? Do you remember hurtful words? They stay with us and shape our self-image. So, yes, words are still powerful; they can bless or curse, build up or tear down.

The Nature of God

One way of understanding God is to compare the Hebrew concept of God with that of their neighbors. Some of the neighbors had their own versions of creation. So what is different?

One example is the Babylonian creation story called *Enuma Elish*. In this account creation is bloody and violent. Marduk, the king of gods, fights a ferocious battle against his female rival Tiamat. Marduk wins, murders Tiamat and slices her in two. He hammers one half of Tiamat into a domed sky and the other half he lays down to form the earth. Marduk then arranges the universe, placing lesser gods in various roles, such as the moon and stars. When they complain that their work is endless and dreary, Marduk goes into creation mode again and makes humans from the blood of Tiamat's second husband. With humans to do the hard work, the happy gods honor Marduk by building a great monument in the city of Babylon and calling it "the gate of god" (More on this later in the chapter.) The many gods of the *Enuma Elish* are anxious, petty, competitive, manipulative, and destructive. It is impossible to know what they will do next. They are locked in an endless cycle of time without a unifying theme or purposeful end.

In contrast to the violent Babylonian gods, the Hebrew God, sometimes identified as Elohim and other times as Yahweh, speaks a perfect and orderly universe into existence. God is sovereign, above all created beings. There are no rivals, no battles, no blood, no gore. And, God is pleased; the results are most excellent. Humans, too, are very good—made in God's image, given free will, and tasked with the care of God's good creation.

Also in contrast, the Hebrew God is primarily a God of grace who loves the created beings. When pride and violence break relationships and destroy the harmony of the garden, God seeks restoration and reconciliation. When the humans feel naked, God clothes them. When the garden becomes dangerous, God removes them. When Cain murders his brother, God protects Cain. When most of the earth is destroyed by human sin, God saves Noah and his family and starts over. God who felt grief about the human's condition of sin, resolves not to destroy the earth again: "As long as the earth endures, seedtime and harvest, cold and heat, summer and winter, day and night, shall not cease" (Genesis 8:22). The rainbow is to be a visible sign of this promise. Finally, God prevents the builders of the Tower of Babel from reaching the heavens, and in doing so saves them from their own folley.

The God revealed in these stories is a personal God with feelings that change over time. Despite initially finidn humanity to be as "good" as the rest of creation, God soon regrets creating humans and is grieved by human wickedness and violence. (Genesis 6:6).

God is *for* the creation—for its fullness and fulfillment. The serpent, simply a created being (not a devil or competing god), plants doubts in the minds of the humans in the garden about whether God really is *for* them. The serpent pictures an insecure God, who selfishly limits humans rather than seeking their fulfillment and welfare. Humans continue to live with this doubt. God's ultimate expression of love and grace is Jesus, who in the New Testament comes to dispel that doubt once and for all, giving his own life for our redemption, because God is *for*, not against, us (Romans 8:31).

These stories tell us that God is both *immanent* and *transcendent;* that God is active in history, that God loves his created beings, and that when sin enters the scene, God wants to redeem and restore fallen humanity. It takes the rest of the Bible to describe God more fully.

The Nature of Humans

Humans in the *Enuma Elish* are made as lowly slaves to provide for the physical needs of the gods. God's humans, on the other hand are created with dignity and freedom, made in the image of God, cherished and loved by God. In the Genesis 1 liturgy, they are created male and female, blessed, and commanded to multiply. In the Genesis 2 story, God uses earth (*Adamah*) to make the man (*Adam*) and breathes life into him, a most intimate act. After all else has been created, God makes woman (*Ishshah*) from the body of the man to be an intimate companion. He recognizes her as "bone of my bone and flesh of my flesh" and calls her Eve (*Chava)*, "mother of all the living." She is the pinnacle, the capstone of creation.

Human life, endowed with the breath of God, is precious. So much so that God provides and cares for them. The humans, in turn, are given power over the rest of creation to "cultivate and to keep" (NASB). These terms call to mind farmers, who cultivate the soil and shepherds who keep or watch over their flocks of sheep or goats.[2] Humans have the capacity for thought and planning, which enables them to care for and watch over creation.

Paradoxically, humans are created from the dust of the earth, but are brought to life by the breath of God. They share both divine and earthly natures. Part of the divine and infinitely precious nature of humans is the freedom and ability to make choices. This means they can choose for or against God. God did not create robots. Having been created in God's image means special status, but not equality with God. The humans in the stories of the Garden of Eden and the Tower of Babel try for equality but, in both cases, fail. In the garden, Adam and Eve see the fruit of the "tree of knowledge of good and evil" as a way to achieve God-like status. The builders of the tower set out to consolidate their own power and control their own destiny.

The story of Lamech, a descendant of Cain, in Genesis 4 illustrates the downward spiral of humanity's capacity for violence. He brags to his two wives: "I have killed a man for wounding me, a young man for striking me. If Cain is avenged sevenfold, truly Lamech seventy-seven fold" (Genesis 4: 23-24). Beyond that, God sees that "every inclination of the thoughts of their hearts was only evil continually" (Genesis 6:5). Now sin has become a desperate human condition. Human acts of sin have boomeranged, producing sinful persons through and through.

So what is sin and how did humans, the most excellent creations of God, turn their backs on the God who loved and cherished them?

---

2 Eugene F. Roop, *Believers Church Commentary: Genesis* (Scottdale, PA: Herald Press, 1987), 41.

Defining the Sin Problem: The Four Fall Stories

The four fall stories in the Primeval *Geschichte* illustrate sin's alienating power in the breaking of four relationships: with God, self, others, and all creation.

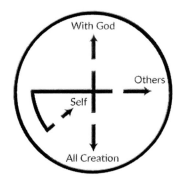

The Four Dimensions of Sin's Results

Fall 1: Pride—The Garden of Eden fall story pictures sin as coming from both the outside (the serpent) and from within the human heart. So when the woman sees that the "tree of the knowledge of good and evil" is a delight to the eyes, and that it can make one wise" (Genesis 3:6), she falls for it. And so does the man. In context, "making one wise" means infinite knowledge or the ability to shape the future, in other words, to become like God.[3]

Sin cuts off Adam's and Eve's relationship with God; they no longer "walk with God in the garden." Sin affects them inwardly; they feel shame and hide from God. Adam blames Eve, illustrating the loss of relationship with others. The ground is cursed, causes humanity to struggle with nature, and results in the loss of relationship with creation. God's harmonious, matrix of creation is like the fabric of a seamless garment. Sin tears it apart, shreds it to pieces. In the New Testament, the Apostle Paul describes it as all creation groaning and longing for renewal (Romans 8:22). While the sin of pride in the garden is directed toward God, its results breaks not only their relationship with God, but also with self, others, and all creation.

Fall 2: Violence—The Cain and Abel fall story depicts sin as an animal crouching outside the door, poised to attack. God warns Cain to master his jealousy (Genesis 4:7). But Cain allows it to simmer and build, until it flares into violence; he kills his brother Abel. Sin begins with an idea that can morph into destructive action. In this story, sin is directed toward a

---

3   Ibid., 41.

fellow human, but it also breaks Cain's relationship with God, self, and all creation.

Fall 3: Violence—The Flood story describes sin as a pervasive inner human condition that produces continuous evil thinking. Evil thinking leads to evil acts, causing the earth to be "filled with violence" (Genesis 6:11). The God of creation responds with sorrow and grief, and therefore acts in judgment: a flood destroys most of humanity and resets creation. Violence is sin directed against others, but also breaks humanity's relationship with God.

Fall 4: Pride—Finally, the Tower of Babel story pictures sin as universal collective pride that drives the people to reach above the "dome" so they can exalt themselves and become like God. This appears to be a particular Hebrew indictment against the Babylonians, since the tower may be a reference to Marduk's "gate of god." Again, this is *Geschichte*, a highly interpreted account of the folly of foreign gods, even though there be a multitude of them. None of them can equal the ultimate power of the Hebrew God of creation. As in the other fall stories, sin flips their intentions against them: instead of becoming a great people equal to God, they are scattered and fragmented. The sin of pride is directed against God, but it ends up breaking relationships with others.

These four fall stories are cumulative in effect: sin and sin's consequences snowball and spiral. The snowball becomes larger with every revolution; the circular movement spirals downward with every turn. Humans are becoming less than their original form. Humans get out of place. Humans trash God's perfectly ordered creation (clearly evident in our current ecological crisis). As a result, the world looks more and more like the chaotic and violent world of Enuma Elish, and less and less like the pristine Garden.

Put more simply, sin is the problem that has plagued humanity's relationship from the beginning of our shared story. And putting a name to the problem is an important step.

The next step is defining a solution, and the solution to the problem of sin is salvation.

When all four relationships are healed or in the process of healing, we can say that a community has *shalom*. *Shalom* is the Hebrew word for a state of existence where a person is in harmony with God, with one's self, with other people and with the physical world. Sometimes we mistakenly associate this word only with the absence of war, but it stands for much more. It happens when everyone has enough to eat and a decent place to live, where everyone has a chance to do dignified labor and relationships are harmonious. It is like the life of the Garden in the beginning, God's perfectly created universe.

Grace and Judgment

A moral, just, and gracious God brings judgment in these fall stories. Moral principles (right and wrong) are woven into the fabric of creation. Everything is connected and interrelated. Human sin harms all creation. That may seem unfair, but it must be so if all creation is an ecological system. The pre-scientific biblical writers could observe that.

These stories reveal that the act of sin has within it judgment on the actor (sinner.) Sin's judgment includes reaping what one sows, one strand of theology in the Bible. Judgment, however, is often misinterpreted as an expression of God's anger. It's not about rage, but about correction through love and grace. Think of a parent who holds the hand of a child to prevent her from running into traffic on the street. Grace has the last word.

God expels the humans from the garden as an act of judgment, but keeping them from reentering is an act of grace. The temptation to eat from the tree of knowledge and attaining equality with God is taken away. The urge to eat from tree of life and living forever in their condition is also taken away. God's mark of judgment on Cain is also an act of grace, since it protects him from becoming a homicide victim. The worldwide flood is harsh judgment, but is mingled with a sliver of grace that washes the world clean and preserves enough of creation along with Noah and his family to start again. And God's judgment in the tower story frustrates the humans from further sinful activity. The same act of God can be both grace and judgment.

If one takes off the blinding glasses of "the Old Testament as law and the New Testament as grace," one sees a gracious God at work in these fall stories. God did not create puppets, but rather humans in the image of God with the capacity to choose good or evil. In that sense God chose to be limited. When these humans use their capacities to sin, God graciously intervenes to make the best of their action, to redeem the situation and bring good out of evil. God's grace and judgment are intertwined. God's judgments seek restoration and reconciliation, not mere destructive revenge.

Matriarchs and Patriarchs

Bible passages: Genesis 12-50

The Primeval Prologue contained in the first eleven chapters of Genesis defined the sin problem that corrupted God's superlative creation as broken relationships in four dimensions—with God, self, others, and creation. The Prologue chapters set the stage for the second and larger part of Genesis, chapters 12-50, where God promises a solution to the sin problem through a specific family, the multi-generational matriarchs and patriarchs.

We can track this family's journey from its beginning in Mesopotamia, literally the "Land between the Rivers" of the Tigris and Euphrates in modern Iraq. At this eastern end of the Fertile Crescent, the first complex societies in the form of city-states emerged around 3,000 BCE. The early kingdoms of Sumerians and Akkadians were followed by the empires of Amorites, Assyrians and Babylonians. These societies appear in the biblical narrative, often as enemies. The Assyrians eventually conquer Israel in 722 BCE and the Babylonians conquer Judah in 587 BCE and sweep them away into exile.

Abraham's father Terah takes the family from Ur "of the Chaldeans" in the "Land between the Rivers" and follows the trade route northward to Haran, at the top of the Fertile Crescent. Here, Abraham, who becomes the father of three faith traditions—Judaism, Christianity, and Islam, is recruited for a special mission. God, identified as LORD (Yahweh), calls Abraham and Sarah (Abram and Sarai) to leave everything they know—homeland, families, customs, and gods—to migrate to an undisclosed destination.

In the Prologue, God created the universe with the spoken word *dabar*. And now, once again, God creates a new reality with the spoken word. Blessings and curses have the power to alter history, to change lives, and to transform the world. This call is as momentous as it is universal:

I will make of you a great nation,
Bless you, and make your name great,
So that you will be a blessing.
I will bless those who bless you,
And the one who curses you I will curse;
And through you
All the families of the earth shall be blessed (Genesis 12: 2-3).

This mission is a "radical new development" in God's creative design to mend the fractured relationships described in the Primeval *Geschichte*.[1] What does this development look like? Very human: sometimes dysfunctional, deceptive, and cowardly; at other times heroic, faithful, and courageous. We follow this family of matriarchs and patriarch from Haran into Canaan, and finally to Egypt.

We track their pilgrimage through the annals of the ancestors or patriarchal and matriarchal narratives, grounded in history and told with *Geschichte*—as we've come to expect. So the events are selective and highly interpreted. Asking why these (and not other) stories were told, passed along, and eventually written can help us understand the *Geschichte* or meaning more fully. The stories are more about meaning than a track record of places and events. More important than geography and chronology is the interplay between God and the chosen family. Yahweh initiates, the humans respond—sometimes cooperating and sometimes complicating God's purposes. In contrast to the Canaanite gods who are bound to specific places, Yahweh is bound to people. Yahweh is a personal God who makes covenants and promises protection.[2]

What do we know about this family? Humans in the Garden were supposed to "cultivate" and "keep" the land and creatures around them . By contrast, the new patriarchs are "keepers," or shepherds, of other people,

---

1   William Sanford LaSor, et al., *Old Testament Survey: The Message, Form, and Background of the Old Testament* (Grand Rapids: William B. Eerdmann Publishing Company, 1996), 33.

2   Ibid., 43

driving their human flocks through the hill country of Canaan, constantly looking for new pastures. In their semi-nomadic patterns, they mingle with "cultivators," kings and city dwellers. These interactions are sometimes harmonious, sometimes contentious, and sometimes dangerous, requiring God's intervention.

The relational, personal Yahweh initiates an unconditional covenant (only God is bound) with Abraham, who is called righteous. Abraham's righteousness, later echoed in the New Testament, is not about an abstract code of ethics, but is defined in relational terms as trusting God.[3] The physical ritual of circumcision begins here and continues in the generations that follow as a visible sign of God's promise of blessing, land, and descendants.

Yahweh's promise to make Abraham and Sarah the parents of a great people is radical and ironic, even shocking! How could they produce an unlimited number of children, so many that they, like the dust of earth and stars in the sky, could not be counted? They are childless, old and infertile! Is this already the end of the story? Without God's providence, yes.

God's radical new development encompasses three prominent themes: chosen, covenant, and providence—central motifs that shape the rest of salvation history.

Chosen

Chosen, called, elected, selected, and recruited are synonyms, though the first three are most common and used interchangeably throughout salvation history. Chosen is among the most misunderstood and misused words in the story of God's people. When "chosenness" is misinterpreted, it becomes the justification for nationalism, militarism, and racial intolerance.

The biblical definition of chosenness is specific and inclusive. Abraham and Sarah are chosen, not as God's favorite and pampered people. They are chosen for a mission to be the solution to the sin problem and to bless all the peoples of the earth. And it is an expression of God's grace. Abraham and Sarah are not saints who caught God's eye for their holy living; they know nothing of Yahweh, but worship multiple pagan gods. They are, however, responsive to God's call and agree to accept the mission.

Another word often misunderstood and misused is nation. God in Genesis 12:1-3 is not proposing to make Abraham's descendants a nation-

3 Eugene F. Roop, *Believers Church Commentary: Genesis* (Scottdale, PA: Herald Press, 1987), 112.

state (*goy*) , but rather a community of faith, a great people (*'am*).[4] God did not envision a political state, ethnically defined, and geographically isolated by borders, inaccessible to all non-citizens. Quite the opposite; the chosen people were to be open, invitational, inclusive. They were to unite and bless all the peoples of the earth.

Covenant

A covenant creates an intimate bond between two people or two parties and is sealed by a solemn oath. The Hebrew origin is carat, meaning to cut, as in cutting a deal, cutting words of a covenant into clay or stone tablets, or cutting of relationships when a covenant is broken or unfulfilled. The covenant between God and Abraham in Genesis 15 is marked by cutting apart animals. With a covenant come responsibilities and privileges, and it typically involves spoken blessings and curses. Yes, again, *dabar*.

Throughout salvation history, the making and renewing of covenants features prominently as a recurring theme. The primary covenants (or renewals) are with Noah, Abraham, Sinai, Joshua, David, Josiah, Ezra, and Jesus. Always, Yahweh, the personal God, initiates covenant relationships and calls people to become partners in mission.

Providence

The third major theme in salvation history refers to God's intervention when humans mess up and threaten to sabotage the solution to the sin problem.   God's providence keeps the chosen, covenant, shalom community—and the story—alive. Though God is always the hero, the story depends on human cooperation; humans are not puppets, moving woodenly as God pulls the strings.

A series of direct interventions throughout Genesis demonstrates God's providence: Yahweh prevents kings from adding Sarah to their royal harem when a frightened Abraham passes her off as a sister; Yahweh gives Abraham and Sarah as son when they are far too old for children; Yahweh saves Isaac from his father's knife ; Yahweh transforms the deceptive and duplicitous Jacob—who cheats his brother and steals his birthright—into a model of faith, renamed "Israel"; Yahweh protects Jacob when Esau plots to kill him; and when jealous brothers sell Joseph, Jacob's favored and rather pompous son, into slavery, Yahweh intervenes to help Joseph survive and become the

---

4   Bernhard W. Anderson, et al., *Understanding the Old Testament, Fifth Edition* (Upper Saddle River, NJ: Pearson Education, Inc., 2007), 192.

manager of resources for Pharaoh's great kingdom during a time of extreme crisis.

Literary Analysis

In general, the organizational methods of the matriarch and patriarch stories in Genesis are built around chronology, characters, and places. The primary characters are Abraham and Sarah (12-25:18), Isaac and Rebecca (21-28), Jacob and Leah and Rachel (25:19-36:43), Joseph and Asenath (37-50). The settings where the story unfolds are Haran, Shechem, Bethel, Hebron, Gerar, and Egypt.

Initially, the stories were told as single, isolated narratives. Later they grew into clusters of stories told and retold around family and clan campfires. Children who heard the sacred narratives from their elders committed them to memory, becoming themselves stewards of their people's collective memory. With remarkable accuracy and skill, the storytellers embedded salvation history in the minds of the next generations. Eventually, scribes replaced storytellers as narratives were gathered, written, and collated into scrolls and books. The Heils*Geschichte* was no longer carried in hearts and minds; it became paper and ink.

To the everlasting credit of the final editors of the book, the variations and versions of a story were not altered to conform to a single literary form, nor were they compressed into a single narrative to avoid differences. The editors compiled the original stories, giving us a rich, multi-hued tapestry of literature. Occasional "rough readings" or contradictions need not threaten our confidence in the authenticity of the Bible. Rather, they should strengthen our confidence in the integrity of the sacred texts.

Some apparent contradictions seem to trouble vast groups of readers. For example, just as we explored the two different creation stories in the previous chapter, two different flood stories are also retained in Genesis. There are also two versions of God's covenant with Abraham. Or, how long did Jacob work for Rachel? We have two possibilities. After the Exodus, the former slaves gather at a mountain to make a covenant with the redeeming God who delivered them. It is called both Sinai and Horeb.

The story of Jacob's son Joseph being sold into slavery contains multiple, seemingly minor inconsistencies. In one account, Joseph's older brother Judah saves his life. In another version, it is Reuben who comes to his rescue. The traders who buy Joseph are described as Ishmaelites in one account, and in another, Midianites.

One of the more striking differences is the use of two names for God. In one strand of literature, God is Yahweh; in another Elohim. Each has a specific purpose and having them both enriches our understanding of God. Of course, it takes many more names to describe a God who cannot be contained by any name!

The Story Continues

To heal the broken relationships, our definition of sin, God calls Abraham and Sarah to prepare for the launch of the chosen, covenant, shalom community. They travel the trade routes of the Fertile Crescent, from the "Land between the Rivers" northward to Haran and then south into the hill country of Canaan. This region, the settings for the annals of the ancestors or the matriarch and patriarch narratives, eventually becomes the promised homeland for the people of God, the many descendants of Abraham and Sarah and countless others who join them.

Though Isaac and Rebecca succeed Abraham and Sarah, Jacob becomes the primary inheritor of God's delayed promises. Even though Jacob, with his mother's help, deceives his father and steals his brother's birthright and blessing, he, renamed "Israel" becomes the father of the clan that becomes a nation. The names of his sons become the names of the tribes of the Children of Israel. Later generations refer to him as their "wandering Aramean" ancestor who migrated to Egypt, the Land of the Nile.

These events lead to the next stage of salvation history. After 400 years of slavery in Egypt, God hears the desperate cries of the enslaved people of Israel and with great drama, frees them from Pharaoh's grasp. This Exodus, coupled with the covenant at Mount Sinai, is "the great watershed of Israel's history."[5] It marks the birth of a nation, the formation of a people, the inauguration of the shalom community. The dramatic Exodus-Sinai event shapes the Children of Israel's understanding of Yahweh as a redeeming God who is active in their history.

---

5 Ibid., 9.

Exodus-Sinai: Liberation

Bible passages: Exodus 1-4, 12, 14, 17-20

The Family of Jacob in Egypt

When the people of God recited Heilsgeschichte, they began not with Creation, nor with Abraham, but with Jacob, whom they recalled as "a wandering Aramean. " The story begins with famine in Canaan. To escape the famine, Jacob's family finds refuge in Egypt, where to their surprise they encounter Joseph, Jacob's son whom the family sold into slavery years earlier. In God's providence, Joseph has risen from slave to become Pharaoh's prime minister. In an emotional scene, Joseph reveals himself to his scheming brothers who sold him into slavery, and he forgives them.

Jacob remains in Egypt, living "as an alien," with his family who are "few in number. " Over the years, Jacob's descendants "became a great nation, mighty and populous." But then a new Pharaoh with no connection to Joseph or the patriarchal family is elevated to the throne. In later recitations of Heilsgeschichte, the past becomes the present, and so they say that the new Pharaoh's regime "treated us harshly and afflicted us by imposing hard labor on us" (Deut. 26: 6).

Though it is difficult to date precisely, the new regime that imposed hard labor on the Hebrews seems to be that of Pharaohs Seti I and Rameses II (1290-1224) of the Nineteenth Dynasty.[1] Egypt, at the pinnacle of its power and influence, was engaged in massive construction projects of new

1 Bernard W. Anderson, *Understanding the Old Testament.* Fifth Edition. (Upper Saddle River, NJ: Pearson Education, 2007), 46.

cities and palaces in the northeast Nile Delta that included Goshen, where family of Jacob was located.

Moses: Yahweh's Messenger

During this period of Egypt's uncontested dominance, when the Children of Jacob are at their lowest point in history, Moses is born. Threatened by the growth of the enslaved people, Pharaoh orders the death of all the slaves' newborn sons. To save her son, Moses' mother hides him in a basket in reeds or bulrushes along a riverbank. From a distance, big sister Miriam keeps an eye on her newborn brother. While bathing in the river, Pharaoh's daughter discovers Moses. When she asks Miriam to find a nurse, Miriam takes Moses to their own mother. In time, Pharaoh's daughter takes him to the palace where she raises him as a member of the royal family.

In spite of his royal cover, Moses identifies with the enslaved people. His secret identity becomes public when he impulsively murders an abusive Egyptian overseer who is beating a slave. Moses, now a fugitive, disappears and finds refuge among Midianite shepherds in the hinterlands of Sinai Peninsula southeast of Egypt. There he meets a Midianite priest named Jethro, and marries his daughter Zipporah.

One day while tending to his father-in-law's sheep, Moses has an encounter that reshapes his life. The core of the encounter is dabar again, and this time the words spring from a flaming bush on sacred ground. God, the Great Recruiter, commissions Moses to go back to Egypt with message for Pharaoh: "Let my people go." But who should Moses say is speaking? The answer from the bush is that this God is not abstract and distant, but rather the relational God of Moses' ancestors, who has "seen the affliction of my people . . . [has] heard their cry . . . and [has] come down to deliver them" (Exodus 3:7-8).

But the answer is not enough for Moses; he wants to know God's name. A name is more than a label in this context, it reveals character and is "filled with power and vitality."[2] God answers, I am that I am, meaning that Yahweh is active in history and in the present in order to shape the future. As for the enslaved people in Egypt, Moses is to identify God as "Yahweh (LORD), the God of your ancestors, the God of Abraham, the God of Isaac, and the God of Jacob...This is my name for all time, and this is how I am to be designated for generations to come" (Exodus 3:25).

2   Ibid., 54.

"Let my people go!"

The very reluctant Moses, with his brother Aaron as assistant, returns to Egypt to confront the Pharaoh—likely Rameses II, who has become Pharaoh in the place of his, father Seti I, from whom Moses fled. Perhaps Moses is facing his royal brother, with whom he spent time as Pharaoh's adopted child. Whatever their relationship, in response to Moses' appeals to free the slaves, a great contest begins to boil between the powers the two men represent: Yahweh, the God of justice who has heard the cries of his people, and Pharaoh, considered in the Egyptian worldview to be a personification of the gods.

After the first appeal of Moses and Aaron, Pharaoh presses the slaves to work even harder, adding to their duties the gathering of straw that had formerly been supplied by a third party.

During the second appeal, Aaron's staff becomes a snake, which the royal magicians replicate, but Aaron's superior snake swallows all the others.

Then the signs and wonders (or plagues) recorded in Exodus 8-10, descend on Egypt in the following sequence: water turns to blood, frogs, gnats, and flies infest the land; the cattle die; boils cover humans and animals; hail destroys crops; locusts devour what is left; and then a heavy darkness blankets the land.

Finally, an Angel of Death strikes down the firstborn sons of Egypt, but "passes over" the enslaved people's homes that have been smeared with the blood of lambs. During this night the enslaved people, awaiting deliverance, eat the lambs and bread baked without yeast, called unleavened bread. To the present time, Jewish people still commemorate this liberation annually as the Passover Seder.

When Pharaoh still refuses to release the slaves, something tremendously interesting happens. The Bible states that God hardens Pharaoh's heart. But why? Moses is the human avatar of God, and he acts faithfully in his appeals to Pharaoh. The idea that Yahweh would act against Moses—and by doing so inflict even more suffering and death on both the slaves and the Egyptians—seems illogical at best and needlessly cruel at worst. Wouldn't it make more sense if the devil were the one to harden Pharaoh's heart rather than God? Fortunately, an understanding of the biblical writers' historical context and culture gives us an answer. The Old Testament authors were Hebrews, and in the Hebrew worldview, there is no anti-God personified as Satan or the devil. The devil appears later in the biblical story, of course, but in these early books, Yahweh is the only real divine actor in history and is therefore the only possible force to affect Pharaoh's attitude.

Notice also that Pharaoh hardens his own heart (Exodus 8: 15, 32; 9:34). He is stubborn, of course, but he also plays into God's hands. The longer the standoff goes on, the more time the people of Egypt have to switch sides. The plagues are sent "so that you may know that there is no one like me in all the earth (9:14). Yahweh could have by now wiped Pharaoh and his people from the face of the earth (Exodus 9:15), but God let Pharaoh live "to show you my power, and to make my name resound through all the earth" (9:16). Further, these signs are sent "that you may tell your children and grandchildren how I have made fools of the Egyptians and what signs I have done among them—so that you may *know* that I am the Lord" (10:2). And again, Pharaoh does not listen, "in order that my wonders may be multiplied in the land of Egypt" (11:9).

Knowing, in this context, is more than intellectual awareness; it is acknowledging the superior power and purposes of Yahweh. *Knowing* was the discovery of "a whole new reality of political power." This God refused to use Pharaoh's oppressive, coercive means of control; this God exercised power for the benefit of "the weak against the strong," and this God, speaks not with the sword, but with the *dabar* of the prophet Moses.[3]

The strategy works: when the Israelites finally leave Egypt, "a mixed crowd" also goes with them (12:38).

It's also possible that God did harden Pharaoh's heart. Perhaps God did this as a way to prolong the demonstration of God's power over the power of the Pharaoh. In the first couple of plagues, the Egyptian magicians were also able to duplicate the miracle (Exodus 8:7). By the third plague, however, they said, "This is the hand of the LORD" (Exodus 8:18-20). As the battle between the LORD and Pharaoh continued, more and more Egyptians came to believe that God was truly the strongest, so that, by the tenth plague, Egyptians and slaves from other nationalities also put the blood of a perfect lamb on their door and they too were rescued out of Egypt (Exodus 12:38).

The Great Liberation

At last Pharaoh permits Moses to depart with the slaves, and a massive mixed crowd of Jacob's descendants and other liberated peoples walk out of Egypt. This grand event—due to which, early Greek translators named

---

3 Millard C. Lind, *Yahweh is a Warrior: The Theology of Warfare in Ancient Israel* (Scottdale, PA: Herald Press, 1980), 63.

Bible's second book Exodus, from the Greek word meaning "departure" —is celebrated as the foundational event of the nation of Israel, the Old People of God (also called Israelites and the Children of Israel).

But the drama continues. Traveling conditions for the erstwhile slaves are difficult. Although Yahweh leads them constantly—a pillar of cloud by day and a pillar of fire by night—crossing the eastern border of Egypt leads them into a desert. Then, as they at last approach the Red Sea (also called the Sea of Reeds), they see Pharaoh's army tracking them. Pharaoh has, once again, changed his mind. Trapped between the sea and Pharaoh's horses and chariots, the people panic. Has Moses brought them out of Egypt only to be slaughtered here?

Through Moses, Yahweh's dabar saves the day. The words spoken here are Yahweh's original model for warfare: "Do not be afraid. Stand firm and you will see the deliverance the Lord will bring you today. The Egyptians you see today you will never see again. The LORD will fight for you; you need only to be still." In other words, this is not the people's fight; it is Yahweh's. Survival is matter of trust, not military strength.

Moses raises his wooden shepherd's staff over the sea. A mighty wind parts the waters, and the people walk on the dry seabed between walls of water. When they arrive on the far shore, Moses raises his staff again and the walls of water fall back to inundate and destroy Pharaoh's chariots, horses, and men. The army of Pharaoh is sacrificed to preserve and found a new nation—an act in which Yahweh's solution to the sin problem is begun.

Miriam, who had watched over the newborn Moses hidden in the bulrushes of the Nile River, now leads a celebration of deliverance: "Sing to the LORD (Yahweh) for he has triumphed gloriously; horse and rider he has thrown into the sea!" (Exodus 15:21). The Song of Miriam celebrates the wonders of Yahweh's miraculous victory. Yahweh, not Moses is the hero. The slaves' deliverance comes from divine, rather than military, might. The Song of the Sea follows also in praise of Yahweh.

The Lasting Significance of the Exodus

The grand story of Moses is Geschichte, highly interpreted and biased, and seen through the prism of faith. It is turning point or crisis number one of Heilsgeschichte. Echoes of this salvation history sound throughout the Bible. There are the covenant recitals, ritualized confessional retellings as in Deuteronomy 6 and 26; Joshua 24; and Psalms 78, 105, 106, 135 and 136. These memories, passed down over generations, form the bedrock of God's people's self-understanding as well as their ethics: they are to welcome strangers and aliens, because they themselves had been aliens in Egypt. Moses' story also defines Yahweh as the God of liberation with a heart for justice.

More generally, the Exodus also establishes several other important truths about God's will and God's people:

- It is the creating formative event. It created the chosen (missional) covenant shalom people of God out of the unjust Egyptian chaos. The shared event and memory creates a bonded community of people out of a diverse crowd of slaves. This shared event and common memory of being chosen by God creates a conscious identity and a sense of mission and purpose.
- It defines salvation as a historical, political and corporate event, as well as an individual experience, and is Yahweh's mightiest act of salvation until Jesus the Messiah.
- It is the greatest revelation of Yahweh's character in the Old Testament as a God who shows compassion for oppressed and suffering peoples.
- It is the beginning reference event and ultimate act of God's grace to which the people of God are called to remember throughout Old Testament history.
- It fulfills the promise made to Abraham.
- It reveals Yahweh through the burning bush event as actively present in history to bring about his purpose and will.
- It reveals Yahweh's original model for fighting a Holy War.

Holy War Theology

Holy War was not original to the Israelites. All ancient Near Eastern nations had national gods who supposedly fought Holy War for them. Holy War involved a battle of the national gods in the spiritual realm of the gods above the sky/dome. Their armies fought to help their national gods win the battle, because the outcome of the battle between the gods above the dome really determined the outcome on earth. Humans could help their gods win by fighting for them on earth. What happened on earth influenced which god won in heaven, which in turn determines who won on earth—a circular movement.

The Israelites made one very critical change in the Holy War concept they borrowed. As at the crisis at the Red Sea, the Israelites did not fight because Yaweh fought for them. The Exodus, rather than the later historical period of conquest and invasion, reveals the original model for warfare in Israel, trusting in God to conquer evil and bring vindication.[4]

After some time, the Israelites fought modified Holy War, yet specific characteristics or elements of Holy War emerged to keep warfare infrequent and as just as possible. These elements become evident as one reads through the Old Testament, and those elements in turn reveal the theology behind Holy War.

- **Inquiry of Yahweh:** Before going to battle, the people needed to discern whether Yahweh had declared Holy War, because if Yahweh hadn't declared war, God's people would suffer defeat. The defeat at Kadesh illustrates this well (Numbers 14:39-45). Going to battle in Holy War was a matter of faithfulness, not emotion or reason. Gideon discerned the Lord's will twice with the fleece before preparing for battle (Judges 6:36). God, not humans, declared war.

- **Summoning of the people:** The men needed to be summoned for a Holy War because the Israelites kept no standing army. Their culture's existence depended on their trust in God. Their existence with Yahweh as king was a daily miracle and witness to Yahweh's greatness and care. Generations after the exodus, King David sinned when he numbered the people and set up a standing army.

- **Hallowing (purging) of the people:** If a Holy God declared Holy War, then God needed a holy people to participate. The Achan story in Joshua 7 illustrated the disastrous results when sinful people declare holy war. Yahweh refused to fight for them. Abstaining from sexual relations during preparation and during war was another element of hallowing. The men were to devote themselves to one purpose alone. David's first sin with Bathsheba was breaking the rules of Holy War. His attempted cover-up failed because Bathsheba's husband, Uriah the Hittite, remained true to the Holy War rules while David, the supposedly godly king of Israel, did not (II Samuel 11).

---

4   Ibid., 34, 49-51.

- **Terror of the Lord in battle:** The Lord went before the people like a king leading in battle. God then wins the battle in a surprising way, called the Terror of the Lord. The Terror of the Lord could be a natural event like a hailstorm, human panic (Judges 6:7), the plagues in Exodus, sudden massive deaths (II Kings 19:35ff), or the blinding of the enemy (II Kings 6:17-18). The Lord wins the battle. The Psalmist asks, "Who is the King of glory? The Lord, strong and mighty, the Lord mighty in battle" (Psalms 24:8).

- *Cherem* (pronounced "hahreem") or the Ban: Everything is offered to God as a holy sacrifice, a holocaust. Nothing is kept from the battle except when specifically told to do so. Since God wins the battle, everything belongs to God. King Saul's sin involved the breaking of this Holy War rule in battle against the Amalakites. Saul and his army did not kill everything as a sacrifice to God as he had been told to do (I Samuel 15).

This holocaust sacrifice sometimes included property (since the gods pervaded everything) as well as all living things. Killing men, women, children and animals is abhorrent to us today. Following Holy War rules in that historical context meant that destroying people and property was an issue of faithfulness, not of revenge or wanton violence. And since the Lord won the battle, all the spoils belonged to the Lord. The people were not to go to battle for revenge or for personal gain, only out of faithfulness to their divine king, Yahweh.

- **Thanksgiving:** Worship and thanksgiving is appropriate because the Lord not the army won the battle. Yahweh is always the hero and deserves the credit though the people participated. In the story above, Miriam led the people in thanksgiving at the Red Sea (Exodus 15). Deborah celebrates Yahweh's Holy War victory (Judges 5).

- **Returning Home:** "To your tents O Israel" (I Kings 12:16) expresses an important attitude of theocracy. Dissolving the temporary army was a commitment of trust and faith in Yahweh. The army that gathered for Holy War disperses after Yahweh, their king, wins the battle. The people become vulnerable again in their dependence on Yahweh. The people's very existence without a "normal king" was a daily miracle. Their trust in Yahweh was a daily witness and revelation of Yahweh's care and greatness (Joshua 2:1-11).

History of Holy War in Salvation History

The purpose of Holy War was to fight against the evil that had destroyed shalom community and that tried to keep God from creating a chosen people through whom the whole world would be restored to right relationships (shalom).

The original method for Israel to fight Holy War was to stand still—to trust and not fight—and let God do the fighting, as in Exodus 14:13. As in other areas of life, God's people were sometimes more and sometimes less faithful in the way they fought Holy War. Very soon after the Exodus, the Israelites became less faithful and began to fight with Yahweh rather than trusting Yahweh to fight for them, much like the nationalistic cultures that surrounded them. Later, during the Monarchy after they had a king, King David established a standing army that fought for God. Finally in the defeat and exile of Judah, God fought against his own people.[5] This movement and change in the history of Holy War reflects God working with an unfaithful people, not a change in God's ultimate will.

After Adam's sin, God declared war on evil, not on humans. God limits judgment as an expression of grace. Judgment comes as a built-in principle. God "gave them up" to reap what they sowed (Romans 1). The original model of Holy War established in Exodus evolved over time as God adapted to the Israelites' failures to remain faithful.

1. **God Fights for the People**—As discussed above, in the original form of Holy War, the people's role is to be yielded and trusting. The plagues, the drowning of the Egyptian army and the promised hornets (Exodus 23:28-35) to drive out the people from the Promised Land represent this original model of Holy War. However, the people become impatient wanting more security than the "trusting and standing still" way! Standing still and trusting God is hard!

2. **People Fight Alongside God**—During the period of the judges,

---

5   Eller

people fight with God. God calls on Deborah and Gideon and a handful of men to defeat Israel's enemies. Yahweh is still king of Israel. There is still no standing army. When the people fight, they do so as a kind of mopping up exercise after the Terror of the Lord has won the victory.

3. **People Fight for God**—During the period of nation-state Israel, King David establishes a standing army, a sin against the original rules of Holy War (II Samuel 24). The Israelites begin to trust in their army (horses and chariots) rather than in Yahweh, their true king. Out of a loss of patience and faith, they desire a human king to lead them into battle like other nation states. Security becomes a matter of institution rather than trusting in Yahweh.

4. **God Fights against the People**—After generations of increased faithlessness, God finally declares Holy War against Judah, and the Israelites fall to Babylon. After their defeat, the people ask the prophet Jeremiah whether Yahweh is really the greatest God—after all, they have been defeated in Holy War! Jeremiah explains that Yahweh was not defeated at all, but was actually fighting against his own people in judgment so they might repent (Jeremiah 19 and 21). Rather than learning from their failure, God's people harden, becoming institutionalized and turning their backs on Yahweh. The kingdom of Israel shatters, smashed like a clay pot (Jeremiah 19), never to be put together again. The post-exile prophets envision God doing a new thing, a suffering servant Messiah leader who will fight evil again in the original way.

The Final Victory of Jesus

In the New Testament, Jesus fights evil in the original way again. Jesus is both God and human and is completely faithful to God. Jesus defeats evil by exposing the evil powers for what they are; not all-good and not all-powerful. The powers are doubly exposed when they kill Jesus. In killing a sinless Jesus they expose themselves as not all good. When Jesus rises from the dead they are exposed as not all powerful because the most feared power, death, is overcome. The power of evil has now been defeated in Jesus' Holy War.

- Deliverance from Egypt is the original model in Exodus 1-15. God sends Moses and various plagues to convince the Egyptians to let the Hebrew slaves go, and parts the Reed Sea when the Egyptians pursue them.
- Battle of Jericho in Joshua 6. The people march around the city blowing trumpets, and the walls fall down.
- Deborah's victory over Canaanite coalition in Judges 4-5. The Israelite army accomplishes nothing, but victory is won.
- Gideon's battle with Midianites in Judges 6-7. God limits the army to 300 men, has them blow trumpets and smash jars around the enemy camp, and the Midianites turn on each other, making for an easy defeat.
- Samuel's battle with the Philistines in I Samuel 7. They attack the Israelite camp, but Samuel intercedes and in response God sends thunder that sends the Philistines into a panic, allowing the Israelites to win.
- David's battle with Goliath in I Samuel 17. In a fight to the death, a boy defeats a giant by hitting him on the head with just one stone from a slingshot.
- Elisha and the king of Syria in II Kings 6. The king of Syria sends soldiers to capture Elisha, but at Elisha's request God blinds all the soldiers; Elisha leads them to the king of Israel where, instead of killing the soldiers, they treat the soldiers to a banquet, and the conflict is resolved.
- Elisha and Benhadad in II Kings 7. God caused the enemy army to hear the sound of a huge army approaching, so they fled without a fight.
- Isaiah's counsel to King Ahaz in Isaiah 7. When Israel is threatened, God tells them to just have faith and God will take care of the situation.
- Isaiah, Hezekiah, and Sennacherib in I Kings 19 and Isaiah 30:15; 31:1-4. Sennacherib sends a threatening message to King Hezekiah, so Hezekiah prays for deliverance and that night God strikes much of Sennacherib's army dead and Sennacherib withdraws.
- Jehoshaphat and people of the East in II Chronicles 20:1-30. God tells Jehoshaphat's army to just go stand there, and God defeats the opposing army by the time they get there.

Exodus-Sinai: Covenant

Bible passages: Exodus 1-4, 12, 14, 17-20

A Call to Mission at the Mountain

After the dramatic Exodus from Egypt, the ethnically diverse liberated people are on the move. They have seen Yahweh's "signs and wonders" in Egypt and experienced Yahweh's "mighty arm" in spectacular victory over Pharaoh's military at the sea. They have been witness to Yahweh's original model of Holy War, where the only warrior was Yahweh and the people's only weapon was trust.[1]

The events of the Exodus will be remembered and recalled, told and retold, sung and celebrated as the highpoint of Old Testament *Heilsgeschichte*. God's saving initiative calls for the people's response; without it there can be no intimate and continuing relationship. The Exodus is inseparably linked to what happens next at Mount Sinai: the covenant and the Eleven Words.

Three months of travel have brought the people into the desert of the Sinai Peninsula and to the mountain of God, Mount Sinai or Horeb. The Gulf of Suez now separates them from Pharaoh's Empire in Egypt. This short journey has been long enough to establish a pattern of behavior: the people grumble and complain and God comes to their rescue. Yahweh, who freed them from slavery, now provides water, food, and victory in a battle against the Amalakites, a people of the desert whom they will encounter

---

1   Millard C. Lind, *Yahweh is a Warrior: The Theology of Warfare in Ancient Israel.* (Scottdale, PA: Herald Press, 1980), 23ff.

again. The people who have known Yahweh as liberator, now experience Yahweh as the God of providence. The Yahweh of providence intervenes to fix what the people mess up and to keep the story going—as God has done since sin entered the world.

Encamped at the foot of the mountain, the people settle in for a long stay. Here is where the people will meet Yahweh, where they receive their identity as a people, where they enter into a long-lasting relationship with Yahweh, and where they hear their call to be a chosen, covenant, shalom community.

While the people are camped at the foot of the mountain, Moses climbs the mountain multiple times to meet Yahweh. The presence of God on the mountaintop is demonstrated by a spectacular storm, a sign of Yahweh's unparalleled power and majesty. As Yahweh used plagues of nature against Pharaoh, now nature once again signals Yahweh's mastery over the natural elements. On the mountain, Moses receives the Ten Words or Ten Commandments that become the basis for the people's attitudes and behavior as Yahweh's people.

Covenant Shapes the Old People of God

How can a ragtag, mixed group of former slaves become a people of purpose and mission? How can people who were under Pharaoh's lash learn to trust and follow Yahweh in gratitude instead of fear? How will a people who have lived under violence and oppression become a people of peace and shalom? It happens by providence and by covenant.

Providence is the basis for the covenant. The covenant is built on what has already happened. The covenant at Sinai is possible because of the Exodus. Exodus is prologue to Sinai. We refer to both events together as Exodus-Sinai. This linking is explicit in the rest of the "Eagles' Wings" passage in Exodus 19:5-6:

> *You have seen what I did to the Egyptians and how I bore you on eagles'*
> *wings and brought you to myself.*
> *Now, therefore, if you obey my voice and keep my covenant,*
> *You shall be my treasured possession out of all the peoples.*
> *Indeed, the whole earth is mine*
> *But you shall be for me a priestly kingdom and a holy nation.*[2]

---

2 Bernard W. Anderson, *Understanding the Old Testament.* Fifth Edition. (Upper Saddle River, NJ: Pearson Education, 2007), 82-83.

The promise of transformation is based on Yahweh's providence and the people's obedience. With the people's cooperation, they will become Yahweh's cherished possession, a kingdom of priests, and people with a sacred calling. Transforming an oppressed, powerless people into the high status of a holy nation is remarkable. This transformation is formalized and sealed by the Sinai covenant that orders or defines the God-people relationship.

Deliverence Means Transformation

From	To
• Egyptian slavery identity	• People of Yahweh identity
• Serving Pharaoh	• Serving Yahweh
• Slavery	• Freedom
• A mixed crowd	• A people
• Bondage thinking	• Freedom thinking
• Forced obedience	• Gratitude obedience to shalom
• Violence	• Shalom
• Oppressive leadership	• Servant leadership
• Inequality and oppression	• Shalom justice
• No mission or purpose	• Chosen for a mission

First, in the covenant ceremony, Yahweh's identity is redefined. Yahweh the warrior is enthroned and crowned king.[3] Yahweh's rule, called a theocracy, becomes the standard form of government until the people later reject it when they demand a human king. But for now, only Yahweh is king and Moses remains a prophet who speaks for King Yahweh. Second, the people are called to respond, not because of Pharaoh-like coercion, but in gratitude of Yahweh' providence in the deliverance from Pharaoh's slavery. We might think of the Sinai covenant as a founding document or constitution of the newly formed Old People of God. At the heart of this long and complex document are the Eleven Words. God's liberating Exodus is the First Word, followed by the Ten Words or Ten Commandments that outline the obligations and duties of the people. In the Passover Seder, *Haggadah* (the story) is followed by *Halakah* (the commands).

Covenant Structure and Form

The covenant made at Mount Sinai follows the form and structure borrowed from Israel's Near Eastern neighbors. The Hittite form of

---

3   Ibid., Lind, 50.

covenant between a king and his subjects contains six elements. The first three are used in the Sinai covenant, and the others are explicit in later texts.

First, the **Preamble** identifies the king, the superior party of the covenant, typically with names and titles. At Sinai, Yahweh is identified as "the LORD your God."

Second, the **Historical Prologue** gives the historical basis for the relationship, usually identifying the king's character and acts of benevolence. Yahweh "brought you out of the land of Egypt, out of the house of slavery" establishes the historical context, and is echoed in the Eagles' Wings text: "You have seen what I did to the Egyptians, and how I bore you on eagles' wings and brought you to myself." This means grace comes before commands.

Third, the **Stipulations** element requires to the loyalty of the subjects and identifies their responsibilities in serving the king and living peacefully in the kingdom. The ten stipulations of the Sinai covenant are:

You shall have no other gods before me
You shall not make for yourself an idol
You shall not make wrongful use of the name of the Lord your God
Remember the Sabbath day and keep it holy
Honor your father and your mother
You shall not murder
You shall not commit adultery
You shall not steal
You shall not bear false witness
You shall not covet

Fourth, the **Deposit and Annual Public Recital** component specifies where the covenant is to be kept and requires an annual ceremony of retelling. Moses took the covenant and put it into the Ark of the Covenant, along with Aaron's budding staff and a golden vessel containing manna. This hallowed box symbolizes Yahweh's presence in the Tabernacle, the portable place of worship built soon after the covenant is made. The annual recital is omitted here, but appears in numerous other texts, such as Deuteronomy 26.

Fifth, **Witnesses.** In Hittite covenants, the gods and natural elements, such as heaven, earth, rivers, and mountains serve as witnesses. At Sinai, when all the people witnessed the thunder and lightning, the sound of the trumpet, and the mountain smoking, they were afraid and trembled and stood at a distance. Sixth, **Sanctions** specify consequences: blessings for keeping the covenant and curses for unfaithfulness, also common throughout the Old Testament.[4]

The covenant with Yahweh is ratified when the leaders meet God on the top of the mountain, and when people promise, "All that the Lord has spoken we will do, and we will be obedient" (Exodus 24:7). Moses symbolically pours blood of sacrificed animals on the ceremonial alter he has built. Now the people have a king and the king has a people.

Two Kinds of Covenants

The Bible contains two kinds of covenants, **unconditional** and **conditional.** Unconditional covenants are one-sided. God, sovereign and transcendent, makes a promise without requiring any human response as with Noah (Genesis 8:21-22, 9:8-17) and Abraham (Genesis 12:1-3, 15:4-20, 17:21-8). Later God makes the same kind of covenant with Levi (Numbers 25:10-13) and David (II Samuel 7:11b-16).

Conditional covenants, on the other hand, require the cooperation of both parties. God's promises are dependent on the people's obedience and faithfulness. Conditional covenants in salvation history include those made at Sinai (Exodus 20, Deuteronomy 5) and Shechem (Joshua 24). Renewals of conditional covenants are made with Josiah, a later king of Israel (II Kings 23:1-4); Ezra, a prophet (Nehemiah 10:28-31). God always initiates covenants and awaits the people's response. Keeping covenants is reward with blessings; breaking covenants brings on curses (Deuteronomy 27-28).

Throughout the Bible, there is tension between conditional and unconditional covenants. Only with Jesus, who is completely faithful to both types of covenants as both God and human, is the tension resolved. Christians and churches continue to live with tensions or paradoxes, such as faith and works, grace and judgment, predestination and free will.

Covenants may also be categorized as parity and suzerainty. In parity covenants, two parties of equal rank bind themselves to each other in a bilateral agreement. The suzerainty or kingly covenant is like the Hittite treaty, made between a king and the inferior vassal, a more unilateral arrangement. The king also binds himself to conditions of the covenant though the king is sovereign. The Sinai covenant reflects a suzerain, not a parity covenant. Yahweh binds himself in the conditional Sinai covenant.

---

4   Ibid., Anderson, 89-91.

Understanding the Eleven Words

The first of the Eleven Words is the word of grace: "I am the Lord your God who brought you out of the land of Egypt, out of the house of slavery." The word of grace, God's act of grace precedes the people's response. To get the full effect, the First Word of grace should be repeated before each command. The commands, Halakah, sometimes called law, are rooted in the grace of what God had done for them.

The motivation for keeping commandments was—and is—gratitude, not fear. Sinai commands are not legalism or salvation based on people's behavior. Legalism is law without prior grace. That is why the First Word must never be detached from the commands that follow. Libertinism, by contrast, is grace without law or what German theologian Dietrich Bonheoffer called "cheap grace."[5]

The Eleven Words keep the Exodus deliverance and Sinai covenant together. From the very beginning of the People of God's existence, divine grace and divine demand, gospel and law, are always connected. As Old Testament scholar Bernard W. Anderson put it, the "saving experience" and the "commanding experience" are inseparable in Israel's experience and theology.[6]

The commands are a gift, not a burden. The law and the Eleven Words are Yahweh's gracious revelation to a recently delivered, diverse, and uninitiated group of slaves about how to live as God's free community. The primary purpose of the law is to teach them how to be a Shalom community, where relationships are healed as a remedy for sin, not the revelation of sin.

The first command calls for exclusive loyalty to the God of the Exodus. United exclusive loyalty to one God is the first requirement for a Shalom community. The second commandment amplifies the first stating that the loyalty to Yahweh must be taken seriously. The rest of the commandments reveal ways to live in Shalom community.

In accepting Yahweh's covenant offer at Sinai, the liberated slaves say "No" to Pharaoh's claims on them. They leave the old values behind, cross over the water, and are now ratifying what God has done for them. At Sinai, the people accept God's action for them and God's call and claim on them to be the priestly, missional people.

---

5   Dietrich Bonhoeffer, *The Cost of Discipleship* (New York: Touchstone, 1995).

6   Ibid., Anderson, 103.

The People Break the Covenant

No sooner is the covenant ratified than the people renege on their promise. Moses returns to the mountain and stays so long, the people fear he will never return. Their grumbling of discontent grows to a demand for "gods" they can see. Despite the second commandment prohibiting images of God, Aaron the brother of Moses, acquiesces, takes the people's jewelry, and crafts a golden calf as an object of worship. The happy people throw a wild carnival: they drink, dance, and perhaps engage in sexual orgies. Such is the scene when Moses returns with the Eleven Words carved onto a two stone tablets. In a fit anger, Moses shatters the tablets—just as the people have broken the Eleven Words and their covenant with Yahweh.[7]

Will this be the end of the story? Moses begs God not to give up. Once again, Yahweh's character is revealed: the God who carried the people out of slavery on eagles' wings, forgives the ungrateful, fallen, sinful people. When Moses climbs again to the mountaintop and cuts two more tablets for the Eleven Words, he hears a description of Yahweh that contains limited judgment and unlimited grace:

Yahweh, the Lord [is]
a God merciful and gracious, slow to anger,
and abounding in steadfast love and faithfulness,
keeping steadfast love for the thousandth generation,
forgiving iniquity and transgression and sin,
yet by no means clearing the guilty,
but visiting the iniquity of the parents
upon the children
and the children's children,
to the third and the fourth generation (Exodus 34:6-7).

Moving On

The encampment at the mountain is a long one. In literary terms it doesn't end until Numbers 10:36. Numbers is the fourth of the first five books of the Old Testament, which scholars call the Pentateuch (the Greek term for "five books"). Sandwiched between the books of Exodus and Numbers is Leviticus, a long and complex detailing of the people's obligations.

The people who leave Sinai are no longer the same ragtag, miscellaneous

---

7   Ibid., 95.

cluster of people who came to Sinai, without a coherent identity. The covenant has given them an official identity as the People of God. Though they are ethnically diverse, they are—together—called the Children of Israel or Israelites. Although they have already failed, the broken covenant is renewed and reaffirmed.

In the next stage of *Heilsgeschichte*, the travelers spend forty years in an unfriendly desert, learning how to be the chosen, covenant, shalom people of God.

Wilderness Wanderings

Bible passages: Numbers 3:1-20; 10-14; 16; 20-23. Deuteronomy 14-20; Leviticus 16-19, 25-26

The Desert Crucible

When the cloud lifts over the Israelite camp, the journey from Sinai to the Promised Land begins (Numbers 11:10). The moving cloud is Yahweh's signal that they are to leave Sinai, the place of the covenant, where they have made camp for nearly a year. Tribe by tribe, the Israelite multitude sets out for Canaan, the land promised to Abraham, Sarah, and their descendants (Genesis 12:1-7).

The physical distance to Canaan is relatively short, but because of their misguided worship of the golden calf idol and the incident with the twelve spies described later in this chapter, the people are doomed to 40 years of desert living. In the crucible of the desert, the people are tested, molded, and shaped. The story of these years is "a complex story of unfaithfulness, rebellion, apostasy, and frustration, set against the background of God's faithfulness, presence, provision, and forbearance."[1]

The grumbling begins before they reach Sinai. They complain about the lack of water at Marah, Massah, and Meribah. After Sinai, the grumbling and complaining intensifies. When they complain about the lack of food, God sends them daily manna, a sweet bread-like substance. But when they remember the good food they had enjoyed in Egypt, the manna does not

---

1 William Sanford LaSor, et al., *Old Testament Survey: The Message, Form, and Background of the Old Testament* (Grand Rapids: William B. Eerdmans Publishing Company, 1996), 99.

satisfy them. When they beg for meat, God sends them quail.

In a leadership crisis, Aaron and Miriam, the brother and sister of Moses, lead a mutiny against their brother. Others, identified as "rabble," lead another revolt against Moses. And then the "whole congregation" rebels. The patience of Moses and of Yahweh is tested again and again. Typically, Moses intercedes for the people, begging Yahweh not to punish the people as they deserve. But even Moses, the model of servant leadership, has his limits. When instructed to speak *dabar* to bring forth water from a rock, Moses becomes angry and strikes the rock with his staff. Water flows, but his fit of disobedience prevents Moses from entering the Promised Land.

For most of the desert sojourn, the people camp at an oasis at Kadesh or Kadesh-Barnea, about eleven days' travel from Sinai. From this place, Moses sends twelve men to explore the southern hills of Canaan. The spies discover a rich and fertile place, "a land flowing with milk and honey." But they also encounter fortified cities and fearful giants. Of the twelve, only Joshua and Caleb trust Yahweh to fight Holy War for them. The others spread fear and distrust among the people, declaring that the Canaanites are so large that in comparison, "we seemed like grasshoppers." Because the ten skeptics prevailed, Yahweh's judgment descends on the people. All the people twenty years and older will never see Canaan, but will die in the desert. In a measure of grace, the younger generation under Joshua's leadership are permitted to enter the Promised Land.

Four Themes

Fragmented by dissension and despair, doubt and disbelief, the people struggle to comprehend the ways of Yahweh. Yahweh got them out of Egypt; now Yahweh faced the challenge of getting "Egypt" out of the people. They have to shed the brutal and coercive ways of the pharaohs. The young-in-faith people must adopt new values and a capture a new vision. Four things they must learn: to trust a faithful and trustworthy God, to follow servant leadership, to worship Yahweh in gratitude, and to become a chosen, covenant, shalom community.

Learning to Trust a Faithful, Trustworthy God

The Israelites have only known the capricious, exploitative gods of Egypt. Learning to trust Yahweh, a faithful God who keeps promises, who loves and cares for them, requires a radical reorientation. The harsh isolation of the desert provides the context—the laboratory for trusting

Yahweh for their daily provision and constant protection—as illustrated by the following examples:

- The water sweetened at Marah reveals a faithful God who can be trusted to provide (Exodus 15). The manna and quail further reveal a trustworthy God (Exodus 16 and Numbers 11).

- The people learn to trust God daily for sufficient food (manna). Any manna hoarded beyond the day's need spoiled, except for the Sabbath (Exodus 16).

- Successful Holy War against the Amalekites teaches the people to trust Yahweh for their protection (Exodus 17). Holy War victories against Sihon, king of the Amorites, and Og, king of Bashan underscores Yahweh's care for them (Numbers 21). Yahweh protects the people from the curses (*dabar*) of Balaam and instead causes the Mesopotamian prophet to speak words of blessing.

- At Kadesh, the people learn what happens when they do not trust God to fight Holy War; they wander in the wilderness for many years and witness those twenty years and older die before they get to the Promised Land (Numbers 13). The lack of trust also brings the judgment plagues (Numbers 16) and of poisonous snakebites (Numbers 21).

These selected stories reveal a faithful and consistent God, as well as a moral God, who enforces the conditional Mosaic covenant with blessings and curses.

Learning Servant Leadership and Theocracy

The leadership the people knew in Egypt was brutal and coercive. Now they needed to learn how to trust and follow servant leadership. Even Moses had to learn how to organize and delegate from his Midianite father-in-law Jethro (Exodus 18).

Amidst jealousy and conflict, the tribe of Levi is chosen for the priesthood when Aaron's rod sprouts blossoms (Numbers 17). The people learn to respect their leaders from the experience of Miriam becoming leprous after she and Aaron speak against Moses (Numbers 12). Korah,

Dothan, Abiram and 250 Levites challenge the leadership of Moses and Aaron. Consequently, the three men and their families are swallowed up by the earth, and the 250 are consumed by fire. When the "whole congregation" rebels against Moses and Aaron, 14,700 of them are killed by a plague (Numbers 16).

Moses provides an excellent, though not perfect, example of Yahweh-like leadership when he is willing to sacrifice his own life to prevent the destruction of his people. In Numbers 14, he shows more grace than does Yahweh. He works to expedite Yahweh's purpose rather than his own. When he was criticized for marrying a Cushite woman, Yahweh defends Moses, who is then called the most humble person on earth (Numbers 12:3).

Learning How to Worship Yahweh

The slaves had known only oppression and servitude under the pharaohs, who were thought to be sons of the Sun god. In the desert, the people learn to worship Yahweh, not as a cyclical nature god who could be manipulated, but in gratitude for what Yahweh has done for them. Their worship is grounded in remembrance. They are invited to voluntarily and joyfully worship Yahweh, the all-powerful, sovereign God, who delivered them from slavery and who daily provides for them in the desert.

The tabernacle or "Tent of Meeting" is a portable sanctuary that symbolizes the presence of Yahweh. It is placed in the center of the encampment to signal Yahweh's presence in their midst. Yahweh, the God of the Exodus, the God of action, now comes to reside in the midst of the people. But the tent is portable. When it moves, the people move. Yahweh is radically free and cannot be confined by geography, nation, or race. Yahweh's purpose for the Old People of God is to live as a chosen, covenant, shalom community for all people everywhere. Later in the story, Israel builds a permanent temple within the borders of the nation-state—a departure from the original will of God.

The Ark of the Covenant in the Holy of Holies represents a God who combines grace and law, story and command. Worshiping Yahweh is a way of living, not merely a ceremony. Worship worthy of this God combined praise and justice, liturgy and holy living. Most of their offerings were given to the widows, poor, and aliens living among them. Israelite worship, praise, and sacrifice was rooted in grateful memory for blessings already received, not pagan appeasement or manipulation in order to receive blessings.

Yahweh was thought to be the most present between the wings of the Cherubim on top of the Ark of the Covenant. It symbolized Yahweh watching over the Covenant. That Yahweh existed in a space rather than in a concrete symbol was a powerful anti-idol worship concept.

All Israelite worship is rooted in God's mighty act of deliverance in the Exodus. The Passover becomes central and foundational for all Hebrew worship (Exodus 23). The Feast of Tabernacles or Booths celebrates Yahweh's faithful provision and protection in the desert. (Leviticus 23).

The Day of Atonement (today's Yom Kippur) reminds people that Yahweh is a moral and just God, as well as a gracious and forgiving God. It reminds people to confess their sins and to integrate ethical integrity in their worship. The sin scapegoat ceremony is also a forgiveness ceremony without shedding blood (Leviticus 16).

The feast of Pentecost is a reminder and celebration of Yahweh's faithful blessings (Leviticus 23). The sacrifice of first fruits, feeding the priests, the alien and the poor is combined with the covenant recital of God's mighty act of creating a people (Deuteronomy 26). All worship is grounded in remembering Yahweh's act of forming a holy, just, shalom community of right relationships.

Learning to be a Theocratic, Shalom, Missional Community

Learning to trust Yahweh, learning servant leadership, and learning to worship all contribute to Yahweh's continued formation of a chosen, covenant, shalom community in the desert. The kind of society the slaves had known was one of oppression, domination, violence and ruthless power. A dynamic social order that was devoted to people's needs, freedom, equality, and shalom justice was radically different. Yahweh broke and disrupted the oppressive imperialism of Egypt. Now the people are free to begin living toward a new social and political reality.[2]

Where did the structures for this unique social vision come from? No doubt some were borrowed from other peoples and adapted along the way. But the vision for this Yahweh-revealing radical political community was born out of this isolated mobile community's encounter with Yahweh in Exodus-Sinai and wilderness experiences. And all godly leaders after Moses attempted to lead the people toward this vision.

Shalom refers to a sense of well-being, of completeness, of wholeness.

---

2 Walter Brueggemann, *The Prophetic Imagination* (Minneapolis: Augsburg Fortress, 2001), 8-9.

Shalom is the proper ordering of relationships where all four dimensions—with God, others, self, and creation—are healed and whole. Shalom encompasses personal, economic, social and political well-being. Shalom is impossible when there is a significant gap between rich and poor, when there are injustices of any kind.[3]

The purpose of the commands, regulations, or laws received at Sinai is to move society toward shalom justice. The Eleven Words pointed people toward shalom. The Sabbath day rest set boundaries around economic gain. Any manna hoarded beyond the day's need spoiled in the wilderness, discouraging any entrepreneurial ambition and self-sufficiency that would disrupt shalom and their dependency on Yahweh. On the Sabbath people and animals were given rest. The motivation for Sabbath rest was God's deliverance (rest) from Egyptian bondage. Sabbath-keeping was an extension of the rest-giving action of the God of the Exodus.

They were to remember that they had been aliens and slaves in Egypt, and this memory was to be the driving force behind their ethics. The Israelites were to care for aliens and strangers because they themselves had been aliens; they were to remember how they suffered under Pharaoh. "I am the Lord your God" is the shortened version of the first of the Eleven Words, "I am the Lord your God who brought you out of the land of Egypt, out of the house of bondage." The motivating word of grace preceding commands (law) reverberates through much of the Old Testament in texts such as Leviticus 29.

This memory of God's gracious deliverance is to prompt the people to practice shalom justice, where people get, not what they deserve, but what they need. Shalom justice reflects the gracious nature and actions of Yahweh.

It includes an economic principle called Jubilee to be practiced every fifty years—when they reach the Promised Land of Canaan. It begins with a weekly Sabbath Day of rest. When they reach the Promised Land of Canaan, they are to honor the weekly Sabbath, a day of rest. In an extension of the Sabbath Day, they are to practice a Sabbath year. In the seventh year, debts are to be forgiven, slaves are to be set free, and the land is to rest by remaining uncultivated. Those who work the land—and even animals, are to be given a year-long rest (Deuteronomy 15:1-18; Leviticus 25: 1-7).

After seven cycles of seven years, on the fiftieth year, comes the grand

3   Perry B. Yoder, *Shalom: The Bible's Word for Salvation, Justice, and Peace* (Newton KS: Faith and Life Press, 1987), 5ff.

culmination of the Sabbath Year, the Year of Jubilee. In an expression of shalom justice, the economy is to be rebooted or restored. All debts are to canceled, slaves are to be set free, and the land is to be returned to the original owner (Leviticus 25:8-ff).

Why the Year of Jubilee? As a reminder that the land belongs to Yahweh and that the people are permanent foreigners and strangers, dependent on Yahweh's grace and generosity (Leviticus 25:23-24). They in turn, are to be generous: If anyone is in need, "don't be hard-hearted or tight-fisted toward your needy neighbor. You should rather open your hand, willingly lending enough to meet the need, whatever it may be (Deuteronomy 15:7-8).

The rebooting of land benefits those, who through no fault of their, loose their property. It benefits those who have gained land by reminding them that the land belongs, not to them, but to Yahweh.

Remember, you too were slaves, poor and landless! Remember!

In addition to human and animal rest, the land was also to lie fallow and rest during the Sabbath year. Debts were to be canceled. Slaves were to be set free with liberal provisions to help them start again. The Book of Deuteronomy clarifies the motivation: Sabbath-year laws were to be kept with joy and enthusiasm, because "you were a slave in the land of Egypt and the Lord your God redeemed you; for this reason I lay this command upon you today" (Deuteronomy 15:15).

Cities of refuge in Deuteronomy 19 are also expressions of shalom justice. The rules of war in Deuteronomy 20 express a concern for environmental preservation. All laws, including dietary restrictions, were considered religious laws because Hebrew faith was holistic: all of life was sacred.

All these laws are rooted in Yahweh's acts of grace, and are intended to restore and recreate the sense of shalom that was lost when humans first sinned in the Garden of Eden. The consequences and solution are universal. The purpose of all the commands is to create a chosen, covenant, shalom community that demonstrates of redemptive ways of Yahweh.

Interpreting the Wilderness Experience

These stories, long remembered, speak of Yahweh's judgment, always tempered by patience and grace. Prophets later recall these years as ideal, a time before Canaanite influence that led them to compromise their faith in Yaweh. Fewer than two dozen stories cover the forty years, illustrating how selective these stories are. Many events and stories were obviously not remembered. So we might ask why these particular stories are remembered, and also what meaning they carried to both their authors and the later scholars who gathered the scriptures for inclusion in the Bible.

The selected wilderness stories are filled with the people's grumblings and complaints. The picture of Yahweh's people seems to be negative and largely that of unfaithfulness. While this is true, Yahweh's "steadfast love" (Psalm 136) shines through more brightly. Yahweh, and Moses to a lesser extent, is the hero in all these stories. Yahweh the potter keeps working the lumpy and pliable clay taken out of Egypt.

While the desert sojourn seems to be a low point in the history of God's people, later prophets idealized this period. There would be no greater prophet than Moses, and it was a time before syncretism—the blending of Yahweh faith with Baal worship in Canaan. Jeremiah and Hosea, for example, see the people's faithfulness during these days in sharp contrast to the later faithlessness of Israel and Judah:

I remember the devotion of your youth, how as a bride you loved me and followed me in the wilderness in a land not sown. Israel was holy to the Lord the first fruits of his harvest (Jeremiah 2:2).

Therefore I will now allure her and bring her into the wilderness and speak tenderly to her. There she shall respond as in the days of her youth, as at the time when she came out of the land of Egypt (Hosea 2:14-15).

In the crucible of the desert, the isolation from other religions and peoples enabled the youthful people of God to be shaped and molded by Yahweh through the leadership of Moses, Miriam, and Aaron. Israel was being drawn to a social-political-religious model of society emphasizing Yahweh's justice and compassion, a model uniquely different from the imperialism of the Egyptians and of the nation-states of Canaan. The wilderness years were significant formative years when Yahweh began to solve the sin problem by choosing and shaping a missional, chosen, covenant, shalom community.

Entering Canaan

Bible passages: Numbers 13-24, Joshua 1-7, 8:30-35, 20, 23, 24

Roads to the Promised Land

From Kadesh, the twelve spies survey and explore the southern hill country of Canaan. The land is promising, but the cities and people seem formidable. Ten of the twelve spies, forgetting or discounting Yahweh's spectacular Holy War victory over the Pharaoh's armies at the Red Sea, convince the multitude that entering Canaan was impossible (Numbers 13-14). Strangely, some of the people decide it would be better to die fighting than to die wandering aimlessly in the desert, so they fight their way into the land. Without Moses' leadership and lacking Yahweh's approval, they are soundly defeated by the Amalekites of the desert and the Canaanites of the hill country (Numbers 14:29-45). Thus begins 40 years of wilderness wandering.

Since the southern approach was now impossible, they turn eastward to the Transjordan, the land east of the Jordan River. Here settled peoples block their way. First there are the Edomites, distant cousins related to Esau, Jacob's twin brother. Then there are the Moabites and Amorites, and beyond their lands is the kingdom of Bashan.

Moses sends emissaries to the king of Edom, asking permission to travel through his kingdom on the King's Highway, the primary north-south route through the region. The Edomite king refuses them passage (Numbers 20:14-21), so they skirt Edom and travel to Sihon, the kingdom of the Amorites. The Amorites make their intentions clear by mounting a military attack, but the immigrants soundly defeat the Amorites and occupy the entire kingdom (Numbers 21:21-26). Next they attack and defeat the King Og of Bashan, a giant of a man, and take possession of his lands Numbers 21:33-35). The Israelites set up camp on the Moabite plains by the Jordan River (Numbers 26:3).[1]

In the strangest of episodes, a donkey talks and a foreign prophet is hired to curse the Israelites. Aside from the humor of a talking donkey, the king of Moab orders a Babylonian prophet to speak *dabar* against the Israelites. But Yahweh, in a display of universal authority, counters the command and causes the prophet to bless Israel (Numbers 22-24).

Finally, Moses gives a long farewell (most of the book of Deuteronomy) to the people he has led from the Exodus, through the long years in the desert, to the point of entering Canaan. In a series of three "sermons" Moses recounts Yahweh's patience and providence, and once again, renews the covenant. In a final blessing, Moses declares:

Happy are you, O Israel! Who is like you,
a people saved by the LORD,
The shield of your help,
and the sword of your triumph!
Your enemies shall come fawning to you,
And you shall tread on their backs (Deuteronomy 33:29).

God summons Moses to Mount Nebo, where he can see the Promised Land he cannot enter. When Moses dies "at the LORD's command" the people mourn his death for thirty days (Deuteronomy 34:1-8).[2]

Joshua and Crossing the Jordan

The Book of Joshua opens with Joshua's appointment as the new Moses. As Moses led the people through the Red Sea in their exit from slavery, so Joshua leads them through the parted waters of the Jordan River into the Promised Land. In the Exodus, Yahweh's pillar and fire and Moses' staff lead the people. Now the priests, carrying the Ark of the Covenant, lead the people across the river on dry land. In the Exodus, Miriam celebrates Yahweh's Holy War deliverance, and now Joshua sets up a twelve-stone

---

1   Bernard W. Anderson, et al., *Understanding the Old Testament*, Fifth Edition (Upper Saddle River, NJ: Pearson Education, 2007), 107-110.

2   Ibid., Anderson, 111.

monument as a witness to this new chapter in *Heilsgeschichte*:

> *When your children ask their parents in time to come, "What do these stones mean?" then you shall let your children know, "Israel crossed over the Jordan here on dry ground." For the Lord your God dried up the waters of the Jordan for you until you crossed over, as the Lord your God did to the Red Sea, which he dried up for us until we crossed over, so that all the peoples of the earth may know that the hand of the Lord is mighty, and so that you may fear the Lord your God forever* (Joshua 4:21-24).

Holy War in Canaan

The people's first Holy War battle in Canaan is against the fortified city of Jericho and follows a slightly modified model of original Holy War. As Moses led the Exodus from Egypt without fighting, Joshua now enters Canaan without a battle.[3] In yet another example of the ethnically diverse character of Israel, Rahab the harlot assists in the victory by hiding the spies Joshua has sent into the city. She has heard the stories of the Exodus and Red Sea, and the recent victories over Amorite kings, Sihon and Og. She acknowledges Yahweh as the God of heaven and earth (Joshua 2:10-11). When the walls of Jericho fall at the sound of rams' horns, only Rahab and her family are spared. They join the Israelites and she is given an honored place as an ancestor of King David (Matthew 1:5), and is later named as a hero of faith (Hebrews 11:31).

After this dramatic victory at Jericho, however, Israel is badly defeated by a small city called Ai, because they "broke faith in regard to the devoted things." One of the men, Achan, has broken the rules of Holy War by keeping some of the booty, instead of destroying everything as a sacrifice to God (*chereem* or *herem*). In what must have been a horrendous scene, Achan and his family are stoned and the booty is sacrificed to Yahweh. Only then are the people's sins purged, making them again ready to fight Holy War (Joshua 7).[4]

---

3   Millard C. Lind, *Yahweh is a Warrior: The Theology of Warfare in Ancient Israel* (Scottdale, PA: Herald Press, 1980), 78.

4   Like the punishment of Korah, who led a revolt against Moses and was destroyed with his family (Numbers 16), the destruction of Achan's family is an expression of the ancient concept of "corporate personality," where individuals are not isolated from the groups to which they belong; all share in collective responsibility, therefore also, guilt and punishment. See Noel David Freedman, et al., "Corporate Personality" in *Eerdmans Dictionary*

From this point forward, the people more frequently abandon the original model of Holy War where Yahweh fights for them; increasingly, they fight with Yahweh.

Two Views: Were the Canaanites All Driven Out?

An initial reading of Joshua gives the impression that all the land is conquered and all the Canaanites are defeated or neutralized. For instance, "Joshua defeated the whole land, the hill country and the Negeb and the lowlands, the slopes and left no one remaining, but utterly destroyed all that breathed" (Joshua 11:16). But this is not the whole story.

The story of invasion and conquest is told as three decisive campaigns. In the first, the Israelites cross the Jordan River and attack the central hill country. In the second, they defeat a coalition of five kings in the south. In the third sweep, they defeat the kings of the northern territory.

In each case, Joshua defeats "the whole land" and "all their kings" because Yahweh "fought for Israel" (Joshua 10:28-43). The victory is reported as complete: "All the people they struck down with the edge of the sword, until they had destroyed them, and they did not leave any who breathed." The *Geschichte* of these events is clear: "For it was the Lord's doing to harden their hearts so they would come against Israel in battle, in order that they might be utterly destroyed" (Joshua 11:20). This recalls Yahweh's hardening of Pharaoh's heart so that all Egypt could witness Yahweh's power over Pharaoh.[5]

Later, however, Yahweh tells Joshua, "You are old and advanced in years, and very much of the land still remains to be possessed" (Joshua 13:1). Nevertheless, Yahweh orders Joshua to divide out the land among the tribes of Israel, with the confidence that Yahweh will eventually drive them all out. Joshua divides the land in chapters 13-21, with the exception that the two Joseph tribes, Manasseh and Ephraim, are given the large allotment of their father. The tribe of Levi receives no land. They are the appointed relgious leaders, and so they are supported by the other tribes' offerings.

The Book of Judges expands on the suggestion in Joshua 13 that many unconquered people remain around the Israelites. Groups such as the Amorites and Canaanites, who are said to have been soundly defeated

---

of the Bible, 285-287. See also LaSor et al., *Introduction to the Old Testament,* 147-148.

5   Millard Lind, *Yahweh is a Warrior: The Theology of Warfare in Ancient Israel* (Scottdale, PA: Herald Press, 1980), 77-71.

according to the Book of Joshua, are not all conquered after all.

The first chapter of Judges creates even more confusion about who was conquered when. What about Jerusalem? According to Judges 1:8, "the people of Judah fought against Jerusalem and took it." Joshua 10, quoted above, implies that Joshua defeated the king of Jerusalem as part of the victory over the five-king coalition. Yet it is it David, who later in II Samuel 5:6-9, conquers Jerusalem and makes it his new capital. While it appears in Judges 1 that the people take the Philistine cities and territories of Gaza, Ashkelon and Ekron, II Samuel 8:1 reports that it is King David who finally captures and controls the Philistine territories.

What is clear about this complexity is that we have a mix of history and *Geschichte*. While it may seem unsettling that there are different versions of how the conquest of Canaan happened, it shouldn't keep us from seeing the Bible as inspired. We can relax knowing the final editors didn't get rid of contradictory details. The ancient writers weren't as concerned about historical accuracy as modern day society is. It was more important to show Yahweh as the hero, with Joshua as a lesser hero. Yahweh did help the Israelites gain the Promised Land, and when the people disobeyed God, Yahweh withdrew his help.

Why weren't all the Canaanites driven out?

Three reasons—two *Geschichte* reasons and one history reason:

1. Judges gives two *Geschichte* reasons. First, for their disobedience: "you have not obeyed my command, so I will not drive them out before you; they shall become adversaries to you and their gods shall be a snare" (Judges 2:2-3).
2. Second, to test Israel: "to see whether they would take care to walk in the way of the Lord as their ancestors did" (Judges 2:21-23).
3. The history reason is that the Israelites could not drive out the inhabitants of the plain "because they had chariots of iron" (Judges 1:19). The Canaanites had a technological advantage. The Israelites were in the late Bronze Age, while the Philistines and other coastal peoples in Canaan were already in the Iron Age. Not until the United Monarchy do the Israelites catch up and enter the Iron Age. During the time of the judges, the Israelites were dependent on the technologically superior Philistines to make and maintain iron tools (I Samuel 13:19-20), an advantage the Philistines intentionally kept.

Even so, we know from the stories of Holy War that victory does not depend on strength or superior technology. Success depends on the degree of Israel's faithfulness and their dependence on Yahweh. In many Holy War stories, Israelite warriors are reduced to an absurdly small group in order to emphasize Yahweh as the victor.[6] For instance, Gideon, a later judge, cuts the number of his fighting men from 32,000 to a mere 300 (Judges 6). So in the end, the *Geschichte* interpretations outweigh the historic one.

Conquest, Infiltration, and Revolution

We can refer to the primary group of invaders under Joshua's leadership as Invasion or Conquest Peoples. Adding to the complexity of the story and to the diversity of Israel are two additional groups: Infiltration Peoples and Revolution Peoples.

The peaceful Infiltration Peoples are distant cousins who did not become slaves in Egypt. Over time they migrated to the less populated hill country as semi-nomadic shepherds and cattle herders. Some may have arrived even before the enslavement of their cousins. They lived at peace with their neighbors, perhaps marrying Canaanites as they blended into the Canaanite landscape, until their Conquest cousins arrived. Others may have settled the southern part of Canaan before they were enslaved. Some may also have infiltrated during the wilderness wanderings. Related Hurrian and Amorite peoples migrated into Canaan at the time of the patriarchs and after and could have joined the incoming tribes.

The Revolution Peoples were the Habiru, marginal and rootless people, perhaps enslaved by Canaanites. The Habiru took the invasion of the Conquest Peoples as their opportunity to engage in a "peasants' revolt" and free themselves from their oppressors and become free. They joined the invading Israelites in their conquest of Canaanite city-states.[7]

The Shechem Covenant and *Heilsgeschichte*

Nearing the end of life, Joshua calls a grand assembly at the city-state of Shechem, a strategic and central meeting place for the tribal confederacy— as it had been for Canaanites, Egyptians, Hyksos, and others before them. Shechem is also a most significant worship site,[8] prominent in later stories.

---

6   Ibid., Lind, 84-85.

7   Ibid., Anderson, 125-128. Anderson also suggests a fourth possibility as "ruralization," a population explosion in rural areas, followed by attacks against city-states.

8   Ibid, Anderson, 131.

Once again following in Moses' footsteps, Joshua gives a farewell speech and recites *Heilsgeschichte*. Joshua's version includes more details than the shorter covenant recital of Deuteronomy 26. As usual, the *Haggadah*, the first word of grace, is followed by *Halakah*, the people's response of grateful obedience. Surrounded by all the Canaanite peoples and their gods, Joshua's declaration, "choose this day whom you will serve" is critical. To give this group the option of walking away from Yahweh, after all God has done for them, is radical grace from God, a gift that honored their free will. Joshua emphasizes the second of the Eleven Words, by reminding the people that Yahweh is an exclusive and jealous God, not a god who will share loyalty with other gods (Joshua 24:19).

So why the need for the Shechem covenant, when there were also earlier covenant renewals at Gerizim and Ebal? Wasn't the covenant made once and for all at Sinai? As Moses unified the "mixed crowd" of the Exodus, now Joshua unifies an even more diverse crowd at Shechem.

Covenanting is a way to incorporate new people into the faith community of God. By covenant, newcomers make *Heilsgeschichte* their own. The stories of Exodus-Sinai and wilderness wanderings become their story too: "A wandering Aramean was my ancestor...When the Egyptians treated us harshly...we cried to the Lord, the God of our ancestors. The Lord heard our voice...and brought us out of Egypt...and gave us this land." They acknowledge Yahweh and became a part of the chosen, covenant, shalom people of God in order to bless all the peoples of the earth.

Infiltration and Invasion

The wilderness peoples were led by the Joseph tribes. Joshua was an Ephraimite. These Joseph tribes were the largest and received the most land that included the central and sacred meeting places. If a considerable part of the Judah-Simeon tribes had not participated in the Exodus and wilderness experiences that could explain part of the struggle to unify the south with the northern tribes, the eventual split, and why David was able to be king in the south for seven years before ruling over all of Israel.

Scholars generally agree that the patriarchs and matriarchs were part of a larger Hurrian and Amorite peoples. Consequently, when the wilderness peoples led by the Joseph and Benjamin tribes invaded the land, they were joined by these distantly related tribes who had infiltrated earlier and by the socially marginal Habiru who joined in a revolt against the elite wealthy city-state coalitions. This would explain the Gibeonites and others joining the wilderness people of God.

What happened then was probably a combination of an invasion and a social revolution that lasted into the period of the judges. Joshua says "there was still much land to be taken." Boundaries evidently moved back and forth. Some city-states had not been conquered. The Dan tribe, for example, lost so much land that some people had to relocate to the far north. But the historical facts and possible explanations do not distract from the faith *Geschichte* interpretation and message that Yahweh providentially gave the Promised Land to God's people. Yahweh is creating a chosen, covenant, shalom community of people.

The social political situation in Canaan at the time of Joshua facilitated the invading tribes gaining a foothold in the hill country. The Armana correspondence tablets found at Tell el-Armana archeological site in Egypt describe the setting. The land, under Egyptian control, was broken into many small independent city-states that controlled the agriculture land around their city. Some of these city-states had loose alliances. The coalition of five city-state kings that Joshua defeated was such an alliance. Consequently, there was no unified national government or military to stop the infiltrating and invading wilderness peoples.[9]

Former Prophets and Deuteronomistic *Geschichte*

Our story has taken us through the first five books of the Old Testament, Genesis through Deuteronomy. They are called the Pentateuch (five books or scrolls) or Torah (instruction or law).

The books of Joshua, Judges, Samuel, and Kings are called the Former Prophets rather than history. The genre is appropriate since these books are no ordinary historical writing; they are more *Geschichte* than history. Yahweh is active in everything that happens. The theological perspective is like that of Deuteronomy, so it is called the Deuteronomistic history. In this view, Yahweh blesses those who are faithful and curses those who are not.

Since the writers of the Former Prophets continue the views of Deuteronomy, some suggest that the book of Deuteronomy belongs to the Former Prophets more than to the Pentateuch. Deuteronomy functions as a transition book between the Torah and the Former Prophets, since it restates the Torah and lays the theological foundation for the Former Prophets.

The Former Prophets, Joshua through Kings, give a broad overview

---

9   Ibid., Anderson, 122; LaSor, et al, 147.

of Israel's history from conquest to the exile of Judah. Covering nearly 700 years, these books describe the crises of invasion, tribal confederacy, syncretism, monarchy, division of the kingdom, the fall of Israel, and finally, the fall and exile of Judah—the crisis of crises. Interestingly, these texts refer to sources unknown to us: the Book of Jashar (II Samuel 1:18), Acts of Solomon (I Kings 11:41), Annals of the Kings of Israel (I Kings 14:19), and Annals of the Kings of Judah (I Kings 15:7, 23).

The book of Joshua begins with the wilderness tribes about to cross the Jordan. After the miraculous crossing of the Jordan and the conquests (chapters 1-12), the book ends with the distribution of the land (13-21) and the Shechem covenant (22-24). A comparison with Judges reveals that Joshua is a highly interpreted book of the invasion and conquest. Joshua makes the conquest sound quick, easy, and complete. The *Geschichte* is that Yahweh gives the land to the people through Holy War. On the other hand, Judges seems to deliver a more historical account, indicating that the conquest was not so complete, and there was still much land to conquer when Joshua's campaign ended.

The book of Joshua closes with Joshua's death, but the story of the people of God continues in the next chapter on Judges and the Tribal Confederacy.

Judges and Tribal Confederacy

Bible passages: Judges 1-4, 6-7; Deut. 27-30:10

The Shechem covenant, like the Sinai covenant, incorporated the many new people who had joined the people of God—in the wilderness and after entering Canaan, including the Infiltration and the Revolution Peoples. The tribal groups are given territories on both sides of the Jordan River, from Asher and Naphtali in the north to Simeon in the south. They were not alone in their territories. Even though Joshua paints a picture of complete domination of Canaan, the Book of Judges makes clear that many of the native peoples remain.

Why are there still Canaanites in the area? There are three reasons. A history reason: the Canaanites have "chariots of iron" (Judges 1:20), and two *Geschichte* reasons: "you have not obeyed my command" (Judges 2:2), and to "test Israel" (Judges 3:4).

Understanding their own identity is a constant challenge for the people of Israel. Their identity is tied to their memory of Yahweh, who delivered them out of slavery and brought them into the Promised Land. As long as they recite *Heilsgeschichte*, they know who they are; when they forget *Heilsgeschichte*, they become vulnerable to the Canaanite gods and goddesses.

The Challenge of Syncretism

The Land of Promise also proved to be a place of peril. Compared to the refined and sophisticated Canaanites, the ways of the wilderness-wandering former slaves were crude and rustic. The natural process of acculturation threatened Israelite identity, shaped by the memory of Yahweh's providence in their history. But "the most divisive and destructive threat" of all was the worship of Canaanite gods, Baal (lord or owner) and his female counterpart, the goddess Baalath (lady) or Astarte.[1]

The danger was not in abandoning Yahweh for Baal, but in blending Baal and Yahweh worship. This fusion or gradual mixing of two religions is called **syncretism.**

Syncretism, as with acculturation, happens gradually, as the metaphor of the boiling frog illustrates. When you toss a frog into boiling water, he jumps out immediately; but if you place him in lukewarm water and gradually turn up the heat, the frog never notices the danger and unwittingly becomes cooked meat. Contemporary parallels might include the blending of Christian faith with nationalism to produce civil religion; or the blending of Christianity with consumerism which can result in a "prosperity gospel" where God is expected to reward faithfulness with material wealth.

Buying into Baal worship involves much more than adopting a new form of spirituality, or a new ritual; it was the wholesale purchase of Canaanite life, culture, and worldview. Take, for example, the very practical matter of agriculture. The wilderness-wandering Israelites had no way of knowing how to farm the new land, so naturally they watched the farming practices of their neighbors. The Baal-worshiping Canaanites linked agriculture to the Baal fertility cult that involved temple prostitution. Successful farming without Baal worship was unthinkable.

In the Canaanite worldview, Baal is the owner, the lord of the land who controls the cycle of seasons. Agricultural prosperity depends on appeasing and manipulating the Baals (plural since many local sites had their own version of Baal) to ensure fertility. Such a worldview includes several elements:

- First, the gods, Baal and Baalath, live above the dome in the triple-decker cosmology.
- Second, the reproduction of animals and germination of seeds is a pre-scientific mystery, but people observe that sexual intercourse produces offspring.
- Third, what happens above the dome, the sexual activity of Baal and Baalath causes fertility on the earth and determines what

---

1   Bernhard W. Anderson, et al., *Understanding the Old Testament, Fifth Edition* (Upper Saddle River, NJ: Pearson Education, Inc., 2007), 170.

happens on the earth and *vice versa*.

- Fourth, the anthropological concept of "sympathetic magic," meaning that human behavior influences the gods, is applied to the fertility rituals of Baal worship.[2]

So sexual intercourse with temple prostitutes manipulates the gods above the dome to have intercourse. This in turn affects the fertility of plants, animals, and humans. So for the Israelites, the temptation to worship Baal was not so much sexual as economic. Survival and prosperity depends on the manipulation of the gods and not on the providence of Yahweh.

Yahweh, on the other hand, takes an active role in history. Yahweh cannot be manipulated or compromised by worship rituals performed on earth. Yahweh permits "no other gods before me" (Exodus 20:3). Yahweh behaves in a ways that are radical and surprising—sometimes being gratious, sometimes saying no—unlike the predictable and cyclical behavior of the Baal gods. Yahweh's relationship with the chosen people is dynamic to the point where God's plans can change over time.

The conclusion of the Covenant Recital in Deuteronomy 26 contains a significant anti-Baal declaration: "So now I bring the first of the fruit of the ground that you O Lord, have given me." Yahweh, not the Baals or Astartes, is the source of the harvest.

The influence of Baal culture is apparent where Israelites use Baal in the naming of their children. Even Saul and David give Baal names to their children: Mephibaal (Mephibosheth) and Ishbaal (II Samuel 21:8; 4:4; 9:6; I Chronicles 8:34). Gideon the judge is called Jerub-baal, because he zealously fought against the worship of Baal.[3]

The following chart identifies differences between Baal and Yahweh worship:

Elements	Baal Worship	Yahweh Worship
Purpose/Goal	Fertility, prosperity, security, self-suffi-ciency, materialism	Creation of a chosen, covenant, shalom community

---

2 Ibid., 172.

3 Ibid., 175.

Worship	Manipulation of the gods	Remembrance of God's grace with thanksgiving
Ethics	Manipulation of people	Shalom justice where all needs are met and all relationships are healed
View of History	Cyclical, tied to nature and the changing seasons	Linear, with history and future, with the purpose of all becoming God's people

Baal worship comes from a cyclical view of history. In this view, the gods must keep the cycle going--seasons of fertility and rains--if the humans do their part and honor these gods with appropriate ritual and sacrifice. But nothing ever really changes. History never experiences a surprise. The people do their worship rituals, the gods do their part, the earth is fertile, the humans benefit and everything's good. In this worldview, people don't love but rather fear their gods. They don't expect their gods to do anything special for them. It's a system of manipulation.

The prophets understood rightly that it's a small step from manipulating your gods to manipulating people. Therefore, they made the connection between Baal worship and social oppression. If you are used to using your gods, why not use other people?

The Israelites had a linear view of history. They believed that Yahweh could and sometimes did do brand new things, like the Exodus-Sinai deliverance. The "I Am that I Am" did work in real history. Consequently, Yahweh couldn't be manipulated and this radically free God was loved instead of feared. The Israelite *Shema*, their expression of faith repeated daily, expressed this sentiment: "Hear, O Israel: The Lord is our God, the Lord alone. You shall love the Lord your God with all your heart, and with all your soul, and with all your might" (Deuteronomy 6:4-5). Other people groups had something similar to *Shema*, but they emphasized fear instead of love.

Judges

To counteract the influence of the Baals and Astartes, Yahweh appoints judges. The Hebrew word for prophet, *shofet,* translated "judge," is closer in meaning to "ruler" or "deliverer." The judges of the loosely organized tribal confederacy are charismatic military leaders who emerge when the "spirit of the Lord empowers" them with exceptional authority and power. Typically, they respond to a specific local crisis in which a tribe, with the help of several surrounding tribes, gains independence from an oppressor. The judges build no dynasties, since ruling is not about flesh and blood, but about faithfulness to Yahweh.[4]

Many of the Judge stories are memorable Holy War stories closer to the original Exodus model when Yahweh fought for the people. Increasingly, the Israelites choose to fight with Yahweh, and still later fight for God with a standing army and dynastic human king. Often the Terror of the Lord wins the battle as in the Song of Deborah: "Yahweh's strikes terror into Sisera, all his chariots and all his troops" (4:15). In many cases of the slightly modified model of Holy War, humans mop up with an absurdly small group of hastily called-out warriors.[5]

Rather than building on their successes in one battle with a centralized standing army, the command is given, "To your tents O Israel" (I Kings 12:6). Sending the fighting men back home leaves Israel intentionally vulnerable, entirely dependent on Yahweh. A new crisis requires a new start by calling out amateur farmer-warriors.

A standout among the judges is Deborah, also identified as a prophetess, and a "mother of Israel" (Judges 5:7) Her song, the Song of Deborah celebrates a smashing victory at Megiddo against Sisera, a general in the army of Jabin King of Hazor: "Awake, awake, Deborah!/Awake, awake, utter a song!" A second woman, Jael, who single-handedly and brutally kills Sisera, is also celebrated: "Most blessed of women be Jael...She struck Sisera a blow" (Judges 5:24). Although human involvement (fighting with Yaheh), has compromised Holy War, the hero of the poem is still Yahweh. Yahweh uses the forces of nature to win the battle: "From heaven fought the stars" and "The torrent Kishon swept them away" (Judges 5:20-21).[6]

Tola, Jair, Ibzan, Elon, Shamgar, and Abdon are the minor judges. The six major judges are listed here with their tribe and their enemies.

---

4 William Sanford LaSor, et al., *Old Testament Survey: The Message, Form, and Background of the Old Testament* (Grand Rapids: William B. Eerdmann Publishing Company, 1996), 155.

5 Millard C. Lind, Yahweh is a Warrior: The Theology of Warfare in Ancient Israel (Scottdale, PA: Herald Press, 1980), 72.

6 Ibid., 75.

Judge	Tribe	Enemy
Othniel II	Ephraim	Cushan-rishathaim
Ehud	Benjamin	Eglon of Moab with Ammonites & Amalekites
Deborah	Ephraim	Jabin, Canaanites
Gideon	Manasseh	Midianites, Amalekites
Jephthah	Manasseh	Ammonites, Moabites
Samson	Dan	Philistines

Although not on the chart, Samuel is both judge and prophet and serves as a transitional figure between the judges and the prophets and between the judges and the kings.

The Deuteronomistic Cycle

The appointment of judges, the faithlessness of the people, and Yahweh's deliverance follows a pattern, outlined in Judges 2: 11-19, called the Deuteronomistic cycle. The cycle's elements are:

1. The people do evil, abandon Yahweh, and worship Baal.
2. Yahweh allows their enemies to defeat and dominate them.
3. The people cry out to Yahweh.
4. Yahweh hears their cry and is moved to raise a judge.
5. The judge delivers the people from their oppressors.
6. After the judge dies, the people relapsed and behave even worse than did their ancestors.
7. The cycle begins again (#6 becomes #1 again).[7]

This cycle reflects a certain theology, or way of understanding God. The Deuteronomistic historian's view is comparable to cause and effect or sowing and reaping, where faithfulness is rewarded and faithlessness is punished. If a person or a whole people group are good, then they will receive blessings during their lifetime. These blessings usually come in the form of more children or livestock, victory over enemies or other tangible, this-world rewards. If a person or group are disobedient, then they are

---

7   Ibid., LaSor, et al., 154-155.

cursed, resulting in barrenness, defeat, or other punishments.

While Deuteronomistic theology is prevalent through the Former Prophets books, there is also an opposing view. In the Deuteronomistic cycle, when the Israelites cry out to God or repent—which is a good thing—they are rewarded with an annointed judge. Yet the very reality that this cycle happens over and over again, without God losing patience and abandoning the people, shows that God is more complex and more gracious than this simplistic theology can encapsulate. God in *chesed* love doesn't walk away.

Later, Jesus will challenge this theology as well (Matthew 5:3-12). Sometimes righteous people suffer on this earth; their reward must wait until after death.

Transitions

In addition to the transition from wilderness living to settled agriculture, there are others: 1) moving from the relative isolation of their forty-year wilderness experience to interaction with technologically superior Canaanite peoples who worshipped Baal fertility gods; 2) shifting from a Moses-Joshua servant type of leadership model to exposure to Canaanite authoritarian divine right-of-kings models of leadership; 3) changing from a more egalitarian shalom justice, social/political model to exposure to hierarchical exploitive and dominating political and economic models; and 4) transitioning from a linear sense of time and purpose to a cyclical, self-interest, economic sense of history marked by wealth accumulation.

Interpreting the Tribal Confederacy

These stories reveal a low level of faithfulness and ethical behavior among the people during the theocratic confederacy. The judges themselves are pictured more as zealous Holy War leaders than spiritual covenant leaders like Moses and the later prophets. Jephthah, who impulsively sacrifices his daughter, is hardly a figure of wisdom to be emulated by the people of God. Similarly, Samson's strength is overshadowed by his undisciplined infatuation with Philistine women. Samson may actually be a metaphor for the people who married Canaanite neighbors and were seduced by their wives to worship other gods. So Israel, like foolish Samson, exposed and disclosed its strength in Yahweh to their enemies. Later Ezra remembers this temptation when he attempts to avoid syncretism by forcing Judeans to divorce their foreign wives (Ezra 10).

The intertribal warfare reveals the struggle for unity and peace during the confederacy. Even the Joseph tribes fought each other when the Transjordan tribe of Manasseh under Jephthah fought and defeated the Ephraimites. Frequent conflict and jealousy erupted.

The story of the Levite and his concubine at Gibeah (Judges 19) seems to summarize the disobedience and faithlessness of the people. And then comes a concluding pro-monarchy judgment where all the "people did what was right in their own eyes," since there was no king in Israel. This is odd given the Deuteronomistic theology of the rest of the book. It suggests, however, things to come.

Nevertheless, during the later period of monarchy, the prophets looked back on the era of tribal confederacy as a time of greater faithfulness to Yahweh's ultimate will. From the vantage point of their neighbors, the people in this period live in an amazing, unusual political arrangement with an unseen god as king. The people's daily existence and survival is a miracle, a witness to Yahweh's providence. The decentralized tribal confederacy is held together only by their faith covenant with an invisible king. This arrangement amidst their enemies required daily trust, like that of wilderness wanderings. Gideon's refusal to be king and his son Abimelech's arrogant attempt to become king condemn the idea of monarchy and promote theocracy, where only Yahweh rules.

The way that the people sometimes united and responded to adversity strikes a positive note for the health of the theocratic tribal confederacy. The tribes rallied as one (from Dan to Beersheba) to Gideon's call and to the call to judge the Benjaminites for killing the Levite's concubine. While not very efficient, the tribal confederacy functioned in some positive ways. In comparison to the period of monarchy to come, at least God's people during the confederacy were not enslaved by their own kings.

The unique, vulnerable, trusting theocratic "way of Israel" continued to be a radical alternative to the politics of exploitation employed by the pharaohs of Egypt and the self-serving, city-state kings of Canaan. And, using the clay analogy, the people were still pliable in God's hands and had not yet begun trusting in the institutions of a standing army, centralized, dynastic monarchy, and the stationary temple (Jeremiah 18).

History and *Geschichte*

Like Joshua, the Deuteronomistic historian of Judges shows a strong faith bias in telling and interpreting these stories. The stories are written on two levels: an elementary history level; and a larger purpose of showing Yahweh's continued activity in developing a chosen, covenant, shalom people as a witness to their Canaanite neighbors. Securing safe tribal territories is important because Yahweh's purpose in blessing all the families on earth is at stake.

The Canaanite religions offer a choice to God's people similar to the choice offered to Adam and Eve in the Garden. The choice gives them an opportunity to make positive decisions that will lead to growth, a further defining of themselves over against the other peoples, and remaining faithful to their chosenness by revealing the ways of Yahweh.

The struggle between Yahweh faith and that of the surrounding Canaanite cultures and religions continue until the fall and exile of Judah. Reform attempts never completely root out Baal worship and syncretism. In fact, many future Israelite kings nurture the development of syncretism, notably Manasseh of Judah and the supposedly wise Solomon.

Toward a United Monarchy

Bible passages: I Sam. 1-12, 15-16, 18-19, 31; Judges 19; II Samuel 5-6

Spiritual, Moral and Political Decline in *Heilsgeschichte*

The stories in Judges seem to be mostly negative. Even some of the judges make poor decisions. God certainly is the hero and intervenes to save the people. God's steadfast grace shines through. The book ends with the grisly story of the rape of the Levite's concubine. The final editorial is "all the people did what was right in their own eyes" (Judges 21:25).

But wait, all is not lost. Despite all the evil, the people of God are still only a "nation" with the possibility of being God's chosen, covenant, missionary people to all the world. They are still a unique theocracy rather than a "nation-state."

Religious syncretism during the Judges' time period and God not fighting Holy War in Samuel 2, 4 and 8 all pointed toward the need for more central authority:

- The disastrous experience with the puppet king Abimelech (Judges 9)
- Samson's senseless behavior (Judges 13-16)
- The Levite's concubine rape at Gibeah (Judges 19)
- Eli and Samuel's corrupt sons (I Samuel 2, 8)
- The Philistine military victory that threatened the Israelites' very existence (I Samuel 4) led to cries for a different style of leadership (I Samuel 8)

The Israelites' interpretation of the hardships was that Yahweh wasn't dependable in fighting Holy War for them anymore. "We need a king to fight our battles" (I Kings 7:19).

True, Yahweh was not fighting Holy War for the Israelites against the Philistines. Why? Because the Israelites were not living holy shalom lives as per their original covenant with Yahweh. Yahweh couldn't fight Holy War without a holy people. They didn't see, or they denied their evil ways—the real reason they lost battles. Rather than repenting they took the Ark of the Covenant into battle attempting to manipulate Yahweh's presence to win the battle. Yahweh would defend himself (I Samuel 4). They trusted in the magic of a worship symbol instead of repenting and becoming faithful to Yahweh and their chosenness to be Yahweh's chosen missionary people.

The Philistine victory threatened their very existence. So they cried out for a king to lead them into battle (I Samuel 8), even though Samuel had just led some people in repentance and a glorious Holy War victory over the Philistines (I Samuel 7).

The Literature of I And II Samuel

The books Joshua, Judges, Samuel, and Kings all form one story written from a Deuteronomistic view that God will bless faithfulness and let judgment come on unfaithfulness.

Samuel is the transition figure from the book of Judges to I Samuel. The first twelve chapters of I Samuel tell the transition stories of the last judges to the first king. As transition stories, these chapters could belong to the book of Judges as well as to the book of I Samuel. I and II Samuel formed one book in the Hebrew scriptures. But when translated into Greek, the book became too large for one scroll. I Samuel 8-12 provide an interesting picture of two different *Geschichtes*. A careful reading shows that there are pro-monarchy and anti-monarchy literary strands.

Scholars have long noted that in I Samuel 8-12 there are two basic attitudes (and probably sources) related to the origin of the monarchy. One is pro-monarchy (9:1-10:16, 11:1-15) and the other is anti-monarchy (8:1-22; 10:17-27; 12:1-25)...Scholars agree that I Samuel contains two different traditions and sources about the rise of kingship in Israel...[O]ne can see that obviously the anti-monarchy materials have been given dominance so that the final form of I Samuel 8-12 has been redacted (edited) to place qualifications on the historical institution of the monarchy.[1]

The later Deuteronomistic source, having seen the results of kingship, is anti-monarchy, while the earlier source is pro-monarchy. The final editors did not eliminate one view but simply stitched them together, letting the two different views/traditions about monarchy stand. The fact that the final editors did not change the two different traditions to make them agree should give us more confidence in the Bible, not less. They considered the story they inherited to be sacred. This material is more like a stitched together patchwork quilt than a cloth of one color.

Pro-Monarchy Literary Strand (I Samuel 9:1-10, 16; 11:1-11)

Read the pro-monarchy passages listed above all together and you will see a coherent story *celebrating* Israel's monarchy. Stated briefly, the pro-monarchy story reads as follows: Saul finds Samuel to inquire where his lost donkeys had strayed. Saul was from Gibeah and a leading family in the Benjamin tribal area. There are two different stories about how he became Israel's first king. The Lord reveals to Samuel that he should anoint Saul king privately. God gave Saul a new heart with confirming signs that day. God's Spirit possessed him as he neared his home at Gibeah.

Later Saul hears of the Ammonite siege of Jabesh-Gilead. Saul is moved, the Spirit of God comes upon him as it had done with the earlier judges. He slays his oxen and sends pieces to all the tribes, a message to come together for battle. They respond and Saul leads the people in a devastating defeat of the Ammonites. The people ask Saul to be king like they had asked Gideon before (Judges 8:22-23). Saul accepts and Samuel installs him king at Gilgal.

In this pro-monarchy storyline, Yahweh through Samuel creates a king for Israel to deal with the Philistines and new political challenges beyond the capabilities of the theocratic tribal confederacy arrangement. Samuel leads Israel into a new day like Moses and Joshua had done in the Exodus and conquest. No reservations or resistance from Yahweh or Samuel appear in this storyline. The departure from trusting Yahweh in a theocracy to a monarchy seems to be Yahweh's providential action in a new situation to preserve the People of God.

However, a second source or strand—the later Deuteronomistic strand

---

1   John Hayes and Carl Holladay, *Biblical Exegesis: A Beginner's Handbook*, rev. ed. (Louisville: Westminster John Knox, 1987), 107.

possibly coming from the Northern Kingdom's prophetic circles—is strongly anti-monarchy.

Anti-Monarchy Literary Strand (I Samuel: 7-8, 10:17-27, 12:1-15)

Read the passages listed above all together and you will see a coherent story *condemning* Israel's monarchy. This storyline reads very differently than the previous one. After the return of the Ark of the Covenant, Samuel leads Israel in repentance and revival at Mizpah. Then Samuel leads the people in a Yahweh Holy War victory over the Philistines, taking away the need for a king to lead them into battle. Samuel sets up his sons to be judges, attempting to make the charismatic judgeship into a more dependable hereditary institution.

But the Israelites are dissatisfied. Samuel prays and the Lord tells Samuel that the people are not rejecting him but rejecting Yahweh as king. Yahweh tells Samuel to anoint a king as the people want. Samuel is told to also warn them about what a king will do: impose heavy taxes and enslave them. Samuel's most dire warning is that when the people cry out about their king, Yahweh will not answer like Yahweh did in Egypt. But the people keep on demanding a king. So God tells Samuel to give in to the people and anoint a king (I Samuel 8).

The anti-monarchy view is also expressed in Judges when the proud Abimelech sets himself up as a king but is finally killed in disgrace by a woman (Judges 9). Previously the people had asked Gideon to become their king but he refused because he understood the Lord was their king.

> *Then the Israelites said to Gideon, "Rule over us, you and your son and your grandson also; for you have delivered us out of the hand of Midian." Gideon said to them, "I will not rule over you, and my son will not rule over you; the Lord will rule over you"* (Judges 8:22-23).

So Samuel the transition figure summoned the people to Mizpah and anointed Saul king after being chosen by drawing lots. Some people didn't bring a gift for the king, indicating less than full support for monarchy and Saul as king. Samuel reads the regulations for a king to the people which would keep him from becoming like other nations' kings (Deuteronomy 17:14-20). These regulations included that the king must not have many wives, nor acquire much silver and gold, shall read the law every day of his life to learn to fear the Lord, and not exalt himself above other members of the community. Two of Israel's most celebrated kings, David and Solomon, broke these rules in major ways repeatedly!

Samuel gave a farewell address reviewing *Heilsgeschichte* up to date, defending his leadership and denouncing the choosing of a king as sin (I Samuel 12). Yahweh's thunder after Samuel's address confirmed Samel's judgment. The people confessed their sin of asking for a king and asked Samuel to pray for them. He further reminded them to remember God's mighty acts for them or they will be swept away by judgment.

God's Remedial Will: The Major Covenant Adjustment

What makes becoming a nation-state with a human king like other nation-states a sin for the people of God? Having a king puts two boundaries around the people rather than having them remain a unique flexible missionary people revealing Yahweh to the whole world. With these boundaries Yahweh becomes a national god rather than the God of all the world. Yahweh also becomes a God limited to one geographic area rather than the whole earth (Psalms 137). In other words, a king makes Israel focus inward rather than outward. Monarchy redefines "chosen" to mean chosen as God's favorites, with citizenship and geography being the marks of this special favor. Now some people who may want to join the people of God can't, because they are not citizens.

Here Yahweh's agreement to kingship is God's remedial will. The people reject Yahweh as their king (I Samuel 8). Nevertheless, in steadfast love Yahweh continues to work with the more and less pliable people, seeking to shape them into the shalom missionary community that could accomplish its priestly kingdom calling to reveal Yahweh to all the world's people (Exodus 19:5). God's remedial will seek to make the best out of the situation created by the people's unfaithfulness. Some call it God's "permissive" will. However the term "remedial" seems more appropriate to Yahweh's behavior because the word "remedy" suggests a more active and creative involvement.

Yahweh continued to care for and stay engaged with the people, attempting to redeem them and make the best out of their unfaithfulness. "His steadfast love endures forever" (Psalms 136). But there would still be long term consequences for God's people for becoming a nation-state monarchy. Samuel warned that after crowning a human king the people would "cry out because of your king...but the Lord will not answer you in that day" (I Samuel 8:18).

This view sees monarchy as a step leading toward slavery under king Solomon, followed by a divided kingdom, the destruction of both kingdoms, and finally Judah and Jerusalem's destruction and exile to Babylon. In the end, God's judgment and grace smashed the "faith and nation-state" and "faith and geography" boundaries so God's people could recover their original mission to all the world's people.

In the crisis of syncretism, God's people often fell prey to the naturalism of Canaanite religions. Now in the crisis of monarchy, they fall prey to nationalism. In their nationalism the people may survive but lose their unique significance. Before the monarchy God's people were a nation, a people, an *am*, like a Cheyenne native American tribe.[2] With the Monarchy nation-state, a *goy* Yahweh's people would no longer be defined as a universal faith community, but as a national identity, which would limit their original mission. Yahweh became just another national and geographic God, while human kings became an institutionalized dynasty that did not trust God to choose the next leader.

Saul's Reign: 1020-1000 BCE

While a charismatic leader, Saul had the no-win task of being Israel's first king. Where should Saul learn how a king of Yahweh's people behaved and led? What were his leadership roles and responsibilities? The theology developed that when a king was anointed, Yahweh would adopt the king as a son to do God's will. The king of Israel was more than a judge, but also not a god like Pharaoh. Saul, Samuel, and the people faced uncharted waters in this crisis.

Saul appeared extremely vulnerable. Samuel, despite having anointed Saul as king, was at the most a reluctant supporter of kingship in the anti-monarchy strand. Furthermore, not all the people supported kingship (I Samuel 10:27). Plus Saul was from the small tribe of Benjamin that included the town of Gibeah, where the Levite's concubine was raped. As a result, Samuel actually seemed to retain the ultimate authority among the tribes and elders. Saul served under him and was accountable to him. The people wanted a king to lead them in battle (I Samuel 8:20). However the political situation remained largely tribal and decentralized and would remain that way through Saul's reign and a part of David's reign. Shechem and other sacred places were religious sites (only later did David capture Jerusalem and make it the capital).

---

2   Bernhard W. Anderson, et al., *Understanding the Old Testament, Fifth Edition* (Upper Saddle River, NJ: Pearson Education, Inc., 2007), 192.

To Saul's credit he did chart a different course from the Pharaoh and Canaanite models of kingship. Archaeological excavations indicate Saul lived in a rustic bunker kind of dwelling. He had only a small band of permanent soldiers, no standing army. He did not amass wealth or create a wealthy class among the people. He also did not have a large harem to produce successors to the throne that would have required taxes.

But Saul broke the rules of Holy War in a battle against the Amalekites by not destroying all the enemies' animals (I Samuel 13). Saul assumed religious leadership by offering a sacrifice when Samuel showed up late during a battle with the Philistines (I Samuel 15). Samuel's condemnation of Saul contributed to the downward spiral toward the end of Saul's reign. Saul lost what support the ambivalent Samuel had given him. Plus, the Spirit of God that had come upon him when he became king left him. We must wonder today why Saul was condemned so severely for these missteps which seem minor compared to David and Solomon's sins later? Perhaps Saul did not repent like David. And in an act of treason Samuel anointed David while Saul was still king! In this situation what could Saul do about it? He sank into deeper and deeper depression and died on Mt. Gilboa in a battle against the Philistines.

David's Reign: 1000-961 BCE

David came from the large southern tribe of Judah and rose to popularity because of military achievements. Rather than singing praises to Yahweh after Holy War victories as Miriam and Deborah had done (Exodus 14, Judges 5), the people began to sing praises to David (I Samuel 18:7). The Philistine crisis was so life-threatening to the tribes that defeating them was agenda number one. David subdued the Philistines during his reign, lessening that threat. King David's personality and military and political skill endeared him to the people, though more in the southern part of his own tribe of Judah than in the northern Joseph tribes.

Young David fled from Saul to the southern Judah area where, in a Robin Hood style operation (I Samuel 25), he amassed resources, followers, and loyalty. After Saul's death David became king in the south for seven and one-half years before becoming king of all Israel. The northern tribes accepted Saul's son Ishbosheth as their king. David's clever and ruthless army commander, Joab, helped David consolidate his rule over all Israel. David shrewdly captured Jerusalem between the north and south and made it the capital. The transition to monarchy took years.

David's sins seem much more serious than Saul's. He committed adultery with Bathsheba and then had her husband Uriah killed in order to cover his sin. Uriah worked for David as one of his personal bodyguards. He also set up a standing army, which Yahweh's original covenant forbade (II Samuel 24). Unlike Saul, David built a palace, amassed wealth, and established a harem. He numbered the people for taxation and a created a standing army. Trust in Yahweh to fight Holy War waned as God's people institutionalized, trusting in their army and king. They began to fight Holy War for Yahweh! To use Jeremiah's clay analogy, the clay (Israel) was hardening and losing pliability in Yahweh's hands (Jeremiah 18). Yet David is celebrated.

King Saul had Samuel to challenge him and keep him honest. When Samuel left the picture, the prophet Nathan played that role. He confronted King David about the adultery with Bathsheba and Uriah's murder (II Samuel 11-12). David's repentant attitude, his defeat of the Philistines, his efforts to bring the Ark of the Covenant to Jerusalem, and enormous popularity kept him on the throne even though his sin wreaked havoc in David's family. Just as Nathan prophesied, the father's sins continued through the lives of the children. David's oldest son Amnon raped his half-sister Tamar, who was also Absalom's sister. David did nothing about it, which angered his son Absalom to kill Amnon and lead a revolt that nearly unseated David as king. David actually had to flee Jerusalem (II Samuel 13-15).

David repented of some of his sins, though he continued to function more and more like the kings of other nations, amassing wealth and centralizing political power in Jerusalem. A patron of the arts, David placed musicians in the capital and he himself wrote many Psalms. But the tribal confederacy vision was not lost completely, especially in the northern tribes. The theocratic vision, decentralized tribal loyalties, and tribal elders remained alive and contributed to Absalom's ability to gain enough support to lead a revolt against his father David. The revolt prompted David to centralize more political power and authority in Jerusalem during the later years of his reign.

King David's last days and words were troubled as he gave orders to have Joab, his commander-in-chief, killed and revenge taken against adversaries. David's dark last days are in stark contrast to the farewell messages of Moses, Joshua, and Samuel. Rather than retelling *Heilsgeschichte* to date, David's last days are full of intrigue in the family, power grabs, and revenge.

Which prince from David's harem would succeed to the throne?

Adonijah, the eldest and obvious heir, was outmaneuvered by a cadre consisting of David's favorite wife, Bathsheba, Nathan the prophet, and Zadok the priest! So Bathsheba's son Solomon became king. Solomon's older brother Adonijah and Joab, David's commander-in-chief, are killed by Benaiah, the new commander-in-chief! Abiathar, the priest who had supported Adonijah, was banished from priestly duties. To say the least, hereditary kingship hadn't solved all the issues of leadership transitions!

Solomon's Reign: 961-922 BCE

Solomon had grown up in his father's palace, and he further centralized authority and power in Jerusalem, extending the kingdom through political marriages. Many—but not all—Israelites flourished from the taxes from newly controlled territories and open trade routes, but Solomon's foreign wives also brought their religions with them into Israel.

Rather than seeing Israel as God's chosen, shalom missionary people for all the world, King Solomon further solidified Israel as a nation-state and a geographically bound kingdom by building a spectacular temple in Jerusalem. The temple centralized worship in the political capital. The growing gap between rich and poor destroyed the shalom community that was to be God's revelation to all the world. Rather than revealing Yahweh's ways to the world, Solomon's oppressive rule took Israel further and further from shalom community and theocracy where Yahweh is king. Solomon's lavish life, building the temple, his army and all the staff needed to support his 300 wives and 700 concubines led to heavy taxation and forced labor. The Israelites were locked back into slavery, but this time of their own making.

Yet Solomon is lauded for his wisdom! Certainly, some of the people enjoyed new wealth. The developing arts and Israel's international power and prestige make Solomon seem wise. But his excesses, his exploitive and oppressive reign, sowed the seeds for the next crisis: the division of the United Monarchy.

Interpreting the Monarchy Crisis

Israel under Saul's leadership had remained largely decentralized with tribal identities. David centralized power attempting to create a more united monarchy, especially after Absalom's revolt. Solomon nearly achieved a united monarchical nation-state, but the tribal loyalties and theocratic vision remained alive. No sooner did the united monarchy seem to solidify under Solomon than it broke apart between the northern and southern tribes, never to be re-united. The conflict between the Leah and Rachel tribes (Jacob's wives) continued to play out.

Less than four hundred years after Yahweh liberated them from Egyptian slavery, the People of God were slaves again, belonging to their own king. Yahweh's theocratic freedom was too difficult, so they sacrificed it for the less vulnerable security of kings. In the face of the Philistine challenge, the people abandoned Holy War, depending on kings and armies instead. They sacrificed their freedom trying to retain their freedom. Israel and their king had truly become like other nation-states.

Rather than being God's missionary people evangelizing the world, the world was shaping them. Syncretism, through Solomon's multi-religious harem, was now even supported by the king. Although some people succumbed to the religious syncretism with naturalism (Baal worship) and nationalism, Yahweh faith continued to thrive.[3]

From a sociological viewpoint was it inevitable that the tribes would ultimately set up a centralized institution of kingship as they developed and matured? That interpretation of the crisis move to monarchy says this was natural and normal—a good move of preservation by the people. God's will simply changed in this new situation when the Philistines threatened their existence. Monarchy was a positive, creative new possibility.

However, from a Deuteronomistic prophetic view, the move to monarchy was a sin, a fall, and not inevitable. This move is God's remedial will at best, an accommodation of Yahweh's steadfast love, working to make the best out of the people's unfaithfulness. The remedial will of God is an ethical recalculation—like a ship's navigator correcting course—due to the people's unfaithfulness to God's original or ultimate will. The "faithful potter" keeps working with the sometimes pliable and sometimes lumpy clay (Jeremiah 18).

To understand the value of Israel's human kings in God's ultimate will, we need only look at who appeared to Jesus generations later on the Mount of Transfiguration. Not one of the kings appeared to Jesus, but instead two prophets: Moses and Elijah. Jesus' kingdom and teachings were in line with

---

3 Rosemary Radford Ruether, *Faith and Fratricide: The Theological Roots of Anti-Semitism* (New York: Seabury Press, 1974), 231. "We must think ourselves back into a framework in which Christianity was within, not outside of, Judaism. The 'Jews,' the 'leaders' who are being attacked, do not represent some 'other people,' but one's own people, one's own 'Church' leaders, who are perceived as antithetical to authentic faith. The schism is not one that divides Christian from Jew, but one which divided Jew from Jew then and which today divides Christian from Christian."

the prophets, not the nation-state kings.

How long could the radical, theocratic community that Yahweh created in the Exodus actually survive? Samuel represented the last of that radical free community. Later the prophets would envision and proclaim that sort of missional community could exist again. Perhaps it is amazing that such a revolutionary social reality like the theocracy did survive from 1280 to 1020 BCE!

Interpreting the Two Views of the Monarchy

The Deuteronomistic writers and editors let both pro- and anti-monarchy literary strands remain in the Former Prophets (Hebrew scriptures), though the anti-monarchy view overrides the pro-monarchy view if we understand Yahweh to be the hero of the story, expressing steadfast love in the face of the people's unfaithfulness. Monarchy is Yahweh's remedial will. Part of this crisis in salvation history is that God's ultimate will can be lost and forgotten when covenant adjustments are made. When reading the Bible's salvation history story, it is important always to remember that much of the biblical story after monarchy represents Yahweh's remedial will.

The prophets retained a long enough memory that they proclaimed theocracy, not monarchy, as Yahweh's ultimate will, although there were some nationalistic prophets. Theocracy remained the reference point of faithfulness. Even near the end of the Northern Kingdom, the prophet Hosea condemned monarchy as the rejection of Yahweh as king (Hosea 8:4, 9:15, 10:3, 9). A comparison of the vision of the kings and the prophets appears in the next chapter.

The two interpretations of this crisis stand in scripture as a symbol and expression of a faithful God's dynamic relationship with the sometimes unfaithful people. The Deuteronomistic writers say that Yahweh's ultimate will did not change in this crisis. The anti- and pro-monarchy storylines represent the ultimate and remedial will of God. Yahweh always seeks redemptively to bring the best out of situations of unfaithfulness. God seeks to reshape the clay (Jeremiah 18).

But the ultimate will of God always trumps the remedial will. A number of scriptures suggest that God's will or actions changed due to unfaithfulness or people's repentance and people's prayers. Abraham bargains with God (Genesis 18). Moses challenges Yahweh and Yahweh does not destroy the unfaithful people (Exodus 33). Yahweh speaks to Jeremiah about how his will changes depending on what the people do (Jeremiah 18:7-10). The

God of the scriptures is not static, but a dynamic God who interacts with both the faithful and unfaithful people whom he chooses for a mission.

The Role of the Prophet

Bible passages: II Samuel 11-12, I Kings 17-22, Amos 1-6, Hosea 1-3

In 1020 BCE, the people of Israel moved from a loosely organized tribal confederacy to a monarchy. Through Samuel, God warned the people that a human king would abuse his powers and over-tax and enslave them. The king would forget about shalom justice and pursue more wealth for himself and his friends. Yahweh would become a national god instead of a God of all peoples.

But God wasn't about to let this turn of events destroy the solution to the sin problem. Yahweh sent prophets to speak the word of *dabar*, to challenge the power of the kings and to keep the theocratic vision alive.

The Prophetic Progression from Moses to the Post-Exilic Prophets

There are many prophets mentioned in the Bible: Isaiah, Jeremiah, Elijah and Elisha to name a few. In a general sense, anyone who speaks on behalf of God could be called a prophet. Moses and his sister Miriam are the archetypes. Moses expressed the vision and mission of God for the new community coming out of slavery in Egypt, an ethnically mixed group of strangers in the midst of forming an identity as God's people. Miriam, functioning as a prophetess, led the new community in doxology for the Red Sea deliverance. Along with brother Aaron, they led the people spiritually. Moses met with Yahweh on Mt. Sinai and then at the Tent of Meeting where he received God's revelation to pass on to the people.

After Moses, the prophetic role of speaking God's word was blurred with other roles. Joshua was primarily a military leader, although he expresses religious concerns in setting up a monument to help the tribes remember to tell the story (Joshua 6). He tells *Heilsgeschichte* at Shechem and calls the people to make a choice whether or not to follow Yahweh (Joshua 24).

Like Joshua, the judges functioned primarily as military leaders. Yet at times their spiritual leadership was emphasized. Saul encounters a "school of prophets" after he was anointed King by Samuel. The "Spirit of Yahweh" possess Saul as he joins in a prophetic frenzy giving him a new heart (I Samuel 10:10). God's message came to the early prophets more through ecstasy and divination. While some later prophets communicated their messages in rather bizarre ways, the "hearing" or receiving of the prophetic word moved from states of ecstasy to the more moral and historically-based preaching the story (*Haggadah*) and the expectations and laws (*Halakhah*).

As the last judge, Samuel claimed a combined role of prophetic, priestly and political leadership, much like Moses did. it's also at this point in history that the distinct role of the prophet starts to emerge. I Samuel 9:9 says, "Formerly in Israel, anyone who went to inquire of God would say, 'Come, let us go to the seer'; for the one who is now called a prophet was formerly called a seer." We can see from this verse there are several Hebrews words that could be translated as prophet, *ro'eh* and *hozeh*. And there is a new name, Nabi, that signals a clearer identity and purpose for biblical prophets. Nabi means one who has been called, or in the active sense, one who announces. And with the coming of human kings, there is a greater need for one who provides Yahweh's divine insight into the new political setting where there is a greater potential for the Kings to abuse their power.

Prophecy rose and fell with the monarchy.[1] The Kings were hard-pressed to stay humble and trust God militarily. The temptation to abuse power was great. And while there were prophets long after both Israel's and Judah's fall, even up to the time of Jesus with the ministry of John the Baptist, the majority of prophetic activity coincides with the monarchy.

Prophetic Categories

All biblical prophets speak God's word to God's people, but they do it in different ways and in different socio-economic contexts. During the monarchy, prophets could be categorized by two social functions. Some

---

1   G.V. Smith, "Prophet," in *The International Standard Bible Encyclopedia*, ed. Geoffrey Bromiley, v. 3 (Grand Rapids: Eerdmans, 1986), 993.

were cultic prophets, working alongside the priests. Others were court prophets who preached and sometimes lived in the the king's court.[2] Nathan was a court prophet who was told by God about David's adultery with Bathsheba and abuse of power as he had Bathsheba's husband killed in battle (II Samuel 11). Nathan confronted David about this sin, probably at the risk of his life. Nathan's courage and integrity stand in contrast to most of the biblical narrative concerning cultic and court prophets. Many times they are cast as accomplices to injustices, asked to bless either oppressive Temple kingly court practices. They were hard-pressed to oppose the very organization that fed them. I Kings 22 describes such a scene, where King Ahab wanted to fight a war. He called up his 400 prophets, asking them to "inquire of the Lord" (I Kings 22:5). They come back giving Ahab the Lord's blessing. Jehoshaphat asked if there weren't some other prophet with which to consult. Ahab said, "There is still one other by whom we may inquire of the Lord, Micaiah son of Imlah; but I hate him, for he never prophesies anything favourable about me, but only disaster.' The messenger for the king goes to fetch Micaiah and whispers to him that all the other prophets are proclaiming victory in war for Israel and Judah and that Micaiah should follow suit. But Micaiah says he can only say what he has heard from God. The two kings ask Micaiah for his word from the Lord, and the narrative takes a unexpected twist. Micaiah tells him to go fight this war. But King Ahab knew the prophet was lying and said, "How many times must I make you swear to tell me nothing but the truth in the name of the Lord?" (I Kings 22:16). Then Micaiah told him his real message from God, that fighting in a war would be disastrous. Ahab was smart enough to know that Micaiah was the true prophet, yet naive enough to believe that he could win in spite of God's command against it. Israel and Judah faced a horrible loss, Ahab was killed and Micaiah was vindicated.

False Prophets and the Rest of Micaiah's Story

One of the difficulties facing the Israelites was determining which prophet to believe when two prophets were giving different messages from God. How was one to know who to trust when both prophets were saying, "Thus says the Lord?" Of course, when the prophecy is fulfilled, then the prophet is proven to be authentic. But by then, it's too late if you listened to a false prophet.

---

2 Aaron Chalmers, *Exploring the Religion of Ancient Israel: Prophet, Priest, Sage and People* (Downers Grove: InterVaristy Press, 2012), 45.

The prophet Jeremiah faced this dilemma when he squared off with Hananiah. Jeremiah begged the people of Judah to submit to Nebuchadnezzar, the king of Babylonia, and allow themselves to be under foreign rule. Hananiah, another prophet, told the people not to worry, that the precious vessels of the Temple that Nebuchadnezzar took will be back in two years and that the Lord would give Judah victory over Babylon. So which prophet should the people listen to?

Sensing their confusion, Jeremiah gave two important strategies for discerning the true prophet. First, the true prophet loves her people so much that she is willing to be wrong. Jeremiah demonstrated this himself. After Hananiah challenged him with a more positive message, Jeremiah said, Amen! May the Lord fulfill the words you've prophesied. Jeremiah loved Judah so much that he would rather be wrong--and possibly killed for it-- than to be vindicated as right and watch Judah fall. Second, it's alway better to put more authority on prophets who give negative messages. Prophets will alway be tempted to give good news, because that's what people want to hear, and likewise, people of faith will always be tempted to accept as truth the good news.

> But listen now to this word that I speak in your hearing and in the hearing of all the people. The prophets who preceded you and me from ancient times prophesied war, famine, and pestilence against many countries and great kingdoms. As for the prophet who prophesies peace, when the word of that prophet comes true, then it will be known that the Lord has truly sent the prophet (Jeremiah 28:7-9).

But are the false prophets, like Hananiah, purposefully trying to fool people? Sometimes, but perhaps not all the time. Back in I Kings 22, Micaiah gives us something to consider. Part of this revelation from God was that the 400 prophets were purposefully deceived in order to entice Ahab to go to war and lose.

After the Division of 922 BCE, there emerged a third category: free-lance prophets. These independent prophets were more free to give stinging critique to the king. Amos, the most famous of these free-lancers, went so far as to say that he wasn't a prophet at all! As opposed to earlier prophets who tended toward ecstatic activity, freelance prophets of this later time, just as inspired, spoke rational and fiery words from God about injustice. Amos is a great example:

Hear this word, you cows of Bashan (wealthy women of Samaria)
who are on Mount Samaria,
who oppress the poor, who crush the needy,
who say to their husbands, 'Bring something to drink!'
2 The Lord God has sworn by his holiness:
The time is surely coming upon you,
when they shall take you away with hooks,
even the last of you with fish-hooks (Amos 4:1-2).

Prophets could also be categorized by their primary way of expressing God's message, specifically writing and non-writing prophets. Writing prophets are remembered for their books, while non-writing prophets are known more for their brave and sometimes bizarre actions or "acted out *dabar.*" These events were written down by other biblical authors. The writing prophets can be further sub-divided by the length of their books. Major prophets wrote long books and minor prophets wrote short books.

Historical sequence is another way to organize the prophets and their primary roles as people who speak the word of the Lord. Broadly stated, there are pre-exilic prophets who lived some time before the exile to Babylon in 587 BCE, exilic prophets or those who prophesied during Judah's time in Babylon, and post-exilic prophets, beginning with the return in 538. And while there are many exceptions to the rule, in general each century had an overall crisis to which the prophets responded. In the 10th century BCE, the prophets dealt with the monarchy crisis and the abusive of power by the kings. In the 9th century, Baal worship as well as state morality was the issue. During the 8th and 7th centuries BCE, social oppression and the unfair treatment of the poor became the rallying cry. In the 6th through the 5th centuries, having lost their nation-states, the prophets helped both Israel and Judah deal with their identity and deep faith questions. By the 4th century, the prophets were helping people look to the future and envision a God of all people groups.

Major pre-exilic prophets:

- From 1000-900: Samuel, Nathan, Gad and Ahijah
- From 900-800: Elijah and Elisha
- From 800-700: Amos, Hosea, Isaiah and Micah
- From 700-587: Jeremiah

Major exilic prophets:

- From 587-538: Jeremiah, Ezekiel, 2 Isaiah

Major post-exilic prophets:

- From 538 on: 3 Isaiah, Haggai, Zechariah

The Role of the Prophet

The prophet was to speak Yahweh's word and lead the people. But how did they do that?

Prophets used *dabar*. The Hebrew word *dabar* stands for the concept that words, particularly words that come from God or God's messenger, have great power to accomplish whatever has been spoken. Prophets are given *dabar* as their only weapon to fight evil. God touched Jeremiah's lips, a symbol of bestowing the power of *dabar* on him (Jeremiah 1:9-10) I Samuel 3:19 says, "As Samuel grew up, the Lord was with him and let none of his words fall to the ground," another picturesque way to illustrate *dabar*. Through their power of *dabar*, prophets brought fire from heaven (I Kings 18:36-39), proclaimed judgment upon their foes (Jeremiah 28:15-17) and raised the dead (I Kings 1717-24) Sometimes the prophets "acted out" *dabar*. God told Jeremiah (Jeremiah 13:1-11) to wear a loincloth around himself but not wash it. Then he was instructed to take this dirty undergarment all the way to the Euphrates River, a long distance, and bury it in a rock cleft. Then after many days, God told Jeremiah to retrieve the now soiled and partly deteriorating cloth. All of these actions were to show the people of Judah that, like a linencloth that clings to the body, so too were they held closely by God, but because of their pride and sin, they would become soiled and good for nothing.

Prophets told the story. When God's people remember how God has rescued them in the past, then they get the right motivation for obedience and worship (Deuteronomy 26:5-10). The prophets knew this principle and they worked hard to help the people remember. They retold the stories of the past, helping people understand a loving, faithful God. Then they worked to help the people see their current situation differently, to see that this loving, faithful God was still at work. The people of Judah saw themselves as safe and God's favorites when Israel fell, but Jeremiah reinterpreted those current events, warning them that they were ever worse than Israel because they saw Israel's fall and did nothing to change their wicked ways (Jeremiah 3). Later, when Babylon threatened to engulf them and they were tempted to fight back, Jeremiah again reinterpreted history, reminding them that their battles were contingent on obedience to God. This time Yahweh was saying, "Submit to Babylon" (Jeremiah 28). What seemed to them to be the worse fate, being exiled to a foreign country, God and Jeremiah saw as a good thing, an opportunity for renewal—a second Exodus (Jeremiah 24).

Part of the telling the story was to help the people feel gratitude. All the surrounding religions believed in a cyclical view of history, where the gods were simply manipulated by worship rituals to give people rain, sunshine and fertility which provided wealth. These people groups didn't worship their gods out of a sense of love for what their gods did in the past. The people deserved their fertility because they did their part: giving offerings and going to their temples. But Yahweh followers worshipped God for a different reason, thanks to the prophets. The story generated generated gratitude for what God had done in the past and reminded them that, unlike the cyclical view of history, Yahweh was radically free to act and not subject to manipulation. The prophets retold the wilderness stories where Yahweh, represented by the pillar of fire and cloud, went wherever God wanted to go. And God rescued the slaves out of Egypt not because they had done rituals to deserve this grace, but because God out of love wanted to free them.

The prophets enforced the covenant. Part of telling the story, called the *haggadah*, was connecting it to the covenant. In conditional covenants, like the Sinai covenant, God had given the people laws as their part of the covenant-keeping. Called the *halakhah*, these laws had the overall purpose of nurturing shalom, or the healing of the four major relationships. The prophets knew this. They reminded the people that how they lived mattered and they called the people to repent.

The prophets critiqued the kings and the priests. The major temptation of the Israelite kings was to abuse their power. The Temple priests also struggled with this temptation, given their great authority over the people and the immense wealth that came to the Temple coffers. Yahweh responded with the prophets. God sent Elijah to King Ahab to confront him about his abuse of royal powers. (Ahab had spread lies about a righteous man, Naboth, so that he could have him killed and then get his vineyard as his right as the king.) As soon as Ahab saw Elijah coming, he said, "Have you found me, O my enemy?" (I Kings 21:20). Elijah had found him alright, and he told Ahab of the disaster God now planned for him.

The prophets afflicted the comfortable and comforted the afflicted. Not only were kings and priests critiqued, but also anyone who got wealthy by oppressing others. Amos scorned those who were at ease in Zion (Amos 6:1) and promised a reversal of fortunes for those who "trample on the needy" (Amos 8:4-10). Isaiah proclaimed that God hated their religious rituals because they didn't do justice (Isaiah 1:12-17):

> *When you come to appear before me,*
> *who asked this from your hand?*
> *Trample my courts no more;*
> *bringing offerings is futile;*
> *incense is an abomination to me.*
> *New moon and sabbath and calling of convocation—*
> *I cannot endure solemn assemblies with iniquity.*
> *Your new moons and your appointed festivals*
> *my soul hates;*
> *they have become a burden to me,*
> *I am weary of bearing them.*
> *When you stretch out your hands,*
> *I will hide my eyes from you;*
> *even though you make many prayers,*
> *I will not listen;*
> *your hands are full of blood.*
> *Wash yourselves; make yourselves clean;*
> *remove the evil of your doings*
> *from before my eyes;*
> *cease to do evil,*
> *learn to do good;*
> *seek justice,*
> *rescue the oppressed,*
> *defend the orphan,*
> *plead for the widow* (Isaiah 1:12-17).

The prophet's message to the poor, the ones being trampled, is in complete contrast to the judgment oracles to the rich. "When the poor and needy seek water, and there is none, and their tongue is parched with thirst, the Lord will answer them, I the God of Israel will not forsake them" (Isaiah 41:17). Through the prophets, Yahweh reminds the oppressed that they have not been forgotten; they are encouraged to remain faithful and wait for the Lord's vindication. Even those who formerly were the oppressors find mercy from God, as Isaiah 40:1 shows. "Comfort, O comfort my people, says your God. Speak tenderly to Jerusalem, and cry to her that she has served her term, that her penalty is paid, that she has received from the Lord's hand double for all her sins."

In all these ways, the prophets not only gave God's word to the people, but they kept the theocratic vision of the wilderness alive. Every part of the prophets' message nurtured an understanding that God is the real king. God can and does overthrow kings who are wicked. God gives power to the powerless and sets captives free. Through the prophets, God provides an alternative way of living, a critique of the king's vision, a way of shalom where people voluntarily give up their power so that others may have the chance to live dignified lives.

The King's Vision vs. the Prophet's Vision

King's Vision	Prophet's Vision
• Economics of abundance and wealth	• Economics of "enough-ness" for everyone
• Politics of power and oppression	• Politics of freedom and shalom justice
• Religion that blesses the status quo	• Religion that calls for revival, reform and readjustment
• Faith in God's presence and favor. God is on our side and easily accessible	• Faith in a sovereign, just God who is radically free to rule
• Worship that manipulates and demands from God	• Worship that expresses humble gratitude. Re-enthrones God and re-covenants with God and others
• Autonomous self-serving leadership that abuses power, oppresses people and uses religion	• Submitted servant leadership that serves God and the people, using power to create a free shalom community[3]

3   Walter Brueggemann, *The Prophetic Imagination* (Minneapolis: Fortress Press, 1978), 36-38.

Oracle Genre

Bible passages: Jeremiah 1, 18:1-11, 27-28; I Kings 21-22

Understanding the prophet's function and meaning determines how one reads and interprets the whole Bible. The words "prophecy" and "prophet" join the words "chosen" and "nation-state" as among the most critically misunderstood words in the Bible. Some mistakenly view prophecy primarily as future predictions, and then they read and interpret the whole Bible through that bias. Consequently, they miss what Yahweh was trying to accomplish in Old Testament history with the chosen, missional people of God. The prophet preaches forth Yahweh's word to a specific historical situation. And in that preaching, the prophet shows God's desire for justice for all. Making the prophet's words about the distant future is a convenient way for Christians today to avoid God's clear call to work for justice.

How we understand the prophetic vision also determines how we interpret Jesus. On the Mount of Transfiguration, Jesus meets Moses and Elijah, not David and Solomon (Matthew 17:1-13). And while Jesus did present himself as a type of king, this alignment with the prophets shows what kind of king he will be. Over and over in the gospels Jesus had the same vision, the same priorities as the prophets. Had Jesus acted like David or Solomon, the temptations in the wilderness wouldn't have been temptations at all! Like these kings, Jesus would have set up a nation-state, including some people and excluding others, and he would have used violence to get what he wanted. But Jesus does none of that and even labels those actions for what they are, a way to bow down to Satan (Matthew

4:1-11). The biblical narrative is clear that monarchy is God's remedial will and that the prophets hold up God's ultimate will. If the monarchy is seen as the ultimate will of God and Jesus is identified and defined through the kings and their vision, one ends up with a militant Jesus, establishment, national civil religion, a carte-blanche approval of the current nation-state of Israel, Jews as God's favorite people, a prosperity gospel and the blessing of society's status quo.

Recognizing Oracle Genre

If our view of the prophets determines our view of the Bible and how Christians are to live their lives, then it must also be important to rightly identify and interpret the prophet's words. Prophetic oracle genre can be characterized in these ways.

This genre sounds like preaching. Prophetic oracles almost always sound like someone telling her audience what to do or what to believe. This genre can take either a poetic or prose form, but either way, the purpose is to convince the listeners or readers to change their ways. Many times this genre uses the phrase, "Thus says the LORD," or some variation of that phrase, as almost a code that this message is prophetic and comes from God. The prophets saw themselves merely as messengers; the words really were coming from Yahweh.

Some oracles are "woe" oracles, expressing deep sadness and sorrow. Ezekiel 26:1-6 is an oracle of woe to the city of Tyre.

> *In the eleventh year...the word of the Lord came to me: Mortal, because*
> *Tyre said concerning Jerusalem,*
> *'Aha, broken is the gateway of the peoples;*
>   *it has swung open to me;*
> *I shall be replenished,*
>   *now that it is wasted',*
> *therefore, thus says the Lord God:*
> *See, I am against you, O Tyre!*
>   *I will hurl many nations against you,*
>   *as the sea hurls its waves.*
> *They shall destroy the walls of Tyre*
>   *and break down its towers.*
> *I will scrape its soil from it*
>   *and make it a bare rock.*

123

It shall become, in the midst of the sea,
 a place for spreading nets.
I have spoken, says the Lord God.
It shall become plunder for the nations,
 and its daughter-towns in the country
 shall be killed by the sword.
Then they shall know that I am the Lord.

One variation to the woe oracle is the covenant lawsuit. Here God brings a "case" against a people group, usually Israel or Judah. As the prosecuting attorney and judge, God through the prophet levels charges against the defendant Israel. There is a summons to appear, a charge, evidence and a verdict. Isaiah chapter 3 is a good example.

Other oracles are promise or salvation oracles. Unlike the woe oracles that "afflict the comfortable," salvation oracles "comfort the afflicted." Ezekiel provides many good examples, such as Ezekiel 36:33-36:

Thus says the Lord God: On the day that I cleanse you from all your iniquities, I will cause the towns to be inhabited, and the waste places shall be rebuilt. The land that was desolate shall be tilled, instead of being the desolation that it was in the sight of all who passed by. And they will say, 'This land that was desolate has become like the garden of Eden; and the waste and desolate and ruined towns are now inhabited and fortified.' Then the nations that are left all around you shall know that I, the Lord, have rebuilt the ruined places, and replanted that which was desolate; I, the Lord, have spoken, and I will do it.

Rules of interpretation for the Prophetic Oracle

The prophet's role is to deliver God's message to the people of a specific time period so they will change their behavior. The majority of the prophets' words and actions sounded like preaching, with the purpose of calling people to repentance or giving them hope in their dire situations. In general, they didn't intend their words to be predictions in the far-off future. "Less than 2% of Old Testament prophecy is messianic. Less than 5% specifically describes the new-covenant age. Less than 1% concerns events yet to come in our time."[1] The prophets were "forth-tellers" and not foretellers.

---

1   Gordon Fee and Douglas Stuart, *How to Read the Bible for All Its Worth* (Grand Rapids: Zondervan, 2003), 182.

The prophets did speak of the future, but it was mostly the immediate future. The prophets saw where the society's actions would lead them and, like a loving but stern parent, they called for repentance in order to avoid the coming judgment. In this sense, the prophets spoke the Deuteronomistic view, which says that the righteous will be blessed and the ungodly will be cursed. The biblical narrative has many instances where the prophet gives the general message that if Israel doesn't repent and change her evil ways, this or that terrible thing will happen. People reap what they sow. The prophets were wise enough to know on an individual level the Deuteronomistic view doesn't always come true, but they were focusing on society as a corporate body, where the sins of some individuals really do impact the whole group.

Avoid treating the Old Testament as merely a shadow of things in the New Testament. Some people see the Old Testament as simply a shadow or typology of events or ideas in the New Testament. This diminishes the real-life acts of God for Israel in that time period and can lead to questionable theological connections. Sometimes the New Testament writers did use an Old Testament passage in a new context, thus giving the passage a second, new meaning in the Bible. An example of this is Hosea 11:1: "When Israel was a child, I loved him and out of Egypt I called my son." Hosea obviously refers to the deliverance of the slaves out of Egypt during the Exodus. Israel is called God's child or son elsewhere in the Old Testament. The plain meaning of this scripture in context is that Israel is the "son" whom God loved and delivered from Egypt. But Matthew takes this verse and gives it a second meaning, where the son refers to Jesus who was taken to Egypt to escape Herod's attempt to kill him (Matthew 2:15). While the gospel writers and Paul sometimes use Old Testament scriptures in this new way, we don't have the license to do the same today. If we allow ourselves to use the Old Testament as a typology for the New Testament, we can easily make the Bible say whatever we want. It would be especially tempting to soften the clear call to social justice that the prophets proclaim.

Cross the hermeneutical bridge. Like all genres, prophetic oracle contains important truth that deserves to be understood properly, in its original context. This genre however, more than other genres, needs the modern reader to understand the historical time period of the prophetic scriptures in question. For example, it's important to understand what "Edom" means for the original audience and the prophets who spoke against it (the book of Obadiah, Jeremiah 49, Ezekiel 35). The Edomites were descendants of Esau and there were bitter feelings between the families of the two brothers (Judah would be connected to Esau's twin, Jacob). Edom had at first collaborated with Zedekiah to fight Babylon (Jeremiah 27:3) but later become allies with Babylon (Ezekiel 25:12-14). When the people of Judah were exiled, the Edomites settled into Judean towns, further infuriating the people of Judah. This background helps the reader understand the pain and anger of the prophet's words and also how the prophecies against Edom were pointed to an immediate future. Edom is not a metaphor for any modern day country today. It was a real place in real time. The prophecies against Edom, or any other ancient people group, cannot be applied to people groups today.

Jeremiah 18 relates how God is like a potter who works hard at the wheel to reshape the clay. Sometimes the potter must smash the clay because the vessel is so marred, so resistant to the shaping of the artist, that it is unfit. When the prophets speak God's word, critiquing the rich and encouraging the poor, reminding the people of the faith story, speaking *dabar,* they serve as Yahweh's hand to try and reshape the clay, the Old People of God. It is a difficult, lonely, but worthy task.

The Prophet's Alternate Vision

With the poetic and powerful words in Micah 6:6-8, the prophet Micah exemplifies how the prophet holds up an alternative vision, the way of the LORD. During Micah's ministry, God's people mistakenly believed that worshipping God equalled doing the right rituals. Micah sets them straight, showing that there has to be more to worship than rituals, for even the most extreme gift is not enough.

'With what shall I come before the Lord,
  and bow myself before God on high?
Shall I come before him with burnt-offerings,
  with calves a year old?
Will the Lord be pleased with thousands of rams,
  with tens of thousands of rivers of oil?
Shall I give my firstborn for my transgression,
  the fruit of my body for the sin of my soul?'
He has told you, O mortal, what is good;
  and what does the Lord require of you
but to do justice, and to love kindness,
  and to walk humbly with your God?

And while giving offerings is not necessarily bad, with the exception of child sacrifice, which God consistently opposes throughout the biblical narrative, they are never enough. God wants worship to be connected to justice (see also Isaiah 1:10-17). "Loving kindness" means being happy for others when they get better than what they deserve, which is also called shalom justice.

"Walking humbly with God" means obeying God. All three of the requirements listed deal in some way with justice. Micah helps his listeners—and us—truly what it means to worship God.

The Kingdom Divides

Bible passages: I Kings 11, 12, 14

When the chosen-for-a-mission people became a nation state they allowed power to be concentrated in a king like other nations. We have seen how the three kings in the United Monarchy increasingly misused their power. Solomon, though dead when the division occurred in 922 BCE, precipitated the crisis with his opulent life, heavy taxes, and oppressive social policies. Samuel's most dire predictions about kingship had come true! Solomon, like David, ignored the rules for the king (Deuteronomy 17:14-20). Yahweh had delivered the people from Pharaoh's slavery in Egypt. Now they were in a slavery of their own making under an oppressive king in the line of David. That oppression had ripple effects for generations. The division between Israel and Judah was never healed completely.

Significant Players in the Revolt and Division
- King Solomon taxed the people heavily and instituted forced labor that continued after his death.
- Jeroboam, a gifted leader from the "house of Joseph," was in charge of forced labor.
- Rehoboam, Solomon's son, was to ascend to the throne.
- Ahijah the prophet prophesied to Jeroboam that 10 tribes would be given to him.
- Pharaoh Shishak gave Jeroboam political asylum and later attacked Judah.

- Shemiah was a prophet in Judah.
- Many old and young advisors to the king also contributed to the problems.

Storyline

King Solomon put Jeroboam, a gifted leader from the "house of Joseph," in charge of the forced labor needed to support his opulent lifestyle, large harem, and building projects. The large Joseph northern tribes Ephraim and Manasseh bore a heavy load in taxes and forced labor for the king. (Remember there was no Joseph tribe but two large tribal areas in the north were given to his two sons, Ephraim and Manasseh.) They also had some of the best land. Judah was the other large tribe in the south. The Judah and the Joseph tribes were the two most influential groups in the kingdom. For centuries, there had been tension between the Judah and Joseph tribes. The southern king, Solomon, added to the tension by enslaving people from the north.

A prophet from Shiloh named Ahijah prophesied to Jeroboam that Yahweh would tear ten tribes from the throne of Solomon and give them to him. *Dabar* could be delivered by actions as well as words. Ahijah tore his new garment into twelve pieces and gave ten to Jeroboam.

Although Jeroboam was put in charge of forced labor, he endeared himself to the laborers forced to work for Solomon and gained a following. When Solomon heard about Ahijah's prophecy he tried to kill Jeroboam, who fled to Egypt where Pharaoh Shishak gave him asylum.

After King Solomon's death, his son Rehoboam was the dynastic successor to the throne. He grew up amidst the wealth of Solomon's palace, sheltered from the conditions of the common people. When it was time for him to be crowned king, he chose a very odd place for the ceremony. He went to Shechem, the old sacred covenant site located in the north. Why go there? Was Rehoboam trying to heal the rift between the North and the South, the House of Joseph (Rachel tribes) and Judah (Leah tribe)?

When Jeroboam heard of this in Egypt, he returned home. With his followers' support, Jeroboam confronted Rehoboam and asked him what kind of king he was going to be. Would he be different from his father and lighten the people's load? Rehoboam asked his advisors for guidance. But then he rejected his older advisors who said to "lighten the load." Instead he accepted the counsel of his younger advisors who had grown up with him in the isolated wealth of the palace. Rehoboam arrogantly rejected the pleas of the northern tribes to be a more just king.

Rehoboam replied, "My little finger is thicker than my father's loins. Now, whereas my father laid on you a heavy yoke, I will add to your yoke. My father disciplined you with whips, but I will discipline you with scorpions" (I Kings 12:1-11).

When Jeroboam heard this response and understood what kind of king Rehoboam meant to be, he and the northern tribes had their own answer: "What share do we have in David? We have no inheritance in the son of Jesse. To your tents, O Israel! Look now to your own house, O David" (I Kings 12:1). Rehoboam put a different man named Adoram in charge of forced labor in an attempt to bring the situation under control. But the northern people fought back. They stoned Adoram to death (I Kings 12:18). Rehoboam fled to Jerusalem and the division grew deeper. Rehoboam might have attacked the northern tribes then, in an effort to reunite the country, but back in Jerusalem, the prophet Shemaiah warned him not to attack his brothers (I Kings 12:22-24).

But in the north Jeroboam, the former slave master, had allies of his own. Pharaoh Shishak, in sympathy with Jeroboam, attacked Judah from the south, even taking treasure from the palace and temple. Now Rehoboam couldn't attack the north even if he wanted to. He had a large national army, but he still couldn't fight battles on two fronts—Jeroboam in the north and the Pharaoh in the south..

With Rehoboam trapped in Judah, Jeroboam established himself as king of Israel. He made the former religious center Shechem into the new capital. He also fortified some of the border cities. To counter the popularity of the temple in Jerusalem, he set up alternate worship sites at Dan in the far North and Bethel near the southern border. He also created an alternate priesthood that claimed roots in the Mosaic period. Many of the Levitical priests had fled to Jerusalem at the time of the division.

It is interesting to note that the biblical writer—who probably came from the south—denounced Jeroboam's action with very strong language (I Kings 14:7ff and I Kings 16:26), and then introduced the northern kings with the words, "He [a king] did what was evil in the sight of the Lord walking in the way of Jeroboam and the sin he caused Israel to commit" (I Kings 15:34). Before that point the biblical writer described Jeroboam's leadership and the subsequent division as being "from the Lord" (I Kings 12).

A Long-Divided People

Just like other divisions there were long-term reasons and immediate causes for the division between the northern and southern tribes. In fact, the cracks were visible well before the rift between Jeroboam and Rehoboam. When David was king in the south, Saul's son, Ishbosheth, the rightful dynastic heir to the throne, was king in the northern tribes. And before that, revolutionary fires in the north had supported Absalom in his revolt against his father David, causing King David to centralize political power in the capital city Jerusalem.

King Solomon continued to centralize political power when he became king. Absalom's revolt that nearly succeeded was put down but it had challenged national unity. There had been a lot of support for Absalom among the northern tribes. Absalom was killed but it would take time to put out the revolting fires and establish national loyalty. The vision of the Mosaic theocracy and tribal confederacy continued in the northern tribes, especially in the Joseph tribes of Ephraim and Manasseh. The vision of being a chosen "nation people" rather than a nation-state was still alive.

The kingdom had been unified only on the surface through David's charisma, shrewd policies and Solomon's coercion. The monarchy was really never fully unified.

Why the division happened	Why the division succeeded
• The history cause is Solomon's forced labor and oppressive tax policies and then Rehoboam's refusal to listen to the pleas of the northern tribes and to his older advisors.	• The history reason is that Pharaoh Shishak attacked Judah from the south, forcing Rehoboam to fortify southern cities rather than attack the northern tribes right away.
• The *Geschichte* cause is the Lord acting through the prophet Ahijah who, in an act of treason, made Jeroboam king of the northern ten tribes by the spoken and acted "dabar."	• The *Geschichte* reason is that the prophet Shemaiah prophesied to King Rehoboam, "Thus says the Lord, You shall not go up to fight against your kindred, the people of Israel." Rehoboam listened to the Lord through the prophet's words and did not attack (I Kings 12).

Interpreting the Division in *Heilsgeschichte* Perspective

The books of I and II Kings were written from the perspective of the south. In writing the history they related Israel's kings to Judah's kings which reveals their location and orientation. For example I Kings 15:33: "In the third year of King Asa of Judah, Baasha son of Ahijah began to reign over all Israel…" The general condemnation reads "He did what was evil in the sight of the Lord, walking in the way of Jeroboam and in the sin that he caused Israel to commit" (I Kings 15:23-26, 33-34, 16:25-26). But when Judah's kings were unfaithful, they were still honored and their sins were mininmized for the sake of the Davidic covenant; II Samuel 7:13 said that David's throne would be established forever. Since David did not kill King Saul when he had a chance, there was an understanding in Judah not to touch "the Lord's anointed" (I Samuel 24:6) however evil they were! There were no coups in Judah unlike numerous ones in the northern kingdom Israel.

The fact of the matter is that Judah's kings in the line of David were not much better spiritually than the northern kings. Judah's kings set up idols even in the Temple and allowed injustices. But Israel's kings were consistently condemned for three things:

1. Israel did not have kings in the line of David (I Kings 15:33). If as Ahijah says it is of the Lord when he prophesied to Jeroboam, why the change in I Kings 14 where he is severely condemned? What changed Ahijah's mind?
2. Israel did not have priests in the line of Levi (I Kings 12:33).
3. Israel didn't worship in the temple in Jerusalem but at Dan and Bethel (I Kings 12).

Interestingly enough, this condemnation reveals that the southern writers gave more loyalty to the Zion Davidic kingship covenant than to the Sinai Mosaic theocracy covenant. The Davidic loyalty is based on the covenant with David that his throne shall be established forever (II Samuel 7). But in I Kings 8 and Solomon's prayer, the throne is conditioned on whether "your children walk before me as you [David] walked before me."

Northern Israel's ambivalence about kingship and their more theocratic vision was actually a higher vision, closer to Yahweh's ultimate will than Judah's monarchy vision representing Yahweh's remedial will.

When one places the critique of the nation-state Israel in the larger

Heilsgeschichte perspective, the southern Jerusalem-oriented writers represent the unfaithful departure from the people of God's original calling to be the missional people to all the earth rather than being a nation-state. They seem to have forgotten God's call to Abraham to bless all people groups. Monarchy seems to be accepted by the southern writers as God's ultimate will rather than remedial will. It is also interesting that Israel's history is more about the prophets Elijah and Elisha than the kings.

Ahijah the prophet stood in the tradition of the prophet and judge Samuel. He also committed treason by appointing Jeroboam king while another king still sat on the throne. The division grew out of a vision for reform and from the Mosaic theocracy tribal confederacy tradition. Did Jeroboam share that vision? One may assume that he did to some extent because he located the capital at Shechem, the original religious covenant center where Joshua led the tribes in re-covenanting after the conquest and the Ark of the Covenant rested until David brought it to Jerusalem. Jeroboam also gave attention to other sacred places such as Penuel and Bethel. Nevertheless, he did become a king, not a judge.

Jeroboam's Most Controversial Act

In a bewildering and possibly sacrilegious move for his new reign, Jeroboam set up images of bulls at the Dan and Bethel alternate worship centers. Various Middle Eastern gods were depicted riding on the backs of bulls, and Jeroboam's bulls would have evoked images of gods other than Yahweh. Scholars debate what this meant to Jeroboam and the people. The Jerusalem temple had Yahweh dwelling between the wings of the seraphim above the Ark of the Covenant. Did Jeroboam envision Yahweh astride a bull instead? He did connect the God of the Dan and Bethel shrines as "Yahweh who brought them out of Egypt." Bernard Anderson writes, "Jeroboam then had no idea of introducing the worship of new 'gods;' rather his intention was to renew Israel's devotion to the God of the covenant."[1] Whatever Jeroboam's intent, the bull was perhaps too close to Baal worship to avoid syncretism in that context. The people misunderstood and Jeroboam's bulls led to syncretism rather than to an exclusive worship of Yahweh who delivered them out of Egypt. The northern prophet Hosea is the first to condemn the bull calf at Bethel, not a historian from Judah (Hosea 8:5-6, 10:5-6).

---

1   Bernhard W. Anderson, et al., *Understanding the Old Testament, Fifth Edition* (Upper Saddle River, NJ: Pearson Education, Inc., 2007), 240.

Conclusion and Interpretation

The division of the kingdom is a critical crisis and turning point in the story of God's people. It was firmly rooted both in history and as an event interpreted from a faith bias. The historic reasons for the division are clear even from the biblical documents. The United Monarchy was never fully united and by Solomon's time only by force. Cracks in the unity appeared from time to time after the first king Saul. David knew that he needed a capital at a neutral site between north and south. He captured Jerusalem and made it both a political and religious center. The Judah and Joseph conflict went way back to the conflict in the Jacob family between Leah and Rachel's sons. The divided people of God often fought each other (I Kings 14:30) and also sometimes became allies against a common enemy or when the royal families intermarried.

The division can be interpreted in two drastically different ways, depending on one's understanding of Yahweh's ultimate and remedial will.

Pro-Monarchy Nation-State View: From a view that Yahweh's ultimate will was for the people to become a nation-state, the revolt and division were completely evil. David was seen as the best king, a man after God's own heart and Nathan—rather than uttering a dark threat about the future of David's house—prophesied that there would be a descendant on David's throne forever. David's charisma, his military victories and political shrewdness were celebrated as the greatest king. Some Bible readers who overlook David's sins believe the monarchy was God's ultimate will. And after all, the "throne of David" dynasty lasted hundreds of years. Solomon, who expanded Israel's power and influence to dominate the Middle East for a while is also seen as a great wise leader of God's nation state and his sins of injustices and forced labor are minimized by some Bible readers today.

Anti-Monarchy View: From a faith *Geschichte* view, Israel's division is God's judgment against Solomon and his anti-shalom policies. The unfaithful Israelites were reaping what they sowed when they became a nation-state with power vested in kings. Succeeding kings increasingly misused their power, including David and Solomon. Nathan prophesied to David after his sin, that Yahweh "will raise up evil against you out of your own house" referring to Absalom's revolt (II Samuel 12:11). Israel also faced challenges from outside its borders in the rough and tumble international politics among the Middle Eastern nation-states.

The monarchy was only Yahweh's remedial will, and theocracy and the Abraham's call to be missional never died out completely during the monarchy. They were to reveal Yahweh to all the world's people groups. In steadfast love (Psalm 136), Yahweh stayed connected throughout the people's unfaithfulness. This tenacious God kept working with people who were free to say no.

Israel and its Fall to Assyria

Bible passages: I Kings 18, II Kings 17

The schism of the United Monarchy leaves the Northern Kingdom, Israel, with the largest and most fertile portion of land. Israel is far superior to Judah economically, militarily, and politically. For this reason, the smaller and more isolated Judah is spared some of the international conflict. Several trade routes cross Israel, making it more desirable and therefore more vulnerable to attack. During most of Israel's existence, Judah was little more than a vassal to the Northern Kingdom. The relationship between the two countries ranged from wars to alliances forged by common defense and royal intermarriages.

Until Israel falls, the biblical writers focus on the Northern Kingdom. Israel's story mostly follows the activities of the northern prophets Elijah and Elisha who get the most coverage. The prophet was called "the man of God." Only after 722 BCE does Judah's story receive much attention. Judah's story mostly follows the kings.

The Deuteronomistic writers summarily condemn Israel because the Israelites are not orthodox. They don't have kings in the line of David, they don't have priests in the line of Levi, and they don't worship in Jerusalem. Israel's lack of kings in the line of David probably led the biblical writers to focus their stories on the prophets who were in conflict with Israel's kings.

As noted in the previous chapter, the revolt against Rehoboam had some theocratic roots, a vision for reform and ambivalence about centralized kingship power. The office of king and the kings themselves were not respected as much in Israel as in Judah. Unlike in Judah, there was no problem in Israel with killing "the Lord's anointed" kings. Consequently there were a number of bloody coups and short reigns in Israel. In contrast, Judah had an unbroken dynasty of kings in the line of David except for one brief reign by a queen. Resistance in Israel to centralized government led to internal instability and external vulnerability to neighboring countries and empires.

Israel's Kings

Political instability and frequent war with Judah during Israel's first 50 years weakened the nation and kept Jeroboam I (922-901) from establishing a long lasting dynasty. After his 21-year reign, a series of bloody assassinations shortened the reigns of the next four kings to one year, three years, one year, and finally to seven days! The low esteem for the office of kings in the northern tribes expressed itself to the extreme.

At last, Omri (876-742 BCE) led a successful coup bringing order and political stability. Omri's four descendants ruled for 35 years. He established peaceful relations with neighboring countries, including marriages of his children with Phoenician and Judaic royal families. He led successful military campaigns enlarging Israel's control in the Transjordan. Omri also moved the capital from Shechem located in an undefensible site in a valley northwest to the city of Samaria strategically located on top of a hill. Later the Assyrians struggled for three years to conquer the capital city, revealing the move's wisdom. Omri's son Ahab married Jezebel of Phoenicia, who was a strong promoter of Baal worship. She persecuted the prophets of Yahweh. Jezebel brought so much evil that her name still carries a negative connotation in some circles.

Omri's dynasty ended with Jehu (842-815 (BCE), who was an army captain anointed king by the prophet Elisha. He led a partly religious, partly political bloody coup to purge the house of Ahab and establish the third dynasty. He killed all of Ahab's family, decapitating his seventy sons, priests, and friends. But the purge killed members of royal families from Phoenicia and Judah as well, hurting international relations and making Israel vulnerable to attacks. The Jehu dynasty fell to Jeroboam II, who restored Israel to economic prosperity and territorial control equal to the days of the United Monarchy. Jeroboam II's son Zechariah reigned for only six months, technically ending the Jehu dynasty.

The Deuteronomistic writer praises Jehu for his religious purge even though he did not destroy the shrines at Dan and Bethel (II Kings 9-10). But the prophet Hosea condemns Jehu for his bloody revolution (Hosea 1:4). The prophets Amos and Hosea preached during the prosperous reign of Jeroboam II (786-746 BCE). But weak kings followed Jeroboam II, and Assyria's westward expansion led to a rapid decline and, ultimately, the fall of Israel to Assyria in 722 BCE.

Israel's Major Prophets

During the tumultuous monarchies of Israel, prophets enjoyed high status and esteem, and several stand out from the pack. The prophet Micaiah, for example, openly disagreed with four hundred other professional prophets' estimation that King Ahab could defeat Syria. Micaiah told Ahab that the battle would go poorly. Ahab chose to fight anyway, and was killed in that battle (I Kings 22:13-40).

The prophets are so important to the biblical story that the Northern Kingdom's story is really more about non-writing prophets Elijah and his successor Elisha than the kings. Elijah and Elisha prophesied throughout Israel, Phoenicia, and Syria and had the power to anoint kings, including one in Syria! Elijah and Elisha represented the Mosaic covenant and laws with an exclusive God who would not tolerate syncretism with other gods, especially Baal. They called the kings and people to the social justice of the Sinai covenant.

Two Non-Writing Prophets

Elijah, the Tishbite from Gilead, was called the "troubler of Israel" by king Ahab. Elijah led the great contest with Jezebel's prophets of Baal on Mt. Carmel. The Elijah stories also include his predicting a drought, the miraculous never-ending oil and flour of the Phoenician widow who took Elijah into her house during a famine, his raising the widow's son to life, his confronting King Ahab about taking Naboth's vineyard, and his ascending into heaven in a whirlwind (I Kings 17-19, 21, II Kings 2).

Elijah anointed Elisha to succeed him. Elisha's miracle stories include making a poor widow's oil supply increase a hundredfold which she then sold to pay her creditors thus saving her children from being taken into slavery. He also raised the dead son of a hospitable, wealthy Shunnamite woman. He purified a pot of stew, multiplied food to feed four hundred men, told the Syrian commander Naaman how to be healed from leprosy by bathing in the Jordan River, and made a borrowed ax head float so it could be retrieved and returned. Elisha was also active politically, participating in various Holy War campaigns, interacting with the king of Syria, anointing Jehu king and supporting him in his bloody religious purge of Ahab's family. Some of Elisha's stories sound suspiciously similar to some of Elijah's.

These stories reveal Elisha's concern for the poor, reflecting the shalom justice vision of the Mosaic covenant. The blinding of the Arameans as the Terror of the Lord is a Holy War story in the vein of the original nonviolent model of Holy War. The king of Aram was sending raiding parties into Israel but without success. Elisha kept telling Israel's king where the Arameans were camped. The Aram king was told that Elisha was telling Israel's king their locations. So the Aram king sent soldiers to capture Elisha at Dothan. They surrounded the city. Elisha prayed that his fearful servant's eyes would be opened. And the servant saw the hills were full of horses and chariots of fire. When the Arameans came toward Elisha, he prayed that God would blind them, which God did. So Elisha led them into the capital city Samaria. When they were all inside, Elisha prayed and the Lord opened their eyes. Israel's king asked Elisha whether he should kill the Arameans, and Elisha said not to. Instead Elisha fed the Arameans with a great feast and then let them go. The story ends with "And the Arameans no longer came raiding in the land of Israel" (II Kings 6:8-23).

Two Writing Prophets

Amos, a shepherd farmer from Tekoa, five miles south of Bethlehem in Judah, became the first prophet in Israel whose oracles were collected into a book. Amos prophesied around 750 BCE during the reign of Jeroboam II, a time of Israel's prosperity and political dominance. When Amaziah, the chief priest at Bethel, told Amos to go home to Judah and earn his bread with the other professional prophets, he replied that he is not a "nabi" nor the son of a "nabi," but that God called him and sent him to prophesy to "my people Israel" (Amos 7:14-15).

Amos thundered against the wealthy and powerful in Israel. He railed against social injustices, calling for a return to covenant shalom community where there was economic and shalom justice. He insisted that acceptable worship at Bethel must be connected with shalom justice.

I hate, I despise your festivals, and I take no delight in your solemn assemblies. Even though you offer me your burnt offerings, I will not

139

accept them... Take away from me the noise of your songs; I will not listen to the melody of your harps. But let justice roll down like waters, and righteousness like an ever-flowing stream (Amos 5: 21-24).

While much of his message was judgment, Amos also expressed compassion and deep love for the people. When seeing the coming judgment on Israel, Amos cried out to God, interceding for the people, "O Lord God, cease, I beg you. How can Jacob stand? He is so small" (Amos 7:5).

The second writing prophet, Hosea, prophesied after Amos, around the time of Jeroboam's death in 746 BCE and then afterward when Israel's rapid decline had already begun. In contrast to Amos, Hosea was a pleading prophet with a message that Yahweh loved Israel by choosing and liberating her out of Egypt and watching over her in the wilderness. He saw Israel as the beloved child of God. "When Israel was a child, I loved him and out of Egypt I called my son" (Hosea 11:1). Using the marriage analogy, Hosea pictured Israel as an unfaithful wife full of harlotry in chapter two. But Yahweh's irrational grace still sought to restore the relationship with this wayward wife. Amos said that Yahweh's judgment expressed God's love and grace, seeking to bring back the wayward people to covenant relationship. But Hosea also challenged Israel:

What shall I do with you, O Ephraim? What shall I do with you O Judah? Your love is like a morning cloud, like the dew that goes away early. Therefore I have hewn them by the prophets, I have killed them by the words of my mouth, and my judgment goes forth as the light. For I desire steadfast love and not sacrifice, the knowledge of God rather than burnt offerings (Hosea 6:4-6).

When Israel was a child I loved him, and out of Egypt I called my son. The more I called them, the more they went from me; they kept sacrificing to the Baals, and offering incense to idols. Yet it was I who taught Ephraim to walk, I took them up in my arms; but they did not know that I healed them... They shall return to the land of Egypt and Assyria shall be their king, because they have refused to return to me (Hosea 11:11-5).

International Players During Israel's Existence

Soon after the division between Israel and Judah, Egyptian Pharaoh Shishak invaded Judah. He also invaded Israel all the way north to Megiddo. Syria was the next country to threaten Israel, taking territory in the northern Transjordan. Israel's relationship with Syria over its 200 year existence included both alliances against common enemies and intermittent wars (see Holy War stories in II Kings 6-7).

The northern kingdom of Israel was a significant player internationally especially during the reigns of Jeroboam, Ahab, and Jeroboam II. The dominating powers in the Fertile Crescent in historical order to that point in the Old testament were Egypt, United Israel, Syria, (North) Israel, and Assyria. As Assyria emerged and extended its control westward, Syria and Israel formed an alliance. But at the pivotal battle of Qarqar in 853 BCE, Shalmaneser III, the Assyrian ruler, was victorious but evidently not to the extent that he could march further westward to capture the capital cities of Damascus and Samaria.

Israel's Fall To Assyria

After the death of Jeroboam II, Israel declined rapidly. Moral and spiritual decline plus political instability contributed to Israel's loss of national strength. Weak kings and coup after coup led to Israel's decline and fall to Assyria in 722 BCE. King Tiglath-Pileser III (called Pul in the Bible) came to power the year Jeroboam II died in 746 BCE. He marched westward from Nineveh, conquering Damascus in 732 BCE and took control of parts of northern Israel. When Pul died in 727 BCE, King Hoshea of Israel decided to revolt and not pay the annual tribute. Then Shalmaneser, the new Assyrian king, invaded Israel and laid a three-year siege of the capital city Samaria but died before he could gain the victory. Sargon II completed the destruction of Samaria. Israel lay in ruins, never to be restored.

The Assyrians deported some 27,000 or about one-third of Israel's citizens and brought in approximately the same number of foreigners in order to weaken the Israelite culture. The two people groups intermarried and their children were called Samaritans. Later on, the people of Judah, eventually to be called Jews, would hate the Samaritans, seeing them as half-breeds. This hatred continued through the time of Jesus.

Judah and post-exilic Jews who defined themselves as ethnically pure considered themselves superior to the Samaritans. The fact of the matter was that the Exodus peoples were a mixed crowd to begin with (Exodus 12:38). This crowd was joined by Kenites in the wilderness and infiltration people and marginal Habiru and the Gibeonites when they moved into Canaan. Other ethnic persons joined the people of God and appear in the lineage of Jesus. The "Israelites" or People of God were never all blue-blooded descendants of Jacob. Their chosenness was to be a faith-based people (identity), not an ethnic group. Yahweh faith survived in Samaria to the time of Jesus.

Judah and its Fall to Babylonia

Bible passages: II Kings 23-24, Jeremiah 18-19

Historical Context: Israel, Judah, and Assyria

Judah and Israel's relationship after the division ranged from close alliance with intermarriage between the royal families to conflict and war. Historically Judah's weaker status and more isolated location contributed to their survival when Israel fell to the Assyrians. But Judah's popular civil religion interpreted their survival differently.

In 734 BCE Israel and Syria invaded Judah to bring it into line for a united stand against the westward march of Assyria. Judah's King Ahaz (735-315 BCE) had refused to join this Israel-Syria coalition against Assyria. In defense against the Israel-Syria coalition, King Ahaz sent a huge gift to the Assyrian king Tiglath-Pileser (Pul) which made Judah essentially a vassal of Assyria for the next sixty years. That vassal relationship included annual tribute that further weakened Judah's economy (II Kings 16:5-8). King Ahaz had to strip the temple in order to pay the tribute (II Chronicles 28:21). The prophet I Isaiah of Jerusalem opposed Ahaz's appeasement of the Assyrians (Isaiah 7). But the king's action did help Judah survive when the Assyrians defeated Israel in 722 BCE.

When Assyria defeated Israel and Syria, Judah did lose some land on its northern border to Assyria, further diminishing it size and significance. Edom, a vassal to Judah on its southeastern border, took advantage of Judah's weakened condition and revolted. Judah lost both land and tribute income.

Three Reasons Judah Survived When Israel Fell

Why did Judah not fall when Israel was conquered by Assyria? One history reason is that King Sargon of Assyria had to return home to deal with political rebellions in the eastern part of his empire. His sweep to the south into Judah remained unfinished. A second history reason is that king Ahaz had appeased Assyria earlier with a huge gift.

But using the Deuteronomistic view, the popular religious *Geschichte* interpretation was that Judah's escape from the Assyrian invasion was another sign that they were more righteous than fallen Israel, so Yahweh saved them. Their popular civil religion helped Judah rely on this false security instead of repenting for economic injustices, idol worship, immorality and glorifying the temple, and the Davidic dynasty, all of which created a false sense of security against which the prophet Jeremiah had warned them (Jeremiah 7). After all, they thought, Judah had kings in the line of David, priests in the line of Levi, plus the temple and Ark of the Covenant in Jerusalem. They believed Yahweh would surely protect them and fight Holy War for them as had happened several times before.

Four Kings Of Judah: Two Evil and Two Godly

The biblical writers don't give Judah's kings much better grades for their religious and political leadership than they gave Israel's kings. Manasseh's evil in Judah certainly rivaled that of King Ahab of Israel. But unlike Israel there were no coups in Judah because the kings were all in the line of David. And David modeled that a sitting king should not be harmed when he had the opportunity to kill King Saul, but refused to do so (I Samuel 24). Yet the Davidic dynasty, civil religion, and the temple in Judah still led the biblical writers to be more lenient with Judah's kings.

Ahaz (735-715 BCE)—Evil King

Ahaz's (also called Jehoahaz) appeasement of Assyria included religious compromise as well as political subservience. He installed altars to Assyrian deities in the temple and went so far as to sacrifice his son to the god Moloch (II Kings 16:3). The prophets I Isaiah (of Jerusalem) and Micah opposed both the political and religious compromises of Ahaz which they saw as the same (Isaiah 2, 7).

Hezekiah (715-687 BCE)—Good King

Hezekiah, the son of Ahaz, led two revolts against Assyria. The first one was largely a religious reform that also had political implications. After this first revolt the Assyrian King Sennacherib invaded the Phoenicia, Syria and Judah area, conquering many Judean cities and isolating King Hezekiah in Jerusalem. Hezekiah made peace by depleting the treasury and further stripping the Temple to pay the tribute to Assyria. Sennacherib also had to return home to deal with political difficulties there (II Kings 19:7). Jerusalem was spared again.

King Hezekiah led a second revolt near the end of his reign that brought the Assyrian army to Jerusalem again. But an epidemic killed 100,000 soldiers in the Assyrian army. The historian Herodotus indicates this event was a plague of mice,[1] which most likely means the bubonic plague, a deadly bacterial infection spread by fleas and intermediate carriers like rats and mice. The plague would be a history reason for the mass deaths. We get a *Geschichte* reason from the biblical writer and prophet I Isaiah, who interpreted the deaths as the Terror of the Lord in Holy War after Hezekiah prayed to Yahweh for deliverance (Isaiah 36-37, II Kings 19). Both Isaiah and the biblical writer's interpretation of this Holy War deliverance, plus the earlier sparing of Judah when Israel fell, fueled Judah's popular religion to believe that Yahweh would always protect Judah and Jerusalem. They believed after all that they were Yahweh's last faithful remnant and so would not be destroyed. They ignored Yahweh's sovereignty and developed an exceptionalist belief that they were Yahweh's favorite people rather than people chosen to complete a mission.

King Manasseh (687-642 BCE)—Evil King

Hezekiah's son Manasseh is seen as the most evil of Judah's kings. The Deuteronomistic writer says that his evil caused Yahweh's judgment, Judah's fall and exile to Babylon. With the prophets I Isaiah and Micah gone, Manasseh restored the places of idol worship, supported human sacrifice—including that of his own son—and outrageously put an Asherah Pole in the Jerusalem temple!

---

1   Herodotus, *The Histories,* ii, 141,5. A.D. Goodly, ed. Perseus Digital Library, http://www.perseus.tufts.edu/hopper/. June 22, 2016. See also William Sanford LaSor, et al., *Old Testament Survey: The Message, Form, and Background of the Old Testament.* Second Edition. (Grand Rapids: William B. Eerdmans Publishing Company, 1996), 215.

Josiah (640-609 BCE)—Good King

Manasseh's grandson was the most faithful king in Judah. He cleared the temple of foreign gods; other places of idol worship were also destroyed and worship was centralized in Jerusalem so it could be controlled. During the temple refurbishing, the workers found a scroll of the Law. It appears that it was the major part of the Book of Deuteronomy.[2] When the prophetess Huldah authenticated the scroll, Josiah repented and led a religious reform. From the Deuteronomistic perspective he feared Yahweh's judgment because of the people's sin (II Kings 22-23). The discovery of the scroll in the temple indicates how far worship rituals had departed from the law of Moses.

From Egyptian to Babylonian Control

During King Josiah's reign, the Assyrian empire was weakened by revolts of conquered territories. Egyptian Pharaoh Necho took this opportunity to reclaim the Egyptian empire's past glory. His armies headed up the Mediterranean coast to conquer Assyria. Fearing being isolated by Egypt, Josiah tried to stop Necho at the Megiddo pass. Josiah was killed and Judah lost the battle of Megiddo (609 BCE). Judah became a vassal to Egypt. Judah's fate was now tied to Egypt's fate.

Meanwhile, Babylonia had defeated Assyria at the Battle of Qarqar and became the emerging Middle Eastern Power. The Babylonian king Nebuchadnezzar defeated Pharaoh Necho's army at the pivotal battle of Carchemish in the Middle East in 605 (BCE), so now both Egypt and Judah became vassals to Babylon! After King Josiah's death in battle, Judah's conquerors installed puppet kings to keep the Judean people in line. It didn't work very well.

First Deportation to Babylonia—Puppet king Jehoiakim (609-589 BCE) revolted against the Babylonians. He died during Nebuchadnezzar's siege of Jerusalem. His son Jehoiachin had ruled for only three months when Jerusalem surrendered to Babylonia. Jehoiachin was taken to Babylon iaalong with 10,000 of Judah's leading citizens. Babylonia hoped that by taking the leaders out of Jerusalem they would be easier to control. The prophet Ezekiel was also taken in this deportation. While the deportation was painful for Judah, they still enjoyed semi-independence.

Second Deportation to Babylonia—Zedekiah, Judah's last puppet

---

2   Bernhard W. Anderson, et al., *Understanding the Old Testament, Fifth Edition* (Upper Saddle River, NJ: Pearson Education, Inc., 2007), 289.

king, ruled for ten years until he also foolishly revolted in 589 BCE. Patience at an end, Babylonia laid siege to Jerusalem, completely destroying the city and temple. To end the dynasty, all of King Zedekiah's sons were killed in front of him and then his eyes were blinded. The blind Zedekiah was taken to Babylonia in chains along with many Judah citizens (II Kings 25). The long siege of Jerusalem led to great suffering. The nation-state Judah was no more! Jerusalem lay in ruins! The trek to Babylonia was long and hard. They could not take the direct route across the desert but followed the Fertile Crescent to the land beyond the Tigris and Euphrates rivers. Thousands of its citizens now lived in exile communities in Babylonia. Only a few poor rural folk remained. The prophet Jeremiah escaped with some who fled to Egypt when Babylonia invaded.

Understanding the Revolts

As described above, the Judeans felt themselves immune from attack, defeat, and suffering in general. This sense of immunity led some of Judah's leaders to rise up against ridiculous odds, with mixed results. However, not all Judeans felt so sure that Yahweh would always step in to save them at the last minute. The prophet Jeremiah warned Judeans to repent and amend their ways, and only then would God dwell with them. "Here you are trusting deceptive words to no avail. Will you steal, murder, commit adultery, swear falsely, make offerings to Baal, and go after other gods you have not known and then come and stand before me in this house which is called by my name and say, 'We are safe!'" (Jeremiah 7:8-10). Worship had become disconnected from morality and shalom justice.

Heedless, the Judeans continued to emphasize the unconditional Abrahamic and Davidic covenants, especially the latter, which promises the establishing of the Davidic dynasty forever (Genesis 12:1-3, II Samuel 7:8-9, 12-19). At the same time, they avoided the conditional Mosaic covenant that involved their responsibility to be faithful to Yahweh as a condition for their well being. Their purpose to be the chosen missionary people without boundaries was forgotten and replaced by the sense of being God's favorite people and a glorification of the monarchy, Davidic dynasty, and nation-state with its anti-missionary national and geographic boundaries.

Faith Crisis of Crises: Will Yahweh Faith Survive?

With Jerusalem, the temple, and Judah in ruins and the people in exile, the biblical story shifts to the exiles in Babylonia. Their land, king, city, and temple are all gone. Yahweh faith had suffered devastating destruction and seemed unlikely to survive. The losses, starvation and suffering of the sieges, fall, and long march to exile raised some critical faith questions. While some of the questions were based on false premises, they were nevertheless serious questions. The exile prophets like Jeremiah, Ezekiel, and II Isaiah held the key to the survival of the people's Yahweh faith. The people asked questions, and the prophets answered.

Is Yahweh faithful to covenant? The prophets answered that God keeps both conditional and unconditional covenants (I Kings 8:23, II Chronicles 6:14, Jeremiah 22). The prophets and biblical writers weave together the conditional covenant traditions with the unconditional traditions.

Is Yahweh the most powerful God? Marduk, Babylonia's national god has defeated Judah's national god hasn't he? The prophets answered that Yahweh is the most powerful God, but Yahweh fought Holy War against his own people. Judgment is an expression of Yahweh's loving discipline (Ezekiel 21, Jeremiah 21:5-19, II Kings 24:2). Yahweh destroyed the boxes of the nation-state and geography.

Has Yahweh abandoned the people? The prophets answered that the people have abandoned Yahweh. Both Yahweh's judgment and continued tenacious engagement of the the people express Yahweh's steadfast love for the people (II Samuel 7:11, Isaiah 54:6-10).

How can we worship Yahweh outside of Yahweh's land and city? Yahweh is everywhere, the throne of God has wheels that move in all four directions (Ezekiel 1:15-21, 10:9-17, 37).

How can we worship without a temple? The prophet Ezekiel says that Yahweh can be worshipped everywhere (Ezekiel 1,10).

How can we have faith when the nation-state ceases to exist? Yahweh is a God of people from every tribe and nation and the God of the whole earth (Isaiah 49:6).

The nation-state Judah lay smashed in pieces like the earthen pot the prophet Jeremiah smashed in front of the Jerusalem elders (Jeremiah 19). Yahweh broke apart the two boundaries the people of God had created in their popular civil religious faith when the monarchy was established. The Babylonian exile broke the geographical box by taking the people of Judah to a foreign land. It also broke the nation-state box by destroying Judah's nation-state.

Yahweh's breaking apart of the land and nation from their faith gave the people a new opportunity to rediscover and be faithful to their chosenness to God's original, ultimate will for a missionary, covenant, shalom community. They could become a transnational people that revealed Yahweh to the whole world, a light to the nations (Genesis 12:1-3, Exodus 19:6).

The Babylonian exile was espeicially difficult because Judah didn't see it coming. The exile prophets were the key to the people's hope for the future. They helped the people have a new world view, a new identity and hope.

Exile Adaptations

Bible passages: Psalm 137; Isaiah 40:1-11; Jeremiah 29:1-15; Ezekiel 36: 26-27, 37:1-14; II Samuel 1:17; I Chronicles 21:1-17

The Babylonian exiles lived in fairly free communities around Babylon in the Tigris and Euphrates River valley. No doubt some abandoned the faith; others acculturated, blending into the Babylonian culture; while still others defined their faith more vigorously over against Babylonian religion. The Babylonian cultural influence is seen in the Jewish religion coming out of the exile. This is especially evident in the creation of the Aramaic language that is a mixture of Hebrew and Babylonian.

Deep discouragement, anger, grief and serious faith questions troubled the exiles. They had lost land, king, and temple. Will Yahweh faith survive? The 137th Psalm expresses the feelings of at least some of the people.

By the water of Babylon
There we sat down and wept.
On the willows there we hung up our harps
For there our captors asked us for songs
And our tormentors asked for mirth, saying
'Sing us one of the songs of Zion.'

How could we sing the Lord's song
in a foreign land.
If I forget you, O Jerusalem,
Let my right hand wither!

Let my tongue cling to the roof of my mouth,
If I do not remember you,
If I do not set Jerusalem above my highest joy…

Happy shall they be who pay you back
What you have done to us!
Happy shall they be who take your little ones
And dash them against the rock!

This Psalm reflects the exiles' belief that Jerusalem is the most important element in their religion, and without it they would be lost. But the ministry and message of the prophets and the religious adaptations the people made were the keys to the survival and renewal of Judah's faith in exile. The primary exilic prophets were Jeremiah, Ezekiel and Isaiah.

Religious Adaptations

With the loss of temple, land, king, and nation-state, the Jews needed to redefine their identity and faith. This identity crisis generated a vigorous gathering and editing of their story. Many of the Old Testament documents were put in final form in the exile. The reclaiming of their story shaped their identity and faith, bringing renewed devotion to Yahweh.

The religious community moved from temple worship to synagogue worship. Since the temple was destroyed, more informal gatherings of worshippers emerged in places called synagogues. Synagogues were not large, so many were established in the exile communities. And because every synagogue needed a copy of the scriptures, many copy scribes were also needed. And since synagogues were on every corner, the exiles gathered to worship once a week instead of once a year.

They moved from altar-centered worship to book-centered worship in the synagogue. Again, without the temple, there could be no animal sacrifices which had been central to their temple worship. Now reading and interpreting Torah and other Old Testament scriptures became the central activity in synagogue worship. The transition to book-centered worship helped the exiles rediscover their story and claim it as their own.

Religious leadership moved from priest to scribe. The scribe emerged as leader because of the need to gather, compile, edit, copy and interpret the scriptures. Priests had much less importance in a world without temple sacrifices. The Old Testament canon emerged largely during and after the exile.

Search for a New Identity

What defines an exile from Judah? The Israelites' new name was "Jews." The word Jew comes from the word Judah. With the worship changes, they became known as the "people of the book." Their emerging identity developed around applications of scripture to life, Sabbath keeping, circumcision, devotion to the Torah, and synagogue attendance. They chose their stories, then their stories shaped them.

Theological Development: From Judgment to Hope

The writer II Isaiah (or Isaiah of the exile) begins chapter 40 with the familiar words, "Comfort, O comfort my people, says your God. Speak tenderly to Jerusalem that she has served her term..." Isaiah speaks further. "Do not fear, for I am with you; I will bring your offspring from the east and from the west I will gather you..." (43:5). "Listen! Your sentinels lift up their voices, together they sing for joy for in plain sight they see the return of the Lord of Zion" (52:8).

In chapter 61 Isaiah writes these words that Jesus repeats in the Nazareth synagogue: "The Spirit of the Lord is upon me because the Lord has anointed me; he has sent me to bring good news to the oppressed, to bind up the brokenhearted, to proclaim liberty to the captives and release to the prisoners..." (Isaiah 61:1). In exile, the prophets start to articulate the hope of a special annointed one, called *Messiah*. This coming Messiah will bring healing and restoration to God's people.

What seems as hopeless as a Euphrates River valley full of dry bones is addressed by Ezekiel's vision (Ezekiel 37). God's word through the prophet's word *dabar* enters into the bones (hopeless exiles) and brings them to life. Yahweh's word brings about the impossible and miraculous, perhaps as miraculous as the first Exodus out of Egypt!

Theological Development: Responsibility

The prophets teach more individual responsibility compared to corporate responsibility. Two aspects of Israelite theology had been that all of history, all generations, are connected and that the people are a corporate body. The people sin and the next generation suffers the judgment. The parents sin and their children suffer for it and may repeat it. The king and leaders sin and everyone suffers. Ezekiel quotes this older theology (Exodus 20:4-6) in proverb form and then challenges it with an emphasis on individual responsibility.

The parents have eaten sour grapes, and the children's teeth are set on edge. As I live, says the Lord God, this proverb shall no more be used by you in Israel. Know that all lives are mine; the life of the parent as well as the life of the child is mine: it is only the person who sins that shall die (Ezekiel 18:2-4).

Ezekiel also emphasizes the individual along with an inward dimension of faith in describing the changed person. "A new heart I will give you and a new spirit I will put within you; and I will remove from your body the heart of stone and give you a heart of flesh" (Ezekiel 36:26).

Theological Development: Redemptive Suffering

The prophets interpreted the woes that befell Judah as redemptive because these troubles revealed Yahweh's steadfast love to many different peoples and because Judah experienced spiritual renewal. Yahweh didn't abandon them. There was horrible suffering during the siege of Jerusalem where people even ate their children but the destruction broke down the two boundaries they had put around themselves and God in the monarchy. The loss of land, king, and nation-state helped them to see their sin and unfaithfulness. The loss and exile offered them new opportunities to be faithful to their chosenness for Yahweh's mission.

However, not all suffering is redemptive. The prophets saw the benefit of the suffering when they looked at all of the exiles, not necessarily individual suffering. While God has the capacity to create renewal from hardship, God doesn't always work that way, and not all hardship is God's plan.

Yahweh's judgment is never simply punishment but intends to bring renewal and repentance so the people may be more faithful. The opposite of love is not hate but abandonment. Yahweh hasn't abandoned his people. II Isaiah describes the redemptive suffering through the "servant Songs" in 42:1-4, 48:1-6, 50:4-9, 52:13-53:12.

Who is the suffering "Servant of Yahweh"? In Isaiah 49:3 the answer is "Israel personified." But in 9:6 the servant's mission is to Israel and does the mission that Israel has failed to accomplish. Not everyone agrees on who the "suffering servant" is. Some think it is a reference to Jesus Christ, or it may refer to a variety of persons and groups.

Theological Development: A New Covenant

Jeremiah and Ezekiel see Yahweh creating a new covenant with the people, a more personal and inward one. "The days are surely coming says the Lord, when I will make a new covenant with the house of Israel and the house of Judah" (Jeremiah 31:31). The word *know* in the following passage means intimate, close knowledge. "I will put my law within them and I will write it on their hearts...No longer shall they teach one another or say to each other 'Know the Lord' for they shall all know me from the least of them to the greatest" (Jeremiah 31:31, 33, 34).

Ezekiel echoes this same theme, sounding like a passage out of the New Testament. "A new heart I will give you, and a new spirit I will put within you; I will remove from your body the heart of stone and give you a heart of flesh. And I will put my spirit within you..." (Ezekiel 36:26-27).

Theological Development: Radical Monotheism

Monotheism is the belief that there is only one god. Other gods do not even exist. While Moses expresses a practical monotheism that stems from Yahweh delivering them from slavery, this belief comes to it fullest expression in passages from II Isaiah of the exile. "I am the first and I am the last, besides me there is no god... is there any god besides me? There is no other rock; I know not one" (II Isaiah 44: 6b, 8b). And again, "...for I am God and there is no other, I am God and there is no one like me..." (II Isaiah 46:9b). Jeremiah also denounces other gods as "vapor or no gods" (2:5, 10:8, 14:22).

Polytheism is the belief in many gods. One finds mention of gods in the Patriarch and Matriarch stories, at Shechem and in the people's syncretism from the conquest through the monarchies. The syncretism of Baal with Yahweh worship is clearly visible during the tribal confederacy. Solomon turns to serious polytheism in his latter days (I Kings 11) as does Manasseh of Judah (II Kings 2). Both kings put altars to other gods in the temple. Was Solomon monotheistic when he accommodated his foreign wives?

Henotheism is the belief that other gods exist, but that "our god" is the greatest. The phrase the "God of gods" expresses this. Joshua's words at the Shechem Covenant imply that other gods do exist but that the people need to choose between them and Yahweh who brought them out of Egypt. "He is a jealous God" is not a monotheistic statement that there are no other gods. Instead it implies that Yahweh will not put up with sharing with other gods or syncretism (Joshua 24). The existence of other gods is also implied in I Kings 9:9.

Radical monotheism helped the exilic prophets realize the universal nature of Yahweh worship. God is a God of all peoples. This vision is expressed in Yahweh being both "creator God and Lord of all the earth" (II Isaiah 40, 41). The people of God are to be a missionary people—"a light to the nations."

Theological Development: Cosmic Dualism

Besides monotheism and its universal and missionary implications, perhaps the most significant theological development in the Jewish community in exile may have been the new belief in cosmic dualism. In this worldview, the earth/world is the battleground between Yahweh and the evil forces referred to as Satan.

Cosmic dualism says that Satan is the source of evil, suffering and death, rather than God's judgment for sin as in the Deuteronomistic view. The source of cosmic dualism was Persian religions, more specifically Zoroastrianism.[1] The Jews in exile incorporated this dualism into their faith. From there this dualism found its way into New Testament Christianity.

Thus, the Bible contains these two worldviews: 1) the view in which Yahweh causes everything including "bad things" as judgment from a Deuteronomistic view, and 2) cosmic dualism that sees Yahweh behind the good and Satan, though less powerful than God, is the cause of evil, suffering, and bad happenings.

Before the exile there is little if any reference to Satan. For example, it is Yahweh who hardens Pharaoh's heart during the exodus from Egypt. And in II Samuel 24:1, Yahweh incites David to sin by numbering the people to set up a standing army. Conversely, in I Chronicles 21, it is Satan who incites David to do this sin. What does the difference in these two versions of the same event tell us? Two things: First, the difference tells us when the materials were written, and second, that the exilic and postexilic biblical editors and writers didn't change the texts they inherited by injecting "Satan" into the earlier II Samuel 24:1 document to make it agree with the later I Chronicles 21:1 passage. They considered the texts they inherited as sacred and so didn't change them. This disagreement between these two scriptures should not undermine our confidence in the scriptures but actually should give us more confidence in how judiciously the biblical texts were handled by the writers and editors. They didn't freely change things to make them agree!

When cosmic dualism is combined with intertestamental apocalypticism and eschatology, a "two-age" view of history emerges. Satan and evil are in

---

1 Stephen L. Harris, *Understanding the Bible,* 3rd ed. (Denmark: Mayfield Publishing Company, 1992), 24-26.

"limited control" now, in this age, even though they have been defeated ultimately by the life and death of Jesus. God will be in complete control in the age to come.

Return and Attempted Renewal

Bible passages: Ezra 9-10, Isaiah 45

Before we pick up the faith story once more, it is valuable to understand the political and military upheavals occurring around the people of God. After a second revolt from Judah, the Babylonians finally struck the Jews in their capital city, destroying Jerusalem in 587 BCE They exiled 99% of the Judean people. Under Nebuchadnezzar, the people of Judah, now called Jews. worked to regain their identity in a foreign land as explained in chapter 20. But another force was at work—the Persian Kingdom, a force that would eventually allow the Jews to return home.

The Persian Kingdom had helped Nebuchadnezzar conquer the western Fertile Crescent, including Judah. Persia remained a significant power to the northeast of Babylonia. The Neo-babylonian empire did not last much longer than its first and greatest emperor, Nebuchadnezzar (605-562 BCE). Murder and intrigue in governmental high places after Nebuchadnezzar's death weakened the empire. The throne changed three times within seven chaotic years. Meanwhile a Persian king to the east defeated the Median king and extended his rule all the way to Asia Minor (Turkey). Nabonidus became emperor of Neo-Babylonia after the seven years of chaos and ruled with his son Belshazzar.

In 539 BCE Cyrus of Persia defeated Nabonidus at the battle of Opis on the Tigris River. Soon after, Babylon capitulated to Cyrus without a battle. The account of Cyrus' victory is recorded on the famous Cyrus Cylinder and in Isaiah 44:24 - 45:13, and Ezra 6:3. The secular account says that the national god Marduk became angry with the emperor Nabonidus for ignoring the temple of Marduk and requiring slave labor. So Marduk ordained Cyrus to march against Babylon where the citizens welcomed him.

Cyrus had radically different policies from the Babylonians about people from conquered territories. He abolished forced labor and returned sacred images to various exiled peoples. Cyrus also allowed the Jewish exiles to go home and provided money for them to rebuild their shrines. In Isaiah 45:1, Cyrus is referred to as the "servant of the Lord" and a "messiah" who helped the Jewish exiles return to Jerusalem. The Persian empire lasted until the Greek leader Alexander the Great conquered the entire Middle East.

Returning Jewish Exiles

The Jewish exiles in Babylon had good living conditions. They lived in their own communities in the Tigris and Euphrates River valley. Many prospered, acculturated, and became involved with the economic, social and some even in governmental life. It was natural for the less acculturated devout Jews to be willing to make the long hard journey back to Jerusalem.

We do know of four groups that returned, totaling about a quarter of those who had been exiled. However the problems in the Nehemiah and Ezra biblical documents makes it difficult to be sure about dates, sequences and details. The four groups are as follows:

- In 538 BCE, when Cyrus was the Persian leader, Sheshbazzar led a group that managed to lay the foundation for the temple. Sheshbazzar was the son of King Jehoiachin of Judah, and a descendent of David.
- In 520 B.C.E, when Darius was the Persian king, Zerubbabel led a group who built the new temple called Second Temple or Zerubbabel's Temple.
- In about 458 BCE when Artaxerxes I was the Persian king, the priest Ezra led the people in a religious reform and re-covenant. Nehemiah assisted in the reform.
- In 445 BCE Nehemiah, the Persian King's cupbearer, led in rebuilding the Jerusalem city walls.

The first group led by Sheshbazzar brought back some temple treasures

Nebuchadnezzar had taken to Babylon. All the first group was able to do was lay the foundation for the new Temple (Ezra 5:14-16). What limited their progress? Much of their energies went to surviving in the still devastated land. Conflicts were also a problem. Judeans who had never been taken into exile felt that the land belonged to them; they had been living there for 40 years. In addition, the exiled Jews felt superior to those who had been left behind. Then there was conflict and actual opposition from the Northern Tribes people who considered themselves faithful to the same Yahweh faith and wanted to help rebuild the temple.

Zerubbabel led the second group in rebuilding the Temple that was called "Zerubbabel's Temple." The prophet Haggai was a strong promoter of rebuilding the temple. In good Deuteronomistic fashion, he told the people that they would prosper after the temple was built (Haggai 2). Zechariah was the second prophet to also promote the temple project. After the temple was built, there was silence about events in Jerusalem.

When the Samaritans heard that the returned exiles were going to build a temple to Yahweh, they offered to help build it, saying, "Let us build with you, for we worship your God as you do..." Zerubbabel and the people rejected them: "You shall have no part with us in building a house to our God" (Ezra 4:1-3). Interestingly enough the biblical writer calls the Samaritan people who offered to help build the temple "adversaries of Judah and Benjamin." Unsurprisingly, the Samaritans then hindered the building projects in Jerusalem after their offer to help was met with scornful ethnocentrism. The old North-South, Israel-Judah hostilities lived on!

The third returning group was led by the influential priest Ezra. They brought considerable money from the Persian king plus more sacred vessels for Temple use. The king commissioned Ezra to appoint magistrates and judges for the peoples "beyond the River." Ezra wasted no time in working at reform when he returned. He discovered that many of the people who were never exiled, including priests, had married non-Jewish women of the land. Ezra made an eloquent prayer recorded in Ezra 9. He then dramatically tore his clothes, pulled out his hair, and went into a state of mourning. He threw himself on the ground in front of the temple, weeping and making confession (Ezra 9-10). A crowd gathered and made a covenant with Ezra that they would divorce all their non-Jewish wives and send them away with their children. Ezra then made them all take an oath that they would do what they had promised, because intermarriage had led to religious syncretism in Israel in the past. But Ezra went a step further with his ethnic purge. In Israel historically when a wife was sent away, the children remained with the father. But in this case the children were also sent away though they were the "seed of their fathers."

The next day Ezra sent out a proclamation that all the people should gather. If they didn't come they would lose their property! This meeting was to begin to apply the oath they had made about their mixed marriages (Ezra 10:7-8). Nehemiah, who was cupbearer to the Persian king Artaxerxes, heard about the sad conditions in Jerusalem. The king made him governor of Jerusalem and sent him with money to repair the city walls. But Nehemiah met opposition from Sanballat, governor of Samaria; Tobiah, governor of Ammon in the Transjordan; and Geshem, an Arab king. In spite of opposition, Nehemiah's leadership and organizational skills enabled him to rebuild the walls.

During Nehemiah's second term as governor, he restored the collection of the tithe so the Levites could serve full time in the temple. He enforced Sabbath-keeping with punishments. Like Ezra, Nehemiah denounced mixed marriages. He physically beat Jews who were married to foreign wives, including the high priest's son. To have a pure and godly community, all foreign influences were rooted out of Jewish life. Ezra and Nehemiah stopped religious syncretism that historically had come through intermarriage with people of the land but in doing so had established an ethnic boundary around God's people—a new way to be unfaithful to their chosenness to be God's missionary people to all the world.

Ethnocentrism: Interpreting the Return and Reform

The story of the returning Jews is both a positive and negative story in the larger Heilsgeschichte story context. Celebrating feasts, telling the salvation history story, confessing unfaithfulness and re-covenanting are all positive. Redefining who is Jewish is a mixed action with a small handful of positive effects but much larger negative ones. The worst consequence was a new boundary that redefined "chosen" to mean God's favorites, this time favorites because of ethnic identity. It's possible that this new boundary was softened when the "the people of the land" joined the returned exiles in a Passover celebration after the temple was completed. The "people of the land" had separated themselves from the pollutions of the nations, a good thing, However, it's not clear whether "the people of the land" were any other than Jews who were left behind in the deportation to Babylon (Ezra 6:21).

160

Ezra and Nehemiah redefined the People of God only as those of pure Jewish heritage, supportive of the Jerusalem Temple, and devoted to the laws, especially Sabbath and circumcision. Jews kept genealogies to prove their heritage. Leaders, priests and Levites especially had to prove their physical Jewish heritage. These definitions eliminated Samaritans as well as others. This definition of a good Jew helped maintain an identity, but it was based on the wrong issues with the wrong attitude.

Instead of asking the non-Jewish wives the missionary question and invitation whether they would become followers of Yahweh, Ezra and Nehemiah asked the ethnic question and expelled them. Rather than being faithful to their chosenness and reaching outward "as a light to all peoples" (Isaiah 49), they defensively focused inward with their exclusion. Yahweh had smashed apart the national and geographic boundaries so they might take the opportunity to be faithful to their chosenness. But now they created a new boundary around God and the people of God! They asked the wrong question; ethnic question, not the faith one. Being devoted to Yahweh, keeping the law, learning the story was something non-Jewish people could do as well as anyone. Ezra and Nehemiah meant well, but they still didn't get it right! How far this departs from Yahweh forming the chosen missionary people out of a mixed ethnic crowd in the Exodus and various peoples joining them in salvation history!

The return from exile was a new second Exodus in which the people of God could be recreated as a priestly missionary people, a light to the Gentiles. This Exodus, like the first, happened so that all people could "know" that Yahweh is the Lord. But the returning Jews rejected even their Yahweh-believing cousins, the Samaritans, and then expelled the Gentiles. The suffering Jews were not the "suffering servant" redeeming the whole world that the prophet II Isaiah envisioned (II Isaiah 42:6, 45:23, 49:6). Ezra is considered the architect of the ethnocentric Judaism of the Pharisees we find at the time of Jesus in the New Testament.

The Story of Jonah

It may seem odd to switch topics from grand political maneuvering and xenophobia to a man trapped inside a fish, but the story of Jonah makes a great deal of sense as a biting allegorical sermon to the ethnocentric Jews. Yahweh is giving the returning Jews a second chance to be a faithful missionary people and a light to the nations.

God calls Jonah to go to Nineveh and preach that they will be destroyed unless they repent. Instead of going there, Jonah heads to the sea. The ship is caught in a storm. The sailors throw all their cargo overboard to save the ship including Jonah. Jonah tells them that he is the cause of the storm and to throw him overboard as well. The sailors want to save Jonah and row hard. Reluctantly they throw him overboard and the storm subsides. Jonah is swallowed by a fish that spits him out on shore after three days.

After God calls Jonah a second time to go to Nineveh he goes and preaches, "Forty days and Nineveh will be destroyed" (Jonah 3:4), hoping that the people will not repent and be destroyed. He goes outside the city to watch the city be destroyed. But the people respond to God right away and God is gracious and doesn't destroy them. Jonah is so angry he wants to die. So God graciously has a plant spring up to shade him. But then a worm comes and destroys the plant. Now Jonah is even more angry at God. Jonah is angry that God would let the plant be destroyed. Then God challenges Jonah about being more concerned about a plant than all the thousands of people in the city. Jonah challenges God, "I knew that you are a gracious God..." (Jonah 4:2). In defense God says if Jonah is so concerned about the plant, should he not be concerned about 120,000 persons in Nineveh?

Jonah's story is not about a fish, who is a minor player. It is about Jonah, who was called—or chosen—to go preach to Gentile enemy Nineveh, capital of the aggressive Assyrian empire. But instead of being faithful to his chosenness, Jonah headed out to the sea where he thought God wasn't present. The sea was thought to be the place of chaos and evil monsters, not a place where God is present. This misconception echoes the view of a geographically bound God, as in Psalm 137, "How can we sing the Lord's song in a foreign land?"

But, surprise! God is present in the sea also. Then comes the first of the ironies in the story. A group of pagan sailors ironically sacrifice everything to save Jonah, when he was willing to let them and a whole city population die. The fish swallows Jonah like Judah was swallowed by Babylonia because of their unfaithfulness. Like the Jews in exile, Jonah experiences some spiritual renewal in the fish. Then the fish spits him out, like some of the Jews were allowed out of Babylonia to return to Jerusalem. This is a second opportunity for Jonah and the Jews to be faithful to their missionary calling.

Freed from his living prison, Jonah reluctantly goes to Nineveh and reveals Yahweh to them, yet he still secretly hopes they won't repent so that

Yahweh will destroy them. The pagan people of Nineveh repent at their first opportunity, in contrast to Jonah, who was only partially faithful even with his second opportunity! Likewise, the Jewish returnees are unwilling to allow Gentiles or Samaritans into God's People.

Afterward, Jonah sits outside Nineveh, hoping to see Yahweh destroy the people. But it doesn't happen! Yahweh extends grace to the repentant city and, apparently, also to the semi-faithful Jonah by giving him a vine for shade. Then a worm destroys the shading vine. Now Jonah gets doubly angry—angry about God's grace to Nineveh and about his own suffering from the loss of shade. Totally self-centered! He complains to God for being a gracious God. Jonah hardly loves "kindness" (mercy) which Micah says God requires (Micah 6:8).

Once again we see the direct similarities between Jonah and Ezra and Nehemiah's ethnocentrism against returnees from exile and their foreign families. All three leaders were unfaithful to their chosenness even after God gave them a merciful second chance.

Reflection on the Allegorical Nature of Jonah

As strange as Jonah's experiences were, it is fair to ask whether his story is a wholly symbolic sermon or a literal adventure of a man who survives being swallowed and later spat out by a giant fish.

The issue with the Jonah story is not whether it is divinely inspired truth but the nature of the literary genre. Is the divinely inspired truth communicated through a historic narrative genre or an allegorical genre in the case of the book of Jonah? Two equally dedicated Christians who hold the Bible equally inspired can disagree about the genre of the Jonah story. The issue is not about the inspired truth of the story but only about the genre or literary vehicle that conveys the truth.

Theologically the return from Exile was a mixed bag. The temple and wall around Jerusalem was rebuilt, Ezra led in a re-covenanting ceremony, and Passover was celebrated. In the midst of these advances, Ezra forced the Jewish men to divorce their non-Jewish wives. He failed to consider that the non-Jewish wives may have wanted to serve Yahweh and become part of God's people. Was Ezra remembering all the past *Heilsgeschichte?* How will Ezra's new ethnocentric boundary influence the continuing *Heilsgeschichte?*

Psalms and Psalm Genre

Bible passages: Psalms 1, 13, 22-23, 44, 58, 88, 145, 149-150

Have you ever written a poem expressing deep anguish? Or have you ever jotted down lyrics to a song in your head? Have you ever made a gratitude list, or spent time writing down all the ways a person—or God—has helped you in the past? If you can say yes to any of these questions, then you have written a psalm.

Psalms, like poetry, are written words and hymn lyrics that work to express human feelings. And unlike most of the rest of the Bible, they are words from humans to God. The Book of Psalms was Israel's hymnal; its contents cover a range of group and individual life experiences. The psalms are a window into the feelings and life experiences of the Old People of God. Their pain, anger, grief, gratitude, joy, and praise—all of these emotions burst from the pages, telling the story not in narrative form, but by their honest prayers and pleadings.

The Book of Psalms

Psalms are found in a variety of biblical books. But the actual Book of Psalms is unique in that it is a collection of poems that scholars believe span almost a thousand years of Israelite history. The Book of Psalms in the present Bible is actually a collection of five books. Book 1 is Psalm 1-41, Book 2 is Psalm 42-72, Book 3 is Psalm 73-89, Book 4 is Psalm 90-106 and Book 5 is Psalm 107-150. Each "book" ends with a benediction. David wrote nearly half the psalms, or had them written in his name, while other psalms were written by Moses, the sons of Asaph, and the sons of Korah, to name a few. The Book of Psalms as it appears today was probably put together after the exile and rebuilding of the Temple.

Characteristics of the Psalms

Like all genres, it's an important skill to be able to identify the Psalm genre so that one can then use the right principles in interpreting it. Probably the best clue that you are reading a Psalm is the way it sounds like poetry, for in essence it is poetry. The Psalms are poetry in that the wording is artistically constructed, it uses metaphorical imagery and its purpose is to invoke and grapple with deep emotions.

The Psalms use parallelism. The ancient Hebrew writers didn't make their poetic phrases rhyme at the end, as we see many times in the English language. However, the lines are related to each other in a stylized way. Their artistic design comes from parallelism, a literary device using distichs, or two lines that relate to each other in a particular way. In parallelism, the lines of the poem/psalm are connected in pairs. Line B relates to Line A in one of three ways:

1. Synonymous parallelism: The second line or Line B repeats Line A in a creative way without really giving any new information. The second line echoes the first line. Here are some examples:

   Give ear to my words, O Lord; (A)
   give heed to my sighing. (B) Psalm 5:1

   Set a guard over my mouth, O Lord; (A)
   keep watch over the door of my lips. (B) Psalm 141:3

2. Synthetic or stair-step parallelism: Here Line B completes Line A or adds more information. Psalm 27:3 provides two synthetic parallelisms where Line B finishes the thought of Line A.

   Though an army encamp against me, (A)
   my heart shall not fear; (B)
   though war rise up against me, (A)
   yet I will be confident. (B)

Psalm 103:2 illustrates a synthetic parallelism where Line B adds more information to Line A.

Bless the Lord, O my soul, (A)
and do not forget all his benefits— (B)

3. Antithetic parallelism: In this form of parallelism, the second line contrasts the first line. Psalm 1:6 is an excellent illustration.

for the Lord watches over the way of the righteous, (A)
but the way of the wicked will perish. (B)

With its signature feature of parallelism, Psalm genre is found not only in the Book of Psalms but in other books as well. Isaiah 1:3 has two synonymous parallelisms: "The ox knows its owner, and the donkey its master's crib; but Israel does not know, my people do not understand." Proverbs 10:1 has antithetic parallelism: "A wise child makes a glad father, but a foolish child is a mother's grief."

Identifying parallelism is important because occasionally the psalm breaks its rules and produces a triplet. The triplet produces a new rhythm in the poem and in that way highlights its meaning. When the psalmist wanted to really emphasize something, he or she wrote a triplet. Knowing this can help the modern reader identify what the original writer thought was important. Psalm 111 features several triplets. It's also famous because, together with Psalm 112, it is an acrostic, or a poem that starts with each letter of the Hebrew alphabet in order. The psalm is composed of typical two-line parallelism for the most part, but the last two verses, the climax of the poem, contain two triplets.

He sent redemption to his people; (A)
he has commanded his covenant for ever. (B)
Holy and awesome is his name. (C)
The fear of the Lord is the beginning of wisdom; (A)
all those who practise it have a good understanding. (B)
His praise endures for ever. (C)

The different rhythm, coupled with the profound statements that sum up the entire psalm, work together to make a clear statement about what is important to the psalmist in this psalm.

The psalms are also like poetry in that they use metaphorical imagery. One of the best ways to illustrate deep emotions is to provide word pictures. The psalms are beautiful testaments to the power of metaphors. Psalm 23 is a great example.

The Lord is my shepherd, I shall not want.
He makes me lie down in green pastures;
he leads me beside still waters;
he restores my soul.
He leads me in right paths
for his name's sake.

Even though I walk through the darkest valley,
I fear no evil;
for you are with me;
your rod and your staff—
they comfort me.

You prepare a table before me
in the presence of my enemies;
you anoint my head with oil;
my cup overflows.
Surely goodness and mercy shall follow me
all the days of my life,
and I shall dwell in the house of the Lord
my whole life long.

Yahweh is not literally a shepherd, nor are we sheep who have been specifically led to a stream of quiet waters. But these word pictures help us gain a clearer understanding of the love and faithfulness David felt as he looked back on how God had rescued him; we can vicariously experience that same deep sigh of relief that David must have felt. Like a trusted shepherd, the LORD led David through multiple troubles, and God's providence and guidance were like being thrown a great banquet in front of one's enemies.

Finally, the Psalms are like poetry in their common purpose to direct emotions to God. The Psalms are expressions of deep feelings. While there are a few exceptions where psalms seek to teach or advise, the majority of psalms almost burst from the page with imagery that arouses our anger, joy or pain. And while these poems are valuable strictly on an artistic level, they gain even more value when we realize that these rants, jubilations and songs are honest prayers made to God, and that God honored them, even the poems that pointed accusing fingers at God. Psalm 13 places the problem right at Yahweh's feet.

> *How long, O Lord? Will you forget me for ever? How long will you hide your face from me? How long must I bear pain in my soul, and have sorrow in my heart all day long? How long shall my enemy be exalted over me?* (Psalm 13:1-2)

By the end of the poem, Yahweh doesn't rebuke the psalmist but gives him relief from his troubles.

Types of Psalms

There are different types of psalms and many times this categorization is tied to the emotions the psalms express. Lament psalms show pain or anger. Laments, which comprise over 50% of the psalms, express the emotions that come from difficult situations. They can be either corporate poems expressing the feelings of an entire people or written by an individual.

Most of the laments have six identifiable elements. The beauty of these poems is that, even in the midst of great pain, there is a certain order. Psalm 22 can illustrate each of the six parts:

1. **Address:** The psalm calls upon God, asking the LORD to be present and hear the psalmist's cry. "My God, my God…" (Psalm 22:1a).
2. **Complaint:** The writer pours out his or her problems and explains why God must take care of these problems. "Why have you forsaken me? Why are you so far from helping me, from the words of my groaning? O my God, I cry by day, but you do not answer; and by night, but find no rest" (Psalm 22:1b-2). "I am poured out like water, and all my bones are out of joint" (Psalm 22:14).
3. **Trust:** The psalmist expresses an overall trust in God. "Yet it was you who took me from the womb; you kept me safe on my mother's breast" (Psalm 22:9).

4. **Petition for deliverance:** Using imperative verbs, the psalmist lists out exactly what God should do to alleviate the problems. "But you, O Lord, do not be far away! O my help, come quickly to my aid! Deliver my soul from the sword, my life from the power of the dog! Save me from the mouth of the lion!" (Psalm 22:19-21).

5. **Assurance of being heard:** After the struggle and pleading, the writer expresses the assurance that God will deliver. This part often parallels the expression of trust. "For he did not despise or abhor the affliction of the afflicted; he did not hide his face from me, but heard when I cried to him" (Psalm 22:24).

6. **Vows of praise:** The psalmist offers praise and thanksgiving for what God has done in the past and what God will do in the future. "From you comes my praise in the great congregation; my vows I will pay before those who fear him" (Psalm 22:25).

Hymns of praise give exuberant exclamations of joy or detail how great God is. Many times they contain a summons to praise and then give reasons why one should praise God, listing God's attributes, and then they extend a renewed call to continued praise. Hymns of praise can be distinguished from thanksgiving psalms in that they are more general; they don't recall or retell a specific act of God's deliverance. Psalm 149 is a good example.

Praise the Lord!
Sing to the Lord a new song,
his praise in the assembly of the faithful.
Let Israel be glad in its Maker;
let the children of Zion rejoice in their King.
Let them praise his name with dancing,
making melody to him with tambourine and lyre.
For the Lord takes pleasure in his people;
he adorns the humble with victory.
Let the faithful exult in glory;
let them sing for joy on their couches.
Let the high praises of God be in their throats
and two-edged swords in their hands,
to execute vengeance on the nations
and punishment on the peoples,
to bind their kings with fetters

and their nobles with chains of iron,
to execute on them the judgment decreed.
This is glory for all his faithful ones.
Praise the Lord!

Thanksgiving psalms recall specific times in the past when Yahweh rescued the people. Filled with gratitude, the individual or a whole people group name the ways God has helped them in the past. Psalm 40:1-3 illustrates the point.

I waited patiently for the Lord;
he inclined to me and heard my cry.
He drew me up from the desolate pit,
out of the miry bog,
and set my feet upon a rock,
making my steps secure.
He put a new song in my mouth,
a song of praise to our God.
Many will see and fear,
and put their trust in the Lord.

Salvation History psalms are similar to thanksgiving psalms in that they too show gratitude to God for their deliverance in the past. Yet Salvation History psalms are even more specific, functioning as creative oral history, naming names. Psalm 135:8-12 is a good example.

He it was who struck down the firstborn of Egypt,
both human beings and animals;
he sent signs and wonders
into your midst, O Egypt,
against Pharaoh and all his servants.
He struck down many nations
and killed mighty kings—
Sihon, king of the Amorites,
and Og, king of Bashan,
and all the kingdoms of Canaan—
and gave their land as a heritage,
a heritage to his people Israel.

Other psalms seem to have been written for a certain worship ritual. These psalms of celebration and affirmation include covenant renewal psalms or psalms that deal with kingship rituals like enthronement or the wedding of a king. The royal psalms can also be laments (Psalm 144) or a thanksgiving hymn (Psalm 18), but by their content concerning the king, they are also called royal psalms. The covenant renewal psalms are Psalm 50 and 81.

Songs of trust focus on the trustworthiness and faithfulness of God. Psalm 27:1 expresses well the overall tone of these psalms. "The Lord is my light and my salvation; whom shall I fear? The Lord is the stronghold of my life; of whom shall I be afraid?"

Finally, Wisdom Psalms provide pithy proverbs meant to educate and encourage faithful obedience to God. They show the least emotion and, in that sense, have more in common with wisdom genre. Psalm 37 has many wisdom genre characteristics. "Depart from evil, and do good; so you shall abide for ever. For the Lord loves justice; he will not forsake his faithful ones."

Interpretation rules for Psalm genre

Both the psalms in the Book of Psalms and psalms found elsewhere in the Bible have their own setting in life that stands apart from the rest of the book. They could very well have been sung orally for years before ever being written down or the writer could have taken an already written psalm and inserted it into his text. And given that most psalms give very little historical detail so we could date them, it's hard to figure out their setting in life. But at the very least, we must honor the psalms by treating them as their own literary units.

Read the entire psalm and strive to find meaning that honors the whole psalm. We must not "cut and paste," or take a verse out of its literary context. For example, individual verses in Psalm 44 all have merit and speak truth. Some of these verses speak of how God has protected them from enemies. These "good news" verses have much more impact when they are read as part of the whole psalm, where other verses give the "bad news" that even though the people have been faithful, they are still being conquered by their enemies. Taken as a whole, Psalm 44 is dense theology, as we hear the ancient Israelites grappling with deep faith questions, daring to honestly think the unthinkable, that God is somehow not able to rescue them and yet demonstrating, by this very prayer, that they still believe in God.

Don't use the Psalms to build abstract doctrines. As with all genres, it's important to remember the purpose of psalms. They are not meant to teach specific beliefs or prescribe how one is to live her life. Their purpose is to provide a vehicle for people to honestly tell God how they feel. Moments of fierce anger or great joy are usually not moments of careful thinking. This is not to say that those types of psalms are less valid, but they must be taken the way they were intended—not as carefully thought-out doctrines, but exclamations of deep feelings in the heat of the moment. King David in Psalm 51 said, "Indeed, I was born guilty, a sinner when my mother conceived me." The historical notes at the beginning of this psalm tell us that David wrote it right after the prophet Nathan confronted him about his adultery with Bathsheba. David got caught and he was feeling guilty. So the claim about being born guilty and a sinner when his mother conceived him is probably an exaggerated way of saying he is a terrible sinner and not an abstract doctrinal statement on how sexual intercourse transmits sin from one person to the next, as some Christian traditions have made this verse out to mean. David is pouring out his heart that is heavy with shame; he's not trying to explain the origin of the sinful nature we all have.

See the metaphors and poetic imagery for what they are: expressive but non-literal ways to communicate truth. Psalm 22:16 says, "For dogs are all around me; a company of evildoers encircles me." It's clear from the whole psalm that David is not talking about real dogs, but evil persons. But the use of the word dogs is beautiful, because it helps us feel David's fear with an image of being surrounded by a pack of feral dogs. Similarly, Psalm 18:2 says, "The Lord is my rock, my fortress, and my deliverer, my God, my rock in whom I take refuge." Again, God is not really a rock. But the metaphor compares God to a rock in that God can act like a protective stone fortress. Whenever we read the Psalms, we must remember that many times the eternal truth of these poems comes to us through metaphor and poetic imagery.

The Psalms Today

We know that the Psalms were precious to the original audience who used many of them as their hymns, and who found solace through existentially experiencing their own pain and joy through the words of another. But they also can be precious to us today.

Nutritionists like to say, "You are what you eat." Theologians and church leaders like to say, "You are what you worship." The psalms can

172

nurture and guide our own worship. The psalms can give us words when we are speechless. They can encourage us to name specific times when God rescued us. They remind us that the chaos of our lives can be put into an order, if only the order of a structured poem. They provide us with hope, calling us to believe again that "Yahweh reigns" (Psalm 93).

The psalms also encourage us to be honest with God. If there were ever doubt that God couldn't handle rough words and accusations, three or four minutes in the Book of Psalms would take care of that. "You have caused my companions to shun me; you have made me a thing of horror to them...O Lord, why do you cast me off? Why do you hide your face from me?" (Psalm 88:8,14). The psalmists over and over again said the almost unspeakable to God—and lived. Did God answer them right away? Probably not. But given enough time, clarity, peace and healing did come, even when the psalmist's specific prayer was not answered in the way he requested it to be answered.

In this honesty, we also relinquish our need for vengeance. Some of the most troubling psalms are the psalms of vengeance, where the babies of enemies get their heads smashed (Psalm 137:9) or the blood of the enemies runs ankle deep (Psalm 58:10). These vicious words don't sound like shalom justice and because of this, we may hold these psalms at arm's length—for good reason. However, all the psalms of vengeance, in the midst of their spewing anger, also put the duty of vengeance squarely on God. Taken as a whole, the psalm of vengeance is good in that it gives an outlet for honest anger. And it's also good in that the psalmist knows the revenge is something only God can mete out.

Finally, the psalms remind us of the importance of meditation and reflection. As we read the meditations of others, from centuries ago, we are silently invited to look inside our own souls. Our enemies may be depression or anxiety instead of a threatening army, but they feel just as scary. We gain the courage to name our own pain and in doing so, find the same healing the psalmists did. The psalms help us stop and take stock of our own emotions; they give us an outlet for our joy that's bigger than words. As we read the psalms, we are forced to slow down and reflect on what's going on inside us. In doing so, the psalms give us a great gift.

Wisdom Genre

Bible passages: Job 38, 42; Proverbs 1-3, 8, 26, 31

"Sticks and stones may break my bones but names will never hurt me." This typical piece of advice parents give to their children might be confusing to a first grader, who already knows that words can sting, but can't articulate why. As the child gets older—junior high, let's say—the catchy sentence makes sense to her, somewhat. Sure, what people say doesn't hurt in a physical way like getting hit with a rock, but it can still be very emotionally damaging. For one thing, reputation among your peers is more important during adolescence than having a black eye. By the time the child reaches her teen years, and the playground threat of being whacked with a stick has lessened, she may disagree completely with her parents about this conventional line of wisdom. But with more maturity yet, she can step back and see another layer of truth: we can—with effort, guidance, and practice—choose whether or not to be hurt by the words of others in a way that we can't choose to be hurt when people physically attack us.

Throughout our lives we encounter moral instruction, advice, warnings, and short recipes for happiness and success. This means we have all experienced wisdom similar to the wisdom genre, at least in its oral form. And like the pithy proverbs our parents share with us, wisdom in the Bible needs careful analysis. There is beautiful, inspired truth in biblical wisdom, but it's nuanced truth that sometimes needs unpacking and always needs an informed view.

Wisdom genre is found predominantly in the books of Proverbs, Job, and Ecclesiastes, although there are wisdom psalms and wisdom elements in several other books. Biblical wisdom is similar to the wisdom sayings of other ancient Middle Eastern cultures and yet there is a distinct emphasis on the need to rely on Yahweh. Wisdom genre is more than just good old-fashioned common sense. "The fear of the Lord is the beginning of wisdom" (Proverbs 1:8).

But what does the fear of the Lord mean? Are we literally supposed to be afraid of God? For biblical wisdom, God is at the center. God is the Creator of the natural world, and our keen and wise observation of this world gives us insight into the character of God. Yahweh is also the source of wisdom. We cannot make ourselves wise, nor can we ever fully understand the mystery or wisdom of God. So the way to "fear" Yahweh is to give God our deepest respect, seek a wisdom that only comes from God, and practice humility, knowing that our wisdom will always fall short.

The Deuteronomistic View of History

Before moving into a full exploration of the Wisdom Genre, we should probably remind ourselves about the Deuteronomistic view of people's relationship with God. One way of understanding God states that God blesses those who are righteous and curses those who are unrighteous. This theology is predominant in biblical wisdom, but it's also challenged. The sages didn't consider their proverbs to be moral absolutes.[1] It was part of the wisdom tradition to critique the tradition.

The following verses are sometimes misinterpreted to mean that if you trust God and acknowledge God in all of your life, you will never have any difficulties.

Trust in the Lord with all your heart,
and do not rely on your own insight.
In all your ways acknowledge him,
and he will make straight your paths (Proverbs 3:5-6).

Here is another example of this view:

Honour the Lord with your substance

---

1   Leo G. Perdue, *Interpretation: A Bible Commentary for Teaching and Preaching: Proverbs.* (Louisville, KY: John Knox Press, 2000), 6.

and with the first fruits of all your produce;
then your barns will be filled with plenty,
and your vats will be bursting with wine (Proverbs 9-10).

There is also an opposing view expressed in the same chapter of Proverbs. The verses imply that good people sometimes face troubles, here interpreted as God's discipline or reproof.

My child, do not despise the Lord's discipline
 or be weary of his reproof,
for the Lord reproves the one he loves,
 as a father the son in whom he delights (Proverbs 3:11-12).

In another verse, a theological challenge comes in a different way: this verse implies that it's possible to be both poor and righteous.

What is desirable in a person is loyalty,
 and it is better to be poor than a liar (Proverbs 19:22).

Characteristics of Biblical Wisdom

Practicality—At its core, biblical wisdom is practical. Being wise means not only right understanding but also right living. Wisdom literature is full of short sayings that emphasize making right choices. Proverbs provides many examples: "A gossip reveals secrets; therefore do not associate with a babbler" (Proverbs 20:19). "The lazy person does not plough in season; harvest comes, and there is nothing to be found" (Proverbs 20:4).

The Hebrew word for wisdom is *chokmah*. In its original context, it's understood not only as the antithesis of being foolish, but also to be skilled in one's labor. Bezalel, a man who was so skilled at woodworking and carpentry that he was the supervisor for the building of the tabernacle, was said to have *chokmah* (Exodus 35:30-36:7). Most of the time, chokmah or wisdom doesn't mean something quite that practical, but it always leans to the simple moral instructions that help us in our everyday life.

Many times this genre teaches through contrasts. Wise persons are set against fools, and the righteous are compared to the wicked. The distinctions between the two groups are clear and whether the literary form is a short parable or a longer instruction, the message is the same: be wise and righteous. Proverbs 12:15 says, "Fools think their own way is right, but the wise listen to advice." In Proverbs 15:6, the righteous and wicked are contrasted, "In the house of the righteous there is much treasure, but trouble befalls the income of the wicked."

Biblical wisdom, however, does not categorically say that everyone who is righteous will be blessed. Much of the wisdom canon does support the deuteronomistic view where, simply put, God will bless you if you are faithful and curse you if you are unfaithful. But there are challenges to this view, such as the entire book of Job. Job is a righteous man who suffers tremendously. Three friends come to visit him and they each try to tell Job that he's suffering because of his sin. They exemplify the deuteronomistic view. Surely God is punishing Job for some awful transgression. But the reader knows what neither Job nor his friends know: Satan has asked God for the permission to torture Job with these various sufferings.

When reading the book in its entirety, we can see that a theology that says God blesses good people and curses bad people is too simplistic. What happens in life is not always what God desires or what seems fair. When God finally speaks to Job, we realize it's also too simplistic to demand that God answer our "Why me?" questions. God tells Job that humans can't understand everything. Like Job, we can't "know when mountain goats give birth" (39:1) nor were we there when God laid the foundation of the earth (38:4). There are limits to our wisdom and understanding. God tells Job that the ways of the Lord are far above human understanding and that God has a right to do what seems unfair to us. So biblical wisdom encourages its readers to be righteous and wise, but holds out no guarantee that just because we are faithful, we will be blessed in this life.

Social Setting—The unique social setting of biblical wisdom is a second characteristic. Often a sage—a wise person who has been given the task of instructing others—is imparting his or her wisdom. This can happen at home, within the family setting, at a "school," or in the royal courts. Eventually the oral sayings of the sage, perhaps preserved only in memory for hundreds of years as part of an oral tradition, are written down and collected into books.

Literary Forms—Wisdom genre has unique literary features that many times enhance the meaning of the content. While there are many literary forms, most of them have the following characteristics: they are precise, short, and written to be easy to remember. If wisdom is concerned with order and beauty (and it is) then the written form of wisdom supports these themes by writing in an orderly and artistic fashion. The common literary features in biblical wisdom are parables, poems, allegories, riddles, alliteration, acrostics, rhetorical questions and beatitudes. In general they fall under the category of sayings or brief, particular expressions of truth, which is called a *mashal* in Hebrew. A collection of sayings is called a *mashaliim.*[2]

All of these literary styles of writing show order and beauty. Acrostics, for example, are poems that use the Hebrew alphabet to organize the content. The first line of the acrostic begins with the first letter of the alphabet and then each new line starts with the next letter. The order of the alphabet is always the same, which subtly emphasizes the importance of order, like the order of creation ordained by God. There's artistry in making the alphabet fit the content. And finally acrostics, as well as the other short pithy sayings such as proverbs and beatitudes, are easy to memorize. Either by their poetic parallelism or by the obvious order of the words, these wise sayings roll off the tongue and are easy to remember.

Use of Imagery—The authors of wisdom genre use concrete words, many times from nature or everyday life, that conjure up images in the reader's mind. Jeremiah 17:11 says, "Like the partridge hatching what it did not lay, so are all who amass wealth unjustly; in mid-life it will leave them, and at their end they will prove to be fools." The prophet uses wisdom genre to paint a word picture for us. We can envision a partridge stealing another bird's nest and how that image from nature captures the greed of those who accumulate wealth through unjust ways.

Using examples from nature can be both a blessing and a potential stumbling block. The imagery of this literature makes it easy to remember. But the metaphorical nature of the saying also means it's easy prey to be misinterpreted. One can't take most of the wisdom sayings literally or as completely true at all times. They are true in a deeper sense in that they point to a principle of how a life lived in faithful obedience to God tends to work.

Examples of literary forms in wisdom literature

- Proverb: "A good name is to be chosen rather than great riches, and favour is better than silver or gold" (Proverbs 22:1).

---

2 Ibid., 27.

- "Better than" proverb (Psalms 37:16): Better is a little that the righteous person has than the abundance of many wicked.

- Beatitude: A beatitude is a short saying that begins with the word "happy." Happy are those who find wisdom, and those who get understanding, Proverbs 3:13

- Alliteration: Alliteration is a literary technique where a particular sound is used frequently, as an intentional way of making the text more memorable and more "musical." Alliteration gets lost whenever we translate from one language to the another one. Ecclesiastes 3;1-8 is a good example.

- Allegory: In an allegory, one thing stands in for another thing. In the following allegory, folly is personified as a prostitute.

> *The foolish woman is loud;*
> *she is ignorant and knows nothing.*
> *She sits at the door of her house,*
> *on a seat at the high places of the town,*
> *calling to those who pass by,*
> *who are going straight on their way,*
> *'You who are simple, turn in here!'*
> *And to those without sense she says,*
> *'Stolen water is sweet,*
> *and bread eaten in secret is pleasant.'*
> *But they do not know that the dead are there,*
> *that her guests are in the depths of Sheol* (Proverbs 9:13-18).

- Rhetorical question: "If you have raced with foot-runners and they have wearied you, how will you compete with horses? And if in a safe land you fall down, how will you fare in the thickets of the Jordan?" (Jeremiah 12:5).

Overall wisdom literature seeks not only to give the original audience simple mandates to follow for success—although that is part of its purpose—but also to help the reader accept a new worldview. In this worldview God is sovereign, transcendent, the source of wisdom. Yet such a God is not necessarily that personal. Having created the world with a divine order, now God and humans need only to let that order play itself out. If a person uses discipline, honors God and observes the natural world, she or he has a key to long life, happiness and is able to avoid conflict and failure. In this understanding of reality, humans can control their destiny and live in harmony with all if they honor this divine order and obey God.

Interpretation Principles

First, we must **remember that wisdom sayings are not contractual promises between us and God.** Wisdom literature gives general guidelines, not automatic guarantees. For example, we all know people who live in substandard housing. It's also clear that some of those people are widows. Yet Proverbs 15:25 tells us this: "The Lord tears down the house of the proud, but maintains the widow's boundaries." Does the reality of homeless widows mean this verse isn't true or that God can't keep promises? We also know of proud and greedy people who live in splendid mansions that have obviously not been torn down.

The ancient sages would tell us that if we draw these conclusions, we're missing the point. This verse points to the reality that God favors the poor and that eventually, God will right all the wrongs of this world. The particularity of the word widow represents all marginalized people. And while many marginalized people may die homeless and many stingy people may die in a mansion, in the end, there will be justice. It is to this larger truth that biblical wisdom points.

Similarly, we can't take proverbs and other sayings in a complete literal way. We can't do this either because the proverb is metaphorical or it refers to a general understanding of life that doesn't always work in a literalistic way. For example, Proverbs 20:17 says, "Bread gained by deceit is sweet, but afterward the mouth will be full of gravel." Even though we will not have our ill-gotten food turn into gravel as we chew, the point still applies. The short-term gratification we may receive from deceitful dealings will eventually catch up with us and bring us harm rather than good.

We must read the whole literary unit. Many people make the mistake of taking one verse out of a wisdom chapter and focusing just on it. But the biblical authors meant for the wise sayings to function as a whole, even if it looks like the individual verses have little in common. In Proverbs 26:4-5, it appears as if the writer is contradicting himself. "Do not answer fools according to their folly, or you will be a fool yourself. Answer fools according to their folly, or they will be wise in their own eyes." So should we answer fools or not? First, we must be careful to see the word "fool" in its cultural context. These verses are not referring to people who may have mental disabilities, but rather people who intentionally choose to reject God's teachings. Second, the two verses put side by side help illustrate a complex truth. When one is dealing with a fool, it's at times important to reprove them and at other times it's better to be silent. We don't have to throw one verse out and call the other verse true.

Using the whole book is an important hermeneutical principle in all the wisdom books, but is particularly needed in the book of Job. Without the context of the whole story, one might take the words of Job's three friends as the intended message of the book—what God wants us to believe—when the truth is that they provide the foil for the real message, that human suffering cannot be so simply understood as the result of human disobedience.

Remember that wisdom genre is pithy on purpose. Wisdom sayings are meant to be easily remembered, so they are colorful and many times written as metaphors. If these short proverbs weren't pithy, they wouldn't have been remembered or have been successful as teaching tools. But in their brevity and metaphorical winsome, they can't be taken as theoretically accurate. Proverbs 15:19 is a great example: "The way of the lazy is overgrown with thorns, but the path of the upright is a level highway." The verse is picturesque, colorful, easy to remember, but it's not a verse to be read with wooden literalism. This is not about the plant life that surrounds lazy people and it's not about righteous people being able to avoid all hills and valleys. It is an artistic statement that packs a literary punch and illustrates a general but deep truth about how laziness makes your life more difficult.

We must always put the truth of biblical wisdom into the context of the whole biblical narrative. Just as one short proverb can't express truth in its entirety, neither can biblical wisdom express all that can be said about God. The theology of "you reap what you sow" sits in creative tension to Jesus' words where he calls the persecuted the blessed ones (Matthew 5:10). And we shouldn't use any of these wise sayings as a way to support an unjust status quo. We can't look at people in poverty and quote them some proverb on how poor people are lazy. It's simply not true that poor people are categorically lazy, and laziness in itself is usually not the real problem in a society dealing with poverty. Furthermore, many other parts of the

Bible, including the gospel stories of Jesus, exhort us to change the current corrupt system that oppresses people instead of blaming individuals. But if we aren't careful, we can celebrate the order and simplistic theology found in wisdom literature because we benefit from the current oppressive system and we can conveniently keep marginalized people down by blaming their marginalization on their sin.

Finally, **we must cross the Hermeneutical Bridge.** While this interpretation principle is true for all genres, proverbs can look so simple that we think they have no unique cultural background. But many of the everyday images expressed in these sayings have different meanings in today's society. We don't have kings (Proverbs 21:1) or use garments for pledges (Proverbs 20:16) or pass on ancestral inheritance (Proverbs 22:28), but we can still glean eternal truth from these sayings if we "cross the bridge" and research the historical-cultural background of these verses and what they meant to the original audience.

The Fear of the Lord is the beginning of wisdom. There is much to gain in a fervent, honest study of biblical wisdom. We wrestle with the complexity of life when good people suffer. We accept the challenge to work hard and live with integrity, knowing there will be a reward, if not in this life, in the next. We humbly seek to learn more about God and receive from God the gift of wisdom.

Intertestamental Times

Bible passages: Isaiah 43, 55; Jeremiah 31:31-34; Daniel 1-11; I and II Books of Maccabees

The 400-Year Gap

It takes only a single page flip in most Bibles to move from the Old Testament to the New Testament. But there is a chronological gap of about 400 years between Malachi, the last book of the Old Testament, and Matthew, the first book of the New Testament. This Intertestamental Period is sometimes called "400 years of silence" because there is no new prophetic message after Malachi—at least none that survived.[1] The flow of history, of course, did not stop; we just have to use other sources to track the story of the people of God.

In addition to secular histories, Flavius Josephus, a Jewish historian writing for the Romans, is our best source. Born in Jerusalem in 37 CE, Josephus wrote the seven-volume *A History of the Jewish Wars* in which he participated, and the 20-volume *Jewish Antiquities,* a history of the Jews from creation to the Roman era. As a historian, he has been faulted for his shallow analyses, imprecise chronology, overstated facts, and the embellishment of his own significance.[2] Nevertheless, we are dependent on his history to help fill in the gap between the testaments.

---

1   John MacArthur, *The MacArthur Study Bible, New International Version* (Nashville: Thomas Nelson, 2013), xiv.

2   Gary William Poole, "Flavius Josephus," *Encyclopedia Britannica,* Accessed June 1, 2016, www.britannica.com.

The Old Testament ends with the story of the return from exile in 538 BCE and the rebuilding of the temple and the walls of Jerusalem under Cyrus the Great. Cyrus, the founder of Persia (present-day Iran), is known in world history for issuing the first known Charter of Human Rights. For his kindness to the Jews, the prophets call him Yahweh's "anointed one" or "messiah"—high praise for a Gentile king.[3]

Alexander the Great and Hellenism

The Persian Empire collapsed in 333 BCE, when Alexander the Great defeated the Persian army at the Battle of Isis in northern Syria. As Alexander's armies swept through most of the known world, they saturated conquered territories with Greek language, culture, and religion, known as Hellenism. His education as a student of the Greek philosopher Aristotle made Alexander a champion of all things Greek.

Alexander died in Babylon at age 32, having pushed his empire "to the ends of the earth."[4] Alexander's generals divided the empire among themselves and then competed for more territory. From Egypt, General Ptolemy I and his dynasty ruled Canaan, now called Palestine. A hundred years later in 198 BCE, the Syrian Seleucid dynasty defeated the Ptolemies and gained control of Judah, now called Judea. All the dynasties promoted Hellenism, but the Seleucids were brutal in forcing the Jews to embrace the Greek worldview at the expense of Judaism. Syncretism was once again a grave danger.

The Diaspora and the *Septuagint*

The majority of Jews (75%) were disbursed in lands beyond Palestine (called the Diaspora), while the remaining 25% lived in Palestine.[5] Those in the Diaspora tended to accommodate Hellenism, while those in the

---

3   Isaiah 45:1. Cyrus is named twenty times in II Chronicles, Ezra, Isaiah, and Daniel.

4   "The First Book of Maccabees," *The Apocrypha and Pseudepigrapha of the Old Testament, Vol I* (Oxford: Clarendon Press, 1963), 67.

5   First-century population estimates vary, but there is a consensus that Jews in the Diaspora greatly outnumbered Jews in Palestine. "By the 1st century CE perhaps 10 percent of the Roman Empire, or about 7 million people, were Jews, with about 2.5 million in Palestine." Naomi Pasachoff and Robert Littman, *A Concise History of the Jewish People* (Lanham, MD.: Rowman and Littlefield, 1995), 67. For a more conservative estimate, "In the first century CE, of 4.5 million Jews worldwide, fewer than 15 percent lived in Palestine." Eugene Boring, *An Introduction to the New Testament: History, Literature, Theology* (Louisville, KY: Westminster John Knox, 2012), 163.

homeland were more inclined to resist acculturation. The result was competing ideologies, worldviews, and political visions.

A consequence of the proliferation of Greek language was the need among Hellenistic Jews for a Greek translation of the Hebrew Bible. The legendary tale is that between 300 and 200 BCE, seventy Jewish scholars gathered in Alexandria, Egypt and worked independently for seventy days. When comparing their finished work, they discovered the miracle that every copy was identical.[6] However it happened, the *Septuagint* (Latin for seventy and abbreviated as LXX), gave all Greek speaking people access to the Hebrew Scriptures.

The apocalyptic writings in the *Septuagint* comforted and encouraged the persecuted Jews suffering under enforced Hellenism. The writer of Daniel, surely one of the *Hasidim*,[7] disguises past and current events as though he were predicting the future. In veiled language, Daniel recounts the deeds of tyrants such as Alexander the Great, the Ptolemies, and the Seleucids, calling Antiochus IV "desolator" (Daniel 9:27) and "contemptible" (Dan. 11:21) for oppressing the Jews and desecrating the temple.[8]

The uncompromising attitude of the *Hasidim* during the Maccabean Revolution is evident in the heroic story of Daniel and his three friends, Shadrach, Meshach, and Abednego, who are thrown into a furnace for refusing to worship a false god:

If our God whom we serve is able to deliver us from the furnace of blazing fire and out of your hand, O king, let him deliver us. But if not, be it known to you, O king that we will not serve your gods and we will not worship the golden statue that you have set up (Daniel 3:17-18).

The apocalyptic Book of Daniel looks forward to the time when God will honor the martyrdom of the faithful, shatter the forces of evil, and establish the full expression of God's eternal reign on earth.

---

6   See Irenaeus, *Against Heresies* 3.21.2. Earlier accounts of the translation of the *Septuagint* are perhaps more realistic. Aristeas says that the seventy-two translators were assembled in a secluded house and worked together to create their translation. *Letter of Aristeas* 301-306.

7   W. Sibley Towner, *Daniel* (Atlanta: John Knox, 1984), 7.

8   Bernhard W. Anderson, et al., *Understanding the Old Testament* (Upper Saddle River, NJ: Pearson Education), 577.

While the *Septuagint* had a unifying effect, the two worldviews, Greek and Hebrew, divided Jews in Jerusalem from the Hellenistic Jews in the Diaspora. In the Greek worldview, many gods existed from Apollo to Zeus, quite the opposite of the Hebrew monotheism of Yahweh. The Hebrew concept of shalom, an all-encompassing sense of wholeness and wellbeing, was narrowed in the Greek world to *eirene,* inner tranquility. For the Greeks, truth could be known through observation and reason, whereas the Jews in Jerusalem understood truth as divine revelation. The Hebrew concept of the human as a single entity where spirit and body were connected and interrelated differed from Greek dualism of body and matter versus the spirit. Salvation in this view meant escaping from the body to the realm of the divine spirit. Dualism was expressed in two opposite ways: If the flesh is evil, Hedonists claimed, one can do anything that gives pleasure without harming the spirit; asceticism on the other hand, punished the flesh in order to free the spirit.

Antiochus IV and Enforced Hellenism

In Judea, the suppression of Judaism and the enforcement of Hellenism reached a crisis point in 176 BCE when Antiochus IV became emperor. Claiming to be the human form of the Greek god Zeus, he named himself "Epiphanies" (god revealed) and forced people to worship him. Others preferred to call him "Epimemes" (the madman).[9] In an effort to eradicate Judaism and to consolidate his power, the emperor banned Jewish worship, burned copies of the Torah, and imposed the death penalty for observing the Sabbath, circumcising sons, and even carrying the Torah.

In the cauldron of oppression, Jews revolted. Antiochus, in response, slaughtered thousands; sold women and children into slavery; raided the temple; seized the temple's sacred treasures; and defiled the temple by erecting a statue of Zeus, sacrificing a hog on the altar, and splashing the blood throughout the temple. Jews were forced to sacrifice pigs to Zeus and eat the swine's flesh.

The Maccabean Revolt, 167-160 BCE

Jewish outrage against Greek rule reached the boiling point in 167 BCE. In the village of Modein, northwest of Jerusalem. An elderly priest, Mattathias, refused an order to sacrifice a pig on an altar to Olympian Zeus. He used the knife to kill a Syrian soldier and a Jewish collaborator,

---

9   Rabbi Paul Steinberg, Celebrating *the Jewish Year: The Winter Holidays: Hanukkah, Tu B'shevat, Purim* (Philadelphia, PA: 2007), 17.

sparking the Maccabean revolt. After destroying the altar, Mattathias rallied the men of Judea with his challenge: "Let everyone who is zealous for the law and...would maintain the covenant come forth after me!" (1 Maccabees 2:27). After that, Mattathias and his five sons disappeared into the hills. From the desert hills, the fugitives and the freedom fighters who joined them, fought a guerrilla war against the Seleucid oppressors and the collaborating Hellenized Jews.

A year later in 166 BCE, Mattathias died, having selected his oldest son Judas to lead the resistance. His ruthless military tactics earned Judas the name Maccabeus, the "hammer." Surprisingly, the revolutionaries won a series of victories over Antiochus's army and reclaimed Jerusalem. In 165 BCE, Judas led the cleansing and rededication of the temple in a ceremony called the Feast of Lights—still celebrated today as Hanukkah (meaning "rededication").

Judas, and then his brothers Jonathan and Simon, continued the battles against their oppressors. The revolt of Mattathias' family in 167 BCE escalated to the Maccabean wars that achieved nearly a century of Jewish independence, beginning in 142 BCE.[10]

Hasmonean Dynasty and *Hasidim:* Two Visions

Jewish independence was characterized by internal dissension, political intrigue, violence, and competing ideologies. The Maccabean family—properly called Hasmoneans, after Mattathias's grandfather Hasmonius—competed for wealth, power, and position. The office of High Priest often went to the highest bidder, and eventually, this religious office became political and morphed into kingship.

The great debate among the Jews was how they as the People of God should relate to the world. In a general sense, here are the collective responses of the two most influential Jewish groups of the time, the *Hasidim* and the Hasmoneans:

- The *Hasidim*, purists and traditionalists, withdrew, separating and insulating themselves against the polluting influence of the world. Their goal was religious freedom and a recovery of the separated, covenant, holy People of God. Two more offshoots of Judaism, the separatist Pharisees and the withdrawing Essenes, are products of the *Hasidim*.

---

10   Ibid., Anderson, 570-571.

- The Hasmoneans resorted to accommodation, compromise, and violence to gain political and religious freedom and to recreate a nation-state monarchy. The Hasmoneans influenced the formation of the Sadducees, who accommodated, and the freedom-fighting Zealots.

Roman Occupation

Jewish independence was fleeting and fragile. Intense ideological and political differences among the Jews led to bloody military clashes in 94 BCE. In one episode during the eight-year civil war (94-88 BCE), the Pharisees trapped the Sadducees and High Priest/King Alexander Jannaeus in the temple where they had barricaded themselves. The standoff ended with the slaughter of thousands of Pharisees and their supporters at the hands of the Sadducees, the king, and his foreign mercenaries.[11]

In 63 BCE two Hasmonean brothers, Hyrcanus II and Aristobulus II, sons of Alexander and Alexandra Salome, were locked in a bloody civil war for the Jewish throne. With large bribes in hand, both brothers arranged meetings in Damascus with Roman General Gnaeus Pompeius Magnus, better known as Pompey. Having recently conquered Seleucid Syria, the general, surely amused by the sibling rivalry, saw his opportunity to add Palestine to the empire. Pompey assaulted the walls of Jerusalem with siege engines and battering rams. When the Romans broke through three months later, the slaughter began. Some 12,000 Jews of Jerusalem died at the hands of Pompey's soldiers. It was an ominous sign of things to come. Pompey sent Aristobulus II to Rome in chains, made Hyrcanus II puppet ruler of Judea, annexed Palestine to the province of Syria, and launched 700 years of Roman domination.

It is under these conditions that the curtain reopens on the long drama of the Bible, with the beginning of the New Testament.

---

11   Don Blosser, et al., *Jesus: His Life and Times* (Lincolnwood, IL: Publications International, Ltd.), 163-172; Anderson,167.

The Historic Jesus

Bible passages: Matthew 1-4, Luke 1-4

Jesus! The name means so many different things to so many people. For some, this name represents a famous Jewish prophet born more than 2000 years ago who was executed by the Roman government. For others, he is the divine son of God who came to earth in human flesh. For others, he's just one more historical figure from the past. Many people claim Jesus to be both human and divine, both the enigmatic rabbi and God in flesh. Who is Jesus? And how does Jesus connect with the rest of the biblical story?

Like all the events of the Bible, it's important to know Jesus in his historical and cultural context. Christmas-time pictures of brightly-lit stables, and Easter greeting cards with gleaming lilies around the cross make it more difficult for the average person to truly see his context.

Another barrier to really understanding his context is the habit of reading Jesus from a post-resurrection perspective. Knowing the end of the story—he's alive!—we jump from the cradle to the cross and pay little attention to the life and teachings of Jesus.

A third barrier to really understanding Jesus is the American civil religion haze that clouds our minds. We know certain Geschichtes about Jesus, as they have been formed in us by our various church affiliations, and so we use that theological lens to view the historical events. We read about the cross of Jesus, already knowing that he is resurrected and, for many of us, already having a specific idea about what that death means.

All these barriers can push us toward a narrow, non-historic view of Jesus. This view spiritualizes Jesus in such a way that it's hard to remember his humanity, lived out in a particular place and time. We miss the significance of his decisions, his teachings and ethics. We miss the political, social and historical dimensions of the Kingdom Jesus was establishing.

Political and Social Jesus

Christmas songs like "Silent Night" and "O Little Town of Bethlehem" plus romanticized views of shepherds give us a false view of the Palestinian world into which Jesus was born. The social and political environment was more like Central America in the 1980s or like present day Palestine/Israel itself than some peaceful middle-class, rural United States community.[1]

The bitter loss of freedom to the Romans in 63 BCE after eighty years of independence was still alive. People remembered the Roman General Pompey slaughtering 12,000 Jews in his takeover of Judea and Jerusalem.[2] The Roman conquest had been brutal, with villages destroyed and people crucified and enslaved. This resentment, the memory of Maccabean independence, and visions of a restored Kingdom of David smoldered below the surface. Local revolts burst into flame before and during the life of Jesus. The Romans crushed each of them mercilessly along with the later major revolts of 66-70 CE and 135 CE. The Jews had their list of martyrs for the faith.[3]

When the Romans gained control in 63 BCE, they made Palestine a part of the Syrian province. Caesar made Hyrcanus II, a Jew from the

---

1   Scott Korb, *Life in Year One: What the World Was Like in First-Century Palestine* (New York: Riverhead, 2010), 11. "From what we know about first-century Palestine, my choice of the word "lively"...may be something of an understatement. This was a time of insurgency, banditry, widespread soothsaying and prophecy, political backstabbing and religious uprising, and a good many instances of religious backstabbing and political uprising, all of which, in their own ways, culminated in war that...left more than a million people dead, most of them Jews."

2   Josephus' description of the siege: "But when the battering-engine was brought near, the greatest of the towers was shaken by it, and fell down, and broke down a part of the fortifications, so the enemy poured in apace...But now all was full of slaughter; some of the Jews being slain by the Romans, and some by one another; nay, some there were who threw themselves down the precipices, or put fire to their houses, and burnt them, as not able to bear the miseries they were under. Of the Jews there fell twelve thousand, but of the Romans very few." *Antiquities* XIV, 4.4.

3   Tessa Rajak, *The Jewish Dialogue with Greece and Rome* (Boston: Leiden: Brill, 2002), 100.

Hasmonean dynasty, ruler of Judea. After several rulers were slain or poisoned, Herod the Great (of mixed Idumean and Jewish blood) gained power over the Hasmonean leader Aristobulus II. Herod had Aristobulus II crucified and then beheaded. He also executed 45 Sadducean priests who had supported Aristobulus II.[4]

Herod the Great ruled from 37-4 BCE. He brought stability and engaged in numerous construction projects, including rebuilding the temple, doubling its size. However, heavy taxes made him unpopular. Ruthless and paranoid, Herod killed three of his sons and two of his ten wives as well as other relatives. Out of that same paranoia Herod the Great had the boy babies killed after Jesus was born in Bethlehem, according to Matthew's gospel.[5] He died soon after and upon his death, the kingdom was divided among his three sons.

Judea

Herod the Great's son, Archelaus, ruled Judea. Rioters at the Passover in Jerusalem demanded that he lower taxes, release political prisoners, and restore the High Priest he had replaced. Archelaus promptly killed three thousand rioters. After deposing Archelaus in 6 CE because of his brutality and incompetence, the Romans changed policy and directly appointed a procurator to govern Judea. Pontius Pilate, the fifth procurator, governed from 26 to 36 CE and was involved in Jesus' death. The procurator's primary responsibility was to keep the peace. He had a cohort of 300-500 soldiers, stationed in Fort Antonio next to the temple to put down any Jewish riots. Pilate lived in the coastal city of Caesarea. He came to Jerusalem during special occasions, bringing additional troops to control pilgrims at feast times.[6]

Galilee

Herod the Great's son, Herod Antipas, ruled over Galilee during the time Jesus grew up in Nazareth. He too led with a heavy hand, calling for the head of Jesus' cousin, John the Baptist, among other deeds (Mark

4   H. W. Hoehner, "Herodian Dynasty," in *Dictionary of Jesus and the Gospels*, ed. Joel B. Green et al. (Downers Grove: InterVarsity Press, 1992), 319.

5   For views on the historicity of this massacre, see Peter Richardson, *Herod: King of the Jews and Friend of the Romans* (Minneapolis: Fortress Press, 1999), 297.

6   Donald Kraybill, *The Upside-Down Kingdom*, 25th Anniversary ed. (Scottdale, PA: Herald Press, 2003), 45.

6:27). A certain Judas of Galilee led a bloody revolt against the Romans in the large town of Sepphoris, northwest of Nazareth, when Jesus was about ten-years old. The Roman army surrounded the city, crucified Judas and the leaders, sold the population into slavery, and burned the city. The army continued southward, killing two thousand more rebels. These events were no doubt matters of family conversation in the Joseph and Mary home in Nazareth.

Jesus was born and grew up in the context of an occupied country full of revolts, heavy taxes, and a large gap between wealthy landowners and poor farmers. The Jews were a long way from being the chosen, covenant, shalom community that revealed the nature of God and right relationships. Some seven revolutionary Jewish prophets and messianic leaders led revolts during the childhood and youth of Jesus, plus additional riots and uprisings. The great question was, "What to do with the Romans?" How would Jesus respond to this situation?

The Economic Context

There was no middle class in the economic structure of first-century Palestine. A huge gap separated the richest nobles and priests in cities, who could tithe, "keep the law," and spend freely, and the poor working class that struggled to survive in terrible poverty. Nearly 90% of the population fell into this latter category, eking out a living in a system that seemed to guarantee their failure.[7] They couldn't afford to be "righteous."[8]

The crushing Roman taxes were only part of the economic problem. There were also mandatory Jewish temple taxes and tithes. Scholars estimate that 30-60% of the average person's wages were gone after different organizations had taken their share.[9] Most of the working class farmed land for absentee landlords, many of them as slaves or indentured servants. The most fortunate of the poor were craftsmen and artisans. Their skilled labor gave them slightly more livable incomes, though still far beneath the exorbitant lifestyles in Jerusalem.

---

7 Ibid., 74.

8 "Since on the grounds of equality the temple tax came to two denarii for all who were obligated to pay it, whether they were rich or poor, one can imagine that in view of all the other taxes, they were no small burden for many families." Ekkehard Stegemann and Wolfgang Stegemann, *The Jesus Movement: A Social History of its First Century* (Minneapolis: Fortress Press, 1999), 121.

9 Ibid., Kraybill, 77.

Jesus, who probably worked as a carpenter, was likely on the upper end of this poor class. He would have identified with the majority of the Jews who were despised by the elite. His ministry would have to break down both the arrogant superiority of the upper class (Romans and priests) and the festering hatred of the oppressed masses.

The Religious Context

Jesus lived in a religiously pluralistic world. Even among the Jews, there were several "Judaisms," with four major parties with multiple sub-groupings. The four major Jewish religious groups had several common values, however. They each had a strategy for living with the Roman occupation. The idea of a coming Messiah was a subject of concern for at least some Jews, including the possibility that this Messiah may be the One who could get out them free from under Roman rule. Each Jewish party valued sacred scriptures and had some relationship with the temple in Jerusalem. And each of these four groups, as they interacted with Jesus, felt great disappointment, for he didn't meet their Messianic expectations.

The Messiah

The word *messiah* comes from the Hebrew word that means "anointed." The earliest definition of messiah, therefore, was one who was anointed or given a special task. This task was usually that of delivering the people. A messiah could be any leader and even the Persian King Cyrus was called a messiah for allowing the Jews to return to Judah after their exile in Babylonia (Isaiah 45:1). Yet the exile experience itself was formative in developing a new definition for messiah. The exilic and post-exilic prophets comforted people with the news that God would send the Messiah, not just any deliverer, but a special One who would make all things right. The term moved from something that any number of persons could be called, to the title for the person who would finally set them free. A messiah transformed into the Messiah. And while it is not possible to find a homogeneous definition of Messiah, even from within the same Jewish party, there was a lot of excitement when it came to thinking about this Anointed One.[10]

The expectation for this special person was high during the time of Jesus. Other men had called themselves the Messiah and had drawn a

10   William Scott Green, "Introduction: Messiah in Judaism: Rethinking the Question," in *Judaisms and their Messiahs at the Turn of the Christian Era*, ed. Jacob Neusner et al. (Cambridge University Press, 1987), 10.

following. To a person, they were executed by the Romans, and after their death, their group disbanded. Was Jesus the real Messiah? Or was he just another self-proclaimed leader?

The Many Possible Messiahs

The major Jewish party of the Sadducees, more than the other Jewish groups, loved the Temple and sought to protect it. This group felt the favor of Rome more than the other groups and thus they had the privilege of controlling the Sanhedrin, the ruling court for the Jews. The Romans appointed the High Priest, a lucrative and powerful position, and the highest official religious position in the land. At this time, the title went to the highest bidder, usually a Sadducee. Sadducees had different views than the Pharisees, another group, about how to follow the law. And while scholars debate whether or not Sadducees even believed in a coming Messiah, what they did want was a leader or system that supported the Temple. They wanted protection for a Temple system that benefitted them so well.[11] And their solution to the problem of Roman oppression? Compromise your values to accommodate the Romans.

The Pharisees formed another major Jewish party. Around 6,000 Pharisees and scribes, men skilled in writing and interpretation of the Law, led the synagogues in the villages and towns of Palestine and the Diaspora. For the Scribes and Pharisees, the Law of Moses, not the animal sacrifices that the Sadducees and priests cherished, was at the heart of their religion. The Pharisees believed they could rid themselves of the awful Romans by persuading every single Jew to obey all the Sabbath laws completely for two straight Sabbaths, which would prompt Yahweh to act, sending the Messiah who would free them from Rome. Scriptural liberals, they embraced as sacred many writings beyond the Five Books of Torah. They believed it necessary to obey not only the laws as written in *Torah,* but also commentaries such as the *Mishnah* written to delineate Moses' Law more clearly. Thus, they longed for a Moses-type or a law-abiding Messiah, one who encouraged obedience to even the smallest laws.[12]

The Essenes formed yet another Jewish religious party. Frustrated with

---

11   Lawrence Schiffman, "Messianism and Apocalypticism in Rabbinic Texts," in *The Cambridge History of Judaism*, v. 4, ed. Steven Katz (Cambridge University Press, 2006), 1060. See also Anthony Saldarini, *Pharisees, Scribes and Sadducees in Palestinian Society* (Grand Rapids: Eerdmans, 1988), 302-303.

12   Ibid., Saldarini, 290.

the compromise they saw in the Sadducees, they fled as a group to the Dead Sea area. They sought purity in every form, and believed that a withdrawal from evil would aide in their search for purity. This withdrawal was also their answer to the problem of Roman oppression: simply leave and live a cloistered life away from evil influence. They longed for two Messiahs, a priestly one and a kingly one, with the priestly messiah having authority over the kingly Messiah. For at least some, the coming of the Messiah would signal the end of the ages.[13]

The Zealots had a different solution to the Roman problem. For them, obeying Yahweh meant fighting the oppressors, usually through guerilla warfare. They looked back to the time of David as the glory years. They strove to bring Israel back as a free nation-state. They wanted to be ready to die for God as martyrs; they reviled the pagan Hellenistic environment they found themselves in. So they envisioned a Military Messiah, one who had the power and know-how to wipe out the Romans.[14]

While it is possible to discern distinct characteristics of the four Jewish parties during Jesus' day. we must also careful to hold those characteristics loosely. There were many forces pulling at the Jews of First Century, just as it is with Jews and Christians today. The Pharisees and Essenses were spiritual descendants of the *Hasidim*. They sensed the possibility of Hellenism watering down their faith, but that didn't make them completely insular. The Zealots and the Sadducees, spiritual ancestors of the Hasmoneans, may have related more with the Hellenistic world, but they also honored the Jewish scriptures and worked hard to stay loyal to their beliefs. It was a difficult time to be "in the world but not of it" as Jesus himself advised his followers.

The three annual pilgrimage feasts were a common experience for all Jews in first-century Palestine.[15] These feasts—Tabernacles, Passover, and Pentecost—celebrated God's providence in the past. Jews were expected to attend one per year. Tabernacles, or Succoth, was a feast commemorating God's providence in the wilderness. Passover was the most passionate festival, celebrating the Exodus when God rescued the slaves from Egypt

13   Paolo Sacchi, *The History of the Second Temple Period* (London; New York: T&T Clark, 2000), 397.

14   Martin Hengel, *The Zealots* (Edinburgh: T&T Clark, 1989), 377.

15   Kimmo Ketola, "A Cognitive Approach to Ritual Systems in First-Century Judaism," in *Explaining Christian Origins and Early Judaism*, ed. Petri Luomanen et al. (Leiden: Brill, 2007), 97.

as the Death Angel passed over the homes with blood on their doorposts. Scholars estimate that anywhere from 300,000 to 500,000 pilgrims came to Passover in Jerusalem.[16] Pentecost happened 50 days after Passover. This festival, also called the Festival of Weeks, was a time to express thankfulness to the LORD for the blessings of the harvest.

Enter Jesus

We learn about Jesus primarily through four biblical narratives or gospels called Matthew, Mark, Luke and John. The gospels are not a complete biography of Jesus. We can account for only fifteen specific days in his life and three-year ministry. The gospels are highly selected stories with the clear purpose of convincing readers that Jesus is the Messiah so they will believe in and follow him (John 20:31). Yet the gospels are reliable in giving us a good picture of the historical Jesus

Jesus in the Gospel of Luke

The writer of Luke, more than the other gospels, desired to identify Jesus both to his Jewish roots and as the Messiah for the entire world. In the birth narrative, Luke connects Jesus to historic Roman rulers; Jesus is the rival political Lord, who, like the Roman emperor, also brings good news and is called the Savior (Luke 2:10-11). In Luke's genealogy, Jesus is connected to Abraham and David, but is also shown to be the son of Adam and the son of God (Luke 3: 38). Jesus is Jewish and also part of all people groups.

Not only is Jesus' birth a political challenge to the emperor, but it's also a statement against the wealthy. Mary's song of praise, the Magnificat, identifies her child as one who will bring a social, political and economic revolution; "he has scattered the proud...brought down the powerful and lifted up the lowly...has filled the hungry and sent the rich away empty" (Luke 1:51-53). Jesus, born into the poorer class, is wrapped in bands of cloth (rags). What does it mean that shepherds are the first to hear the good news (Luke 2:8-16)? Shepherds were at the bottom socially. They were considered dishonest sheep-stealers and couldn't testify in court.

Finally, Jesus' incarnation is for all peoples. Mary and Joseph bring the eight-day old Jesus to the Temple to be dedicated. Simeon, a righteous man who had been in constant vigilance waiting for Messiah, held the

---

16   E. P. Sanders, *Judaism: Practice and Belief, 63 BCE - 66 CE* (London: SCM Press, 1992), 128.

tiny infant in his arms and said Jesus would be the "salvation," the one who delivers...all peoples, a light for revelation to the Gentiles and for glory to your people Israel" (Luke 2:30-32). Later, In Luke 3, John the Baptist challenges the Jews' trust in their ethnicity for salvation, "Do not begin to say to yourselves, we have Abraham as our ancestor, for I tell you, God is able from these stones to raise up children of Abraham." This proclamation, combined with the many Gentiles who begin to follow Jesus in Luke, highlights Jesus as the Savior and deliverer of all peoples.

Jesus truly was for all types of people. Women join the disciples (Luke 8:1-3) and Mary is treated like a disciple when she is affirmed for "sitting at his feet" to learn from him (Luke 10:38-42). He moves beyond Jewish ethnocentrism when he teaches and heals among Gentiles on the east side of the Sea of Galilee (Luke 8:26-39). He heals an occupying Roman soldier's servant (Luke 22:51). Healing a widow's son was an act of economic compassion and justice because she was dependent on her son for survival in her old age (Luke 7:11-17).

Jesus' love for Samaritans and Gentiles extends to the other gospels as well. In John 4, Jesus tells his disciples that they must go through Samaria. This seems odd to the disciples, for the province of Samaria was a place to be avoided. Samaritans, "distant cousins" of the Jews, were hated more than even the Gentiles. As the offspring of Israelites and foreigners brought in by the Assyrians in 722, Samaritans were half-breeds, therefore tainting precious Jewish blood, while Gentiles were simply not Jewish. But Jesus is insistent. And while they go into town for food, Jesus speaks with a Samaritan woman, an unacceptable thing for a Jewish Rabbi to do. Not only that, but he asks her for a drink and drinks from her cup, an even more unacceptable thing to do! Their conversation leads to her conversion, and she runs into their town to tell them that she has found the Messiah! Jesus reached out to all kinds of people: rich and poor, Jew, Gentile, and Samaritan, men and women, slave and free. Jesus revealed God's indiscriminate love. The kingdom was and is open to all.

Baptized and Empowered for Mission

The baptism of Jesus is often interpreted merely as an example for later followers with no particular meaning for Jesus. But his baptism held much meaning; it was Jesus' ordination for ministry. Jesus experienced the Spirit empowering him for his mission. "Jesus, filled with the power of the Spirit, returned to Galilee" (Luke 4:14). Then Jesus and the crowd gathered there heard a voice from heaven say two phrases that came from Old Testament scriptures. "You are my son, the Beloved; with you I am well pleased." The first phrase, "You are my son," is derived from Psalm 2:7, the Psalm used to coronate the Davidic Kings. Jesus was being inaugurated as king. In the Old Testament when a King was enthroned, it was believed that Yahweh adopted him as a son to do God's work. In contrast, "With you I am well pleased" comes from Isaiah 42:1, a passage identifying a gentle servant. Here Jesus is identified as a Suffering Servant. Putting the two phrases together, the crowd beheld a paradox. Jesus was a Servant-King, and empowered and commissioned as a real king, not some spiritualized savior. Recall how Israel's kings selfishly misused power. People had never seen a humble servant king! They couldn't have imagined it!

What Kind of King Not to Be: The Temptations

How would Jesus go about his mission as a servant king? How would he use his power to establish his kingdom? Jesus went into the wilderness to find out. Here Satan tempted him. The temptations were not so much personal temptations as they were all different ways to set up a kingdom, be a king, and establish a following. The word if in the phrase "If you are the Son of God" may be better translated as since or because, which means that Satan was implying that Jesus indeed was the Son of God. And Satan's real goal was to persuade Jesus to bring about his kingdom in ways that violated his own principles.

The first temptation was a temptation to set up the kingdom by giving the people food—to appeal to their self-interest. Satan tempted Jesus to turn rocks into bread and while Jesus himself was hungry, the implication ran deeper than feeding the hungry. Like the Emperor, Jesus could curry the favor of the people by giving out freebies. Satan was tempting Jesus to be an economic Messiah, a Bread Messiah. Jesus also faced this temptation in John 6. After feeding the five thousand, people came to make him king!

In the second temptation, Satan took Jesus on a high mountain and offered him all the political and military power in the world. This temptation was to be a dominating military ruler and force people into his kingdom. Jesus faced this temptation again in the garden. He replied to Peter, "Do you think that I cannot appeal to my Father and he will at once send me more than twelve legions of angels?" Jesus struggled with the temptation to defend himself violently and establish the kingdom that way (Matthew 26:53).

The third temptation, and the most manipulative way to establish the kingdom, was to be a spiritual superman Messiah and overwhelm people with his spiritual power, to operate beyond human limits. Jumping down from the Temple roof and bouncing right back up unhurt would certainly gain a following to establish the kingdom. Jesus faced this temptation again when he went into the Temple with the cheering crowd at his back after his entry into Jerusalem. And he faced it even earlier in his life when he performed miracles. Many times after Jesus healed a person, he would command that person to be quiet about the miracle. Jesus didn't want people following him just because he had razzle-dazzle powers. He wanted them to follow him freely, out of love (Mark 1:40-45).

These temptations were all "top down" approaches to establishing the Kingdom of God. They were all ways of coercing people to become followers of Jesus. People would become part of God's People either for the free food and other provisions, or because they were awed by the miracles or because they were being forced to join politically or militarily. In other words, Jesus was tempted to bring shalom in a non-shalom way and simply hope that the ends (God's kingdom) would somehow justify the means (coercion).

Yet in the end Jesus said no to these temptations. He chose to establish the kingdom from the "bottom up," servant style, like the Exodus that began with lowly slaves. This is an important distinction for Christians to make, for the method of establishing the kingdom would determine the kind of kingdom it would be. And those who call themselves Christians today are called to bring in the Kingdom in the same, "bottom up" way—a way in which the end partakes of the means.

What Kind of King to Be: Nazareth Synagogue

Jesus' method for bringing in God's kingdom was further identified in the Nazareth synagogue passage from Luke 4:18. Jesus went back to his hometown and he was asked to be the *Torah* reader for the day. He read from Isaiah 61:1-2 and claimed this Jubilee passage of social justice as his platform as the promised Messiah:

The Spirit of the Lord is upon me because he has anointed me to bring good news to the poor. He has sent me to proclaim release to the captives, and recovery of sight to the blind, to let the oppressed go free and to proclaim the year of the Lord's favor (Luke 4:18).

For modern-day Christians, this passage is usually spiritualized, turning inward rather than outward, and it's all about Jesus changing our attitudes rather than dealing with physically oppressed captives. The "poor" is interpreted as poor in spirit. Captives are those who are spiritually captive to sin. The blind refers to the spiritually blind seeing truth. The oppressed are those oppressed by demonic spirits. And "the year of the Lord's Favor" means that one experiences God's favor through Jesus.

It's true that Jesus can free us spiritually and help relieve us from our spiritual blindness. However, Jesus meant much more than a kind of spiritualizing that separates inner piety from a concern for justice for all people. The "year of the Lord's Favor" is code for Jubilee, the system for economic justice established during the wilderness wanderings. Furthermore, Jesus would go on in his ministry to actually heal blind people and speak out against social injustice. Good news to the poor meant re-establishing economic shalom justice to the many desperately poor in Palestine. Here, as elsewhere in Jesus' ministry, he cared about the healing of all four broken relationships that sin had damaged.

The Nazareth synagogue event has yet another amazing dimension. At the end of the scripture reading, Jesus claimed he was the Messiah. His family and friends were astonished. Knowing their thoughts, he acknowledged their unspoken disbelief that this hometown boy could be the Messiah. He also struck at the heart of their own ethnocentrism. Jesus said:

> "Truly I tell you, no prophet is accepted in the prophet's home town. But the truth is, there were many widows in Israel in the time of Elijah, when the heaven was shut up for three years and six months, and there was a severe famine over all the land; yet Elijah was sent to none of them except to a widow at Zarephath in Sidon. There were also many lepers in Israel in the time of the prophet Elisha, and none of them was cleansed except Naaman the Syrian" (Luke 4:24-27).

The hometown crowd was livid with anger. How dare Jesus tell stories of God showing favor to Gentile enemies, a Phoenician widow and a Syrian military captain, in the same context of God showing his favor to them, the Jews! Could it be that God wanted the same Jubilee blessing of shalom to fall on Gentiles as well as them? Even though the two Old Testament stories were known to be sacred stories to the Nazareth crowd, they couldn't bear to be reminded of this inclusive grace. Feeling a threat to their ethnocentrism, they pushed Jesus toward a cliff to throw him down to his death. Jesus miraculously walked through the angry crowd, but the message was clear. Jesus had come to heal both spiritual and physical brokenness and that healing was meant for all who would receive it.[17]

Jesus further connected the social, economic, and spiritual in the Lord's prayer. Jesus taught his followers to ask God to forgive them as they have forgiven the monetary debts owed to them. It simply meant that they were to ask God to treat them spiritually as they treated others economically! In the kingdom that Jesus was establishing, the spiritual, social, political and economic realms were all intertwined. It was only after Zacchaeus gave away much of his money that Jesus said, "Today, salvation [deliverance] has come to this house" (Luke 19:9).

Conclusion

Jesus was born and raised in a volatile society crippled by poverty and oppression. He lived in a religious setting where different groups had different visions of God's ultimate will. In the midst of this, he was ordained as servant-king. He was tempted by Satan to use his divine powers to bring his kingdom in such a way that he would never be crucified. His hometown of Nazareth rejected him when he called himself Messiah. Was it that he was just too much of a hometown man for them to believe it? Or was it that he challenged their ethnocentric beliefs?

Different Jewish groups wanted a different Messiah, everyone wanted deliverance from the hated Romans. Would Jesus be that deliverer? Would he be the one to save them? And what would that salvation look like? And how would it come to them? These were the questions that rumbled through the villages as Jesus went from town to town.

---

17 "No reader of Luke could be in doubt. Jesus had come to point Israel to the purpose of her history, which was to be God's instrument to bring light to the nations...What may have been isolated incidents in the past, when prophets like Elijah went on God's command to Zarephath in Sidon to feed a widow...or when Elisha was empowered to give healing to a leprous Syrian, would now become the normal pattern." C. Marvin Pate et al., *The Story of Israel: A Biblical Theology* (Downers Grove: InterVarsity Press, 2004), 127.

The *Geschichte* of Jesus

Bible passages: Matthew 5-7, Luke 19:28-24:53

Jesus is not a new phenomenon that simply cancels out the previous biblical narrative and starts a new one. And yet Jesus does represent something not seen before. The Bible speaks of a new covenant, and for Christians, that new covenant begins with Jesus.

> *The days are surely coming, says the Lord, when I will make a new covenant with the house of Israel and the house of Judah. It will not be like the covenant that I made with their ancestors when I took them by the hand to bring them out of the land of Egypt—a covenant that they broke, though I was their husband, says the Lord. But this is the covenant that I will make with the house of Israel after those days, says the Lord: I will put my law within them, and I will write it on their hearts; and I will be their God, and they shall be my people. No longer shall they teach one another, or say to each other, "Know the Lord," for they shall all know me, from the least of them to the greatest, says the Lord; for I will forgive their iniquity, and remember their sin no more* (Jeremiah 31:31-34).

> *Then he took a loaf of bread, and when he had given thanks, he broke it and gave it to them, saying, 'This is my body, which is given for you. Do this in remembrance of me.' And he did the same with the cup after supper, saying, 'This cup that is poured out for you is the new covenant in my blood* (Luke 22:19-20).

But how does Jesus connect with *Heilsgeschichte?* Throughout the biblical story, Yahweh has been creating a people of God as a way to restore the broken relationships and bring shalom to all. Jesus follows this pattern completely. He doesn't come just to make a payment for our sins or just to heal the broken relationship between humanity and God. And like the Old Testament, Jesus works at creating a People of God, a profoundly different community, made of all different ethnicities and socio-economic backgrounds, a community of grace, forgiveness, and love.

Jesus in the Context of *Heilsgeschichte*

The creation was good. But humans wanted to be equal with God and became violent, destroying shalom and breaking relationship with God, others, self, and all creation. God chose Abraham for the mission (Genesis 12:3) to be a chosen, covenant, shalom people to reveal God to the whole world so these broken relationships could be restored.

Yahweh created the Old People of God out of a mixed group of slaves through the common bonding experience of the Exodus and the covenant with Yahweh at Sinai. They were to be a priestly, missional people to the whole world. Functioning as a theocracy, they were further formed in the wilderness. In Canaan they were unfaithful to their chosen-ness when they acculturated with the Canaanites rather than helping them become a part of the People of God.

The people become even more unfaithful to their chosen-ness when they abandoned the theocracy to become a nation-state with an earthly king. They put two anti-missional boundaries around themselves: 1) a political box, in which Yahweh became a national god rather than the God of all the earth; and 2) a geographic box, in which Yahweh existed within a geographical area, not in the whole earth. Out of steadfast love, Yahweh kept working with the people through his remedial will.

In the fall and exile of Judah Yahweh smashed apart these two boxes the people had put together. Taken into exile to Babylonia, the people lost their kings, nation-state, and land. This was judgment but also a gracious new opportunity to be faithful to their calling to be the outreaching, shalom community. The prophets envisioned a people faithful to their chosen-ness, a "light to the nations."

The return from exile without the geographical and nation-state boundary and without a king was like a second Exodus, a second chance for the people to be faithful to their chosen-ness. Ezra led a renewal that helped save their identity but unfortunately he didn't get it right either He put together Yahweh and ethnicity. Yahweh became the God of the ethnic Jews. This ethnocentrism is now the third anti-missional boundary. The newly isolated Jews became defensive and ingrown rather than missional and outreaching, creating a new false boundary around God and the people of God.

During the intertestamental period, the continuing issue of how the people of God relate to the larger culture again split the Jews. Some adapted and acculturated with Hellenism while the conservative *Hasidim* were fiercely faithful to their faith, but, alas, still ingrown.

It is in this religious heritage context that Jesus is born Jesus is born and spends his formative years. Like the political and social context, the questions remain: How will Jesus interpret the behavior of the different groups of Jews? How will Jesus attempt to bring in God's kingdom in the context into which he was born.

The Teachings of Jesus

The four gospels contain many teachings of Jesus. These teachings are radical in that they go beyond the normal understandings of common decency and ethics. And in today's North American culture, where Jesus has been domesticated, smoothed over and spiritualized, they seem jolting— and refreshing. These teachings are not for the faint-hearted, and yet, by the help of the Holy Spirit, they are part of our calling as followers of Jesus. The following chart lists some of these teachings and then contrasts them with the values of a world outside of God's kingdom.

Values in God's Kingdom	Values in the Human World
• Jesus is Lord and he rules	• Humans rule
• Good news and a bias for the powerless	• There is a bias for the strong and powerful
• Jubilee ideal for economy, shalom is alive	• Debt, bondage
• Shalom justice and peace	• War, strife and injustice
• God's people break barriers and work at healing all broken relationships	• Supports barrier and division
• The kingdom is open to all	• There are exclusive groups

• Restoration of the proper place and purpose for the law and institutions	• Law and religious institutions rule instead of Jesus
• Deliverance, forgiveness and gratitude	• Bondage, condemnation and bitterness
• Serving and healing with compassion	• Controlling and hurting with anger
• Servant leadership	• Dominating leadership
• Love of enemy and nonviolent confrontation of evil	• Hatred, retribution, violence, revenge
• Righteousness beyond the natural	• "Righteousness" that focuses on externals
• Faithfulness, honesty, integrity	• Unfaithfulness, deceit, corruption
• Kingdom can't be stopped	• System is fallible and failing

The Sermon on the Mount (Matthew 5-7)

The Sermon on the Mount is a concentration of Jesus' teachings about the values and characteristics of the kingdom. These chapters could have been catechetical material for the early church—that is, resources that help prepare people for baptism. The Sermon is filled with high standards and abundant grace. Christians are called to love their enemies, (Matthew 5:43- 48) trust God completely for every need (Matthew 6:25-34) and seek a relationship with God that goes beyond both word and deed (Matthew 7:21-23). We are not to be content with merely controlling our external behaviors, which Jesus calls the righteousness of the Scribes and Pharisees (Matthew 5:17-20). Instead through the help of the Spirit, we are transformed on the inside. Here are some examples of that inner transformation from Matthew 5:21-48.

- Instead of just keeping yourself from murder, get rid of your anger.
- Go beyond avoiding adultery; don't even look at another person as a sex object.
- Don't settle for equal retaliation, as in an "eye for an eye," but do good to the one who hurts you.
- These transformations seem impossible. Of course, says Jesus, but as you see yourself as powerless, or poor in spirit, this opens the door for transformation. This transformation from Jesus can go as far as to even help us love our enemies:

You have heard that it was said, "You shall love your neighbor and hate your enemy." But I say to you, Love your enemies and pray for those who persecute you, so that you may be children of your Father in heaven; for he makes his sun rise on the evil and on the good, and sends rain on the righteous and on the unrighteous. For if you love those who love you, what reward do you have? Do not even the tax-collectors do the same? And if you greet only your brothers and sisters, what more are you doing than others? Do not even the Gentiles do the same? Be perfect, therefore, as your heavenly Father is perfect (Matthew 5:43-48).

In these verses, Jesus gave two clear reasons why we should love our enemies. First we are children of the Heavenly Father and, like earthly children, we should be emulate our parents' best behavior. Therefore, we should love our enemies because we are to be like God, who sends rain and sun to evil people.

The second reason why we should love our enemies is explained by the simple logic of "more than." If we don't love our enemies and do good to them, what more are we doing than non-religious people? The answer is obvious: nothing.

Jesus called for active love of enemy, not just a passive willingness to not harm the enemy. We are to greet them, love them, and in our own way, send them "rain" and "sun." But Jesus is also clear that we must respond to injustice, not as doormats, but as active and nonviolent participants.

He taught further in Matthew 5:39-41: "But I say to you, do not resist an evil doer. But if anyone strikes you on the right cheek, turn the other also; and if anyone wants to sue you and take your coat, give your cloak as well; and if anyone forces you to go one mile, go also the second mile." Turning the other cheek is not a passive response. In Jesus' culture, hitting the cheek with the back of the hand was done to insult and humiliate an inferior more than to injure them. A right-handed person would strike the person he wants to humiliate on the right cheek. If the one who was struck turns the other cheek, then the striker would have to use the left hand in order to hit with the back of the hand. The left hand was used for unclean tasks. To strike with it would humiliate one's self. To hit with the fist would be treating the person as an equal. Far from passive, Jesus called for his followers to assertively take charge of situations and put the ball back in the offender's court.[1]

---

1   Walter Wink, *Engaging the Powers* (Minneapolis: Fortress Press, 1992), 175-77.

Jesus called his followers to creatively take charge of their responses to violence, domination, and humiliation. To respond in kind is to become what you are against. Jesus called for creative love that helps offenders discover what they are doing. Passivity can actually contribute to the violent person's behavior. It tends to reinforce one's self-view of inferiority and the offender's superiority. Only the creative, loving response breaks the cycle of dominating violence and opens up the possibility of the enemy changing.

The Teachings Put to the Test

After only three years of ministry, Jesus was arrested, taken before Pontius Pilate and sentenced to death by crucifixion. It was an unusually painful and humiliating way to die. Christians believe that this death, sometimes simply referred to as the "cross" is an integral part of salvation. But not only is it a key to our atonement, the cross also teaches us how to live.

After Jesus asked the disciples about who he was, he told them "If any want to become my followers, let them deny themselves and take up their cross daily and follow me" (Luke 9:23). Jesus told them to follow him, his decisions, teachings, and loving service to others. This obedience and following in the way of Jesus is called discipleship, and almost always, it eventually leads to suffering. The "cross" in this passage and cross-bearing in general are often spiritualized to mean agreeing to do God's will when it conflicts with our own will or misunderstood to mean enduring some illness or inconvenience that Paul refers to as a thorn in the flesh (II Corinthians 12:7).

But these notions miss the mark. Taking up our cross is not about allergies or annoyances but being will to suffer in our discipleship.

Christians behaving like Jesus—befriending the marginalized, speaking out against oppression, refusing to be violent—these actions will anger those in power and challenge an unjust status quo. So, like Jesus, they will be persecuted. Bearing the cross is taking on persecution for following Jesus. Suffering discipleship is one part of what the cross symbolizes.

If the cross only represented Jesus paying for our sins, then it would make no sense that he should ask us to carry a cross. None of us can make that sacrifice for the world. But Jesus asked his followers to carry their crosses before he ever got on one himself! So the cross must mean something more than a sacrifice for sin. Like Jesus, Christians may suffer for the Kingdom of God.

The Romans crucified political revolutionaries in public to make examples of them. Jesus was killed on a cross by the Romans because he set up a historic, political, and religious revolutionary kingdom that demanded first allegiance to himself as the king. That was a challenge to the power of the Roman Caesar and to any government today! The threat had to be dealt with.

It's important to understand Jesus in this historical-cultural context. It's important to take his teachings seriously, and not avoid simply spiritualizing them into convenient beliefs that excuse us from "carrying our crosses." It's important to accept the kind of kingdom Jesus sought to establish--a kingdom of non-coercive love, open to all people. And all of us are invited to become part of this New People of God, to follow Jesus, and let him transform us so that we can be this seemingly impossible thing to be, the chosen, covenant, shalom community. This invitation, this new way of life, contains great joy.

Human and Divine

When Jesus taught with authority and did mighty deeds, the people asked, "Who is this man?" and "What is this?" And while each gospel writer answered these questions in a slightly different way, they each made the same paradoxical claim: that Jesus is 100% human and 100% divine.

Most of the New Testament writers refer to Jesus Christ the Lord. The name Jesus refers to the human man from Nazareth. Christ comes from the Greek word Christus which translates into the Hebrew word Messiah. Lord can mean a political ruler and in using this name for Jesus, the early Christians were declaring their allegiance to him over the Roman Caesar. Lord can also be an appropriate way of saying or alluding to the sacred name of Yahweh. In this sense, Jesus was being connected to God in a more direct way. First-century Jews were cautious about using any language that even came close to "Yahweh," to the extent that they didn't say the phrase "I am." John recorded Jesus saying "I am" eight times in his gospel, a clear sign that for John and his audience, Jesus was deeply connected to Yahweh.

One of the early heresies the Christian Church had to deal with was not a denial that Jesus was divine but that he was not really human and historic. That problem continues today when persons read Jesus from end to beginning, or do not know the Old Testament Heilsgeschichte and the historical contexts in which Jesus lived. Without historical context, the life, decisions, ministry and teachings of Jesus become a non-historic, scripted puppet show with God pulling the strings. The drama appears on the stage of history but it is not real life or history like today. When people envision that kind of spiritualized Jesus, he becomes irrelevant for the way we live today. Then people must come up with other ways to define what a Christian is, other than "following Jesus." Jesus becomes a spiritual idea— an impossible ideal—rather than a person, a historic and eternal Lord.

On the other hand, there is something different about Jesus. He claimed a special relationship with God. He was conceived by the Holy Spirit, and as an adult had the power to heal diseases, forgive sins, calm stormy waters. God raised him back from the dead.

The Jesus of history and the Christ of faith are sometimes referred to as the "front" and "back" side of Jesus. The front side of the Jesus of documented history anyone can see, such as his birth, baptism, teachings, healings, trial, crucifixion, and burial. The back side, or the Christ of faith, would include the virgin birth, miracles, resurrection, and ascension. It takes faith to see that side of Jesus.

Misunderstanding Jesus and the Kingdom

The people of Jesus' time, even his closest disciples, did not understand what kind of Messiah he was or the nature of the kingdom he was establishing. Their misunderstanding reveals how deeply they still thought in terms of a violent, top-down Davidic nation-state. When Jesus talked about going to Jerusalem and suffering, Peter confronted him with "God forbid it, Lord! This must never happen to you." Jesus replied, "Get behind me, Satan! You are a stumbling block to me" (Matthew 16:22-23).

One of Jesus' disciples, Judas, was a clear example of this misunderstanding. Even after three years of learning from Jesus, he still thought that God's kingdom was established through a nation-state. When Jesus and the disciples were in the garden of Gethsemane, Judas came and kissed his cheek. This was a sign to the Roman soldiers who had come to arrest Jesus that this was their man. But why would Judas do this? Scholars suggest that Judas, failing to understand the nature of the kingdom, was trying to force Jesus' hand to establish the kingdom with spiritual power or violence. When he saw that Jesus did not come out fighting, he killed himself in remorse.

Peter also misunderstood Jesus. Jesus rebuked Peter and healed the High Priest servant's ear when Peter used a sword to defend Jesus. He said to Peter, "Do you think that I cannot appeal to my Father and he will at once send me more than twelve legions of angels?" (Matthew 26:53). Jesus says in John 18:36, "My kingdom is not from this world. If my kingdom were from this world, my followers would be fighting to keep me from being handed over to the Jews." He does not say that his kingdom is not in the world, but that the Kingdom has a loving, nonviolent nature in contrast to a violent, coercive kingdom.

The two disciples walking to Emmaus after the crucifixion illustrate the point. Jesus joined them and asked what they were discussing and what they were sad about. Luke ends his account of the events in Jerusalem with "But we had hoped that he was the one to redeem Israel."

Then beginning with Moses and all the prophets, he interpreted to them the things about himself in all the scriptures" (Luke 24: 21, 27). Later when Jesus appeared to the disciples he "opened their minds to understand the [Old Testament] scriptures" (Luke 24: 21, 27, 45). They had expected a violent, political Messiah who would restore a free nation-state.

The final misunderstanding came before Jesus ascended. The disciples asked him, "Lord, is this the time when you will restore the kingdom to Israel?" (Acts 1:6) They still expected the restoration of the nation-state Israel. They didn't understand the nation-state as a decision of unfaithfulness to their calling or chosen-ness. Even after the death, resurrection and appearances, the disciples still didn't understand what kind of kingdom Jesus was establishing!

What is Salvation and How Does Jesus Bring It?

Jesus was executed by the Roman authorities during Passover in 33 CE. Surrounded by two others, he suffered a painful and humiliating death on a cross. But why? Most Christians would answer this question by saying that Jesus died for our sins (I Corinthians 15:3). But what does that mean and how does the death of one man somehow take care of our sins? And what does it mean to be saved?

Jesus is the continuation of God's solution to the sin problem. He doesn't represent some new strategy. God began working to solve the sin problem in the Old Testament by creating and shaping a People of God, made out of all peoples. This community understood themselves as chosen for a mission. That mission? To live as a counter-cultural community that nurtures shalom and draws others in. Jesus is the epitome of this solution.

Jesus is an extension of the Exodus-Sinai event, only much better. God cared about the physical oppression the slaves endured in Egypt and so

God, through Moses and the miracle of the plagues, rescued the slaves. God healed their broken relationship between themselves and the physical world, that is, their need for survival and a life free from bondage. Jesus also did something about the oppression and physical ailments he encountered. He healed the lame and the blind; he fed thousands. He challenged unjust systems of oppression. He brought an "exodus type" of deliverance or salvation.

But sin also breaks the relationship between humans and God and between us and our inner selves and other people. God cares about this spiritual bondage too. On Mt Sinai, the rescue from that bondage began as God gave the slaves the Eleven Words. Likewise, Jesus came to help us be freed from our guilt and shame. He forgave sins and helped people begin to love themselves. Jesus transformed all who would let him and those who trusted him to do this found the ability to forgive others and themselves and follow God out of heartfelt love and gratitude. Jesus brought, and still brings, this spiritual salvation.

Today, some followers of Jesus are tempted to see only the physical part of salvation. They emphasize how Jesus challenged injustice and worked to help the poor. They are right in that Jesus did these things and that salvation includes all of life and that it starts right now. Christians should do these things. But if this side of salvation is emphasized too much, then these Christians can become legalistic about doing good deeds or believe that Jesus will only love them if they "perform." They feel burned out trying to fight injustice and help people while depending solely on their own willpower.

Other followers of Jesus make the opposite mistake. In fact, this second mistake is so common that it has a name: forensic atonement. In this view, only the spiritual side of salvation matters. Jesus' death is the only important event in his life and what really matters is getting people to admit they are sinners and ask Jesus to forgive them of their sin. In this view, salvation is a future event for the most part; it is about getting to heaven after you die. Jesus' teachings and his life have little influence on how one should live. The only broken relationship that needs attention is our relationship with God. How one feels about oneself or others or even the physical world has little bearing.

But this view also falls short of the biblical vision of shalom and salvation. God not only wants to be reconciled to us through the forgiveness of sins, important as that is, but also to free us from the woundedness we

211

carry inside of us. God wants to change us so much that we can love the unloveable and have healthy bodies and a healthy physical earth. In biblical salvation, all the relationships that sin breaks get healing.

Christians use the word atonement as a way to capture the mystery of Jesus' death and why he died. The word comes from this configuration: at-one-ment, or the reality of being at one with God. The Bible honors this complex mystery by using many metaphors for atonement. In one metaphor, Jesus' death was like someone paying ransom money to set a slave free (I Peter 1:17-19, Matthew 20:26-28), in this case Jesus setting us free from our slavery to sin. Another metaphor is someone going before a judge on our behalf, and paying the "wages" for our sins (Romans 3:19-25). In substitutionary atonement, Jesus becomes the substitute (Galatians 3:13). In this symbol, Jesus is both the one who needs the "payment" and also the one who makes the "payment." All of these metaphors are called forensic atonement metaphors or theories. The word forensic brings up the image of a courtroom and judge. In all these metaphors, what really matters is that something clears the guilt of the person and "pays" for the sin. Jesus does this through the cross and then God is able to forgive people.

In the "Christ as the Victor" metaphor, Jesus fights with the evil powers and wins (Colossians 2:13-15). The decisive battle is the cross. He wins the battle by fighting with love. In this refusal to destroy evil by being evil and by countering hatred with love, he unmasks evil for what it truly is...terrible and ineffective. It is this final metaphor that probably best illustrates the biblical view of salvation. In all the other metaphors, sin gets "paid for" but it doesn't get defeated. In other words, God can now forgive humans because of what Jesus did on the cross but the real problem--the evil--still exists. Perhaps this illustration will help. A narrow view of salvation, like the forensic atonement views, would be like an alcoholic being forgiven of her drunken behavior. The people she hurts forgive every time she "falls off the wagon." This forgiveness is a wonderful gift, one that shouldn't be minimized. But she still gets drunk every weekend. In the "Christ as Victor" view, or the more biblical approach to salvation, not only does this person get forgiven, but she also receives the power to get sober. She is not only forgiven, but also restored and set free. All four of the broken relationships in her life find healing.

Biblical Salvation Works to Heal All the Broken Relationships

Forensic Atonement/Salvation	Biblical Atonement/Salvation
• The cross works for us.	• The cross works inside us, changing us.
• Forgiveness from sins is the most important thing.	• Forgiveness and restoration are both important.
• God is the one who needs to change.	• Humans are the ones who need to change.
• God is angry about our sins and now through Jesus can forgive us.	• God sent Jesus to the world out of love, not anger. (John 3:16)
• Only important relationship is the relationship with God. Ethics are optional.	• Salvation means a healing of all 4 relationships. We live differently (ethics) because we want to and have been changed in such a way that we can live differently.
• The optimal word is "saved."	• The optimal word is "healed."[2]

When we think about atonement, we must always remember that God sent Jesus to the world because of God's great love for us. "For God so loved the world that he gave his only son, so that everyone who believes in him may not perish but have eternal life." (John 3:16) We must also embrace the continuity of the biblical narrative. Genesis 1-11 shows us how sin breaks four major relationships and how we define sin determines how we define salvation. Jesus came to heal all those broken relationships. The chart below illustrates this well.

How does Jesus save us?
Jesus saves us through his birth, life, teachings, death, resurrection and Spirit.

Birth
By coming into the world to reveal God's love and forgiveness to humans, Jesus helps us accept God's love for us. That he was born to poor people helps break down unfair stereotypes and thus help heal our relationship with others.

---

2   Rob Bell. Lecture, Youth Specialties Conference, San Diego, Feb 15-16 2002.

Life

By re-revealing God's ways through his decisions and acts, Jes helps heal our relationship to others. Central to that is the community he nurtures, a community that loves indiscriminately.

Teachings

Jesus re-reveals God's ultimate will so humans may know how to live a faithful life that helps God's kingdom come on earth and by restoring the intent of the law and putting the law in its original serving place. This heals our relationship with our inner selves, with others and with God.

Healing Acts

Most people during the time of Jesus believed that disease meant you were a worse sinner than others. So when Jesus healed people, they were able to stop blaming themselves, which healed their broken relationship with their inner selves. Because the healings dwelt with physical bodies, Jesus was also healing the relationship between us and the physical world. His miracles were often connected with compassion for the marginalized, poor, and suffering, thus healing our relationship with others.

Death

Jesus died for our sins, healing our relationship with God. But it's more than that. By not fighting back and loving us to the end, Jesus reveals God's extreme steadfast love to humans in a way they can believe it, trust God and surrender "all of ourselves we know to all of God we understand." Had Jesus fought back at the end and saved himself, humans would not have trusted him. The way Jesus fought evil on the cross also teaches us how to fight evil.

Resurrection

Jesus heals our relationships with the physical world by defeating the biggest enemy of the physical world: death. Colossians 2:17 says Jesus also defeated Satan and the evil powers that had humans under their control. Death, the ultimate power, was exposed and defeated. It is not all powerful.

Spirit

The Spirit transforms our minds, hearts and wills, giving us the ability to live for God 's purpose and mission in the world and help God's kingdom come and will be done on earth as in heaven.

Introducing the Powers

Who killed Jesus? Physically, Roman soldiers killed him, but that's too simple. Many different religious, political, and social forces and powers collaborated to kill Jesus: Sadducees in the name of the Temple, Pharisees and Scribes in the name of piety and law, Zealots in the name of the nation-state, Judas in the name of effectiveness, and Pilate to preserve his office. Jesus undermined their control and authority.

The New Testament writers speak of evil as the "fallen powers." Powers refer to the capacity to make things happen. Organizations and institutions have invisible powers or systems within them. God created the powers as good. Humans need them to be human. But the powers deified themselves wanting to be God. Rather than serve, they want to dominate. Their weapon is their ability to fool people that they are all good and also all powerful. Humans cannot be human without the powers but are lost in their complex invisible webs. In fact people often don't realize how they are controlled. Jesus refers to this during his own execution when he says, "Father forgive them, they don't know what they are doing" (Luke 23:34).

When Jesus challenged the "fallen powers" of the various entities—law, Temple, Sanhedrin, position—they reacted and finally killed Jesus. The last straw was when Jesus challenged the Sadducees' lucrative control of the Temple tax and sacrifices that ripped off the poor. Nationalism, legalism, templeism, and traditionalism are among other fallen powers (isms) that killed Jesus. Had Jesus only preached an individualistic, pietistic, future salvation gospel, or merely about life after death, he would not have been a threat to any "power group." There would have been no reason to kill him. But when he established a group of followers with himself as the leader, and when he spoke against the unjust ways that certain powers were being used, Jesus challenged their leadership and control. The powers either had to submit to his leadership or get rid of Jesus, so they got rid of him. But they weren't expecting a resurrection!

Jesus healing the lame man in Mark 2:1-12 is one example. A lame man was brought to Jesus, lowered to him through a roof, so that Jesus could heal him. But the first thing Jesus did was say, "Son, your sins are forgiven." The scribes then "questioned in their hearts." Knowing their thoughts, Jesus challenged them by asking whether it was easier to forgive a man's sins or heal him from his paralysis. He then asked the man to walk and he did! We must ask why the scribes weren't happy about this miracle. They were caught in the grip of the "powers." They were threatened by Jesus because forgiveness of sins was only supposed to happen in the

Temple. But the lame man couldn't go to the Temple because he was lame and therefore unclean and because he probably didn't have enough money to pay the Temple tax. The Temple, originally meant as a good thing, had become a system that cared more about money and control than people being healed.[3]

Jesus deliberately healing on the Sabbath is another example. According to Sabbath law, healing a person on a Sabbath day was considered work and was therefore a sinful thing to do. It would seem that this law would be easy to abide by, for one only needs to wait until the next day to bring healing to the sick and lame. But Jesus publicly and purposefully heals sick people right in front of the religious leaders! Why would he do that, knowing this law-breaking would get him in trouble? Jesus saw that an institution originally set up to do good—the Law—had become more important in its own eyes self than the good it was created to do. The Law had gotten out of order. Sabbath was created so that people could find rest. A man suffering from a withered hand (Mark 3:1-6) surely needs a "rest" from this terrible disease. But when Jesus healed him, he sensed the anger from the Pharisees. He said, "Is it lawful to do good or to do harm on the Sabbath, to save life or to kill?" his response left them speechless, but they began planning for his demise. They were people caught up in the powers, letting a good thing like Sabbath become a law of bondage and pain.

From the powers' perspective, the salvation or atonement Jesus accomplished is a revelation that lets humans know God freely offers forgiveness and wants to restore the broken relationships. Like the Old Testament Exodus salvation event, Jesus delivers those who follow him from their slavery under the fallen powers to freedom!

God raised Jesus back to life after three days in the tomb. And even though Jesus told his disciples this would happen, they were still overcome with grief when he died and struggled to believe the good news when they heard it. In the resurrection God vindicated Jesus; God demonstrated categorically that Jesus did the right thing by loving humans to the end and not fighting back.

The resurrection also spelled the ultimate defeat of the powers. Since death is the ultimate "power" people fear most, the resurrection of Jesus is the ultimate defeat of the powers. The powers, including death, are now limited in their dominion over humans. The powers are not destroyed

---

3 William R. Herzog II, *Jesus, Justice and the Reign of God: A Ministry of Liberation* (Louisville, KY: Westminster John Knox Press, 2000), 126-131.

but disarmed so they can't fool humans into thinking they have the last word. Paul says, "Where, O death, is your victory? Where, O death, is your sting?" (I Corinthians 15:55). Salvation is not only about persons, but also putting the powers into their place.

Where does evil come from?

Some people would say that Satan or the devil is the source of evil. Others speak of the fallen powers. The Bible supports both views. Remember the story in Genesis 3, where evil came to Adam and Eve both from an outside source, the serpent, and also from their own inner desires? So too, there are personal demonic forces that Jesus and others fought in the biblical narrative and there is also evidence of the evil effect of the fallen powers.

What Does It All Mean?

Cleopas and his friend walked slowly down the road toward Emmaus. Their hearts were heavy. Their dearest friend, the one they believed to be Messiah—had been crucified. A stranger joined them, wanting to know what they were talking about. "Are you the only stranger in Jerusalem who doesn't know the things that have taken place there in these last days? Then they told him about Jesus and how they had "hoped he was the one to redeem Israel." Even more disconcerting, the women disciples were saying that Jesus was alive, and that angels had told them this news. The stranger started sharing Old Testament scriptures with them, showing them how "the Messiah must suffer and then enter into his glory." As they neared their village, they invited him to eat with them. The stranger took the bread, blessed and broke it and gave it to them. At that moment, their eyes were opened. The stranger was none other than...Jesus (Luke 24:13-35).

What does it all mean? Perhaps we are like Cleopas and his friend. We don't know what to make of the death or resurrection of Jesus. We struggle to make connections between the Old and New Testaments. We ponder the miracles and his interactions with so many different people. Is it possible to truly live out the teachings of the Sermon on the Mount? Can we become so transformed that we can love our enemies?

And are we like Cleopas and his friend in that we don't recognize him as he stands close to us? Are there misunderstandings about Jesus that we may yet have? What part does faith play and how does it interact with the importance of good study and deep questions? May we continue to seek out this risen one. May our hearts continue to "burn within us."

Pentecost and the Jerusalem Council

Bible passages: Acts 1-4, 9-10, 15; II Corinthians 5:16-21; Ephesians 2:11-22.

Jesus was killed on a Friday, raised to life on Sunday, spent forty days with his followers and then ascended into heaven. So, was that it? What happens next? The disciples felt unprepared, a little scared and at a loss for how to move on. What should be the next step? Jesus had told them to wait. It seemed like there was something more to be done, something more that was needed.

There was something more. God's solution to the sin problem had been accomplished, but now it needed to be fully realized. And that realization would come about through Pentecost and the Jerusalem Council.

The next big events in the biblical narrative, Pentecost and the Jerusalem Council, were really a continuation of the Jesus story, as the early church began to realize the implications of who Jesus was and what he taught. This connection is important for several reasons. First, Jesus promised to send the Holy Spirit after he ascended (Acts 1:8) and the promise was fulfilled at Pentecost. This marks the birth of the new People of God. Second, both Pentecost and the Jerusalem Council complete God's solution to the sin problem. It was not until these two events that the followers of Jesus fully understood that God was calling all people into this new community, both Jews and Gentiles, and that Gentiles were equal partners in this "new creation." Finally, the book of Acts continues the story, demonstrating how the early church lived out its call or mission.

Pentecost and the Jerusalem Council were also needed because the disciples (soon to be called apostles) still misunderstood the nature of God's kingdom. Before Jesus ascended, they continued to ask the wrong question, "Lord, is this the time when you will restore the kingdom to Israel?" (Acts 1:6). They were still thinking about the nation-state that Yahweh had smashed in Judah's fall and exile. Jesus didn't answer their question but said, "You will receive power [*dunamis* or *dynamite* in Greek] when the Holy Spirit has come upon you and you will be my witnesses...to the ends of the earth" (Acts 1:8).

The Holy Spirit

Acts 16:7 spells out explicitly what the rest of the Book of Acts implies, that the Holy Spirit is the Spirit of Jesus that works in the followers of Jesus. The Spirit worked with a few persons in the Old Testament, but the birthing of the New People of God at Pentecost ushered in a new time, where all believers would be filled with the Spirit. The coming of the Spirit is part of the Doctrine of the Trinity, which states that God the Father, God the Son and God the Spirit can function as separate entities but yet in a mystery, are truly one.

Pentecost Experience

The event recorded in Acts 2 is truly miraculous. It was Pentecost, the feast that occurred fifty days after Passover and celebrated the harvest given by God. One hundred twenty disciples were together and heard the sound of a violent wind in the house. "Tongues of fire" appeared and rested on each of them. "All of them were filled with the Holy Spirit and began to speak in other languages as the Spirit gave them ability" (Acts 2:4). Pilgrims from the Jewish Diaspora who had come to Jerusalem for the feast heard the disciples speaking in familiar languages. Through the open windows, they heard the 120 disciples speaking about Jesus and they were able to understand the story in their own tongue. It was a true miracle.

Pentecost echoes many key signs that occurred earlier in *Heilsgeschichte*. The different languages echo the Tower of Babel story, but now the judgment from this story is reversed! Where before in the Tower of Babel, speaking in tongues broke the community apart, now the same sign brings different people groups together. The lost relationships are restored. The wind and fire of Acts 2 are two other signs. They harken back to Yahweh's action in the Exodus to create the Old People of God. A strong wind dried up the sea for the people to pass through. The pillar of fire led them in

219

the wilderness. These signs point to the fact that Christ-Pentecost is the new Exodus, the creation of the Radical New People of God. And like the Exodus, they are bonded together by this common experience. God has chosen them through Jesus and now empowers them to be faithful to their calling to be the missional, covenant, shalom community that reveals God to the ends of the earth. They continue the mission of Jesus by the kind of community they are and what they say. This new People of God is called the church. It's also called the Body of Christ with the Holy Spirit as its life.

At Pentecost Peter preached a sermon where he connected Jesus to *Heilsgeschichte*. Three thousand Jews, many of them Diaspora pilgrims, believed in Jesus as Messiah and were baptized. Miracles followed with much worship and fellowship, celebrating Jesus and what God had done among them. The same fearful disciples who fled the Garden of Gethsemane when Jesus was arrested now spoke boldly about Jesus as the Messiah; they were willing to suffer persecution. Peter and John were called before the Sanhedrin and told to be quiet about Jesus. They responded with, "We can't keep from speaking about what we have seen and heard" (Acts 4:19). In a second appearance Peter said, "We must obey God rather than any human authority" (Act 5:29). The powers were humbly put into their rightful place.

One of the early Christians, Stephen, was arrested and stoned to death. Before being stoned to death, Stephen recited *Heilsgeschichte* and connected Jesus to the story, the "longest" covenant recital yet (Acts 7).

Diaspora Jews

The Persian Cyrus allowed the exiled Jews to return to their homeland. Only 25% of them did return, for a variety of reasons. Many of those who remained in Babylonia and others places, however, did return to Jerusalem for one or more of the annual festivals. Jews who didn't live in Judea were called Diaspora Jews.

Radical New Creation: The Solution is Realized

What is this radical new creation and how is it tied to God's solution to the sin problem? From the beginning, God has planned to heal the problem of sin through the creation of a People of God. This is a unique community; we've used words like missional, shalom and covenant to describe it. This community lives in such a different way that other people are attracted to it. They see a group of people who love everyone, even enemies, who share their possessions so that everyone has enough, a community who loves and obeys God in all they do, who live lives without the overwhelming burden of shame, a group of people who care for the physical earth and their own bodies. And this community is open to all people everywhere, anyone who is willing to follow God. This is a community of shalom, where all four of the relationships are in the process of being healed.

Unfortunately, the Old People of God quickly fell away from these high ideals, even though the prophets worked hard to bring them back to God's ultimate will. After hundreds of years of preparation and struggle, Jesus came to re-reveal God's ultimate will and bring both forgiveness of sins and the transformation needed for people to live free from sin, to live in shalom with each other and God. At Pentecost, the miraculous deliverance of Exodus-Sinai happened again. The Spirit descended and the New People of God were born.

Can Just Anyone Be a Part of this Radical New Creation?

The ethnocentric box established by Ezra still held sway over the early followers of Jesus. Even the disciples who had been with Jesus for three years believed only Jews could be part of this new community. But God called Abraham and Sarah for a mission, not as God's favorites. That mission was to be the vehicle through whom all families could be blessed (Genesis 12:3). God's intention was about to take a new and daring step forward. Anyone willing to follow Jesus as Lord could be part of this new People of God.

Several key events helped the early believers "get it." First, 3,000 Jews were baptized at Pentecost, many of them Diaspora Jews who came from a variety of countries. Second, Philip baptized an Ethiopian official who had come to the Pentecost Feast (Acts 8:26). Third, Philip then proclaimed Jesus as the Messiah to Samaritans, a people group held in suspicion by the Jews (Acts 8:4-25). Those who accepted the message also received the Holy Spirit. The long standing Jewish-Samaritan animosity was beginning to heal; that broken relationship was being restored! Now Jew and Samaritan ate together. Before, they wouldn't even greet each other!

The final example was possibly the most mind-blowing. The disciple Peter had a vision during his daily rooftop prayers. In this vision, a sheet came down from heaven full of all kinds of animals, both clean and unclean. A voice from heaven told Peter to rise, kill and eat. Peter resisted, saying, "By no means Lord; for I have never eaten anything that is profane or unclean" (Acts 10:14). Just then messengers from the Roman centurion Cornelius came to his door. Cornelius, a God-fearing Gentile, also had a vision where an angel prompted him to send for Peter. The pieces starting falling into place for Peter. Two Gentile men asking Peter to visit a Gentile military officer—these actions were unheard of for a faithful Jew. Peter remembered the words from heaven, "What God has made clean, you must not call profane" (Acts 10:15). Peter went with the men to Cornelius' house and told all gathered there about Jesus. He said, "I truly understand that God shows no partiality, but in every nation anyone who fears him and does what is right is acceptable to him" (Acts 10:34). Peter then baptized Cornelius and other Gentiles.

Peter continued preaching, "You know the message he sent to the people of Israel, preaching peace [shalom] by Jesus Christ; he is Lord of all" (Acts 10:35-36). While Peter was preaching, the Holy Spirit fell on all who heard. The Jewish believers who were with Peter were astonished that the gift of the Holy Spirit had been poured out "even on the Gentiles!" (Author's emphasis) Their choice of words revealed their ethnocentrism.

This event was the turning point for a new understanding of the makeup of the People of God. Just like in the Exodus event, where God created a people out of all the slaves who were willing to put blood on their doors, now with the combination of Pentecost and Samaritans and Gentiles becoming Christians, the same phenomenon was happening. This new People of God also was composed of a "mixed group." The new believers were finally realizing what God wanted all along—a People of God out of all people groups.

More Miracles: the Saul to Paul story

In Acts 9, we find another story that nurtures the new People of God. A Pharisee named Saul vehemently opposed these new followers of Jesus. Because Jesus had been hung on a tree (the crucifixion), he couldn't be Messiah for, as the scriptures said, "Everyone hung on a tree is cursed" (Deuteronomy 21:23). Saul gained permission from the authorities to kill every Jesus-follower he could find. But to his surprise, he was the one found by Jesus, who appeared to him on the road to Damascus in a vision. Saul had a 180 degree turnaround and, with the help of the believer Ananias, he became a Jesus follower himself. His name was changed to Paul and his passion changed as well. He became the first missionary, with a particular longing to help Gentiles hear about Jesus. At every new city where he'd go, he would begin talking about Jesus at the Jewish synagogue. If the Jews there would kick him out, and many times they did, he would go to the Gentiles with the same story. Paul's heart longed for every person to know the Jesus he encountered on the Damascus Road.

But the ethnocentrism ran deep. Many Jewish Christians questioned the idea of Gentile believers, even to the extent of opposing their full participation in the church. The early church faced its first real test. What should they do with Gentile believers? Should they exclude them completely, make them become Jews by asking the men to get circumcised and obey the food laws or accept the Gentile believers as equal brothers and sisters in the church?

The Jewish Christians met in Jerusalem in the year 49 CE to discuss the issue. Would there be an "old creation" or a "New Creation?" Peter, Paul and their friend Barnabas carried the day, retelling the story of Cornelis. The council decided there should be no distinction between Jew and Gentile believers. Jesus, and not ethnicity, will rule!

This is the culmination of everything! From the beginning, God had dreamed of a People out of all people groups. The decision at the Jerusalem Council to not put difficult stipulations on the Gentiles, essentially asking them to become Jewish, is a big step forward in having that dream fulfilled. Jesus—his life, teachings, death and resurrection—combined with Pentecost and the Jerusalem Council was the salvation event! The solution to the sin problem had been accomplished and was being realized! There was (and is) a new creation of Jews and Gentiles, equal partners in this new shalom community. The relationships between God, others, self and all creation had been and are still being restored. This is what Yahweh had been working to achieve throughout *Heilsgeschichte*!

The Radical New Creation in Paul's Writings
Paul writes in II Corinthians 5:16-17, "From now on, therefore, we regard no one from a human point of view...So if anyone is in Christ, there is a new creation: everything old has passed away; see, everything has become new! All this is from God who reconciled us to himself through Christ, and has given us the ministry of reconciliation ..." In the Greek manuscripts the pronoun after the word Christ is missing. It reads "if anyone is in Christ, new is creation." The translators have to supply the pronoun. The NIV translators chose the pronoun "he" making the individual the new creation. The RSV and NRSV translators chose the word "there" which

makes the new creation the church. This is in keeping with the "corporate thought" of the biblical world; when one is "in Christ," one is in a "new creation." In this context, that new creation is the combination of Jews and Gentiles, a radical new social order where Jesus rules.

The idea of an isolated, individual Christian is a notion of modern western individualism not found in the biblical world. In the biblical "new creation" there is neither Jew nor Gentile, male or female, slave or free (Galatians 3:27-29). This doesn't mean that one ceases to be a certain ethnic race or gender but that God doesn't favor one over the other. Nor does this mean that personal transformation is unbiblical or unimportant. Other passages in the New Testament refer to the individual being born again and transformed. So choosing "there" In II Corinthians 5:16-17 rather than "he" is not denying personal salvation. It is rightfully emphasizing the miracle of Jews and Gentiles, as equals, worshipping Jesus together.

Paul repeatedly describes this miraculous new social-political order as the church, the body of Christ.

> *But now in Christ Jesus you who were far off have been brought near by the blood of Christ. For he is our peace; in his flesh he has made both groups into one and has broken down the dividing wall, that is, the hostility between us....that he might create in himself one new humanity in place of the two, thus making peace, and might reconcile both groups. So he came and proclaimed peace to you who were far off* [Gentiles, Samaritans] *and peace to you who were near* [Jews] (Ephesians 2:13-17).

The dividing wall in the passage above refers to the wall in the outer court of the Temple that threatened death to anyone from any other "nation" or ethnic group that came beyond the wall! The wall read, "Let no one of any other nation come within the fence and barrier around the Holy Place. Whosoever will be taken doing so will himself be responsible for the fact that his death will ensue."[1]

In one sense, not only did Christ tear the curtain in the Temple (Matthew 27:51) but he also broke down the wall outside! Paul writes in Galatians 3:27-29 the same strong message:

---

1 William Barclay, *The Letters to the Galatians and Ephesians* (Lousiville: John Knox Press, 1958), 129.

As many of you as were baptized into Christ have clothed yourselves with Christ, there is no longer Jew or Greek, there is no longer slave or free, there is no longer male or female; for all of you are one in Christ Jesus and if you belong to Christ, then you are Abraham's offspring, heirs according to the promise."

The same thought is echoed in Colossians 3:11-12. "In that renewal there is no longer Greek and Jew, Circumcised and uncircumcised, Barbarian, Scythian, slave and free. But Christ is all and in all."

Again in Galatians 6:15 Paul writes, "Neither circumcision nor uncircumcision means anything; what counts is a new creation."

The Mystery is Now Revealed

Paul writes about the mystery that is now known to the followers in Ephesians 3:4-11. And what is this mystery? That God wanted the Gentiles to be part of the People of God all along.

...a reading of which will enable you to perceive my understanding of the mystery of Christ. In former generations this mystery was not made known to humankind, as it has now been revealed to his holy apostles and prophets by the Spirit: that is the Gentiles have become fellow heirs, members of the same body, and sharers in the promise in Christ Jesus through the gospel...and to make everyone see what is the plan of the mystery hidden for ages in God who created all things so that through the church the wisdom of God in its rich variety might now be made known to the rulers and authorities in accordance with the eternal purpose that he carried out in Christ Jesus our Lord (Ephesians 3:4-11).

Paul writes in a benediction in Romans 16:25-26 about the "mystery" of the radical new creation, this chosen, covenant, shalom community:

Now to God who is able to strengthen you according to my gospel and the proclamation of Jesus Christ, according to the revelation of the mystery that was kept secret for long ages but is now disclosed, and through the prophetic writings is made known to all the Gentiles, according to the command of the eternal God to bring about the obedience of faith to the wise God through Jesus Christ to whom be glory forever! Amen.

The mystery was hidden not because God wanted it hidden! The universality of the kingdom of God was hidden because the Old People of God were unfaithful to their chosen-ness to be the missional, covenant, shalom community to reveal Yahweh to all people through words and actions. Their unfaithfulness looked like this:

- They misinterpreted "chosen" to mean "favorite."
- They syncretized their religion with Baal worship rather than evangelize in Canaan.
- They changed nation to nation-state.
- They put two boundaries around Yahweh when they abandoned theocracy for monarchy, thus limiting God rather than revealing Yahweh to all peoples.
- By combining Yahweh and nation-state they made Yahweh into a national, one-country god.
- By combining Yahweh and geography, they limited Yahweh to a given geographic area.
- Ezra and the returning Jews put a new ethnic boundary around Yahweh.

This mystery, the creation of a People of God out of all peoples, was what God was trying to accomplish throughout *Heilsgeschichte* all along. This was and is the solution to the sin problem. And now through Jesus Christ, Pentecost and the Jerusalem Council, it finally happened. The Church was born.

That solution, the church, still continues today. We still proclaim that Jesus is Lord, just as the early church proclaimed in its worship. Paul wrote that the Kingdom has come, the Kingdom is coming and the Kingdom will come (Romans 5:1-11). The biblical writings come out of the dynamic relationship between a tenaciously engaged, faithful God and the sometimes faithful and unfaithful people. We who are Christians, however, must choose to be faithful to our calling. Are we setting up boxes that keep others out? Do we have our own "Gentiles" that we want to exclude? Have we made something else besides Jesus Lord, something like consumerism or nationalism? These are important questions to ponder.

226

History of the Church

The New People of God are born at Pentecost (Acts 2). The nature of the New People of God, called the church, is tested at the Jerusalem Conference in 49 CE (Acts 15). Would it continue to be the radical new creation (II Corinthians 5:17), where Jesus is Lord and Jews and Gentiles are united? Or would the New People of God limit people's access to God by drawing boundaries or boxes—ethnocentric, or nation-state, or geographical boxes?

The New People of God are first called "People of the Way," and later, "Christ-followers" or Christians." For the first 50 years, Christians are thought to be a sub-group of Judaism. On the Sabbath (Saturday), they meet in synagogues with Jews. On Sunday, they meet with fellow Christians for fellowship and worship. When Paul, the most dynamic missionary of the early church, enters a new city, he first meets with Jews and then with Gentiles. He baptizes all who are drawn to Jesus and the radical new creation—both Jews and Gentiles.

As long as they are considered Jewish, Christians are relatively safe. But soon they separate. When the Jews revolt against Rome, in 66 CE and the Romans destroy Jerusalem in 70 CE, the Christians are marginalized. In the 90s the gap between Christians and Jews widens. Their sacred writings also divide them. Jewish scholars meet in Jamnia near the Mediterranean coast in 90 CE to define their canon of scriptures, the Old Testament. When Paul and the disciples, now called apostles, write the story of Jesus and of the church, they create the Christian canon, the New Testament. By 100 CE the Christian church is largely Gentile.

But as the Christians come to be more distinct from Judaism, they become more vulnerable to Roman persecution as an illegal religion. Christians also risk alienation from their families and communities. Claiming Jesus as Lord had religious, social, economic implications. Nevertheless, the church grows rapidly and spreads from Jerusalem to Judea, Samaria, Galilee, Antioch, Egypt, and throughout the Roman Empire.

Persecution: The Blood of the Martyrs is the Seed of the Church

As the church spreads, challenges confront it from within and from without. From within, false teaching (heresy) confronts orthodoxy (right belief) and orthopraxy (right living), threatening the unity of the church. As the Old People of God faced syncretism with Baal worship and Hellenization, so too, the New People of God have to guard against the influence of false religions and alien cultures.

From the outside the church, Romans, and eventually Jews, are threatened by the growth of the church and target Christians as dangerous. But persecution, sporadic at first, strengthens the church and causes it to grow. In his *Apology for Christians*, Tertullian of Carthage, the brilliant defender of Christianity, taunts Roman authorities:

> *Crucify, torture, condemn, grind us all to powder if you can; your injustice is an illustrious proof of our innocence...But do your worst, and rack your inventions for tortures for Christians—it is all to no purpose: you do but attract the world, and make it fall the more in love with our religion; the more you mow us down, the thicker we rise; the Christian blood you spill is like the seed you sow, it springs from the earth again, and fructifies the more.*[1]

The Romans, by the favor of their gods, believe themselves to be the world's peacekeepers and saviors. Christians who pledge loyalty to Jesus alone, will surely anger the gods, and threaten the peace and prosperity of the empire. Treasonous Christians, "haters of the human race," are targeted.

Emperor Nero launches the first crusade against Christians in Rome in 64 CE. To incite fear and hate, Nero accuses them of setting fire to Rome.

---

1 Tertullian, Apology for the Christians. WM Reeve, AM. Trans. and Annotated. The Ancient & Modern Library of Theological Literature, vol. 31, 50, 143.

Sarcastically, Turtullian remarks, "Even if the sky does not move or the earth does [move], Christians are blamed!"[2] The brutal Emperor Domitian initiates the second persecution in 81 CE. He names himself "master and god" and demands an oath of loyalty from all citizens. They are to offer incense on a pagan altar and declare "Caesar is Lord." For Christians, only Jesus is Lord, so most refuse and many are imprisoned or executed. In 250 CE, Emperor Decius orders a vicious campaign against followers of Jesus.[3] In 303 and 304, Diocletian destroys church buildings, confiscates Christian books, and orders all Christians to worship pagan gods.

As Jesus died at the hands of the Romans, so did many of his followers. Polycarp, the aging bishop of Antioch, is burned at the stake. Perpetua and Felicity are executed in 203 CE. Origin, a prolific writer, died in 253 or 254 after refusing to acknowledge the divinity of Emperor Decius.

The joy and courage of many Christian witnesses (martyrs) at the point of death prompt many others to become Christian also.

For the first three centuries, Christians are eager evangelists and passionate pacifists. In addition to Tertullian, other Church Fathers like Origin, Polycarp, and Justin defend the Christian faith against such heresies as Gnosticism (knowledge as truth), Marcionism (rejection of the Old Testament), and Montanism (emotional expressions of ecstasy). Councils of leaders are convened to define truth from error, and to promote orthodoxy. They crystalize core theological concepts in short summaries or creeds, easy for people to understand and quote. The most well-known statement is the Apostles' Creed:

I believe in God, the Father Almighty,
creator of heaven and earth.
I believe in Jesus Christ, His only Son, our Lord:
who was conceived by the Holy Spirit,
born of the Virgin Mary;
suffered under Pontius Pilate,
was crucified, died and was buried;
he descended to the dead.
On the third day He rose again;
he ascended into heaven,

2   Ibid., 40, 2.

3   Innocent III on the emperor and the papacy, October 1198. Quoted in Tim Dowley, ed., *Introduction to the History of Christianity* (Minneapolis: Fortress Press, 2002), 264.

he is seated at the right hand of God the Father,
and he will come to judge the living and the dead.
I believe in the Holy Spirit,
the holy catholic church,
the communion of Saints,
the forgiveness of sins,
the resurrection of the body,
and the life everlasting. Amen.

As the church grows, it becomes more complex; organizational structures and hierarchy develop. Leadership is stratified and eventually, the pope, considered the successor to the Apostle Peter, emerges as the highest office.

Church and State, Cross and Sword

In 312 CE, Roman Emperor Constantine makes a dramatic turnaround. He is about to fight Maxentius, his rival for the Roman throne, when he reports having a vision. He sees in the sky a symbol of Jesus Christ and hears a voice, ordering him to use the symbol to conquer his enemy. He wins the battle under the banner of the Christian God. He defeats another rival, Licinius, and in 313 issues the Edict of Milan, ordering the toleration of Christians, thus ending persecution. The church and the state begin to merge and the cross and sword begin to fuse together. But, how does one rule an empire by the Sermon on the Mount? Does an empire forgive its enemies? Does an emperor turn the other cheek or go the second mile?

This ironic and destructive merger is complete when in 380 Emperor Theodosius declares Christianity the only legitimate religion of the empire. All other religions, including Roman pagan religions, are prohibited. The formerly persecuted Christians, become the persecutors! Now the sword of the state becomes the instrument of the church in its bloody ritual of discipline.

In the fusion of the cross and the sword and the marriage of church and state, faith is no longer voluntary, the teachings of Jesus are no longer normative, and servant leadership and nonviolence are lost. Armies are marched through rivers for baptism and the sword became the missionary arm of the church.

It is a convenient arrangement: the state protects the church with its sword, and the church blesses the state's military conquests. The emperor replaces Jesus as Lord. Since the empire can hardly be run by the ethics of Jesus, emperors turn to the monarchy of the Old Testament and the oppressive kingship models of Egypt, Assyria, Babylon, and Syrian Seleucids. The boxes of nation-state and geography are recreated. While some historians call this paradigm shift the "triumph of the church," others, Anabaptist-Mennonites among them, believe it to be the church's downfall. The radical new creation is no longer a welcome place for all ethnicities. The nonviolent church of the first 300 years becomes a nation-state that rules with the sword.

Two Levels of Christianity

Combining the church and the state meant that everyone who lived within a Christian territory, was automatically both a citizen and a Christian. Because commoners could not be expected to live the radical life of Jesus, a two-tiered system develops, one for common people and another for "holy people." Monks isolate themselves from the corrupting world of commoners, settle on the edge of the desert and engage in prayer, Bible reading and meditation. An outstanding example is Benedict, who about 540 CE, created a set of rules for prayer and work still followed today by the Catholic Benedictine Orders. Monasticism spreads throughout Europe and monasteries became centers of education, arts, and worship.

Church Fathers

Among the important leaders of the church after Constantine, are Jerome (345-420 CE), and Augustine (354-430). Jerome is born in northeast Italy, becomes the leading Bible scholar of his time. He produces the *Vulgate Bible*, translated from the original Hebrew and Greek into Latin.

Augustine, born in North Africa (now Algeria) in 354 CE, is baptized in 387 CE. He becomes the bishop of Hippo in 395. His many writings make him the father of Western Church doctrine. Because the church has become a servant of the state, it is suddenly necessary to justify violence. Augustine provides the rationale for state-sponsored violence and devises the criteria for the "just war" theory. He dies in 430, about the time when the Vandals, a tribe of European "barbarians" invade and destroy his city of Hippo.

The Fall of Rome and the Founding of Islam

Meanwhile, in 410 CE, Germanic tribes of northern Europe attack and destroy the city of Rome, the Western center of the Catholic Church. By 476, the Roman Empire falls marking the beginning of the Middle Ages or the medieval era in Western Europe that lasts until the 15th century.

An alternative religious tradition is developed in the Middle East. Mohammed (570-632 CE), founds Islam, the third faith tradition, along with Judaism and Christianity that claims Abraham as father. In later generations, Islam threatens European Christians. In 722 CE, in the battle of Tours, France, Christians defeat Muslims, thereby determining the religion of Europe.

The Church Splits and Abuses Power

Islam is not the only danger to Christianity. In 1054, disagreements over theology and practice split the church when the bishops of Rome and Constantinople, excommunicate each other. What had been two centers of the church become two churches, the Roman Catholic Church and the Eastern Orthodox Church. When the Western Roman Empire falls in 476 CE, the Eastern Byzantine Empire and the Eastern Orthodox Church centered in Constantinople thrive for another 1,000 years. After many attempts, the Ottoman Turks capture Constantinople in 1453, making it the center of Islam.[3]

During the European medieval era the church, once a persecuted minority, becomes wealthy and powerful. Popes and the emperors compete for control over the other. In an attempt to recreate the Western Empire, Pope Leo III demonstrates his supremacy by crowning the Frankish King Charlemagne emperor of the Holy Roman Empire in 800 CE.

Charlemagne chafes under the pope's domination until the king gains the upper hand. Still they compete. During the next 700 years, the church often wields the greater power, threatening excommunication as a weapon to keep rulers in line. This is effective in an era when it is believed there is no salvation outside the church. Pope Innocent III formulates the following analogy:

The Creator of the universe set up two great luminaries in the firmament of heaven; the greater light (the sun) to rule the day, the lesser light (the moon) to rule the night. In the same way . . . he appointed two great dignities; the greater (the church) to bear rule over souls, the lesser (the king) to bear rule over bodies . . . Furthermore, the moon derives her light from the sun, and is in truth inferior to the sun in both size and

press to spread reformation ideas. Luther, a German priest and university professor, sparks the Protestant Reformation, when in 1517 he posts his 95 Theses or complaints against the power of the pope and the Catholic Church. He targets the selling of indulgences—the practice of selling forgiveness of sins for self or others. Pope Leo X excommunicates Luther, whom he describes as "a bull in a vineyard" destroying all that is sacred. Luther cannot be stopped. While reading the Book of Romans, he has a serendipitous realization of God's grace that transforms his impression of God as angry and demanding. Grace becomes the primary theme of his teaching and preaching.

Luther's reformation succeeds in the German states, and eventually leads to the founding of the Lutheran Church in Germany and Scandinavia. For all of his radical teachings, the union of church and state does not change. The church is still territorial, either Catholic or Lutheran. So the religion of the territory's prince determines the faith of its citizens.

Ulrich Zwingli and the Swiss Reformation

Luther's reformation of the church in Germany leads to other reforms in Switzerland and England. The Reformed Church emerges in Switzerland, and the Anglican Church is born in England.

In Zurich, Switzerland, Ulrich Zwingli (1484-1531) is the reformer who preaches against the abuses of the Catholic Church and the power of the pope in Rome. His Biblical preaching and vision of a church free from the domination of Rome causes excitement and enthusiasm. Public debates spark conversations in the streets and taverns and destruction of images and other symbols of Catholicism.

Anabaptists

Among Zwingli's disciples are Conrad Grebel, Feliz Mantz, and George Blaurock. Their lives are transformed as they catch a vision of a church based on the teachings of Jesus. They become impatient, however, with the slow pace of reform and Zwingli's dependence on the city council for permission to make changes. They believe he is also retreating from his earlier, more radical teaching of a voluntary church free from state control.

The young radicals threaten the progress of Zwingli's reform, so the city council orders them to be quiet or be banished from the city or worse. What to do? The radicals gather in the house of Felix Mantz's mother to consider their response. In that meeting on the evening of January 21,

1525, they defy the city council by baptizing each other.

This simple act of baptism breaks the thousand-year tradition of church-state union. For the first time since Constantine, they will be a free church, free from the state. They will baptize only adults who choose to follow Jesus and they will follow the teaching of nonviolent Jesus. They are called Anabaptists, rebaptizers. In rejecting the state's control and its protection, they know they will suffer persecution. But that is the way of Jesus.

Persecution does, indeed, come from both Catholics and Protestants. Nevertheless, the Anabaptist movement spreads widely in Europe. In 1530 the Anabaptist movement reaches North Germany and the Netherlands, where in 1536 a Catholic Priest, named Menno Simons is re-baptized and joins the movement. He becomes the leader of the Anabaptists in the North and soon his followers are known as "Menists," Mennonists," and finally, "Mennonites." Eventually, the Swiss and South German Anabaptists, who call themselves Swiss Brethren, also take on the name Mennonite. And eventually, many migrate to other parts of the world including the American colonies, beginning in 1683. Today the fastest growing Anabaptist-Mennonite churches are in Africa, Asia, and Central and South America. These churches now outnumber white European and North American Mennonites. Other Anabaptist descendants are the Hutterites (formed in 1528), the Amish (formed in 1693), the Church of the Brethren (formed in 1708), and the Brethren in Christ (formed about 1780).

Other Faith Traditions

As of 2010, there were 2.2 billion Christians in the world. Islam was second with 1.6 billion adherents. But Islam is growing faster and the number of Muslims is expected to increase by 73% so that by 2050 Christians and Muslims will be about the same level. Hindus will number about 1.4 billion.[5]

The Roman Catholic Church is the largest church in the United States with 67 million members. Protestant denominations number over 200. The Southern Baptist Convention with 16 million is the largest Protestant Church. Though not a denomination, the total number of nondenominational or independent churches would total more than 12 million members.

---

5   Pew Research Center, Religion & Public Life, Accessed June 22, 2016. http://www. pewforum.org/2015/04/02/religious-projections-2010-2050/.

Today the total church membership reported in the 2012 *Yearbook of Churches* is over 145.5 million members, a decrease of 1.15% since 2-11.[6]

Current Challenges

The Christian Church in North America, is transitioning from the modern era to the postmodern, and from Christendom to post Christendom. It is challenged by the influence of an increasingly violent and secular society, by nationalism, militarism, individualism, materialism, and existentialism (only now matters), and civil religion.

We ask, what does it mean to follow Jesus? How will God's kingdom come on earth as it is in heaven? Will the church be the radical new creation, where Jesus is Lord and all are welcome? Will the church challenge injustice? Will the church welcome the immigrants, care for the marginalized, and the poor and disenfranchised? Will the church make any difference at all?

And the final question: Will you continue the story?

---

6   Fast Facts about American Religion, Hartford Institute for Religious Research, Hartford Seminary, Accessed June 22, 2016. http://hirr.hartsem.edu/

Gospel Genre

Bible Passages: Mark 1-6, Luke 6-14 and John 1-8

The Story of Jesus

For many Christians, the gospels are their favorite part of the Bible. They devour the miracle stories, where Jesus tames the Sea of Galilee or feeds 5,000 people with one child's lunch. They ponder the teachings of Jesus; his words ring true, with a beautiful mixture of seemingly impossible standards and grace. What's not to love about Jesus?

But in our enthusiasm for this genre, we tend to forget that this is a specific category of literature, with its own set of interpretation rules, and a specific audience and purpose in mind.

Gospel genre in the Bible can be complicated in that Jesus didn't write a gospel. Instead we have other authors, four of them, reflecting on Jesus and his teachings. And even when they share the same story or give the same teaching, each writer changes a few details. This seeming disparity can feel stressful to the young biblical scholar, but it can also be fertile ground for discovering how the early church wrestled with the individual they considered both God and human, Messiah Jesus.[1]

The Non-Canonical Gospels

The Christian Bible has been locked down as a piece of literature for over 1500 years. Every book, every story in the Bible, including the four

---

1   Gordon D. Fee and Douglas Stuart. *How to Read the Bible for all It's Worth.* Grand Rapids, MI: Zondervan, 2003, p. 128.

gospels, is considered by theologians to be "canon," or the established and agreed upon collection of sacred writings. But the books that appear in the Old and New Testament represent only a tiny fraction of the writings that exist from those periods of human history. The final selection of books that comprise both the Old and New Testaments are canon. They are part of the faith story. Other books written during these periods of history, even if they mention Yahweh or Jesus, are considered non-canonical—outside the canon. They are historically valuable, but they exist outside the faith story.

For a long time there was no Old or New Testament as we know them today. People disagreed with each other about which books were truly inspired by God and authoritative in their lives. Consensus regarding Old Testament books was established at the Council of Jamnia in 90 CE.[2] Three centuries later, in 397 CE, church leaders at the Council of Carthage decided which books went into the New Testament. But even now, Christians may use canons containing slightly different books, or with the books listed in a slightly different order.

History provides us with many non-canonical accounts of Jesus' life that, for various reasons, are not included in the Bible. The four gospels in the Bible—Matthew, Mark, Luke and John—are our canonical gospels. But there were other gospels written; we call these books the non-canonical gospels. So why were these gospels left out? In general, the ancient church leaders valued older manuscripts, possibly even written by eyewitnesses to Jesus, over the younger ones because the older books were closer to the actual life of Jesus. They wanted books whose theology meshed with the Old Testament; they worked to avoid gospels that seemed heretical (contained untrue doctrines) such as the gnostic gospels which deemphasized the humanity of Jesus. They also strove to include books that many different congregations found meaningful and useful.

---

2   Some scholars argue that the formation of the Old Testament was a much longer process and cannot be pinpointed to Jamnia in 90 CE. For example: "We used to assume that canonization took place in three successive stages corresponding to the three parts of the Hebrew canon [Law, Prophets, Writings]. In this theory, the Torah was formalized around 400 BCE, the Neviim-Prophets around 200 BCE, and the Ketuvim-Writings added to the collection at a rabbinic assembly or council held at the city of Jamnia (Jabneh) near the end of the first century CE. However, it seems unlikely the process of canonization was based on the authority of an assembly. More importantly, we have reason to believe that the books of the OT canon were considered authoritative scripture earlier than the dates of the three stages, and we are not even certain that the so-called Council of Jamnia actually took place." Bill T. Arnold, *Introduction to the Old Testament* (New York: Cambridge University Press, 2014), 21-22.

We must also ask the question: why four gospels instead of just one? The early Church leaders understood that Jesus was more complex than any one gospel could express. They valued the different "camera angles" the four canonical gospels offered. At the same time, these leaders believed that the four gospels shared enough of the same view of Jesus that they had integrity. The same Jesus was recognizable in each one.[3]

Some of the more famous noncanonical gospels include *The Gospel of Thomas*, the *Protevangelium of James*, the *Infancy Gospel of Thomas*, the *Gospel of Peter*, the *Gospel According to the Hebrews* and the *Gospel of Nicodemus*. Also called the Apocryphal Gospels, these writings give details about the life of Jesus that aren't included in the four Canonical Gospels. The Protevangelium of James, for example, tells the story of Mary's conception, birth and upbringing and then tells about the birth of Jesus. The Gospel of Thomas tells us more about the boyhood of Jesus, and pictures him doing many miracles even as a young boy.[4]

Characteristics of Gospel Genre

Bias—The word "gospel" means good news. It's derived from the Greek word *euangelion* which is also the origin of our words "evangelist" and "evangelism." The first four books of the New Testament—Matthew, Mark, Luke and John—call themselves gospels. The book of Mark begins in this way: "The beginning of the euangelion [good news] of Jesus Christ, the Son Of God." Interestingly, many Roman emperors proclaimed that their reign was good news or gospel as well.

It's obvious that Jesus didn't write the gospels. They were written *about* him by four different writers from the group of his original followers or people close to them. Yet neither are they "news reports" transcribed for video viewing. As the original apostles began to die, the early church realized that it needed to preserve the stories about Jesus and his teachings. These stories had been passed down through oral tradition by those "eye witnesses" of Jesus' life and ministry, and now they needed to be more permanently preserved for the next generations of Jesus' followers.

At first glance, it seems like the gospels are narratives. Gospel genre seeks to tell a story that "reads" as if it actually happened, just like our

---

3 Luke Timothy Johnson. *Living Jesus: Learning the Heart of the Gospel.* (San Francisco: Harpercollins Publishing, 1999), 119.

4 For more information, see "Canon," by F. F. Bruce, and "Gospels (Apocryphal)" by R. J. Bauckham in *Dictionary of Jesus and the Gospels,* edited by Joel B. Green, Scot McKnight and I Howard Marshall, (Downers Grove: InterVarsity Press), 1992.

favorite books or movies. But gospel genre is also different from narrative genre in that it contains more *Geschichte*. In other words, the gospels have a positive bias or view of the person whose story they are telling. The gospels want their readers to believe in and follow Jesus. And they are up front in this bias. John 20:30-31 says, "Now Jesus did many other signs in the presence of his disciples which are not written in this book. But these [stories] are written so that you may come to believe that Jesus is the Messiah, the Son of God, and that through believing you may have life in his name."

All of the gospels are narratives about Jesus, and they are more than just neutral retellings of what happened in Jesus' life. They have a unique concept of history in that they are more concerned with meaning than with exact times, dates and chronology. The gospels want you to follow this person called Jesus.

Inclusion of Other Genres—The gospels are not just stories about Jesus. They also contain teachings and sayings of Jesus. So the gospels are chock full of sermonettes, parables, catechism material, songs and allusions or echoes of Old Testament writings. Some of this material originated—was written—before the gospel itself. These documents with a previous life were originally created to help the church worship or teach new believers about Jesus. Some scholars specialize in form criticism, which is the study of literature that has an "earlier life" and then gets used in another document. Serious Bible study requires that one investigates all the *Sitz im Leben* of a piece of literature and gospel genre is no exception.

Highly Selective—Jesus did many more more things than what could be contained in a thousand books (see John 20:30-31). So readers of the gospels must ask, "So why did this story make it in, while others didn't?" For example, we have many stories of Jesus healing on the Sabbath and yet we can assume that Jesus healed people on other days as well. Realizing this, we start to ask about the special significance of Sabbath healings. The gospel writers made these choices on purpose and when we wrestle with why certain stories were included, we get closer to really understanding the story itself, and therefore, Jesus too.

Gospels do contain biographical information, but they are not intended to be biographies in the modern sense. Except for Jesus' birth and one incident from his childhood, we know nothing of him before he began his public ministry at about age 30. Other gospels, like the Gospel of Thomas, have more childhood stories of Jesus, but these gospels didn't make it into the canon.

Church Document—As L.W. Hurtado says, "The close association of the Gospels with early Christian worship and proclamation suggests that we should see them as church documents with a certain biographical character rather than as biographies with a religious tone."[5] The gospels writers wrote in the context of local congregations or gatherings of Jesus followers. They desired to preserve the story and teachings of Jesus in a clear, truthful way, and in doing so, strengthen their congregations. They also, at least on some level, had a desire to reach the world with their stories of Jesus. Jesus commanded his disciples to go and "make disciples of all nations" (Matthew 28:19). Therefore these early church communities saw their writings as part of this bigger vision as well. The writers hoped their literary works would be read by many and would influence many to become followers as well. The gospels are the "memoirs of the apostles" who wanted to strengthen the church through their writings.

Therefore, the gospels are written on two levels. One level is what Jesus said and did—a retelling of the historic Jesus. The second level is the retelling of the interpreted story (*Geschichte*) with a focus on the needs and concerns of the church to which the gospels was addressed. We call this the writer's context or *Sitz im Leben*, the latter being a German term used to denote the original social and cultural context of a particular Bible passage. Literally, it means "setting in life." When interpreting the gospels, we must take into account three of these settings in life: the original place and time of Jesus' life, the historical context of the gospel writer and his or her congregation, and the literary context of the gospel story.

Backward-Looking—The gospels were written from a resurrection point of view, as opposed to an on-the-spot report or diary. Many things the writers recorded wouldn't have been understood at the time they took place. However, at the time of the writing, these events were understood differently as the writers looked back through the astonishing event of the resurrection. Other post-crucifixion events also brought new meaning to the narrative of Jesus, such as Pentecost and the Jerusalem Council, but the surprise of the resurrection was clearly the biggest change. For example, the synoptic gospels take pains to show that the disciples didn't comprehend Jesus' words that he would suffer, die and then be raised back to life (Mark 8:31, 9:30-31, and 10:32-34). The original eyewitnesses were keen to note how they didn't "get it" because this misunderstanding was in such great contrast to post-resurrection, when they finally do understand.

---

5   L.W. Hurtado. "Gospel Genre," Ibid., 276.

One of the characteristics of Gospel genre is that it talks about the Kingdom of God. In general, "kingdom" is used to refer to a geographical territory that falls under the jurisdiction of a particular ruler or king in a country ruled by a monarchy. In contrast, the "Kingdom of God" in the New Testament refers to God's kingly rule or sovereignty. The Kingdom is not *where* but *when* God rules.

Principles of Interpretation

Given the characteristics above and remembering some general interpretation rules for narrative genre, here is a good list of rules of interpretation for gospel genre.

Remember the faith bias and purpose of the gospel writers. The gospels are clearly intended to bring about faith in the reader. It's helpful to remember that the gospels could have had a different emphasis. On one hand, they could have contained even more Geschichte and been written as strident apologetics or to defend a person or belief. The gospel writers could have also aimed at complete neutrality, just telling the facts as accurately as possible, but they didn't do that either. The gospels find a middle road, where they lovingly represent Jesus in an honest way that makes sense to their context.

Read the gospels as a whole. Just like almost every other kind of literature, one can "cut and paste" a certain sentence out of the gospels and, stripped of its literary context, make it say almost anything. We misinterpret the Bible when we don't see it in its full literary context. When Jesus tells the Syro-Phoenician woman in Matthew 15:24 that he came only for the lost sheep of Israel, we gulp at the seemingly rude, ethnocentric statement. Yet in the context of the whole story—particularly in the context of Matthew which includes God's love for foreigners at the beginning and the end of the story—this single statement of Jesus get its proper nuance.

Seek to understand the extra contexts of the gospels. Every Bible passage has two contexts: the historical-cultural context and the literary context. For gospel genre, we must endeavor to understand not only Jesus' time and place but also the setting in life of the church in which the gospel was written, as well as the writer's own *Sitz im Leben*. We must also pay attention to gospels that choose to tell the same story, sometimes even sharing almost identical wording (we call this the synoptic problem—see below). We can better understand a gospel passage if we check to see if the other gospels also include the same story or teaching, and if so, what major or minor changes occur in the storytelling. If the other gospels shorten the story or add details, if they change some details or give a slightly different emphasis, the reader/interpreter has "struck gold." We ask why this or that detail got left out? Why did Matthew insert this new paragraph? Why did Luke put this story in between these two events, instead of using the same chronological order as Mark? Reading with a critical eye and asking questions will always bear fruitful learnings.

The Synoptic Problem

The first three gospels are unique in that some of their passages are almost identical. If these gospels were written today in a college setting, the professor would probably accuse the writer of plagiarism. But using another person's writing without giving them credit wasn't seen in such a negative light in first-century Palestine. So it's likely that one gospel was written first and then the two other gospel writers used his manuscript to write their own gospel. Figuring out why the first three gospels are so similar, who wrote the first gospel, and how this changes our view of the gospels is called the synoptic problem. Synoptic means "same eyes" or "to view together." It's as if Matthew, Mark, and Luke saw through the same eyes when writing their gospels.

Many scholars believe that Mark wrote the first gospel. Why? First, almost all of Mark is found in both Matthew and Luke, and when Matthew and Luke agree with each other, they also agree with Mark. Both Matthew and Luke have extra material not found in Mark. So the logic goes like this: Mark must have been written first because if one of the longer gospels was written first and Mark used that, why didn't he include the other material? And the most logical reason to explain why Matthew and Luke agree so thoroughly with both each other and with Mark, is to conclude that they both used Mark as their primary source.

Matthew and Luke probably shared another source, which scholars call *Quelle* (source in German). *Quelle* contains many teachings of Jesus, including what we call the Sermon on the Mount found in Matthew chapters 5-7. Both Matthew and Luke use *Quelle*; Matthew puts most of Jesus' *Quelle* teachings in a concentrated form in chapters 5-7, and Luke scatters those teachings throughout his book. Both Matthew and Luke also have stories and teachings of Jesus that are unique to their gospels. We call Matthew's unique stories "M" and Luke's unique stories "L."

What About John?

John is an equally important gospel and holds an honored place in the canon. But John is not a synoptic. Even though the writer of John tells many of the same stories, he doesn't use the same words the synoptic gospels do. If he did have the same original source, he chose not to copy it in the same way the synoptic gospel writers did.

There are several striking differences between John and the synoptic gospels.

- A different day of the week for the Last Supper.
- A different day of the week for the crucifixion of Jesus.
- A different reason Jesus is killed. In the synoptics, the tipping point happens when Jesus clears the Temple. In John, the leaders decided to kill him after he raises Lazarus from the dead.
- The relationship between faith and physical healing. In the synoptics, the typical phrase is "Go, your faith has made you whole" (Luke 17:19). In John, typically the healing comes first as a sign of the coming of the Kingdom, which then results in faith (John 9).

It may be disconcerting to think that John has such different details than the synoptic gospels. But we must remember that these first-century writers didn't share the same burden we have for being historically accurate in every aspect. Most scholars believe that Jesus cleared out the temple at the end of his ministry, during his last week on earth. The writer of John probably knew this fact too, but because he wanted to portray Jesus as the New Temple, he took that historical event and placed it toward the beginning of his gospel. John was comfortable taking those liberties because this metaphor for Jesus was important to the overall message of his gospel.

There is a sense in which God's sovereign rule, while constant from the beginning of creation won't be realized in its fullness until the age to come. But there is also a sense in which the kingdom or rule of God does break into the present age in a new way in the life and teachings of Jesus. He brings the "here and now" of that which is "yet to come." Jesus begins the "now of the not yet." This "already"of the "not yet" kingdom reality was validated by Jesus' miracles, parables, the resurrection and the establishment of the church.

Snapshot of the Synoptic Gospels

Mark

- This is probably the first gospel written and may have been written as early as 65 CE.
- John Mark is the probable author, writing to a predominantly Jewish audience.
- This gospel is possibly based on Peter's preaching; there is an oral style to the writing.
- Mark writes of a Messianic secret. "Who is this man?" People see Jesus, but don't understand him.
- The disciples are portrayed as clueless
- There is sense of urgency. "Immediately" is a favorite word.
- Jesus brings in the Kingdom of God. He has power over nature and demons.
- There is no infancy material.
- Mark gives more space to the Galilean ministry and less to Jerusalem.

Luke

- This gospel was probably written shortly after 70 CE, by Luke, a physician and travelling companion of Paul's.
- He writes to a ethnically mixed audience of both Jews and Gentiles.
- He avoids overtly pointing out Old Testament prophecies, for the sake of his Gentile readers, and yet subtly gives more Old Testament allusions than any other gospel writer.
- He specifically addresses the book to Theophilus, a Greek name which means "Friend of God." This could be an actual person or it could refer to the type of person who should read the book.
- This gospel connects Jesus to the larger world history. The birth story is referenced to secular rulers; the genealogy goes back to Adam.
- This gospel emphasizes prayer, the Holy Spirit, women, and lifts up all marginalized groups.
- This is the gospel that most directly speaks to the dangers of wealth.
- Luke is called the social gospel; Jesus meets human needs and teaches about caring for the poor.
- This gospel seeks to refute the charge that Jesus and the church are political revolutionaries. Pilate declares Jesus innocent three times, Herod finds no grounds for judgment, and the Roman centurion says Jesus is an innocent man.

Matthew

- This gospel was written shortly after Jerusalem fell in 70 CE. It addresses a predominantly Jewish audience.
- The purpose is to show Jews that God's kingdom comes through Jesus.
- Jesus is emphasized as the Divine Teacher.
- Jesus is also pictured as the new Moses, a true Israelite who supersedes Moses. Like Moses, he comes out of Egypt, as shown in the infancy narrative.
- Matthew includes the Sermon on the Mount as a whole sermon, in chapters 5-7. This contrasts and connects the Old and new Testament teachings and serves as Jesus' inaugural address.
- Matthew's genealogy starts with Abraham and goes to Jesus, in contrast to Luke who starts with Jesus and goes back to Adam.
- Matthew emphasizes the Kingdom of heaven. There are 22 kingdom parables, more than the other gospels.
- Matthew uses a harsher tone against hypocrites and the Pharisees.

Conclusion

The gospels are a goldmine of rich information about the historical Jesus and the context in which he lived and taught. Gospel genre is complex, in that it contains other genres, such as parable genre and narrative, and yet it functions differently than narrative genre in that it contains more *Geschichte*. The gospels are up front about this their bias for Jesus; the gospel writers wanted to share what they believed to be very good news, the news of Jesus, the one they believed to be the Son of God.

Parable Genre

Bible passages: Matthew 13:1-50, 18:21-35, 20:1-16, 25:1-46, Luke 10:25-37, 20:9-18, 15:1-31

> *"Have you understood this?" They answered, "Yes." And he said to them, "Therefore every scribe who has been trained for the Kingdom of Heaven is like the master of a household who brings out of his treasure what is new and what is old"* (Matthew 13:51-52).

Try to imagine what it must have been like to have heard this very short story through the lips of Jesus, and to know that he wanted you, his audience, to take an important meaning from it. Maybe you would have been standing by the road, a part of the crowd, listening to Jesus teaching on a hot summer day. Maybe you would have heard it while sitting on the beach by the Sea of Galilee or in a busy marketplace. The writer of Matthew positions this story as the final parable of a series that begins by the seashore and ends up in a house. Does knowing the setting help us understand the story better?

Jesus told some of these tiny stories, or parables, to large groups. Other parables, including this one, he shared only with his disciples. Does his audience matter? Should we intuit some special meaning from this story because Jesus chose to share it with those closest to him?

Or, jumping ahead a couple thousand years to the present, can we use the surrounding verses of Matthew 13 to help us interpret these few lines? Can we understand why Matthew included this parable at all? What does the "Kingdom of Heaven" mean? Is it the same thing as the Kingdom of

God? And what does Jesus mean by the word "scribe," "master of a household," and old and new "treasure"? *What does this story mean?*

Welcome to the parables of Jesus.

What is a Parable?

Perhaps we can understand parables best by first understanding how they function. Jesus loved to use parables; there are over forty parables and related sayings recorded in the gospels. They are primary teaching moments for Jesus. We can define a parable as a story or saying with two levels of meaning.[1] Yet they are more than merely illustrations for an abstract concept; more than just symbolic vehicles to deliver a theological understanding. Parables are, in one sense, the message themselves. Jesus used parables to change how his audience perceived reality. In that sense, the parables created—and can still create—meaning. In that sense, the parables created, and can still create, a liminal space where we experience truth.

Parables tend to be short and to the point. They use characters, objects and settings from everyday life. The Greek word *parabole* has a broader meaning than the English word parable. The Greek word can describe a proverb, a riddle, a comparison, a contrast, or a story. Many times there is a shock value to the parables, a moment of surprise or a twist in the story, which usually happens close to the end. Finally, the parables call for a response. They demand a change or they invite the listener into a new reality.

Parables vs. Fables

A parable is different from a fable, which is another genre type where there is a storyline. Fables also work on two levels of meaning and also call for a response from its listeners, but unlike parables, fables contain elements that don't happen in real life. Donkeys talk (Numbers 22:22-39) and bushes and trees have a debate (Judges 9:8-15). The story as told couldn't happen in real life, while parables describe situations that actually could happen.

True Parables

There are several kinds of parables. While all the different short stories and sayings that Jesus used to create meaning are called parables, only the longer stories that contain traditional story elements like plot, character,

---

1 *Dictionary of Jesus and the Gospels,* Edited by Joel B. Green, Scot McKnight and I Howard Marshall (Downers Grove: InterVarsity Press, 1992), 594.

setting, and conflict are true parables. But unlike a narrative, which would also share those story elements, the point of a parable isn't the story itself. The point, rather, is the message. Some famous true parables include the parable of the Good Samaritan (Luke 10:25-37), the Prodigal Son (Luke 15:11-31) and the story of the wedding banquet (Luke 14:15-24).

Simile and Metaphor

Sometimes Jesus says things like, "The Kingdom of Heaven is like a mustard seed" (Matthew 13:31) or "You are the salt of the earth" (Matthew 5:13). These short sayings are called similes or metaphors. Jesus is not communicating to his audience that the Kingdom of God is exactly like a mustard seed, yeast, or a net thrown into the sea that catches fish of every kind (Matthew 13), but rather that each of these ordinary comparisons sheds new light on the nature of the kingdom.

Likewise, Christians aren't salty per se, but as we live out our lives in discipleship, our lives can be like the characteristics of salt. Christian disciples, like salt, can make the world more flavorful and can help preserve our world. Jesus uses these similes and metaphors to help his listeners encounter a new spiritual truth.

Interpreting Parables

Parables are difficult to interpret precisely because of their main purpose: to elicit a response from the audience. Culturally, we are very unlike Jesus' original audience, and so we struggle to respond to a parable in the same way they did. We don't get all the cultural references. We miss out on any nonverbal communication or social cues Jesus might have conveyed. We don't understand the historical-cultural background, the implied assumptions made by both Jesus and his listeners.

In many ways, a parable is a like a good joke. A good joke also has a double meaning and it's funny because the hearers of the joke both "get it" and they're surprised. If you have to explain a joke, it's not funny. Likewise, the original audience of Jesus' parables "got it." They automatically understood the context, and in that understanding, they could be jolted by the surprise twist that revealed their world to them in a new or unexpected way.

When we have to research and figure out the cultural and historical background of a parable—when it has be explained for us—we don't get the punchline right away. We struggle to feel the emotional impact of the parable, just as we would struggle to find humor in a joke written in Chinese or Farsi and then translated word-for-word into English. Jesus' parables don't automatically help us see ourselves or our world in a new way, because they were never meant to describe us to begin with.

Yet that doesn't mean that parables can't illuminate our culture or our current world. We just have to do some extra work first. Research into the cultural and historical background of a parable is essential if we want to truly understand it. Take the parable of the prodigal son (Luke 15:11-31), for example. It's easy for us to assume that we completely understand it because all cultures have troubled father-and-son relationships, self-righteousness, and greed. We all know of family situations where one sibling is more rebellious than the other.

What we might not understand is that in first-century Palestine, asking your father for your share of the inheritance is akin to telling him to drop dead.[2] The entire tone and meaning of the story change when we apply this single layer of nuance. And most parables are rife with cultural understandings that aren't immediately apparent to us as contemporary readers.

Complicating matters further, we must also consider that there are really two intended "audiences" for any Bible stories, both the original listeners who heard Jesus tell the story in person and the early church listeners, for whom the Biblical authors recorded their stories. Both of these audiences bring their unique cultural and historical backgrounds.

Therefore, as with all genres, it is essential to research the cultural and historical background of each parable and the background of the writers and their audience.

Literary Context

Like in other genres, the authors placed parables intentionally next to other passages to enhance their meaning. Three parables in Matthew 25 make this point. In the preceding chapter, Matthew relays Jesus' teaching about the future filled with persecution. After this time of suffering, he says, the Son of Man, Jesus, will come again. Then starting with Matthew 24:45 and running through chapter 25, Mathew gives three parables meant to encourage believers who anticipate these difficult end times. For example, in Matthew 24:45-51, the master comes back before the slaves

---

2   Kenneth E. Bailey, *Jesus through Middle Eastern Eyes: Cultural Studies in the Gospels* (Downers Grove, IL: IVP Academic, 2008), 281.

expect him. The point? Jesus may come back before you think he will and it's important to stay faithful.

Matthew 25:1-13 provides another parable about five wise bridesmaids and five foolish ones. The groom they so eagerly await comes later than they anticipate and the foolish ones are asleep. The message? Jesus may come later than you anticipate, so stay awake and be faithful.

The third parable of the Talents (pounds), Matthew 25:14-30, offers variation on the theme of being faithful and encourages disciples to take risks for the Kingdom of God. In this parable, the two persons who invest their talents are praised and the person who "plays it safe" is condemned. A good way to invest, Matthew continues in 25:31-46, is to care for the poor, hungry and those in prison. These are also good strategies for "staying awake" until his coming. Matthew's message to be faithful in the troublesome end times is all the more powerful given the positioning of these parables together.

It's also important to investigate how the other synoptic gospels treat the same parable. The changes that each writer chose as they reworked the parable can alter a parable's meaning or demonstrate how parables can have more than one meaning in a different context. The parable of of the Talents found in Matthew 25:14-30 can again be used to prove the point. In the literary context of Matthew 24 and 25, the parable's call to radical risk-taking for the sake of the kingdom is given in the context of the coming age when Jesus will return. The writer of Luke includes the same parable, but he puts it in a different context. "As they were listening to this, he went on to tell a parable, because he was near Jerusalem, and because they supposed that the Kingdom of God was to appear immediately" (Luke 19:11). Luke had just written about Jesus' encounter with Zacchaeus, where Jesus showed love to a hated tax collector and in response, Zaccheus gave half of his possessions to the poor and four times the amount of money to anyone he had defrauded. Zaccheus essentially gave away all his money, and in that context, the parable of the talents has a different feel. It still calls for risk-taking, using whatever resources are available for God's service, but the original readers see this risk-taking as a response to God's grace, like the example of Zacchaeus and as a call to keep risk-taking, given that the kingdom will not appear immediately.

Parables are Not Allegory

With the exceptions of Matthew 13:1-9 and 13:36-43, Jesus' parables should not be interpreted as complete allegories. An allegory is a story in which every character and most, if not all, of the details of the story represent something other than what they are. In other words, allegories are wholly symbolic stories with little meaning outside their densely coded symbolism. The danger of conflating parable and allegory is therefore apparent: we are prone to misinterpret what Jesus means with his parables if we try to force symbolic connections that Jesus didn't intend.

Throughout much of church history, people have made allegories out of Jesus' parables. Augustine's allegorizing of the parable of the Good Samaritan (Luke 10:25-37) is a case in point.

> *Just then a lawyer stood up to test Jesus. "Teacher," he said, "what must I do to inherit eternal life?" He said to him, "What is written in the law? What do you read there?" He answered, "You shall love the Lord your God with all your heart, and with all your soul, and with all your strength, and with all your mind; and your neighbour as yourself." And he said to him, "You have given the right answer; do this, and you will live."*
>
> *But wanting to justify himself, he asked Jesus, "And who is my neighbour?" Jesus replied, "A man was going down from Jerusalem to Jericho, and fell into the hands of robbers, who stripped him, beat him, and went away, leaving him half dead. Now by chance a priest was going down that road; and when he saw him, he passed by on the other side. So likewise a Levite, when he came to the place and saw him, passed by on the other side. But a Samaritan while travelling came near him; and when he saw him, he was moved with pity. He went to him and bandaged his wounds, having poured oil and wine on them. Then he put him on his own animal, brought him to an inn, and took care of him. The next day he took out two denarii, gave them to the innkeeper, and said, "Take care of him; and when I come back, I will repay you whatever more you spend." Which of these three, do you think, was a neighbour to the man who fell into the hands of the robbers?" He said, "The one who showed him mercy." Jesus said to him, "Go and do likewise."*

Many scholars now believe that this church father misinterpreted the parable.[3] Here is how he changed the ordinary people and objects in the parable and made them into spiritual concepts:

- The man who went down from Jerusalem to Jericho = Adam
- Jerusalem = the heavenly city of blessedness from which Adam fell
- Jericho = the moon, and thereby signifies Adam's mortality
- Thieves = the devil and his angels
- Stripped him = took away his immortality
- Half dead = fallen humans are half alive and half dead spiritually
- Priest and Levite = the priesthood and the ministry of the Old Testament
- Good Samaritan = Guardian; therefore, Christ himself
- Bandaged his wounds = binding the restraint of sin
- Oil = comfort of good hope[4]
- Wine = exhortation to work with a fervent spirit
- Donkey that bears the wounded man = Christ's body
- Inn = church
- The next day = after the resurrection
- Two silver coins = promise of this life and the life to come
- Innkeeper = Apostle Paul

This way of interpreting the Good Samaritan parable suggests a meaning that could not have been Jesus' original intention. At the time Jesus shared this parable, there was no church and Paul was not yet a believer. It seems clear that Jesus is saying something about what it means to love our neighbor, which is the question from the lawyer that prompts this parable (Luke 10:29). Augustine's allegory doesn't come close to answering that question. He is also making a clear challenge to ethnocentrism; a Samaritan is the hero.

We can also use allegory to avoid responding to the call of discipleship Jesus makes in his parables, to avoid "carrying our crosses" and following Jesus in ways that might lead to suffering. "For many centuries, allegory reigned supreme as a method of interpretation, and the fatted calf in the parable of the prodigal son became a symbol for Christ because the calf was

---

3 Fee and Stuart. *How to Read the Bible for all Its Worth* (Grand Rapids: Zondervan Publishing, 2003), 150.

4 Augustine, *Quaestiones/ Evangeliorum//, II, 19* –slightly abridged as cited in Dodd, C.H., *The Parables of the Kingdom* (New York: Scribners, 1961), 1-2.

killed. Through allegory, interpreters were able to locate their favorite ideas almost anywhere, and confusion and finally meaninglessness conquered."[5]

On the other hand, some parables do have certain allegorical elements. After all, parables are extended metaphors; they obviously can and should be seen as stories with two levels of meaning. But we must be able to distinguish between certain elements of a story that have symbolic meaning without making the entire parable into a code for an abstract doctrine. The context is important.

The parable of the creditor with two debtors in Luke 7:41-42 is a good example.

A certain creditor had two debtors; one owed five hundred denarii, and the other fifty. When they could not pay, he canceled the debts for both of them. Now which of them will love him more?

Knowing the context for the parable helps us understand it. Luke 7:36-50 tells the story of Simon the Pharisee who invites Jesus to a meal. A woman from the village known as a "sinner" approaches Jesus with a bottle of expensive perfume. Weeping, she kneels before his feet and washes them with her tears and her hair. Simon remarks to himself that if Jesus were any kind of a real prophet, he would know what kind of woman she is and put a stop to this behavior. So Jesus gives Simon this three-sentence parable. The story makes it clear that Jesus isn't really talking about a debt of money here; he is referring to a "debt" of sin. The sinful woman loves Jesus more, having been forgiven more. And in his self-righteousness, Simon fails to realize he is just as much a sinner as she is.

True, at other times Jesus uses the word "debt" to talk about about money; one of his major themes is economic justice. But the context of this parable helps the reader see that "debt" takes on a different meaning for this particular story.

Different Points of the Parable

In the story of Simon and the sinful woman in Luke 7, the two points of reference, Simon and the woman, would have each heard something different from the parable Jesus told in their midst. And they both would have been right. The woman would have heard a loving affirmation while Simon would have felt Jesus' judgment, and this was all from the same parable.

---

5   Ibid., Bailey, 282.

This is true for most of the parables. Depending upon their social location or life background, the original audiences of Jesus' parables would have felt either comforted or confronted. Going back to the parable of the prodigal son mentioned above, it is easy to assume that the only message of this parable is the reality of God's unconditional love, as shown through the father who forgave his wayward son. But Jesus, in his original setting had to help his fellow Jews accept the reality of God's open-arms love for the Gentiles. The Jews would have related well to the older brother; like him, they had worked hard at keeping the faith. They were tempted to resent the Gentiles, the younger sons, who got to come home and receive God's blessing.

The Twist Ending

So many parables include a surprise ending that biblical scholars created a term for the study of parable endings: the rule of end stress.[6] Some well-known examples of these surprise endings include the parable of the laborers in the vineyard found in Matthew 20:1-16 and the parable of the great dinner in Luke 14:15-24. In the parable of the laborers in the vineyard, the workers who only worked an hour got the same wage as those who had worked all day—surprise! In the parable of the great dinner, the first people invited to the dinner all had excuses not to attend and so—surprise!—the host invites people who never got such invitations, the poor, crippled, blind and lame. Both of these shocking twists would have produced deep (and rarely positive) emotional responses from the Jesus' contemporary Jewish audience, many of whom understood themselves to be the legitimate and sole heirs to God's grace.

Even if a parable doesn't have a surprise ending, many times an important point is made at the end, so it is still essential to study the endings of parables for clues to their interpretation.

Interpretation Based on Jesus' Life and Teaching

Jesus' parables can be difficult to interpret because they are at least partially symbolic. Jesus is creating meaning through a comparison of one thing to another, and it can be easy to misinterpret that comparison, particularly if we only view the parables through the lens of our own personal belief system à la Augustine's interpretation of the good Samaritan. We must see the allegorical elements in a parable without completely allegoriz-

---

6 *Dictionary of Jesus and the Gospels*, 594.

ing the parable itself. In other words, we must realize that Jesus is speaking on two levels of meaning, but we can't make those metaphors mean something that Jesus never intended.

The most reliable way to do that is to compare our own interpretations to all of the other teachings of Jesus. After all, Jesus did not exist or teach in a vacuum. We should always be asking whether our interpretations support or sabotage what Jesus said elsewhere. If an interpretation is at odds with the rest of Jesus' message, or if includes elements that would have made no sense to the original audience, then we know we've missed the mark, and we should continue searching for a better, more consistent interpretation.

Conclusion

The parables of Jesus are serious theology. They teach truth and create meaning in ways that reason alone can't accomplish. They strike deeply into our emotions. The characters and plots, the surprise endings, open up our minds in new pathways to the identity of God and how we are to respond. Parables call us to action; they demand a response. For all of these reasons, it's important to read them and take great care in interpreting them. They are the treasures.

The author of Matthew knew the power of parables, how they can help us experience truth in a new way. So he carefully crafted chapter 13, using seven parables in a row. Then as a crowning point of the chapter, he ended with these words, "Have you understood this?" They answered, "Yes." And he said to them, "Therefore every scribe who has been trained for the Kingdom of Heaven is like the master of a household who brings out of his treasure what is new and what is old." Matthew 13:51-52 As we do careful study of parables, we too can be like a master of a household, bringing to others sacred truth, the rich treasure of the parables of Jesus.

Epistle Genre

Bible passages: Romans 1:1-15, I Corinthians 1-9, Galatians 1:1-3, Philippians 1-4

Most of us have written letters. On some level, even a short email or text could be construed as a letter. Letters are important ways to communicate and like other genres, they have a special purpose, specific characteristics and certain interpretation rules to follow lest we misinterpret their meaning. The Bible is chock full of letters: this genre takes up a fourth of the New Testament. Of the twenty-seven books of the New Testament, twenty-one are cast in the form of letters, almost half of which are written by the Apostle Paul. And like our own desire to be understood, so too these letters deserve our real effort to interpret them well.

The Apostle Paul

A man named Paul wrote most of the letters of the New Testament. Understanding his story is key to understanding what he wrote, so before plunging into another genre study, let's ponder his life.

Paul had the rare opportunity to understand two very different worlds. He was born into a deeply religious ethnic Jewish family; he loved and followed the Old Testament scriptures. We know from Acts 22:3 that Paul studied under Gamaliel, the most renowned rabbi of his day in Jerusalem. But he also knew the Greek world. He grew up and was educated in Tarsus in Cilicia, which was a Hellenistic Roman city, only surpassed by Athens and Alexandria. His Jewish teaching made him well-versed in the Old Testament Scriptures and his Greek training made him fluent in rhetoric and

258

written communication and able to understand Hellenistic culture. He truly thrived in two very different worlds.

Paul was originally named Saul. His Jewish background led him to a career as a teacher of the law, a Pharisee among Pharisees. As such, he hated the followers of Jesus. Saul believed that he was obeying God by doing everything he could to stop The Way, this new movement of misguided people who thought that Jesus was Messah. In Saul's his mind, this Jesus couldn't be Messiah because he didn't observe Torah laws correctly, he didn't get rid of the Roman problem and most of all, he was executed in the most humiliating way, by death on a Roman cross. The scriptures were clear that anyone hung on a tree was cursed (Deuteronomy 21:22-23). Saul was granted the authority from the high priest to find and bring bound to Jerusalem anyone from Damascus who belonged to this dangerous group. [1]

But on his way to Damascus to persecute Christians, something miraculous happened. Saul encountered the risen Jesus Christ (Acts 9:1-25). With a blinding light, Jesus came to him on the road to Damascus saying, "Saul, Saul, why do you persecute me?" Struck blind, Saul asked, "Who are you Lord?" Jesus replied, "I am Jesus, whom you are persecuting." Saul's life made a complete turn-around. He went to the house of Ananias, a follower of Jesus, who had also received a vision about Saul in which he was told to visit this man even though Saul was looking to persecute him. Ananias obeyed, told Saul about Jesus and Saul became a follower of Jesus. Saul was given a new name—Paul. Like Jacob in the Old Testament who was given the new name of Israel after he wrestled with God, this new name symbolized a new identity, a new beginning. God healed his eyes through Ananias and his spiritual eyes were opened too.

Everything changed for Paul. First, his understanding of Jesus changed. Once he understood Jesus as Messiah, his understanding of salvation history changed and thus also his loyalty and behavior. He went from persecuting the church to becoming a missionary for the church, a missionary with a special calling to help Gentiles become part of the People of God.

Paul travelled to many places telling anyone who would listen about Jesus. He always started in the Jewish synagogues, but once he got kicked out of those, which was the typical reaction of his fellow Jews, he took to the marketplaces and other public venues. He started many small house churches, and not able to stay with them for a long time because of his calling to evangelize in other places, he wrote letters to these congregations

---

1 Jacob W. Elias, *Remember the Future: The Pastoral Theology of Paul the Apostle* (Scottdale, PA: Herald Press, 2006), 42-43.

with encouragement and theological teaching. Again, his immersion in both the Old Testament scriptures and in a Hellenistic culture served him well. Most of the letters in the New Testament come from Paul.

Paul's letters are a great gift to us today. Even though he was writing to specific congregations set in cultural contexts much different from our own, his words enrich our own theological understandings. Four themes stand out. Paul wrote about the complexities of who Jesus is and how one follows Jesus. We call this study Christology. This theme is particularly rich in the books of Ephesians, Philippians and Colossians. Another theme is Soteriology, or the study of salvation. This theme is highlighted in the books of Romans, Galatians and I and II Corinthians. The study of the doctrine of the church, found most clearly in the books of I and II Timothy and Titus is called Ecclesiology. Finally Paul wrote about the end of the ages and the second coming of Christ in the books of I and II Thessalonians and we call this study of the end times Eschatology.

Characteristics of Epistle Genre

While there are many letters in the New Testament, there isn't a genre called letter genre. Instead scholars use the name epistle genre. An epistle is an artistic literary form that copies the elements of a true letter, but is intended more as a communication for the general public. An epistle, then, is a sermon or homily dressed up like a letter. A letter, on the other hand, is a piece of writing not originally intended for public use but intended only for the person or persons to whom it is addressed.[2]

Paul's letters are true letters; he wrote primarily if not exclusively for a specific audience in a historical and geographical context. He wasn't sitting with quill in hand, thinking, "Now I wonder what people in the early 21st Century will think of these ideas?" That is not to say Paul's letters can't have any meaning for us, for they have much to offer. But it does mean that we must remember the primary audience.

While Paul's writings are true letters, there are true epistles in the New Testament as well. II Peter, I John and Hebrews are some examples Paul's book called Romans reads the most like an epistle. This may be because Paul didn't visit the church in Rome and therefore needed to write something less personal and more "sermon-like."[3] It is important to note that

---

2   Gordan D. Fee and Douglas Stuart, *How to Read the Bible for All Its Worth* (Grand Rapids: Zondervan Publishing, 2003), 594.

3   Ibid., 56.

some of what are considered epistles in the New Testament actually come closer to being sermons. Hebrews is thought to be a homily on Psalm 110. James seems to be more like a collection of sermon notes on a variety of ethical topics.

A Question of Authorship

Are all of the writings attributed to Paul actually written by Paul? Scholars disagree about whether or not Paul actually wrote all the books that claim him as the author. This may seem strange to our modern ears that there would be any question as to Paul's authorship. Why would the real author lie about such a thing? But the ancient Middle Eastern world had a different worldview about authorship. Sometimes the real author would give credit to someone else for writing the book as a way to honor that person. In this worldview that was not considered a lie, but rather a way to show respect or communicate the inspiration behind the writing. Given this practice, it might be that some of the letters claiming Paul as author were written by someone else. For example, scholars have noticed a different writing style in Ephesians than in I and II Corinthians. Did Paul take on a new literary voice or did someone write Ephesians in Paul's name? The following chart illustrates the possible ways one could understand authorship for the Pauline epistles.

Epistles most likely written by Paul	Epistles possibly written by Paul	Epistles written by other authors
Romans	Ephesians*	Hebrews
I and II Corinthians	Colossians*	James
Galatians	Titus	I and II Peter
Philippians	I and II Timothy	I, II and III John
I and II Thessalonians		Jude
Philemon		

*Many scholars believe Paul did write Ephesians and Colossians, but there are some who question his authorship.[4]

All of the books in the chart above are called epistles, whether they are true letters or not. Despite this one major difference, letters and epistles share many common characteristics and call for the same interpretation rules. So what are those characteristics?

---

4 Jerry L. Sumney, *The Bible: An Introduction* (Minneapolis: Fortress Press, 2010), 335.

Prescriptive: One of the ways we can categorize literature is to see it as prescriptive or descriptive. Prescriptive writing refers to pieces of literature that seek directly to tell its readers what to do or believe. Like a prescription for medicine that a doctor writes out for a pharmacist, these passages give specific directions for behavior, morals and doctrine. Therefore the message for the original audience is stated explicitly. Epistle genre is highly prescriptive.

Unique Literary Form: Letters written during the time of Jesus and Paul followed a strict literary pattern. Every letter began with a formal greeting and continued with particular elements that followed in a particular order. Whether the letter was from Paul to a congregation or from a Roman official to his subjects or from a husband to a wife; almost all letters flowed in the same way.

1. Name of the writer
2. Name of the recipient
3. Greeting
4. prayer wish or thanksgiving
5. Body of the letter
6. Final greeting and farewell[5]

"Occasional Documents": Letters arise out of and in response to a specific occasion. There's always a previous story underneath the message of the letter. And because the epistle writer wasn't thinking primarily of who might read his or her letter in the future, the writer doesn't write about everything that's going on. The letter's recipients know all the background details and so they don't need the backstory. So at times modern readers have the answers but we aren't one hundred percent sure what the questions were, kind of like hearing only one side of a telephone conversation.

Amanuensis: In several of our biblical epistles, it's clear that the real writer, Paul, had someone else do the actual writing for him. An amanuensis is a professional secretary or letter writer. Such a trained amanuensis made use of a system of Greek shorthand while Paul dictated the letter he wanted to send, and would then have to transcribe what was dictated into ordinary Greek script. Paul often wrote his closing comments and final greeting with his own hand (I Corinthians 16:21, Colossians 4:18, II Thessalonians 3:17). Some of the differences in vocabulary and style that

---

5   Ibid., Fee and Stuart, 56.

have been picked up between some of Paul's letters leave us to wonder how closely Paul proofread the work of the amanuensis he employed.[6]

Principles of Interpretation

In all our inductive study and genre work, our goal is to find the meaning for the original audience. We can't make a passage of scripture mean something to us that it couldn't have meant to the original listeners.[7] Epistles are no exception. They have specific and important interpretation rules to follow so we can avoid misinterpreting the text.

As with every genre, it is our duty as modern readers to cross the hermeneutical bridge into the time and culture of the letter. We must remember that these epistles are first-century documents. They were written for a variety of different congregations scattered throughout Asia and Asia Minor. They sought to communicate truth to people who had different understandings on such important things as what makes up a household, who can and cannot speak, what should be worn on one's head, and what should and shouldn't be eaten.

The book of I Corinthians can give us a good illustration of the importance of crossing that bridge. Paul was writing to a church which contained some Christians from a Hellenistic background. Influenced by their Greek culture, these Christians were particularly disgusted by the idea of a body being raised from the dead. Given their worldview on the importance—or rather the non-importance—of the physical world, the thought of a dead corpse coming back to life and walking around repulsed them. So the resurrection of Jesus was foolishness to them (I Corinthians 1-3). And the practice of Christian men using prostitutes didn't seem that wrong, given their belief that the human body was unredeemable anyway and so what they did sexually had little ethical import (I Corinthians 6).

Paul understood their worldview and yet, as a Jew, didn't share some of those beliefs. He had to reinterpret the story of Jesus for them and he had to do it in a way that made sense to them. Modern readers of this book will understand the theology of I Corinthians more accurately if they understand these competing worldviews.

---

6   Sean A. Adams, "The Relationships of Paul and Luke: Luke, Paul's Letters and the 'We' Passages of Acts," in *Paul and His Social Relations*, ed. Stanley Porter and Christopher Land (Leiden: Brill, 2013), 128. For a dissenting view, see Aida Besancon Spencer, *Paul's Literary Style* (Lanham, MD: University Press, 1998), 59.

7   Ibid., Stuart and Fee, 30, 74.

Derivations in Literary Form

Since ancient letters followed a strict literary pattern, it's important to notice when the writer chose not to follow that pattern. The deviation itself may be a clue to the meaning of the passage. Occasionally Paul did deviate from the standard letter form. One example would be his letter to the Galatian church, a letter that contains no words of thanksgiving. Because this deviation, or any change in the literary form of a letter, would seem odd if not outright rude, we have to ask why Paul chose not to include a thanksgiving section to his letter. Even if the answer seems obvious—that Paul was mad at this congregation—it's wise to notice, do research and ask questions.

Reading the Whole Epistle in One Sitting

Can you imagine receiving a letter and not reading the whole thing at once or just reading the last page? You would never spend time trying to interpret or go over one paragraph again and again without a feel for the whole letter, nor would you feel like you knew what the letter was saying without a sense of it as a whole. So it is with these sacred letters. We honor them and get closer to the original meaning of the text when we read the whole epistle and work to interpret the specific messages from certain parts in light of the whole document.

An example of a passage that sometimes gets pulled out of its literary context is Ephesians 2:8-10. Many Christians have memorized these two verses with taking a serious look at the third.

For by grace you have been saved through faith, and this is not your own doing; it is the gift of God—not the result of works, so that no one may boast (Ephesians 2:8-9).

These beautiful verses carry a profound message of God's grace and a caution to not try to earn our salvation through good deeds done through our own strength. Yet without verse 10, we may misunderstand Paul and believe that what we do—our ethics—have no importance at all. Verse 10 adds, "For we are what he has made us, created in Christ Jesus for good works, which God prepared beforehand to be our way of life." It's important not to pull individual verses out of context. Another way to understand this concept is to digest passages in paragraphs instead of in verses, and to respect the letter's natural and logical divisions. Most Pauline epistles have a clear division between the doctrinal part of the letter, which usually takes about the first half, and the practical exhortations, which come in the second half.

The Writer's Cultural and Contextual Moment in History

Since epistles are occasional documents and have a story "underneath" them, we need to do as much as we can to reconstruct that story. We study the historical and cultural backgrounds. We note who the recipients were and what we are told about them. We list and research any specifics mentioned such as the occasion for the letter or plans for the future. Paul's tone and attitude often speak as loudly as his words. Sometimes he is gentle and patient. Other times he can be very confrontational or defensive if he feels he is under attack. All genres need our careful research, but epistles in particular need this attention because we are hearing only one side of the "conversation."

Today's church can be thankful that the early church had conflicts, concerns and weaknesses, for it is out of concern for these weaknesses that Paul and other church leaders wrote letters that helped Jesus' early followers, and they can help us, too. If we take the time to research the contexts out of which these letters were formed, we can find a rich treasure-trove of theological gems that can help us with our different but equally important conflicts and weaknesses.

Apocalyptic Genre

Bible Passages: Revelation 4-5, 13-14, 19:11-16, and 21

The Lamb standing yet slaughtered (Revelation 5:6); a woman clothed with the sun, the moon under her feet and a crown of twelve stars on her head (Revelation 12:1); locusts with human faces, wearing crowns of gold, with teeth like lion's teeth and tails like scorpions (Revelation 9:7-10). What kind of sci-fi movie have we just walked into?

Apocalyptic genre, found primarily in the Book of Revelation and in the last half of the Book of Daniel, is a beautiful, intriguing—and strange type of literature. From the myriad of wild word pictures, the seemingly endless references to numbers, the breath-taking scenes of worship and the terrifying scenes of judgment, to the back and forth of earthly and future kingdoms, apocalyptic genre can feel other-worldly. It is a difficult genre to exegete and we must be humble as we venture forth on this daunting task. But the fruits of our exegetical labor will be worth all of our efforts.

Apocalyptic Genre and Apocalyptic Theology

Part of what makes our task so difficult is the fact that there exists both an apocalyptic genre *and* a theological understanding called apocalypticism. Like other genres, apocalyptic genre has its own set of characteristics and interpretation rules. Apocalyptic theology is not a style of writing but a set of beliefs. The word apocalyptic comes from the Greek word *apokalypsis* which means unveiling or revealing. So an apocalypse would be a piece of writing that helps reveal something, hence the name Revelation for the last book of the Bible. One could chuckle at the meaning of "unveiling," because with the frequent use of unfamiliar symbols in Revelation, apocalyptic genre can feel more like a "veiling" of truth.

Apocalypticism

Before delving into either apocalyptic genre or apocalypticism itself, it's important to understand the historical background that helped nurture these things. Think back to 587 BCE, Judah's fall to Babylonia. The people of Judah were devastated by their exile and overwhelmed by their persecution, a suffering that theologically didn't make sense to them.[1] This confusion was further solidified in their persecution under the Seleucids during the Intertestamental times when the Syrians tried to force Hellenism on the Jews.

Their suffering, both in the exile and later under the Seleucids, created gut-wrenching faith questions. What did it mean to be God's elect? Why hadn't the words of the prophets come true yet? Where was the Messiah who was supposed to restore Israel? Suddenly the Deuteronomistic view that God blesses those who are faithful and curses those who are unfaithful seemed inadequate to address their reality. Good people were suffering. Wasn't God active in the world anymore?

Enter Zoroastrianism, a Persian mythology or religion introduced by the sixth-century Iranian prophet, Zarathustra or Zoroaster, that places a heavy emphasis on dualism: good vs. evil, truth vs. falsehood, light vs. darkness. It believed that history is the outworking of a cosmic conflict between the forces of good and evil. The influence of Zoroastrianism on Judaism and subsequently Christianity, comes from the Persians during the Exile (587-538 BCE) and is seen in the emerging concept of the Devil or Satan as the one in control of the forces of evil. It also reinforced the notion of the triple-decker universe that saw the forces of good in heaven above the earth and the forces of evil below.[2]

In their exile, the people of Judah had contact with Persians who had

---

1 John Bracke, *Jeremiah 30-52 and Lamentations* (Louisville: Westminster/John Knox, 2000), 146. "In the ancient world, the destiny of nations was understood to be linked to the gods of a nation. If Babylon had defeated Judah, a common understanding would have been that the god of Babylon...had defeated Yahweh, the God of Israel and Judah. In fact, many in Judah thought that the Babylonian victory of 587 B.C. signaled the supremacy of the Babylonian deity, so the exile created a faith crisis."

2 Norman Cohn, *Cosmos, Chaos and the World to Come: The Ancient Roots of Apocalyptic Faith*, 2nd ed. (New Haven: Yale University Press, 2001), 82, 86.

an explanation for what seemed to be unjustifiable suffering. The Zoroastrianism answer follows that blessings and curses from God can come after one dies. Sometimes the evil seems to be in control, but really it isn't. There is a cosmic battle going on where the evil forces struggle for power against the good force or God. Your job? Hang on and be faithful for in a short while, God will miraculously intervene.

The mixture of gut-wrenching faith questions and the exposure to Zoroastrianism brought about a theological transition. The Jews moved from a general understanding that God was fulfilling promises through present political structures and historical events to a bewilderment over the seeming absence of God because their world was so cruel, to the belief that God would deliver them out of this present age into a new, transformed order. Apocalypticism was born.

It's not that God's people had never developed any theology for a next age. There was a long history of thinking about the next age, which is called eschatology or a study of the "last things." Before the emergence of apocalypticism, **prophetic eschatology** also believed in an age to come, but the focus was on working with God in human history to bring about God's kingdom.[3] Jesus spoke out of this understanding when he taught his disciples the Lord's Prayer, "Thy kingdom come, thy will be done, on earth as it is in heaven" (Matthew 6:10). In this view, evil is more likely to be viewed as a punishment of the wicked.

The background of apocalyptic literature and theology, therefore, came out of a time when Judah was undergoing severe persecution with little hope for change. Apocalyptic literature functioned to give hope to a persecuted and powerless people; it called them to be faithful, regardless of their suffering. Ultimately, God was sovereign and the reward for faithfulness would far outshine whatever pain they were currently enduring.

Apocalypticism is a theological system with certain characteristics, or a certain way of understanding God and the world. Most of the time, apocalyptic theology uses an apocalyptic style of writing, and most of the time an apocalyptic style of writing, or apocalyptic genre, contains apocalyptic

---

3   Ibid., 165. "The revelations that the apocalyptist received from God were very different from the revelations received by the biblical prophets. There is no suggestion in the apocalpyses that human beings can, by their obedience or disobedience, affect the shape of things to come. The future is already determined, in fact its course is already inscribed in a heavenly book. And its outcome will be different from anything foretold in classical prophecy. There will be a final judgment. There will be an afterlife when human beings, including the resurrected dead, will receive their just rewards and punishments."

theology. Most of the time the ideas or the theology of apocalypticism is expressed in a certain genre style we call apocalyptic genre, although there are some exceptions to the rule so it's critical to understand the differences between the two. Eugene Boring defines apocalyptic theology as a "particular kind of eschatology, which in turn is a particular understanding of the doctrine of providence."[4]

Apocalypticism is the eschatological belief characterized by the following points:

- The power of evil (Satan) is now in control of this temporal and hopelessly evil age of human history. This explains why there is evil in the world, an evil that surely a loving God could not be entirely responsible for.
- The righteous are now afflicted by Satan's demonic and human agents.
- Satan will soon be overcome and his evil rule ended.
- God, the power of good, will intervene to end Satan's rule.
- God will create an entirely new, perfect and eternal age under God's direct control.
- This glorious, everlasting age will be for the enjoyment of his righteous followers from among the living and the resurrected dead.[5]

Characteristics of Apocalyptic Theology or Apocalypticism

Apocalypticism is dualistic. A theory that is dualistic is one that divides reality into two irreducible parts or sides.[6] Everything fits on one side or the other. There are several kinds of dualisms, and apocalyptic theology should not be confused with other dualistic schemes of thought, such as Greek dualism. Unlike Greek dualism, biblical apocalypticism does not divide the world into the two categories of physical and metaphysical, even though it doesn't deny these two categories either. Instead, everything is divided in these three pairings: good and evil, this age and the age to come, and earth and heaven. So in apocalypticism, the characters tend to be either entirely

---

4   M. Eugene Boring, *Interpretation: A Bible Commentary for Teaching and Preaching: Revelation* (Louisville: John Knox Press, 1989), 35.

5   Ibid., 42.

6   "Metaphysical dualism assumes that there are two irreducible substances in the universe (i.e., matter vs. nonmatter; body vs. soul)." Bennie R. Crockett, Jr. "Dualism," in *Eerdmans Dictionary of the Bible,* ed. David Freedman (Grand Rapids: Eerdmans, 2000), 358.

good or evil; there is the present age which began as good but because of sin, was handed to over the reign of Satan; and the battle between good and evil rages on two levels, earth and heaven.

Apocalypticism emphasizes the sovereignty of God. In apocalyptic theology, God is ultimately sovereign over everything. The power of evil is allowed to have its day because and only because God allows it. Even then, if understood correctly, the power of evil is limited. Revelation 9:1-5 says that the locusts, part of the evil side, were given authority to do their damage. They were told not to damage the grass and they were only allowed to torment the people for five months. So no matter how chaotic and evil the world seems, God is in control of history. No matter how persecuted the followers of Jesus are, they can have hope. This is the positive side of this theology.

The more negative side to this theology is the belief that nothing can really be done about the evil that now seems to have control in the present age. So the only thing faithful followers can do is to sit and wait for God's miraculous intervention. They are to endure their suffering, and possibly even martyrdom, all the while believing in hope for the real One in power, God, to swoop into the evil world and make all things right.

The Apocalyptic View and the Prophetic View

Most of the Bible supports a prophetic view. By this we mean that righteous people are called upon to work with God to fight injustice, evangelize and other actions that help build the chosen, covenant, shalom community.

A few parts of the Bible take a different view, called the apocalyptic view, in which evil is so bad that the righteous don't have responsibility to work with God to bring shalom. They can do nothing but sit and wait for God's cataclysmic intervention to save them.

When Christians use the apocalyptic view as the guide for their ethics while living in a time and place where they face little persecution, they are misusing the apocalyptic view. Interestingly, the Book of Revelation, which stems from the great persecution early Christians suffered under the Roman Empire around 95-100 CE, calls itself a prophecy and encourages the original readers who were suffering to actively fight evil.

Unfortunately, many Christians like this part of apocalyptic theology for the wrong reason. They use apocalypticism as a "weapon," claiming a particular tragedy came from God to punish others, including other Christians, who disagree with their theology. "End times" scenarios become a tool of fear and hatred. Another way apocalypticism is misused happens when Christians use it as a way to relieve them of any responsibility of working with God to create a shalom community. They let this theology be their excuse for not telling others about God's love for them or fighting injustice the way Jesus did in his earthly ministry. There is an appropriate time for this theology—when Christians are being heavily persecuted. But when Christians forget the context of apocalypticism, they misuse the theology to get themselves "off the hook."

Characteristics of Apocalyptic Genre

Apocalyptic literature is like apocalyptic theology in that, content-wise, it is dualistic and usually reflects a concern for the end times. All the apocalyptic genre in the Bible was created during times of duress and persecution. But apart from any theology, this genre has certain characteristics.

Apocalyptic genre contains vivid word pictures. It's highly symbolic, using imagery, color, animals, heavenly beings and natural disasters, to name a few things. Angels, dragons, beasts and creatures so grotesque they are barely imaginable march across almost every page. Each of the images holds symbolic meaning that is culturally shared. The original audience *gets it,* in much the same way that people in the United States get it when they see an elephant or a donkey in a political cartoon. This overwhelming mix of symbols is the most reliable clue that we are using this specialized genre. Read this sample from Revelation 9:7-12:

> *In appearance the locusts were like horses equipped for battle. On their heads were what looked like crowns of gold; their faces were like human faces, their hair like women's hair, and their teeth like lions' teeth; they had scales like iron breastplates, and the noise of their wings was like the noise of many chariots with horses rushing into battle. They have tails like scorpions, with stings, and in their tails is their power to harm people for five months. They have as king over them the angel of the bottomless pit; his name in Hebrew is Abaddon, and in Greek he is called Apollyon. The first woe has passed. There are still two woes to come.*

Many times these images are set in a symmetrical pattern, which artisitally supports the dualism. Revelation has an evil trinity which is offset by

271

the good side's Trinity of Father, Son and Holy Spirit. The mark of the Beast in Revelation 13 is balanced by the mark of the Spirit in Revelation 14. Both the Lamb and the Beast who comes out of the sea have a mortal wound.

Many people wonder if there is a special purpose in the dense symbols. Were these symbols meant to hide or encode the intended message from the persecutors? While this may be true, it's also possible that the evil was simply so terrifying that that ordinary language couldn't contain it. Like the painting "Guernica," where Pablo Picasso used nonliteral, abstract images to depict the real-life bombing of the Spanish town Guernica, so too apocalyptic genre uses graphic, unrealistic images to highlight the emotions of real-life persecution.

Apocalyptic genre uses numerology. Numerology refers to the practice of assigning special meaning to numbers. Many apocalyptic writings use numbers as part of their symbolism. In a similar way, this genre tends to use cycles or a series of events. In Revelation, there are seven seals, seven trumpets and seven bowls. The suffering advances in each series, starting with a fourth of the earth being afflicted in the seals, to a third in the trumpets and one half in the bowls. Here is a list of key numbers in the book of Revelation and what they symbolize:

3 = Trinity. Not only is there the trinity recognized by most Christians—the Father, Son and Holy Spirit—but also an unholy trinity of the Dragon, the Beast from the sea and the Beast from the earth.

4 = the earth number. In our natural world, there are four directions and four seasons, so the number four represents the natural world. In Revelation, the four living creatures mean more than just four; they represent all the creatures of the earth.

6 = the human number. Six is just short of the divine number, which is seven. So too, humans fall short of the divine. Therefore, the mark of the Beast is 666.

7 = the divine number. There are seven churches, seven seals, seven trumpets, seven bowls, and Jesus the Lamb is praised with seven attributes.

3.5 or 42 = the time of suffering. Exactly half of seven, 3 and a half years or 42 months was the time of suffering the Jews experienced under Antiochus IV, the Selucid king who tried to destroy them in the time around 164-167 CE. Three and a half years is also known as the "time, two times and a half time" as specified in Daniel 7:25.

12 = the People of God number. There were twelve tribes of Israel and twelve disciples of Jesus. Likewise, the book of Revelation is filled with many references to twelve. The holy city of new Jerusalem has twelve gates and twelve pearls.

Sometimes 12 and 12 are added together, making 24. Twenty-four elders bowing down before the Lamb represent the entire people of God. In chapter 7 there are 144,000 who are sealed with the mark of God. Here 12 is multiplied by 12 and then multiplied by a thousand, which is the symbol for infinity. It is not, therefore, a good interpretation to claim that only 144,000 people will be saved by God, because the numbers are symbolic rather than literal. John's further words prove this point, when he describes a multitude that no one can count, right after proclaiming the number of sealed to be 144,000 (Revelation 7:4-9).[7]

Apocalyptic genre usually has anonymous writers, a practice called psuedonimity. It was common practice in the early church for writers to attribute their writing to famous and respected church leaders as a way to gain authority for their writing. This was not considered plagiarism or falsehood. Interestingly, the main source of apocalyptic genre in the Bible is the book of Revelation, and some scholars believe that the claimed author, the apostle John, actually did the write the book.[8]

Principles for Interpretation

With all the wild images, apocalyptic genre can easily be the most misinterpreted genre in the Bible. **Using the Hermeneutical Bridge is key to avoiding misinterpretations.** Serious readers must perform inductive

---

7 "Despite no definite article standing before this number in the Greek text, it is almost impossible to believe that the hearers would not think of the 144,000 sons of the tribes of Israel described earlier in Rev 7:1-8 when encountering this number. Thus, when the 144,000 reappear in 14:1, this image of the transformed Israel has itself been transformed in the light of the innumerable crowd, suggesting that the 144,000 are now forever identified with the innumerable crowd (see 7:9), not unlike the way in which the Root of David is now forever identified with the slaughtered Lamb." John Christopher Thomas and Frank Macchia, *Revelation* (Grand Rapids: Eerdmans, 2016), 251.

8 Robert H. Mounce, *The Book of Revelation,* Revelation ed. (Grand Rapids: Eerdmans, 1998), 15.

Bible study, researching the cultural and historical background of these scriptures, working to understand the worldview of the original audience. Take for example the word "sea," a word used frequently in Revelation. Understanding that for most ancient cultures the sea was viewed as chaos or evil helps the reader properly interpret many passages in Revelation. Revelation chapter four creates a word picture of God sitting on a throne in the middle of the sea and the sea is as "of glass." Knowing that the chaotic sea represented all that was evil in the world, the original audience took comfort that God was in the midst of the chaos and better yet, God had tamed the sea so that it was smooth as crystal.

Part of using the hermeneutical bridge is putting ourselves in the place of the original audience. In the case of Revelation, that would be a first century church member to whom it was written. And that original audience faced the threat of suffering at the hands of the state. Given this context, for whatever else it may mean, Revelation can't mean that Christians won't suffer.[9]

Keep the historical connections in mind when interpreting this genre. Just because apocalyptic genre uses a lot of imagery, doesn't mean that it is other-worldly and that it has nothing to say about how to combat evil in the world they lived it, or that we live in now. The writer of Revelation was very concerned to comfort persecuted Christians who were suffering from the Roman Empire, a very real entity in their lives.

Given this reality, it's also important to **remember that the symbols don't necessarily represent just one historical thing.** True, the symbol of the Beast rising out of the sea in Revelation always means world empire.[10] But for the original audience, that meant the very historical and real Roman Empire. In other contexts, the attributes of the Beast could just as easily be applied to any empire that demands complete allegiance to it, even our own empire in the United States. That doesn't mean that John predicted a specific contemporary empire to be the final Beast. It simply means the symbols can both have specific historical significance and also be applied to our times today.[11]

Remember that some symbols are constant throughout the apocalyptic writing and other symbols are fluid. Additionally, some symbols are specific and some more general. The seven lampstands mean the seven

---

9 Stuart and Fee, *How to Interpret the Bible for All Its Worth*, (Grand Rapids, MI: Zondervan, 2003), 257.

10 Ibid., 255.

11 Ibid., Boring, 55.

churches; this symbol is specific and unchanging. On the other hand, the four horsemen of Chapter 6 probably do not relate to any specific war or famine, but to the general chaos and evil of war and famine in general.[12]

When the writer tells us the meaning of the symbols, we must take this interpretation seriously. Sometimes the writer gives the readers an interpretation key to the symbol. First, this functions to remind us that we can't take these symbols literally. John tells us in Revelation 12:9 that the great dragon is none other than Satan. The fourth horse in Revelation 6:8 is Death, and this horse had Hades following closely behind him. Revelation 17 details a woman who is called a whore. She is sitting on "many waters," and later said to be sitting on a scarlet beast. This beast has seven heads and and ten horns (Revelation 17:1-8). Then, in the next verses, the writer explains what the symbols mean, which is also a big clue for us that we must be careful not to take any of the symbols literally. Revelation 17:9-16 gives meaning to each of the symbols. Of particular importance are verses 15-16.

> *And he said to me, "The **waters** that you saw, where the whore is seated, are peoples and multitudes and nations and languages. And the **ten horns** that you saw, they and the beast will hate the whore; they will make her desolate and naked; they will devour her flesh and burn her up with fire."*

In this passage, not only do we receive the meanings of the symbols, we also receive a meaningful theological insight. The whore, the ten horns and the Beast are all on the evil side, yet they destroy each other. The ten horns and the Beast devour the whore's flesh. This is a vivid word picture of the the truth that evil destroys itself.[13]

Be careful to not overuse the "analogy of Scripture" method when interpreting apocalyptic genre. Analogy of Scripture means that one section of Scriptures must be interpreted in light of or by another section of Scripture. In a general way this is proper to do since Christians believe that all Scripture has been inspired by God. But this practice can be misused in such a way that one is tempted to twist the meaning of one passage just to fit another one. We shouldn't use other scriptures as the hermeneutical key to unlocking books like Revelation.[14]

---

12   Ted Grimsrud, *Triumph of the Lamb* (Scottdale, PA: Herald Press, 1987), 62.

13   Ibid., 133.

14   Ibid., Stuart and Fee, 254.

On the other hand, it is important to notice how apocalyptic writings sometimes echo the Old Testament. The writer of Revelation makes direct or indirect references to the Old Testament over 250 times.[15] Readers who can see these connections are better able to understand the apocalyptic symbols and events. For example, the plagues in Chapter 9 resemble the Exodus plagues that God used to set the slaves free from Egypt. The original readers would have recognized this reference and remembered two things: that God was faithful to rescue God's people during a time of great oppression and second, that the plagues in and of themselves served as a way to get the Egyptians to repent and join God's people. Likewise, Revelation 9:20-21 implies that plagues currently happening also have the same purpose even if they are largely unsuccessful:

> *The rest of humankind, who were not killed by these plagues, did not repent of the works of their hands or give up worshipping demons and idols of gold and silver and bronze and stone and wood, which cannot see or hear or walk. And they did not repent of their murders or their sorceries or their fornication or their thefts.*

See visions for what they are—visions. In much the same way we give important consideration to our own nocturnal visions we occasionally receive, we need to seriously consider the apocalyptic visions. But just as we don't allegorize every detail of our own nighttime visions, so too should we not give a special meaning to every detail in an apocalyptic dream. See the visions with your controlled imagination and as just that—visions. Most of the details in a apocalyptic piece of writing have no specific meaning apart from their contribution to the total vision.

Apocalyptic genre asks us to use a different kind of logic than our rational, linear, "put this on a two-dimensional chart" type of logic. Several times John in Revelation uses several visions to describe the same ultimate reality. If pressed to make these different visions match in a logical way, it seems like the visions contradict each other. But the point is not to make logical sense in literal-reality world. For example, in Revelation 6:14, "every mountain was removed from its place." But in verse 15, "the kings of the earth, the magnates, generals, rich and powerful, everyone, slave or free, hid in the caves and among the rocks of the mountains."

Apocalyptic writings, like other visions, are not necessarily chronological.

---

15   Ibid., 249.

Revelation is organized around a series of sevens, and at the end of each set of sevens, there is an "end." This doesn't mean that the end of the ages comes several times, but it's an artistic way to give several different camera angles to the same end.[16]

The apocalyptic realities are so mind-blowing that they need more than one way to describe them, and conflicting details don't negate the truth of the visions. If we insist on harmonizing every symbol and forcing the text to "make sense," if we insist on making logical sense of the vision, we miss the point. Says Eugene Boring, "Conflicting pictures should not be harmonized with a 'both/and' or 'partly/partly.' Each should carry its full message even when it cannot be logically harmonized with other pictures.... as propositional, objectifying language, these statements can only compete with each other; but as pictures, both communicate christological reality and neither picture should be sacrificed to the other."[17]

Maintain symmetry with symbolism and literalism. There are many sets of opposites in apocalyptic genre, pairs of characters or things that are diametrically opposed to each other. Revelation has the Lamb, *arnion* in Greek, and the Beast, *therion* in Greek. The Lamb has the marks of slaughter and the Beast has a fatal wound. Possibly the most familiar symmetry is the mark or seal of the Spirit which is paired as an opposite to the mark of the Beast. Whenever we encounter these paired opposites, we must interpret them in the same way. Revelation 13 talks about the mark of the Beast that is put on one's forehead or hand. Some Christians read this and then are afraid of getting any physical mark on their head or hand in case they may accidentally receive the mark of the Beast. Yet few if any Christians are worried when they have no mark of the Spirit on their foreheads, as is mentioned in Revelation 14:1. If we aren't careful, we make one part of the symmetry literal and the other part symbolic. This does a great disservice to the interpretation of apocalyptic genre.

Don't "calendarize." Any attempt to correlate people, places or events in apocalyptic genre with current people, countries or events with the purpose of predicting a future event is called calendarizing. Calendarizing results in separating Scriptures from their historical context and leaves one open to gross distortions of meaning. We can juggle the numbers around to predict that Jesus will come back to earth again in so many months. Another person will use the same numbers and claim that Jesus is returning in

---

16 Ibid., Boring, 32.

17 Ibid., 58.

a hundred years. When we assume books like Revelation were written only for people of the 21st century to predict future events, we leave the book little to no meaning for the original audience, an audience that needed encouragement for their political situation.

The basis for this interpretation principle comes from Jesus himself, where he says in Matthew 24:36, "But about that day and hour no one knows, neither the angels of heaven, nor the Son, but only the Father." Again, in Acts 1:6-8, Jesus tells to his disciples that it is not for them to know about dates and times. The main purpose of Revelation and other apocalyptic genre is to encourage those who are suffering for their faithfulness, not to predict the future.

A Special Word About the Book of Revelation

For some readers, the book of Revelation can feel more like Tolkien's *Lord of the Rings* than the Bible. We may be tempted to not read it at all because it seems so fantastical and hard to interpret. Yet it's important because it's in the Bible and because it's a somewhat unique apocalyptic book. Unlike most apocalyptic writings, it proclaims itself as a prophecy. Seven times John says the book is prophetic (1:3, 19:10, 22:7, 22:9, 22:10, 22:18, 22:19). This means that even though the evil is almost overwhelming, Revelation has more of a prophetic view than an apocalyptic view. The seven Asia-Minor churches in chapters 2-3 of Revelation were being called to stand forth and do something. They were to follow the Lamb wherever he goes (Revelation 14:4b). This fact makes Revelation especially important for our study today, even though we risk misinterpreting it. Most Christians use one of the following four views to understand the book as a whole.

- The **in-that-history** or **preterist** view might be described as the "backward look." People who use this view believe Revelation was written for the benefit of the seven churches addressed in chapters 2-3 and other Asia Minor churches like them. These churches were real churches and not symbols for a distinct time period. The main purpose of John's vision was to strengthen these churches as they suffered persecution. This view would emphasize that today's readers cannot take spiritual truths from this book that would not have made sense to the original audience.

- The **all-of-history** view could also be called the "sweeping look." This view goes along with some forms of dispensationalism (see chapter on hermeneutics) that divides history into different time periods called dispensations. Many times the seven churches are seen as symbols for seven dispensations. According to this view, John's purpose was to forecast history in its successive stages. Each dispensation (each church) of Revelation fits or matches with a different age of history. If we can figure out what has already taken place and where we are today, we can use Revelation to determine what is yet to come. This view isn't necessarily preoccupied with the future but can tend to be that way.

- The **end-of-history** view is a "forward look" which could also be called the futurist view. Here Revelation records events and visions dealing primarily with the end of history. With the exception of chapters 1-3, the book intends to give information and details about the second coming of Christ and the end times. This view, even more than the all-of-history view, emphasizes reading Revelation as a document for today's church. In this view, Revelation has little meaning for its original audience.

- The **above-history** view can also be called the "timeless look." This view is most concerned with the ahistorical meaning that can be gleaned from the visions. Sometimes called the idealist or philosophy of history view, it would be most interested in eternal truths and spiritual principles found in the text. Revelation doesn't relate much to real historical events, but is more about theological truths.

All four of these views have some validity, but all four are not equally helpful in understanding Revelation. The dispensational and futurist views both read into the book meanings and predictions not there. The timeless look can separate Revelation from its historical context too much. But the most congruent view with the whole biblical narrative is the preterist or backward view, which takes into consideration the historical background of Revelation and takes seriously John's purpose of encouraging the churches suffering from oppression.[18] As Stuart and Fee argue, "The book (Revelation) was not intended to prophesy the existence of communist China, for example, or to give us literal details of the conclusion of history."[19]

With striking images, weird numbers, scary scenes of natural disasters and glorious scenes of worship, it seems like apocalyptic genre is not for

---

18 Ibid., Grimsrud, 18. See also Boring, 47-50.

19 Ibid., Stuart and Fee, 263.

the faint-hearted. But, like all genres, a working knowledge of its characteristics and interpretation principles can give us what we need to appreciate
these writings and to gain truth for ourselves.

Part II
Study Methods

Bible Study Types and Tools

There's a funny story about the Bible student who, wanting to please God, vowed to close her eyes, open up her Bible, point to a page, open her eyes and then do whatever her finger was pointing to. At this point, the story diverges into many different endings, each of them funny, because, depending where your finger rests, you can be doing a lot of strange things. Being jealous of Moses in the camp (Psalm 106:16), for example, sitting inside tombs and eating swine's flesh (Isaiah 65:4), or tearing your robe into twelve piece and giving ten to Jereboam (I Kings 11:30). We laugh because some elements of the Bible are so far outside our experience that they seem completely inapplicable to a contemporary audience. So what is a good way to go about studying the Bible and keeping its messages meaningful to our lives today?

Types of Bible Study

People study the Bible in many ways, from casual reading at one end to deep inductive Bible study at the other. Different methods of Bible studies serve different purposes. If we understand not only the purpose of each kind of Bible study, but also also their strengths and weaknesses, we will be able to choose the type best suited for our needs.

Devotional Bible Study

Devotional Bible study most closely aligns itself with the "point your finger at a passage and then let God speak to you" anecdote above. It's a combination of Bible reading, meditation and prayer. The most important principle here is to read the Bible as if God wrote it directly to you. It doesn't matter what the verse, passage or story meant to the original readers; the only important meaning is what you hear God saying to you. The meaning or interpretation of the text is located in you, the reader. So a number of different people could do devotional Bible study on the same text and each come up with a different meaning. Most of these interpretations would be accepted as valid because the meaning is personal to the individual.

The strength of Devotional Bible study is that you read with your heart. It takes faith to believe that God can speak to you through this ancient text; practicing this faith is healthy. And this type of Bible study requires no special training of knowledge; anyone can do it.

The weakness of Devotional Bible study is that there is much opportunity to misinterpret the text and/or make the Bible say whatever the reader wants it to say. Without properly understanding the historical and cultural background of the scripture passage and without taking into account the different genres involved, the reader could insert her own biases into the text, and in doing so, possibly justify all sorts of atrocities. The Bible ends up having many different meanings according to the context, thoughts, and experiences of the reader.

Devotional Bible study has its place. It is reading with one's emotions and sometimes that is a wonderful way to hear the voice of God. But this type of Bible study is inadequate for forming doctrines or deciding on what is right or wrong to do.

Topical Bible Study

This method of Bible study takes a life question and seeks to find all the biblical passages that address that topic. For example, you may take the issue of sexuality and you try to find all the Bible verses that address this issue. You would use a concordance, which is an alphabetical listing of all the important words in a book and where those words can be found in that book. There are entire books of concordances, such as *Strong's Concordance*, but many Bibles also have an abbreviated concordance in an appendix. The person using this method would look up all the Bible passages that say something about the chosen topic, do some limited cultural-historical research on those verses, and then condense the content of the verses into a general interpretation or meaning for this given issue. The purpose is to find out what the entire Bible says about a given topic and subsequently get guidance on that topic.

The strength of the Topical Bible study is that you are exposed to a wide range of biblical passages related to your chosen issue. You get a breadth of knowledge.

The weakness of the Topical Bible study is that you "cut and paste" the Bible verses. Even if you do limited cultural-historical context work on each verse, the very practice of reading just that verse instead of reading and studying the entire chapter or section of chapters in the Bible means you are likely to take the selected verses out of context. You are trying to understand one verse that is only meant to be understood in its literary context. More often than not, you misinterpret the individual verses and then come away with a distorted interpretation of the issue you sought to understand. You get breadth but sacrifice depth.

Guided Bible Study

A Guided Bible study is research-based Bible study done by a biblical scholar and then simplified for a general audience. Typically if you are doing a Guided Bible study, you are answering questions in a study book that will lead you to a better understanding of the contexts of the passage. The assumption is that if you follow the scholar's study guide, you will understand the correct meaning of the text. This type of study is more objective than either the Devotional or Topical Bible study.

A Guided Bible study is good for helping you see things that might be overlooked such as repetitions, emphases, relationships, the meaning of words in their original context, and cultural and historical information. The person who prepares this kind of study probably has more expertise in biblical study than the person using the study guide.

On the other hand, the same study guide that can be helpful to you also tends to limit what you see. You end up seeing the passage through the eyes of the guided study author rather than what you might see for yourself. You take on the bias of the scholar who designed the study, and you may underestimate your own ability to research and understand the text.

Inductive Bible Study

In an Inductive Bible study, you research the cultural-historical and the literary contexts of the Bible passage and, as opposed to the Guided

Bible study, you do this work yourself. You are seeking to understand what the passage meant to the original audience and then, given the different contexts today, you determine the unchanging truth of the passage and apply that to today's society and your life. You attempt to read the Bible as if for the first time, laying aside assumptions about the meaning of the text.

Just as in the Guided Bible study, Inductive study is excellent at helping you gain an understanding of the historical, cultural, and literary contexts of the passage. After an Inductive study, you are more likely to understand the meaning for the original audience. Inductive Bible study helps us lay down our beginning assumptions about what the text means, giving us a more objective approach to the scriptures.

One problem is that this kind of study can become so dependent on research that we employ the mind exclusively, neglecting the heart and will. We can use the inductive method as a way to "hold the Bible at arm's length," always ready to study more contexts and do more research, but not ready to apply the truths to our own lives.

Deductive and Inductive Reasoning

Another way to understand the four types of Bible study is through the lens of deductive and inductive reasoning. Both types of reasoning are sound, but they begin at different points. Deductive reasoning begins with a hypothesis, an assumption of the truth, or a stated generalization. Given this assumption, the person then uses outside resources or data to prove whether or not the original hypothesis is true. So, in deductive reasoning, you begin with a generalization and work to prove or disprove it. This could be like the detective who is given the name of a suspect. The detective will start by following this person and in the process of his investigation, he then rules out the suspect or gathers more proof that he suspects the right person.

Inductive reasoning purposely puts all assumptions aside and tries to not be influenced by any hypothesis or assumption. Instead, you begin with raw data. You collect neutral facts, and in this research process, you are able to form a hypothesis. Instead of beginning with a generalization, as in deductive reasoning, this process starts with raw facts. This process is what we see in popular detective fiction, including Sherlock Holmes. At the story's outset, the detective has no clue who performed the crime, so he simply gathers pieces of evidence from the scene of the crime—things like fingerprints, scuff marks on the floor, bits of cloth—and in that search, eventually is able to name a suspect. (Curiously, the character of Sherlock Holmes claims he uses deductive reasoning to solve crimes, when his process is entirely inductive.)

Or, to use a medical analogy, pretend you are visiting to the doctor for a mysterious ailment. You are escorted into the examination room, where the nurse takes your pulse, weighs you, and takes your blood pressure. The doctor continues this investigation, asking you questions about your appetite, looking into your eyes and ears and listening to your heart. Both the doctor and nurse are conducting inductive research. They are gathering facts before they make a judgment, in this case called a diagnosis.

Once the doctor diagnoses you, she gives you medicine and specific directions for your self-care. She also asks you to come back in two weeks. When you come back to her office, she again does careful observation, but it's different. Now the doctor begins with the diagnosis she gave you two weeks ago, and as she collects medical information about you, she is weighing that against the diagnosis she gave you before. Did the medicine work? Was the diagnosis right or is there something else wrong with you? Now the doctor is doing more of a deductive process. She is starting with your diagnosis--what she assumes is the medical problem--and is now using her collected information to validate that diagnosis.

There are two Latin words that Bible scholars use that relate to deductive and inductive reasoning. *Eisegesis* is like deductive reasoning in that the meaning or interpretation of what you are studying comes from inside you. *Eisegesis* is a Greek word that means "to read into." You begin with your assumptions or opinions. To do *eisegesis* to a biblical text means to put your own meaning to the text without consulting any outside resource. In this way *eisegesis* is similar to being subjective. Subjective information is one's opinion. This opinion might be well-informed and based on accurate data or it might be just one's preference or intuitive response. But if a finding is subjective, then it's probable that another equally valid opinion could be made about the same subject or text. But in both cases, the meaning resides in the person.

Exegesis is like inductive reasoning. In Greek *exegesis* means "to read out of." The person who does *exegesis* on a biblical text will work hard to put his assumptions aside and simply look at the text itself as neutrally as possible. He will start with the particular details or facts of the text and only draw conclusions after much study. The meaning or interpretation of the text comes from outside of the person who is doing the investigation. *Exegesis* is similar to being objective. Objective information considers many points of view and strives to be as unbiased as possible. While it may be impossible for any person to be completely unbiased, we strive toward objectivity when we intentionally put aside what we think the biblical text means and work to understand the text in its original contexts.

Many times we approach a passage thinking we already understand it. In the process we read our own meaning into the passage. This is called eisegesis. (Eis is a Greek preposition meaning 'into.') But interpreting the Bible correctly demands that we listen to what the text itself is saying, and then draw the meaning out of the passage. This is called exegesis. (Ex is a Greek preposition meaning 'out of.') If we let a passage be defined by what it and the surrounding verses say, then we have taken a large step toward interpreting the Bible properly. Only by watching the context carefully and by letting the passage speak for itself do we give Scripture the respect it deserves. Of course, it is impossible to dismiss totally our own bias and subjectivity. Our interpretation will always be colored by our culture and our opinions about the passage, or perhaps by our theological beliefs, which are partially based on the passage. But this should not discourage our attempt to let the passage speak for itself as freely as possible, without being weighed down with our personal opinions and views.[1]

Four Types of Bible Study at a Glance

Bible Study	Subjective/Objective	Method of Discovery
Devotional	Highly subjective	*Eisegesis*
Topical	Subjective	*Eisegesis*
Guided	Objective	*Exegesis*
Inductive	Highly objective	*Exegesis*

Tools for Inductive Bible Study

Biblical scholars, including beginners, use a variety of tools to conduct Inductive Bible study. They use Bible dictionaries, Bible commentaries, concordances and atlases. They also hone in on four types of criticism, or four ways of examining the biblical text. Overall, we use the phrase "biblical criticism" to describe this type of study. Biblical criticism is the

---

1 "Interpretation of the Bible," *Nelson's Illustrated Bible Dictionary*, ed. Ronald Young-blood (Nashville: Thomas Nelson, 2014), 172.

careful examination of all the data and phenomena associated with the recording, preserving and interpreting the Scriptures.[2] When scholars use the word "criticism," they are emphasizing the importance of critical or analytical thinking. It is a positive concept. The use of the word criticism should not be confused with any negative attitude toward or attempt to undermine the Bible.

Lower and Higher Criticism

Biblical scholars use the term "criticism" to signal the investigation or in-depth study of a text. When students research the historical-cultural contexts or the literary contexts and try to figure out the origins of a certain text, they are engaging in criticism. Likewise, the terms "lower criticism" and "higher criticism" don't mean that higher criticism is better than lower criticism. These two phrases are just ways of categorizing different types of study.

One type of lower criticism is **textual criticism.** In this study, scholars compare ancient manuscripts, trying to find the oldest one, assuming that the older a manuscript is, the closer it is to the original manuscript and therefore closer to the message the original author intended. Scholars work to figure out which manuscript is the oldest or most reliable by comparing the differences in the Hebrew (for Old Testament) or Greek (for New Testament) texts.

In the ancient world before the invention of the printing press, scribes copied the biblical text word for word. Sometimes, because the animal skin or the papyrus they were writing on was expensive, these scribes didn't make spaces between the words in order to get more text on a "page." So one task of textual criticism scholars is to decide where one word ends and another one begins. Sometimes whole sections of scripture are found in different parts of the Bible. Here scholars must try to determine why the text "moved" from one old manuscript to another. When scholars find any anomalies between ancient manuscripts, they ask questions, trying to find the "best" reading. Many times the reading that is the most difficult or contains the fewest words is considered the best reading because it's presumed that the ancient editors were more tempted to add words and soften the obscure teaching than the other way around.

A classic example is John 7:53-8:1-11, the story of Jesus and his

---

2   David Schroeder, "The Scholar of the Bible," *Mennonite Life* 19, no. 2 (April 1964): 65.

interaction with the Pharisees who bring to him a woman caught in the act of adultery. In some ancient manuscripts, this story is found after Luke 21:38 or Luke 24:53 as well as different places in John. This is not to say that Jesus' encounter with the woman caught in adultery didn't happen, but it's clear that the story has a peculiar history. Therefore we have to consider the possibility that the story wasn't included in the oldest copy of John. The other possibility is that the story is original—in one of the gospels—but because of the incredible grace shown to the woman, it was so radical that it got cut out of some manuscripts. Textual criticism scholars study stories like this one in order to better understand the origin and "life" of such texts.

Beginning scholars usually don't delve into textual criticism. Many Bibles do note these variations and it's wise to read these footnotes and do more textual study if needed.

Literary criticism is part of higher criticism. Literary criticism strives to understand how the literary features of the text itself function. Here scholars study the genre of the text and whether or not the author deviated from the understood genre rules. They also study how the literary unit is structured, the relationship the text has with surrounding texts and the meaning of the words in their literary context. This is important work, because different genres communicate truth differently and words take on different meanings depending on how they are used in a sentence. Many ancient authors also used a certain structure to enhance meaning. Repetitions and parallelism worked to make certain phrases stand out. When scholars take careful note of these things, they get closer to the original intention of the author.

Beginning scholars should do literary criticism. By making a vertical chart, determining the genre and studying the interpretation rules for that genre and noting the repetitions and how words are used in the passage, students take great leaps toward understanding the meaning of a text.

Another part of higher criticism is **historical-cultural criticism,** sometimes called historical-critical work. Just like words take on different meanings depending on how they are used in a sentence, they also take on new meanings depending on what they mean during the time period in which they were written. Cultural practices and understandings, historical events and assumed understandings of their reality shape the worldview of the speaker or writer and the modern reader must have some grasp of that ancient context or the original meaning is lost. For example, in

North American culture in the 21st Century, the concept of firstborn has a different meaning than it did during the time when Genesis was written. Today, to be the firstborn child seems like either a slight privilege or the burden of more responsibility as the oldest child. But in ancient Israelite culture, the firstborn son received double his father's inheritance and also a special blessing. This privilege was so important that laws were set up to protect it.

So the goal for all biblical scholars, even beginning ones, is to study the historical and cultural background of their text. They ask questions like, "What historical events helped shape this story?" or "What were the assumptions about [marriage, honor, authority, power, ownership, responsibility, etc.] in this time?" Students investigate the social, political, economic, cultural and religious contexts of their chosen passage and when they do so, they gain a better understanding of the meaning of the passage for its original audience.

Form criticism is the final area of study and it's also part of higher criticism. Some Bible passages within the same book seem to have a different literary origin than the rest of the book. The first two chapters of Philippians offer a great example. Most of the book is in the epistle genre, and the author, Paul, is telling a certain congregation in Philippi what to do and believe. But suddenly in chapter 2, the letter doesn't sound like a letter, but rather like a hymn or a poem. Did Paul take a hymn written by someone else and stick it in his letter? Studying this phenomenon is called Form Criticism. Part of truly understanding a literary unit is to understand its original *Sitz im Leben,* or setting in life. If an author uses something that has already been written, then that piece of writing has a different *Sitz im Leben* than the rest of the book. While most beginning scholars don't do form criticism, it's important work to do. Scholars find it fascinating to figure out the real life situation of all the different passages within a book.

Inductive Bible study takes time and perseverance. You may need to spend hours pouring over Bible dictionaries, write down details so you don't forget them, skim many Bible atlases to finally find that small town, re-read the passage over and over again to pick up repetitions and special literary structures. It can feel exhausting. And there is some expertise required, which the next chapters seek to address. But your willingness to put aside your beginning assumptions of what you think the text means and to passionately search for the literary and historical-cultural contexts is the most valuable tool you own.

Inductive Bible Study

While all four types of Bible study mentioned in the previous chapter hold merit, the inductive Bible study method provides a wonderful way to understand the biblical narrative in its original contexts. The inductive process encourages us to put aside our biases about the text, dig into the history and culture of the story, discover and ponder the literary context and perhaps most importantly, this process helps us realize that the average person can do quality *exegesis*. The Bible is accessible. We can discover the meaning for the original audience and have greater confidence that we are not misinterpreting the text.

Inductive Bible study refers to a careful analytical study that seeks to allow the Bible to speak for itself, to read "out of" (*exegesis*) rather than read "into" (*eisegesis*). The inductive reasoning process begins with details or facts, moving from the particular to the general conclusion. The deductive reasoning process begins with the conclusion or hypothesis and moves from the general to the particular.

So How Do We Begin?

Our goal is to see the Bible without bias. While it's not possible to clear our minds completely of preconceived ideas and interpretations, we can help the process by admitting up front what we think the text says and then letting those ideas go. Our aim is to allow the Bible to speak for itself. Being observant is another great tool we must use. As we approach the text, we should assume that we will miss details the first three or four times we read the passage. It is only upon multiple readings that we start to see small, even contradictory, details. All of this takes hard work and commitment, but getting to the meaning for the original audience is worth it.

The Bible story itself is our primary source. We also use scholarly books such as Bible dictionaries, commentaries, concordances and atlases. These are our secondary sources.

Imagination is another great tool for inductive study. The best inductive scholars ask, "What doesn't make sense in this passage?" This skill is like pretending you are visiting from another planet, and while you're able to read and understand the language itself, you are completely unfamiliar with the culture, history or assumptions of the original audience. In this creative, imaginative process, questions bubble to the surface. "I wonder how they define family in Genesis 38?" "Why did she touch the edge of his cloak in Luke 8:40-48?" "Why didn't all of people get out of his way and let him pass in Mark 2:1-12?" "Why did he salt the city in Judges 9, and what does that even mean?"

Four Basic Steps of Inductive Bible Study

A. Observation: take off your current cultural "glasses," cross the Hermeneutical Bridge and put on the biblical worldview "glasses"

1. Write out your initial reactions. Read the passage. Write one paragraph where you express your initial reactions and questions.
2. Write 25-30 facts from the passage as you read slowly and carefully.
3. Who? List all the persons or groups of persons in the passage. List a specific name only once. If the same person is given a new name or designation, include this new information. List by verse number.
4. Where? List all the geographical locations and draw a map locating all the places.
5. Literary contexts
   a. Salvation History context: In one paragraph, describe where this passage fits in Salvation History (Describe the major themes).
   b. Book context: Create a horizontal book chart, where you divide the book into its major sections. In each section, write a phrase for each major story.

c.   Immediate literary context: Write a paragraph for each of the 2-3 Bible passages immediately before your Bible passage. The paragraphs summarize the passages. Then write a paragraph for each of the 2-3 Bible passages immediately after your Bible passage.

6.   Cultural-Historical contexts: Make a list of all the words, phrases or implied concepts that you think may have a different meaning in biblical times than today. Find 27-30 concepts. Using only Bible dictionaries or approved resources, look up two definitions for each concept and then write a paragraph in your own words about what you learned. Include only what is significant for the cultural context of your passage. After each definition, note your source. Supply a Works Cited page.

B. Analysis: discover how the writer communicates. Break the passage into smaller parts and discover how they work together.

1.   Genre: Identify the type of genre(s) in the passage. Write 4-5 principles for interpreting this genre.

2.   Vertical chart: Break the passage into paragraphs or parts. The left column details literary relationships, the middle column summarizes actions in each paragraph, the right column describes moods for characters.

3.   Summarize the passage: Summarize the passage without interpretation.

C. Interpretation: find the meaning(s) of the passage for the original audience

1.   Brainstorm and list all kinds of interpretations, and put these interpretations into a category: absurd, possible, probable and quite sure. Use complete sentences that start with an action verb.

2.   Create an Interpretation/application chart (you will finish this chart in step 4): Create a two-column chart and fill in the left side, which is the meaning for the original audience side. Follow these steps:

   •   Choose your 3-4 "quite sure" interpretations. Beginning with your primary interpretation, write out the interpretation in a clear sentence that honors the historical-cultural context.

   •   Still working with the primary interpretation, now write a paragraph or two in the chart that shows your evidence and reasoning for choosing this as your primary interpretation. Use proof in the story itself, historical-cultural evidence (use A6) and literary context proof

- Repeat the process with your other interpretations

3. Interpretation essay: Write a 2-4 page essay where you logically prove that your interpretations are valid. Include an introduction paragraph that summarizes the story, one paragraph for each interpretation and a conclusion.

4. List significant questions: We can never answer all the questions. List the questions you still have.

D. Application: discovering the meaning for our society now and for you personally

1. Finish the Interpretation/application chart: Determine which part of the interpretations (C2) are historically-culturally based and which part is the eternal truth still applicable to today's society. Using the eternal truth, fill in the chart by now stating in complete sentences the application for contemporary society. For each application statement, write a short paragraph in the chart that demonstrates how this application is still needed today.

2. What do I hear God say to me through this passage? Write 1-2 paragraphs about what you hear in this passage that applies to you. If you are not Christian, still reflect on the truths and write a response.

3. Personal response: In a paragraph, describe your response to D2. Will you change your actions or beliefs? Will you say yes or no to God? Honest wrestling with God is better than dishonest pious cliches.

Rationale for the 4 Steps of the Inductive Bible Study Processes and Their Order

Observation step: this step must come first so that you can see the details or facts in their original contexts, thereby alleviating most of your bias. You can't interpret a passage well without first seeing what all is in the passage.

Q: Why write down your initial reactions?
A: This process helps you admit to your assumptions and intentionally put them aside. It also engages you with the text.

Q: Why write down 30 facts?
A: This activity helps you see more details in the text.

Q: Why list all the people and people groups?
A: This list helps you notice the "little people."

Q: Why list all the places?
A: This process helps you place the story into the physical world; it helps you begin to see the story. Sometimes the places give clues to the interpretations.

Q: Why study the literary contexts?
A1: The writers were intentional in placing your passage. You will understand your passage better as you see its relationship to its surrounding passages.
A2: The Salvation history context helps you see how your singular passage contributes to the Big Story.
A3: The book context helps you see how your singular passage relates to the overall purpose of the book.
A4: The immediate literary context helps you see common themes, contrasts and comparisons to the surrounding stories.

Q: Why study the historical and cultural contexts?
A: Words take on meaning in their contexts. If you don't know the context, you will misinterpret the passage.

Analysis step: After studying the context for your passage, you must now study how the story itself works.

Q: Why identify the genre and note the interpretation principles?
A: Different genres communicate truth differently, and if you misidentify the genre, you will misinterpret the text. Once the genre has been identified, then you need to remind yourself how to properly interpret its message.

Q: Why create a vertical chart?

A: The vertical chart is a way to break the story down into its parts. In doing this, it's easier to see how the writer intentionally used literary techniques to heighten the meaning of the passage. You find repetitions, reversals and other emphases. You see the logical progress of the passage.

Q: Why summarize the passage without interpretation?

A: This process helps you understand the difference between describing and interpreting. It helps you practice withholding interpretation until enough research has been done.

Interpretation: After the work of observation and analysis, you are ready to find the meaning of the passage for the original audience. You must know the meaning for the original audience before you can safely determine the meaning for your society.

Q: Why list all kind of interpretations, even silly ones?

A: This process helps you see the difference between absurd and valid interpretations. Brainstorming also unleashes creativity that many times leads to better interpretations.

Q: Why make an interpretation/application chart?

A: Writing interpretations takes careful thought and several re-writes until you say what you mean to say. The chart helps you see your reasoning more clearly and it prepares you for your essay.

Q: Why write an interpretation essay?

A: This step, more than any other, serves to help you check your logic and evaluate your sources, thus helping you find accurate meanings for the original audience.

Q: Why list remaining questions?

A: Sometimes listing these questions alerts you to new research or a possible new interpretation. It's also a way to admit that there will always be more to a passage than we can know.

Application: having completed the first three steps, you are now ready to apply the eternal truth to your society and yourself.

Q: Why complete the interpretation/application chart?
A: Crossing back over "the bridge," you are now able to apply the eternal truth to today's culture. Finishing this chart will help you think more critically about the culture you live in.

Q: Why write about the meaning for me personally?
A: For many people, this is the reward for all the work of the inductive Bible study. Hearing what God says is the ultimate purpose of any Bible study. Waiting to determine the meaning in your life until now helps ensure that you heard God more accurately than if you had done a Devotional Bible study.

Q: Why write about how I will respond to what I heard?
A: Writing down your response helps you be intentional. By pushing yourself to respond, you don't allow yourself to avoid the main purpose of the Bible study.

Tips for Observation

The Observation step can look daunting, but it can also be the most rewarding. Discovering the worldview of the Bible is a fascinating process, like exploring a new world! Here are some ways we've discovered to get the most out of Observation:

Engage the passage emotionally as well as intellectually. Sometimes we fear the emotional reactions, because we think that our very emotions will take over and blind us to our biases. While this could happen, it's also deadly to repress our emotional reactions to the text, because those very reactions are themselves something we need to notice. We must ask, "Did the writer intend to foster these feelings, and if so, why?"

Read and re-read the passage. Many beginning Bible scholars think that one or two readings is enough, and they miss crucial details.

Remember that your most difficult task during the observation and analysis step is to hold off your interpretations. If you aren't mentally aware of how easily you can slip into assumptions, you will start to do *eisegesis* and miss the true meaning of the text.

Engage with the geography of your text, especially if you are studying a narrative. Knowing the "where" of your story helps you ask better overall questions of your story.

Remember that every Bible text has at least two contexts: the literary context and the historical-cultural context. The historical context usually includes both what is historically happening at the time of the narrative and what is happening when the author wrote the story. The literary context includes the whole biblical context, the context of the book where the passage is found, and the immediate context of the chapters before and after the passage.

Remember that words take on their meaning in context. For example, the word bat can either mean a small mammal that lives in a cave or a wooden stick used in the game of baseball.

Tips for Analysis

Remember that each genre communicates truth differently, so properly identifying the genre of a passage by observing its literary characteristics is crucial to good interpretation. If you demand certain genres to be literally true, then Jesus becomes an actual door...and a sheep.

Determine the basic written unit of study. Usually the paragraph is the basic unit of study for the inductive process. But short Bible passages might only be one paragraph and yet need to be divided into smaller units for literary study. If the text is only one paragraph long, then look for natural divisions and words that signal something new is happening.

Note words that in English signal transitions or comparisons. Those words include *also, but, yet, if, since, so, because, therefore,* and *although.*

Note the literary structure of the passage. Are the actions or events organized chronologically? How does the passage build to a climax? Is there a surprise ending? Does the passage feel like it has resolution or is it purposefully leading you to the next literary passage? What are the repetitions and what purpose did the writer have for making these repetitions?

Look for a chiasm. A chiasm is a pattern of organization where the beginning of the passage relates in some way to the end of the passage, either by being similar or completely opposite. Then, working its way inward, the passage has matching pairs, until the center of the passage. The pattern may look like this: A, B, C, C, B, A. Sometimes the very center of the passage has no matched pair and this part may hold special meaning. Here the pattern would look like this: A, B, C, X, C, B, A.

Remember the difference between history and *Geschichte*, especially when writing the summary of the passage. If you aren't careful, you will insert your own *Geschichte*.

Tips for Interpretation

Take your time when you assign meaning to facts and when you connect one fact to another. For example, you could easily surmise that adultery is wrong by the story in II Samuel 11, where David commits adultery with Bathsheba and then all sorts of bad things happen to him. That is a good interpretation, but it's not the only one, nor is it the primary interpretation. There's more to the story.

Take enough time to really interpret the passage well. Because it's easy to misinterpret, you must choose words carefully and give adequate time for reflection and evaluation of the interpretations you created. Try to catch the nuances of the passage. Determine what is explicit in the passage and what is implied.

Make your interpretation statements specific to the culture and the passage. For example, if the story has something to do with King Saul, then make your interpretation say something like, "Don't trust King Saul to be your king," or "Support the prophet Samuel as he dethrones King Saul." Later you can glean the eternal truth from this interpretation so that it is more applicable to your situation, but remember that for the original audience, they were trying to figure out how to obey God in the midst of real people and real situations. Avoid general or vague interpretations, such as "Trust God," or "Obey God." Every Bible passage has these general interpretations and therefore, a statement this general is not useful.

Begin your interpretation sentences with an imperative verb, as a way to avoid simply writing a statement. All your interpretations must state what the original audience was to do differently or what new truth they were to believe. For example, "Saul failed to obey the rules of Hole War" is simply a statement; it doesn't tell the reader what to do. However, "Obey the Holy War rule of *cherem* unlike King Saul who lost his throne for neglecting this rule" is a good interpretation because it tells the original audience what to do: Obey *cherem*. It's also a quality interpretation because it is specific to the story and culture.

Remember that the aim of biblical interpretation is to discover the plain meaning of the text, not some hidden or mysterious meaning. In general, God and the biblical writers didn't try to hide truth from the readers to make the meaning hard to understand. If things seem hidden in the Bible, it is because we don't understand the cultural-historical context.

Interpret the Bible; do not simply take it as it stands. Some people claim they don't interpret the Bible, but are able to completely understand God's meaning without their own bias. But that is impossible. To read is to interpret. Just the fact that we are not reading the passage in its original language means that we are reading the translator's interpretation. But even if we were proficient in the original language, it's human nature to experience or understand something through our own worldview. It's nearly impossible not to interpret subconsciously. Given this fact, we have two choices: interpret the Bible haphazardly without any self-awareness of our bias or interpret the Bible with a disciplined methodology that, using the tools of biblical criticism, helps us see the text as neutrally as possible.

Be humble in your interpretations. As humans, we can't interpret perfectly. This is why we label our best interpretations as "quite sure." We must live out the tension of being sure enough of our interpretations that we discipline ourselves to live by these truths, even to the point of sacrificing our lives and at the same time, we must always be humbly open to new insight from the Holy Spirit.

Be able to support your interpretations with good research and logic. Take what you discovered in the observation and analysis steps and apply analytical thinking or logic to that research. The combination of these elements will be the proof that your interpretations are valid. The interpretation essay is the place where you can spell out your reasoning and highlight your research.

Test your interpretations with the rest of the Bible. While the inductive process outlined in this book doesn't include a correlation step, where one checks his interpretations with other passages in the Bible, this is an excellent practice for those who know the Bible well enough to make correlations. If your interpretations for a particular passage find no correlate anywhere else in the Bible or they disagree with major portions of the Bible, you need to re-evaluate the validity of your interpretations. This doesn't mean that everything will always agree in the Bible. Some people begin with that assumption and then don't allow themselves to see the disagreements. Truth may be paradoxical or two-sided.

Remember that it's okay to have unanswered questions. It's actually a mark of good inductive Bible study if you have these questions. It shows that you've unearthed complex truths and thought through many hypothetical outcomes.

Tips for Application

Remember that the application statement, like the interpretation, can be stated positively or negatively. And like the interpretation, the application needs to tell its audience what to do differently or how to change their thinking or beliefs. The application may be an affirmation and encouragement to keep on doing something, a call to change or repent or a warning against something.

Remember that sometimes all the research into the different contexts of the biblical worldview glean rather straightforward or obvious eternal truths. Sometimes "crossing the Hermeneutical Bridge" is easy and we realize there's not much that changed between the two worlds. But don't dismiss an application if it seems too simple. The message to us might be clear, but difficult for us to do, such as the clear message that God wants us to help those who are poor. Here the interpretation/application challenge is not in understanding a vastly different context, but in living out the costly sacrifice that's plain to see.

Don't assume you understand your own culture thoroughly. Often one of the most difficult parts of the application step is to describe the relevant characteristics of the current society that relate to the application. Sometimes we are blind to the particulars of our own culture.

Take the time needed to honestly answer how this passage applies to you personally. The overall purpose of any Bible study is to hear what God is saying to you and then respond in kind.

Conclusion

"The Bible can't mean what it never meant when the event happened or when it was written."[1] If we allow the Bible to mean something to us that it never could have meant to the original audience, then we are making the Bible say whatever we want it to say. This can justify all sorts of unethical behaviors and lead to faulty theology. Maybe it's possible for the Bible to mean something different for us than for the original audience when we do devotional Bible study, but this can't be true if we are doing inductive study. We read and interpret the Bible looking over the shoulders of the

---

1   Gordon Fee and Douglas Stuart, *How to Read the Bible for All Its Worth,* (Grand Rapids: Zondervan, 2003), 30, 74.

original observers of the event they interpret or we look over the shoulders of the first readers of the documents. We work hard to connect the Bible to its history.

The biblical writers were not unconscious or in a trance writing for the future. They used language, metaphors and concepts that made sense to their worldview and context. Had the Bible been written for today's social, political and worldview context, the people of biblical times would have found the writings difficult to understand. The biblical writers were writing for their time and society.

The biblical writers were also selective in their writing. Many other events happened during these times that the authors chose not to include in the biblical narrative. But the events, poems and beliefs they did choose to write about held special meaning for them. A good question to ask in inductive Bible study is "Why was this remembered?"

The biblical writers interpreted events. This is not to deny the work of God in the process, but it is simply admitting that these human writers made interpretive decisions as they listened to God's voice. So the revelation of God comes in both the events themselves and in their interpretations. The writers were inspired and at the same time wrote in ways that made sense to them in their worldview. When we do thoroughly inductive Bible study, we honor their endeavors and we honor the Bible.

The Impact of Worldview on Bible Study

What is a Worldview?

We can define worldview or cosmology as the mental map of reality we carry in our minds. It's what we believe to be true or not true about our world. It is the assumptions we make and the presuppositions we hold that shape our opinions.[1] Am I the center of the universe, or am I a part of something much greater in scope? We all have a worldview, though we may not be conscious of it.

Our worldview is shaped by our families, schools, churches, communities, countries, and by personal experiences and observations. Our conscious universe may be local and self-centered, or it may be global in scope. We are mistaken if we think everyone sees the world as we do. A Kenyan proverb makes the point: "He that has never traveled thinks that his mother is the only good cook in the world!"

Typically, our perceptions of ourselves, our communities, our nations are rather limited. Education and travel expand our horizons by exposing us to other ways of seeing the world and thinking about reality. C.S. Lewis has observed that:

A [person] who has lived in many places is not likely to be deceived by the local errors of his native village: [the scholar] has lived in many

---

1   James W. Sire, *The Universe Next Door: A Basic Worldview Catalog*, 3rd ed. (Downers Grove: InterVarsity Press, 1997), 16.

times and is therefore in some degree immune from the…nonsense that pours from the press and the microphone of his own age.[2]

Elements of a Worldview

But how do we know our own worldview? How can we recognize other worldviews, including that of the Bible? Consider the following five components that make up a worldview:

1. **Ultimate reality**—The highest power, the *realest* reality. What is it like? When everything material is taken away, what is left? Possible answers: God, gods, good and evil spirits, angels, powers, nothing. What are these gods or powers like?

2. **Cosmos (Universe)**—What is the nature of physical reality and where does it come from? What lies at the center of the universe? Are physical things related? How? What is the nature of the earth? Biblical writers see the earth as flat, sitting on pillars in the midst of a watery abyss with a dome above the earth that holds back water above, and a higher area above where an active God makes everything happen directly like moving the sun and moon from one horizon to the other. Another simpler theory has the earth resting on the back of a giant turtle called, fittingly, the World Turtle.

    Alternatively, scientific theory—shaped over thousands of years as new observations forced corrections of old theories—suggests the earth is a tiny blue marble spinning on the edge of an inconceivably huge galaxy of stars, which itself is a mere speck within a still-expanding universe nearly 14 billion years old. Throughout history, understanding of the earth has been shaped by the information, ideas, and tools we use to observe our universe.

3. **Human nature and destiny**—Are humans good, bad, or somewhere in between? Some possible answers: Born good; born good but become distorted; born evil and learn goodness; created in the image of God; an evolving animal. The Greek philosopher Plato saw humans as good souls imprisoned in evil bodies. The biblical Hebrews viewed humans as integrated wholes.

---

2   C.S. Lewis, "Learning in War-Time," in *The Weight of Glory: And Other Addresses* (New York: HarperCollins, 2001), 59.

As for destiny, when we die we enter another eternal realm. You become extinct. You are transformed to a higher state. You exist in a shadowy existence until a resurrection. You reincarnate.

4. **Highest good and how we can know it**—What is the most important thing to do in life? Possible answers: Become godly ourselves, seek God's Kingdom; seek self-actualization; what feels good (Hedonism); seek the greatest good for the greatest number (Utilitarianism); the state. How do we know it? We know the highest good through revelation from God because we are created in the image of an all-knowing God, or we arrive at it from reasoning and evolved intuition.

5. **History's meaning and nature**—Is history cyclical or linear? Possible answers: realize fully the rule of God on earth or in another realm; merely prepare people for life with God in the next realm; life has no meaning and we should seek to escape it. Is history linear, starting sometime and will end with another realm to follow? Or is it cyclical, a never-ending repetition of time, seasons, life, reproduction, consumption, decline and death?[3]

Why Worldviews are Crucial to Bible Study

Authentic Bible study is a cross-cultural experience. We must understand our own cosmology as well as the ancient cosmologies of the biblical world. Since the Bible was written in other parts of the world, in other times, by people of different cultures, and in different languages, we must understand those worldviews in order to properly understand and interpret the Bible. This means we must disengage from our own worldview, or we will simply read into the Bible our own perceptions and assumptions (*eisegesis*) and misinterpret the Bible. As we have said in this course, "If we don't know the biblical worldview, we will misinterpret. If we don't understand our own worldview, we will misapply the biblical text."

Understanding Hebrew Cosmology

What is the biblical worldview? Elements of Hebrew cosmology reflected in various Old Testament passages. Consider the texts below.

In the biblical cosmology, the earth is flat with four corners (Revelation 7:1, Isaiah 11:12). It has ends (Job 28:24; Psalm 19:6, 22:27; Proverbs

---

3 Ibid., 17-18. Sire lists seven elements of a worldview.

30:4). The earth is set on pillars or foundations (I Samuel 2:8; Job 9:6; Psalm 75:3; Proverbs 9:1). Heaven or the firmament is a dome stretched across the sky (Job 37:18; Genesis 1:6) that separates the waters above from the waters below. The dome has windows (Genesis 8:2; II Kings 7:2, 19; Isaiah 24:18; Malachi 3:10), and a door (Revelation 4:1). Rain comes from the windows of heaven (Genesis 3:11).

The phrase "in heaven, or on earth, or under the earth" (Revelation 5:3, 13, 12:12; Philippians 2:10) reflects what might be called a triple-decker universe. God and good are up above in heaven, the dragon and evil are below, and the sea is the source of evil (Revelation 12:17, 13:1).

Incidentally, Jesus claims authority over the sea by calming it (Matthew 8:2). Demons return into the sea when they are cast into pigs and sent fleeing (Luke 8:33). The earth is the stage where the spiritual forces of good and evil battle it out.

The Hermeneutical Bridge

So how do we transport ourselves into the biblical world? If we had access to a time machine, we could do it quickly. Wouldn't it be easy if we could travel with *Back to the Future's* Marty McFly in Dr. Emmett "Doc" Brown's time-traveling Delorean? Or if we could step into the magic wardrobe with Lucy, Edmund, Susan, and Peter to be transported, not to mythical Narnia, but to Canaan in about 2000 or 1700 BCE? Since we don't have either of those options, we use another tool to bridge the gap between our world and the biblical world—the Hermeneutical Bridge. "Hermeneutics" is simply the art and the science of interpretation. So the bridge helps us enter the biblical world in order to understand and interpret the text as the writers intended and as the first hearers and readers understood it.

We begin by taking off our 21st century, worldview glasses. Temporarily, we leave them behind as we step onto the bridge and cross to the other side. When we enter the world of the Bible, we do three things: observe, analyze, and interpret what we find there. Only then do we return to our side of the bridge for the application.

Crossing the Hermeneutical Bridge

Hebrew Biblical Culture	Today's Culture
Observation	Application
Analysis	
Interpretation	

307

Since the biblical worldview is unlike our own, we must cross the Hermeneutical Bridge to understand biblical images and terminology. We believe that the Bible is the inspired, revealed word of God, and we believe the truth doesn't change, but cultures do change. If we are to take the Bible seriously, we must understand its context. Words take their meaning from their context.

Words take on meaning in their literary and cultural historical contexts. "I love you, too," can be said romantically, between family and friends, or even sarcastically to mean the opposite. What is missing in Bible study is the voice inflection and body language which often determine a word's meaning.

Word meanings change over time. New words are coined, old words change or have additional meanings. Consider words that have changed in recent times: trip, pot, fix, grass, bread, square, chicken, tough, rock, roll, and cool. So how do we know what biblical words, used many centuries ago, mean? Here are three steps:

- First, we need to understand the biblical worldview in order to understand the meaning of words, stories, metaphors, and analogies in their context.

- Second, we also need to understand our own worldview so we can apply the biblical teachings appropriately, consistent with their original meaning and intent in the Bible.

- Third, we need to understand the nature of different literary genres in order to interpret properly.

Our cosmology has changed also. Our view of the world and universe is based on science. Today we use scientific observation and explanations, considering cause and effect. We no longer say that God is directly making everything happen as in the biblical cosmology.

The Bible and Science

Is the Bible, its authority and revelation, discounted because the biblical cosmology isn't true according to modern scientific methodologies? Of course not. The Bible nowhere claims to make us "wise to science," but "wise to salvation." It does not pretend to answer modern questions of science. To insert scientific explanations into the biblical text is to dishonor the Bible. We can't make it say what it was never meant to say.

308

One of the oldest clashes between science and religion had to do with the solar system. For centuries people believed in a geocentric universe, where the earth is the center and the sun revolves around the earth. Renaissance scientist Nicholas Copernicus (1473-1543), challenged this view and presented the alternative hypothesis that we live in a heliocentric universe where the sun is the center and the earth (with other planets) revolves around the sun. Fearing the church's backlash, he waited to publish his theory until he was on his deathbed.

In the 17th century, Galileo Galilei (1564-1642), an Italian astronomer, proved the heliocentric model of the solar system. Church leaders were threatened, because they believed the Bible supported the geocentric model (Psalm 19:5-6). Galileo was called to a hearing and threatened with imprisonment and possible tortureHe recanted and lived the rest of his life under house arrest. Only in modern times did the church acknowledge its mistaken worldview: in 1992 Pope John Paul II issued an official retraction and apology.

The church continues to get into difficulty when it does not consider the cultural, historical context of biblical passages. The Bible is not science but rather, *Heilsgeschichte*.

As a student at Hesston College in the early 1970s, I was impressed in reading the poet James Russell Lowell, who in 1844, said:

Careless seems the great Avenger; history's pages but record
One death-grapple in the darkness 'twixt old systems and the World;
Truth forever on the scaffold, wrong forever on the throne, —
Yet that scaffold sways the future, and, behind the dim unknown,
Standeth God within the shadow, keeping watch above his own.[4]

Indeed, all the world, science included, is God's realm.

Worldviews of Greek Philosophers

Unlike Eastern or Hebrew thought, the Western world seems intent on seeing the world as divided into opposing ideas and concepts, and is focused on the individual. René Descartes, the French philosopher, represents the Western worldview: "I think, therefore I am." The more communal, relational, inclusive Easterner will say, "I am because we are." Do we emphasize thinking and knowing or do we focus on being and meaning?

---

4   James Russell Lowell, "The Present Crisis," Bartleby.com. Accessed June 3, 2016. http://www.bartleby.com/42/805.html.

It may be useful to consider the context for modern cosmology by turning to the Greek philosophers who have shaped the Western worldview. Consider the following four:

- For Socrates (470-399 BCE), knowledge is the ultimate reality. "The unexamined life is not worth living," he said. For him knowledge is the source of freedom, and one discovers truth by asking questions. The human is the measure of all things for there is no transcendent, metaphysical or spiritual reality.

- Plato (427-347 BCE), on the other hand, thought ultimate reality existed in the metaphysical (non-physical, beyond the five senses), in a "realm of forms" or ideas. The material world is merely a shadow of the ultimate reality of ideas. A chair, for example, is not real; what we see as a chair is only a shadow of a perfect idea of a chair. He demonstrates this in his famous cave analogy. Humans are chained in a cave, facing the wall where they could see only the shadows of real beings walking behind them. The shadows are cast by a fire behind them. Plato argued that the shadows were the physical world. What's real is the ideal form of our physical world, and God is the god of perfect form.

  Knowledge is subjective and we learn by contemplation and observation, using deductive reasoning.

- Aristotle (384-322 BCE), sometimes called the father of science, believed reality existed in both the physical and metaphysical realm. But one understands the metaphysical by observing the physical with the five senses. One learns about reality, not merely by abstract thinking, but by inductive reason, by observation.

- Some contemporary faith-based worldviews combine Plato and Aristotle. When Christians both pray for healing and consult a doctor they are combining Plato and Aristotle. The challenge is how to combine these worldviews in a life of discipleship putting faith and trust in God and also assuming personal responsibility.

- Epicurus (340-270 BCE), in contrast to Plato, said that only the material is real. What you see is all there is. Pleasure is the highest good. This philosophy is called Hedonism. God, if God exists at all, does not care about what we do.

We can also conceive of reality and truth from three points of reference: premodern (from ancient times to about 1500), modern (from 1500 to about the 1950s), and postmodern (1950s to the present).

Premodern, Modern, And Postmodern Worldviews

Premodern	Modern	Postmodern
Knowledge is divine	Knowledge can be free from human bias.	All knowledge is human and thus value laden. Scientists have human bias.
Truth comes from contemplation, prayer and revelation.	Truth comes from a reproducible experiment.	Truth comes from an evaluation of the process of study.
Knowledge is scarce and comes only to the "contemplative person."	Knowledge is scarce, and comes from the rigor of science.	Knowledge is everywhere and must be evaluated.
Qualitative	Quantitative	Contextualizes the quantitative
Truth tends to be context bound.	Truth can be generalized or is context free.	Truth must have a contextualization and generalization. Truth cannot be imposed; it must be chosen.
The "gods" are the sources of authority.	Empirical evidence is the source of authority.	Authority must be shared and is shared according to your values.
Weakness: It misses the whole because it tends to focus on the spiritual or philosophical.	Weakness: It misses the whole because it tends to focus on the physical cause and effect.	Weakness: It misses the whole because it tends to portray truth as relative

Requires superior intellect	Requires formal education	Requires critical (in the finest sense) thinking

Conclusion

Clearly, the biblical world is premodern, and we now live in a postmodern world, although those of us who are older may still think in modern terms. However we see ourselves, what is crucial here is understanding the premodern biblical world. When we take the Bible out of context and unhook it from history, we can make the Bible say and mean most anything. When misused, the Bible has been used to teach slavery, male dominance, prohibit the use of doctors, medicines, contraceptives, support the divine rights of kings, and capital punishment.

Most people consider some elements of worldview in their Bible study, though often unconsciously. We have made the case for the importance of intentionally using the inductive study process, worldview concepts, and the hermeneutical bridge. When we use them, the Bible speaks to us in the ways the authors intended and as the original audiences understood them. Only then can we appropriately apply the eternal truth to our time and place.

Part III
Hermeneutics

Formation of the Canon

The Purpose of the Bible

What is the Bible's purpose? When and how did we get the Bible? To answer the first question, let's start with what the Bible says about itself. "All scripture is inspired by God and is useful for teaching, for reproof, for correction, and for training in righteousness, so that everyone who belongs to God may be proficient, equipped for every good work" (II Timothy 3:16-17). The Bible is the *Heilsgeschichte*, the story of God, the story of Jesus, who is the fullest revelation of God, and the story of God's people. From it we learn how to live as God's people.

The Canon

We refer to the Bible as a "canon," which comes from the Greek word *kanon*, meaning a tool for measuring, a standard by which something is judged. For example, in order to determine if a wall is perfectly vertical or whether a table is level, we need a tool, such as a carpenter's level or a plumb line. The books of the Bible "measured up" as books considered inspired by God. Now taken together as the whole revelation called the Bible, these books provide direction for understanding God's purposes.

In Anabaptist theology, there is also a canon *within* the canon. When scriptures disagree, Jesus settles the argument. The New Testament is the lens through which we read the whole Bible.

The Old Testament Canon

The answer to the second question, "When and how did we get the Bible?" is longer and more complex. First, we consider the formation of the Old Testament canon. Let's recall what happened in the Babylonian Exile, after 587 BCE. When Nebuchadnezzar and the Babylonians captured and destroyed Jerusalem, the people of Judah lost everything. They lost the temple, their homeland, priests in the line of Levi, and kings in the line of David. Since there was no temple, priests were no longer needed. Instead, scribes replaced priests for the task of gathering and editing the scriptures that had been preserved and passed on orally. So in the crisis of crises, the scriptures were preserved by writing.

Fast-forward to another crisis, the destruction of Jerusalem in 70 CE. The Jews, unhappy under the oppressive rule of the Romans, rebelled in 66 CE. As a result, the Romans crushed the rebellion, slaughtered many, and destroyed the city, the temple, and synagogues throughout the land.

With the destruction of the temple and synagogues, "the book" once again became the most significant source for faith and practice. At the same time, Christians, a Jewish subgroup, began collecting and writing the gospels, the story of Jesus, and the epistles, the letters of Paul and other disciples of Jesus.

To preserve their own teachings and traditions, Jewish scholars met in Jamnia in 90 CE. Their mission was to determine which of the many writings should be included in their canon. Some scholars believe that there was a series of meetings. But as Jewish scholars point out, in either case, "the enduring significance of Jamnia lies not in the closing of the Jewish canon, but in ensuring the cultural and religious survival of the Jewish people."[1]

Council of Jamnia, whether a one-time council or a series of meetings, defined Judaism over against the growing Christian Church. This determination of their sacred writings led to the widening gap between Jewish Christians and Jewish Community.

Two criteria determined which writings were to be included in the canon: 1) they needed to be written in Hebrew, and 2) they had to be written before prophetic inspiration ended with Ezra and Nehemiah. The fourteen books rejected for the canon are called the *Apocrypha* (secret or

---

1   Peter Shirokov and Dr. Eli, Lizorkin-Eyzenberg, "The Council of Jamnia and Old Testament Canon," *Jewish Studies Blog, Official Forum of Israel Institute of Biblical Studies.* Accessed June 2, 2016. http://jewishstudies.eteacherbiblical.com/jamnia/

hidden writings) and include books of the intertestamental period, such as the five Books of the Maccabees.

The New Testament Canon

The Christians accepted the Old Testament as their scriptures, but they also added their own sacred writings, which became the New Testament. When the books were written is a bit of a puzzle. Scholars disagree about the dates of writing, but it seems clear that the Apostle Paul's epistles or letters to the churches were earlier than the gospels. In the period between 48 CE and 66 CE, Paul's epistles were copied and circulated in the churches. James, the brother of Jesus, wrote his epistle about the same time as Paul wrote Galatians and I Thessalonians, about 49-51 CE.

The gospels came later. Mark was the first (about 65 CE), followed by Matthew and Luke (about 70 CE), and John (in 85 or later). John's three epistles, I, II, and III John, were written around 90 CE.

Since many other accounts of Jesus and many other epistles or letters were written and circulated, it was necessary to determine which were most authentic and authoritative.

The Councils of Hippo in 393 CE and Carthage in 397 CE, both in North Africa, established the Church's New Testament canon. Once again, two criteria were used: 1) they needed to be written by eyewitnesses to Jesus or closely associated with them, and 2) the content of the writings needed to agree with the orthodox (commonly agreed upon) teachings of the church.[2]

Writings not accepted into the canon by the councils are called the New Testament *Apocrypha* and the *Pseudepigrapha* (false writings). We know of seven Epistles, nineteen Gospels, twenty four books of Acts, and six Apocalypses that circulated among the churches. Until the sixteenth-century Reformation, Christians included the Old Testament *Apocrypha*. But after the Reformation, most Protestants excluded them from their Bible. The Roman Catholic Church, however, uses selections from the *Apocrypha* for readings in their worship liturgy. The Amish make use of the *Apocrypha* as well, especially the Book of Tobit, for wedding sermons.

Translations

In about 400 CE, Jerome (c. 245-420), a monk and biblical scholar, made

---

2   Mark A. Noll, *Turning Points: Decisive Moments in the History of Christianity* (Grand Rapids, Mi.: Baker Academic, Ninth Edition, 2008), 24-38.

a Latin translation of the Greek New Testament and the Hebrew Bible, called the *Vulgate*. Until the Reformation, Jerome's translation was the official Bible for the Roman Catholic Church.[3]

John Wycliffe (1329-1384), the English church reformer, first translated the Bible into English in 1382 as a hand-printed copy. In 1525, William Tyndale published the New Testament and part of the Old Testament. Martin Luther translated the Latin New Testament into German in 1522, and in 1534, he finished the entire Bible. German language speakers still use Luther's translation. The Roman Catholic Church made a new Latin translation from the *Vulgate* in 1582 and 1610, called the Rheims-Douai. The most recent Roman Catholic English translation is *The Jerusalem Bible*. When English Puritans requested a new English translation, King James I authorized the 1611 *King James Version* based on the *Vulgate* and earlier English translations.

The discovery of more manuscripts and the changing English language have called for fresh and newer translations. Among the major English translations of the twentieth century are the *Revised Standard Version* (1950), the *New English Bible* (1960, 1971) the *New International Version* (1973), the *New Revised Standard Version* (1989), and *Today's New International Version*. In addition, there are numerous other more recent English translations. The Bible has been translated into all the major languages of the world.

Paraphrases and Manuscripts

Unlike genuine translations, paraphrases are rewritten versions of the Bible that adapt existing English versions into watered-down vernacular. Paraphrases can make the story feel more accessible, particularly to younger readers, but they should not be used for serious study.

We know of more than 5,000 Greek manuscripts and over 24,000 fragments of the New Testament. The earliest, shortest, and most difficult readings are considered the most authentic. Sometimes variations occurred when manuscripts were copied by hand. Missed words or lines are called errors of the eye. Words that are missed or changed while one scribal monk read as another copied are called errors of the ear.[4]

R.W.F. Wootton has called Bible translation one of the church's greatest

---

3   Ibid., Noll, 112.

4   Bruce M. Metzger, *The Text of the New Testament* (New York & London: Oxford University Press, 1964), 186-192.

success stories of the last century. At the turn of the twentieth century, parts of the Bible were translated into 517 languages. By 1990, portions of the Bible had been translated into nearly 2,000 languages. Complete translations of the Bible number 310. In addition, there are more than 45 English versions of the Bible.[5]

Canon and the Church

After the Council of Jamnia in 90 CE, and after the councils of Hippo in 393 CE and Carthage in 397 CE, we say the Bible is complete and the canon is closed. Since then, no more books have been added to the Bible. When considering the relationship between the church and the canon, we say that before the canon was closed, the church was above the canon, since the church determined the canon. After the closing of the canon, the canon is above the church, that is, the church acknowledges the authority of the Bible for its faith and practice.

5   R.W.F. Wooten, "Translating the Bible," in Dr. Tim Dowly, ed. *Introduction to the History of Christianity* (Minneapolis: Fortress Press, 2002), 654.

The Unity and Disunity of the Biblical Library

When the Bible Seems to Disagree with Itself

Have you ever disagreed with someone about God's will or what you believe God wants people to do in certain situations? And in this disagreement, were both of you quoting scripture? This scenario has happened many times because, at first glance, the Bible has different viewpoints on ethics, or our beliefs about what's right and wrong to do. Two equally devout Christians can both do careful inductive Bible study and still come out with radically different, even contradictory interpretations about God's will. Different Christians have a variety of ways they solve the problem of biblical disunity, whether they are fully aware of their solution or not. The purpose of this chapter is to show how different Christians use different approaches to solve the problem of biblical disunity. In a larger sense, we are studying hermeneutics, which is a term used for the process of studying, interpreting, and applying the scriptures.

It's all about assumptions. Assumptions, our unspoken ideas about how the Bible works, are a big part of hermeneutics. Imagine sitting in the big chair at the eye doctor's office. When the doctor tests your vision, she swings a big metal contraption containing several strengths of lenses over your eyes. As she swaps out different lenses, she asks you to read letters and numbers off a small screen. The letters and numbers don't change, but they do become clearer or fuzzier, depending on the lenses the doctor is using.

The test ends when the letters and numbers are at their clearest, meaning the doctor has arrived at your individual prescription.

Just like everyone who sits in the eye doctor's chair must decide for themselves which lenses help them see the best, Bible readers must decide which hermeneutical approach has the most integrity.

But unlike the eye exam, in which every patient must first try to read the screen with no lenses at all, nearly every reader brings some presuppositions and pre-existing beliefs to the biblical story—and ways of interpreting the story when there are conflicting views. Knowing our own assumptions or presuppositions is so important because what we bring to the Bible determines what the Bible says to us.

Let's repeat that, because it is so essential to understanding how people all over the world read and understand the Bible: *The assumptions and presuppositions we bring to the Bible determine what the Bible says to us.*

Our assumptions are particularly influential when we consider difficult ethical issues. Yet many readers of the Bible are unaware of how they solve the "disunity" problem, let alone how others who may disagree with them solve the problem. So it is crucial to be aware of the assumptions we bring to Bible study.

It's also important to understand hermeneutics so that we can better understand and appreciate each other. Persons who don't agree on what the Bible teaches can talk past each other when they aren't aware of each other's hermeneutical approach or starting assumptions. If they don't know each other's hermeneutics, they will only know that they disagree, but not why! When people disagree without knowing why, it's easy to doubt the other person's sincerity or openness to truth or they may doubt how seriously the other person takes the Bible. But personal attacks or doubts about another person's faith will not solve the problem. Only when we become aware of our own hermeneutical assumptions and approach to the Bible can we become aware of another person's hermeneutical approach in comparison to our own.

This is not a new problem. Down through the centuries Christians have wrestled with what to do about the diversity in the Bible. Marcion in the second century CE went to the extreme of discarding the Old Testament completely because of the contrasts, disunity, and disagreements with Jesus and the New Testament.[1] Some Christians today discard or ignore much of

---

1   Mark A. Noll, *Turning Points: Decisive Moments in the History of Christianity,* 9th ed. (Grand Rapids: Baker Academic, 2008), 35.

the Old Testament all the while saying that the whole Bible is the inspired word of God.

Jesus indicated that he disagreed with some things that were said in earlier times. He said six times in Matthew 5, "You have heard that it was said...but I say to you..." Different churches and people deal with the contrasts and contradictions between the Old and New Testaments differently. Assumptions about the relationship of the two Testaments have an enormous effect on what we allow the Bible to tell us about God's will. If the same God is behind both Old and New Testament, how do we deal with the sometimes night-and-day disagreements? Does God's will change? Is God's will relative to situations and changes with different situations?

A well-developed hermeneutic can help you answer those questions.

Basic Hermeneutical Approaches

There are four basic hermeneutical approaches to the Bible in the Christian tradition: Allegorical, Flat Bible, Dispensational, and the Ethical Christocentric approach. All four hermeneutical approaches attempt to deal with the disunity and apparent disagreements in the Bible. All four deal differently with that disunity.

Allegorical Hermeneutic

The allegorical hermeneutic approach has its roots in Greek philosophy. Philo, a Jewish scholar born in ca. 25 BCE and steeped in Greek philosophical education, brought this approach into the Hebrew scripture interpretation tradition in first century BCE. He used allegory to reconcile Israel's faith with Greek philosophy. The overall allegorical approach includes three related allegorical strategies: spiritualization, typology, and allegory/metaphor. Spiritualizing scriptures is a part of the Pietistic tradition in which scripture takes on uniquely personal meanings that have to do with inward thoughts and attitudes rather than outward actions. The typology approach sees persons, objects and happenings in the Old Testament as a type of Christ or other New Testament realities. Allegory goes further, driving metaphor to its logical end, going directly to "that is this" rather than "that is like this." Except for a few parables such as the Sower (Matthew 13:1-23) and the Parable of the Weeds (Matthew 13:24-30, 36-43) parts of the book of Hebrews, and Paul's description of

Sarah and Hagar in Galatians 4, allegory is not overtly used in the New Testament.

Allegorizing the Old Testament is one way to deal with the disunity and disagreement between the Old and New Testaments. When the Bible states apparently conflicting ways God wants us to act, this approach would take one of those ways and say, "You can't take the plain sense of this text. The elements of this scripture mean something different."

In general, allegorical strategies soften some of the difficult ethical standards of the Bible, making it into a devotional reading that's disconnected from the real life in biblical times or today. Overuse of allegorical interpretation tends to lead to a Christianity that is essentially inward and abstract, a kind of Pietism where salvation and ethics are disconnected. So a devoutly spiritual Bernard of Clairvaux, using the Allegorical hermeneutic approach, could write deeply spiritual hymns like "Jesus the Very Thought of Thee" and at the same time support despicable and bloody endeavors like the crusades.[2]

The allegorical hermeneutic approach was used through the centuries until the Renaissance and Reformation times when new freedoms and the printing press allowed scholars to go back to the original languages and question long standing interpretations. This new flowering of critical thinking and a rediscovery of the teachings of Jesus brought serious questions to this approach. While the Bible does occasionally use allegory, are we allowed to take that liberty ourselves? How can we know that we aren't allegorizing what is meant to be taken literally? What keep us from making the Bible say what we want it to say?

Flat Bible Hermeneutic

Flat Bible Christians solve the disunity problem in a different way. Probably the most common style of interpretation since the reign of Constantine, the Flat Bible approach claims that when the Bible disagrees with itself, it's because God has two different ultimate wills that apply to different situations.

The logic is fairly simple: if the ethics under question are corporate ethics or deal with a group or institution, then Christians should look to the Old Testament to find out God's ultimate will. If the ethic in question

2   Bernard of Clairvaux, "Letter to Eastern France and Bavaria Promoting the Second Crusade," 1146, *Bernard of Clairvaux, the Jews and the Second Crusade (1146)*, Council of Centers on Jewish-Christian Relations, Accessed June 22, 2016. www.ccjr.us.

is a personal matter or dealing only with the individual, then one must look at the New Testament and the life of Jesus for direction in what to do, or God's ultimate will.

Take for example the issue of whether or not Christians should participate in war. War is considered to be a corporate ethical issue; it deals with a relationship of an entire country and the corporate institution of a government that would call for war. So Flat Bible Christians would look to the Old Testament for guidance. Seeing that the Old Testament has wars where God's People fight, they conclude that Christians today should fight in a war for their country.

On the other hand, if violence is not corporate but rather a personal attack, such as a burglar who breaks into your home, then Flat Bible Christians look to the New Testament and Jesus. Since self-defense is a personal issue, one must abide by the teachings of Jesus, who would call us to love our enemies and refrain from personal retaliation. Therefore it would be unfaithful to attack the burglar inside your house.

So a Christian could be personally nonviolent like Jesus and still think it is God's will to kill in war or as a policemen, or to pull the switch as a public official to execute a prisoner. In the Flat Bible Hermeneutic, all scripture has equal authority for our lives, but our personal lives use a different Testament than our corporate lives.

Dispensational Hermeneutic

The Dispensational approach deals with the diversity in the Bible by saying that God has many different ultimate wills for different time periods, called dispensations. Dispensational Christians look at the past, present and future and divide all of time into seven or more dispensations. Then they take the Bible and also divide it into seven sections, or more sections if they believe in more dispensations. Each time period has a particular section of the Bible that pertains to it. Therefore, Christians living in that dispensation only need to abide by the ethics in their particular section of the Bible.

To interpret the Bible correctly with this approach, you must first determine which dispensation a passage is in. Most dispensationalists say, for instance, that the Sermon on the Mount is really for a future dispensation—-the millennium after Christ returns—not for today, and therefore Christians today don't need to follow the Sermon on the Mount teachings (Matthew 5-7). Using the ethical dilemma of Christians going to war, the Dispensational Christians would agree with the Flat Bible Christians but use different logic to come to the same conclusion. Flat Bible Christians think they should go to war because war is a corporate ethical issues and for corporate ethics, one looks to the Old Testament, where there we see God's people engaging in wars. Dispensational Christians also say that Christians should engage in war, but they would argue that the Bible passages meant for our current dispensation allow Christians to go to war. Once Jesus returns and a new dispensation begins, we will then start following the Sermon on the Mount and other teachings of Jesus and we will not be allowed to go to war.

This approach is relatively new, coming into the church since the late 1800s, primarily via John Nelson Darby (1800-1882). Since it is a complex approach, with numerous charts and graphs, dispensational scholars have created extensive footnotes in two study Bibles: the *Scofield Reference Bible* and *Ryrie Study Bible*. These notes "help the reader understand and interpret the scripture." The Dispensational hermeneutic approach is another way to deal with the diversity in the Bible.[3]

Christocentric Hermeneutic

Christians who have a ethically Christocentric hermeneutic solve the diversity problem in a different way. Christocentric is another way of saying "Christ-centered." What can be confusing is that nearly all Christian churches say they are Christocentric. Who doesn't want to be Christ-centered? But by that phrase, many of these churches believe in being Christ-centered spiritually, but not necessarily ethically. In other words, they do put Jesus in the center for their inner, spiritual lives, but don't favor Jesus' words over other scriptures when it comes to ethical issues.

The Christocentric approach acknowledges the inspiration of all scripture and affirms the usefulness of all scripture, but it gives more authority to the words of Jesus over other scripture when those scriptures disagree with each other. The Christocentric interpretation takes seriously the scripture that calls Jesus the "Word" of God (John 1:1-3). If Jesus truly is God incarnated in the flesh, then Jesus must therefore be the clearest picture of what God really wants and who God really is—and the clearest picture of God's ultimate will in ethical dilemmas.

The following scriptures illustrate the point:

---

3 Norman C. Kraus, *Dispensationalism in America: Its Rise and Development* (Richmond: John Knox Press, 1958), 26-30, 111-130.

No one has ever seen God. It is God the only Son, who is close to the Father's heart, who has made him known (John 1:18).

Long ago God spoke to our ancestors in many and various ways by the prophets, but in these last days he has spoken to us by a Son, whom he appointed heir of all things, through whom he also created the worlds. He is the reflection of God's glory and the exact imprint of God's very being, and he sustains all things by his powerful word (Hebrews 1:1-3a).

Jesus is the reflection of God's glory and the exact imprint of God's very being, so when the Bible disagrees with itself, which is what "God spoke to our ancestors in many and various ways (Hebrews 1:1) means, we should look at Jesus as the best revelation (Hebrews 1:2-3).

The Christocentric hermeneutic seeks to recognize both the unity and diversity of the Scriptures. God has one ultimate will that is revealed most clearly and fully in Jesus Christ because he was completely faithful to God in contrast to the Old Testament People of God who were often unfaithful. Because all other persons in the Bible were unfaithful sometimes, we must read between the lines as God works with the "lumpy clay" that sometimes resists being obedient. As Jeremiah 18:1-11 helps us see, God is like a potter working with clay. When the clay pot gets lumpy, God reshapes it. However, unlike clay, people can make choices and when we choose to disobey, God also changes his mind and continues to work with us. This is good because God stays with us, but we still must deal with the negative consequences of our choices. So the primary reason why we see different ethics in the Old Testament as compared to the New Testament is that people, in their free will, chose to disobey God. At this point the biblical narrative becomes descriptive, not prescriptive. In other words, many of the Old Testament passages tell us what happened, but not necessarily what God *wanted* to happen.

Through this interpretation, the Old Testament becomes a story of God's faithfulness and creativity in dealing with a wayward and unfaithful people.

The pot he was shaping from the clay was marred in his hands, so the potter formed it into another pot, shaping it as seemed best to him... "O house of Israel, can I not do with you as this potter does?" declares the Lord (Jeremiah 18: 4-5).

When God works redemptively with the unfaithful, lumpy People of God clay, we call that God's remedial will. It is remedial in that God attempts to remedy or better the person or group and change the situation created by unfaithfulness. Some refer to the remedial will of God as God's "permissive" or "redemptive" will in contrast to the perfect will of God. The word "permissive" may give the impression of a disengaged God who glumly shrugs off unfaithfulness and mutters to a resisting people, "Do whatever you want. I don't care." Understanding the remedial will of God captures the fact that God graciously stays engaged with the disobedient people, seeking to make the best out of the wrong decision they've taken.

The word "redemptive" may come closer to "remedial" but may be interpreted that God is just about forgiving. God seeks to remedy the situation, helping the person or people be all they can be after they have failed to follow God's "ultimate" will. It is like the GPS recalculating when a driver ignores directions because he thinks he knows a shortcut. The destination doesn't change just because the route has been altered.

The Christocentric approach says that God's ultimate will (ethically as well as spiritually) was always the same as that revealed in the completely faithful Jesus Christ. When the Bible teaches something different from Jesus' teachings, we need to look at what disobedience God was trying to remedy. Since Jesus is the fullest revelation in the Bible, his life and teaching become a kind of canon with the biblical canon. When parts of the Bible seem to disagree, the Christocentric hermeneutic takes Jesus' life and his teachings as the overriding authority or revelation.

For Christocentric Christians, this primary attention to Jesus applies not only to our belief systems and personal piety but also to our ethics. Christians who use another hermeneutic might say, for example, that Jesus replaces the Old Testament sacrifices or the Temple (belief system) but would not prioritize the words of Jesus when it comes to the ethical issue of whether or not Christians should support the death penalty.

The Christocentric hermeneutic sees up (faithful) and down (unfaithful) movement in the Bible. The People of God are sometimes more faithful and sometimes less faithful. God graciously keeps working with the people to try to shape them into the most faithful people possible in light of their disobedience. It is crucial not to confuse God's ultimate will personified in Jesus with the remedial ethic in the Bible. It is equally crucial not to teach the remedial ethic as God's ultimate will. In the ethical Christocentric hermeneutic one always begins with God's ultimate will in the Bible, not the remedial will.

The church may work with persons in a remedial or redemptive way in light of the situation their disobedience has created, but the church should not teach that remedial will as God's ultimate will. The issue of divorce can provide an example. Because of circumstances where persons could be physically or emotionally hurt by a parent or spouse, divorce may be recommended, as a remedial solution to a pressing problem. But this doesn't mean that a pastor should preach from the pulpit that divorce is a good option, or the ultimate will of God. The Jesus ethic, not the remedial ethic, is the standard for Christians today.

To return to the analogy of GPS navigation, the voice that says, "Recalculating," when one makes a wrong turn (sinful act) doesn't just abandon you because you made a wrong turn! But on the other hand, the remedial directions shouldn't be used at the beginning of the journey either.

God's forgiveness and gracious remedial will should not lead Christians to "sin so grace may abound" (Romans 6:1), or take God's forgiveness and remedial will for granted. The apostle Paul writes in I Corinthians 6:20, "For you were bought with a price." It cost Jesus his life to reveal God's grace and ultimate will.

Descriptive and Prescriptive Passages

Distinguishing between descriptive and prescriptive passages is a crucial hermeneutical issue. Descriptive passages are scriptures whose purpose is to describe what happened. Prescriptive passages aim to tell the reader what to do or what to believe—they prescribe or give direction. Failure to distinguish these two kinds of scriptures can lead to a view where Jesus teaches contradictory behavior. When Jesus says, "The poor you will always have with you" (Matthew 26:11), he did not mean that it is God's will that there should always be poor people and that any modernday program meant to eliminate poverty goes against the Bible and God's will. The same applies to Jesus' statement, "There will be wars and rumors of war" (Matthew 24:6).

Jesus' Hermeneutic and View of the Old Testament

What was Jesus' hermeneutic? He had only the Old Testament for scripture. Jesus certainly set up some of his teachings in contrast to the Old Testament. But he also said that he did not come to do away with the law but to fulfill it, to fill it out, or in other words, live out the law's intent

328

or purpose (Matthew 5:17-20). Jesus intensifies the law. With his life and teachings, Jesus lived out or revealed what the law pointed to or attempted to create.

Perhaps the clearest picture of Jesus' hermeneutics is found in Matthew 5:21-48. As mentioned earlier, six times he says, "You have heard that it was said [by Moses]...but I say to you." Each time Jesus takes one of the laws of Moses, dear to the heart of every Torah-observant Jew, he contrasts the outer workings of that law with a true change of heart. In Matthew 5:21, for example, Jesus says:

You have heard that it was said to those of ancient times, "You shall not murder"; and "whoever murders shall be liable to judgment." But I say to you that if you are angry with a brother or sister, you will be liable to judgment; and if you insult a brother or sister, you will be liable to the council; and if you say, "You fool", you will be liable to the hell of fire.

Moses set down the law that one should not murder. Jesus affirms that. But he takes it one step further to address the real bondage that enslaves people: anger and hatred. He also raises the bar that Moses set. He goes back to God's ultimate will, where it's not good enough merely to refrain from murder, but not to let anger lead you to violence at all.

Illustration of Marriage and Divorce

The Pharisees tried to trap Jesus by asking him about marriage and divorce (Matthew 19:2-9). They had heard his strong teachings on the permanence of marriage. So they ask him why Moses set up divorce laws. Jesus replies that Moses created those divorce laws because of the "hardness of their hearts" (God's remedial will), but that from the beginning it was not so (God's ultimate will). In historical context Moses' divorce laws were set up to protect women and the less powerful.[4] The laws also attempted to shore up the institution of marriage knowing that society depended upon stable social structures. Thus a man could not abuse a woman by changing his mind and taking back a woman whom he had divorced and who had married another man who also divorced her (Deuteronomy 24).

Jesus' response to the Pharisees' question reveal his hermeneutic approach. How Jesus read and interpreted the Old Testament becomes clear in his answer to the Pharisees. The Pharisees were going back to the

---

4   John Driver, *Kingdom Citizens* (Scottdale, PA: Herald Press, 1980), 85-87.

remedial Law of Moses that came about because of their disobedience and hardness of heart (Matthew 19:8). Jesus went back beyond the law of Moses to the beginning or the ultimate will of God. Jesus was not going to allow the Pharisees to substitute the remedial law of Moses for the ultimate will of God.

Jesus clearly distinguished between God's ultimate will and remedial will in the case laws of Moses and the unity and disunity in the Bible.

Illustration of Violence and Nonviolence

A second illustration from the Bible traces God's response to violence. The peaceful, harmonious relationships in the Garden before sin represents a major part of God pronouncing the creation very good. But sin enters the world through the first humans seeking to become equal with God. Adam blames Eve and Eve blames the snake. Their self-consciousness in being naked also reveals a change in their relationship. Their inner peace is disturbed and their relationship with the creation is forever changed.

The Genesis 1-11 stories reveal the exponential growth of sin and its results. The shalom in the garden is disrupted, and soon Cain kills his own brother out of jealousy. The downhill snowballing violence is illustrated by Lamech bragging about killing a man for only wounding him (Genesis 4:23). Then the flood comes because the earth was "full of violence." The Law of Moses seeks to limit the unchecked, survival-of-the-fittest violence that Lamech proposed. God's remedial will in the law of Moses limits revenge to "one eye for one eye." This kind of justice limits persons from taking uncontrolled vengeance to blinding a person who destroyed one of your eyes (Exodus 21:24, Leviticus 24:20).

Along comes Jesus and teaches the law of unlimited love and forgiveness rather than vengeance. Jesus says "eye for an eye" is not God's ultimate will (Matthew 5:38-42). He teaches his followers to do as God does. God makes the sun and rain come on the just and the unjust, those who deserve it and those who don't. Jesus says this kind of unlimited love is the hallmark of a child of the heavenly Father (Matthew 5:44). Jesus reveals and teaches the ultimate will of God that was previously revealed in the beginning Garden story. The movement in the Bible goes from the garden shalom to the law of the jungle to the law of justice to the Jesus way of forgiveness and love. The up and down movement goes from unlimited love in the garden to unlimited revenge in Cain and Lamech, to limited revenge in the law of Moses, to unlimited love and forgiveness in the life and teachings of Jesus.

Illustration of Holy War

Holy War also illustrates the up and down movement in the Bible. In the original Holy War at the Red Sea, Moses tells the people to "stand still and see the salvation of the Lord, for the Lord will fight for you" (Exodus 14:13-14). Because Yahweh fought, the people did not engage in violence. The way of Holy War among Israel's neighbors was to fight to help their gods fight the gods of their enemies. The Israelites made a radical change from this view. *Because Yahweh fought Holy War for them, the people did not fight in war in the original Exodus model.*[5]

However the rules of Holy War were soon modified to a less radical model where God's people fought with God. Later David established the first standing army. Now God's people attempted to fight for God. This disobedience took the Israelites down to the level of their neighbors. They were no longer different. No longer was their very existence a witness and miracle of Yahweh as it was before the Monarchy. They now trusted in "horses and chariots" like other nation-states. In the next modification, Yahweh fought with the Babylonians against Judah as an act of judgment hoping the people would repent.

Jesus came into this distorted teaching and he fought evil in the original way. Just like the Red Sea event, he stood still before Pilate and Herod waiting for God to act. And God did act in the resurrection where Jesus was raised from the dead. By refusing to fight evil with evil, by trusting God and being nonviolent even in the face of death, the evil powers were exposed for what they really were; not all good and not all powerful. The greatest power of evil, death, was overcome through the resurrection.

When we trace the history of Holy War, we see again that God keeps engaging the people although they are unfaithful. What's interesting in the history of Holy War in the Old Testament is that the movement of faithfulness isn't a clear down and then up pattern. Sometimes in the middle of the Old Testament narrative, the people listen to the prophets and fight Holy War close to the original way, when only Yahweh did the fighting (II Kings 6). But shortly thereafter, they would be back to relying on their military strength instead of God. But despite these variations, there was overall disobedience from God's people until Jesus came and re-revealed God's ultimate will on war. Jesus fought evil like the Red Sea. He stood still. They crucified him, and it looked like evil had won. But God vindicated Jesus by raising him from the dead. Ironically, the evil

---

5   Millard Lind, *Yahweh is a Warrior* (Scottdale, PA: Herald Press, 1980). 46-59.

331

powers defeated themselves when they crucified Jesus. His unlimited love, his refusal to hate—these things unmasked evil for what it truly was.

The three examples above illustrate the up and down ethical "movement" in the Bible and the ultimate and remedial will of God. The movement from the miraculous theocracy (God's ultimate will) to kingship is another illustration of God's remedial will. Jesus came to re-reveal God's ultimate, original will that had become clouded, modified and lost through the people's unfaithfulness. Jesus came to bring the new, but in a deeper sense he came to restore the original intent and condition of the law before the fall of humans into sin. He came to make us truly human again!

While most if not all Christians can see how Jesus re-revealed God's original intent, Christocentric Christians choose to then do as Jesus did. If Jesus "turned the other cheek" (Matthew 5:39) as his way of dealing with personal retaliation, then they do this as well. They fight evil in the same way Jesus did, by standing still in nonviolent actions and through Jesus' help, by loving their enemies. They fight Holy War the way Jesus did: through love.

Deciding on a Biblical Hermeneutic

This study should help you discover the unspoken hermeneutic used in the preaching and teaching you have had in your religious background, if you have such. Now you can explore which hermeneutic makes the most sense to you as you read the Bible with genuine fresh eyes as if for the first time. Regardless of our background, we all have to decide upon a consistent hermeneutic as did Christians through the centuries. Taking the whole Bible as it is, how does it want to be read? Using the Allegorical approach or Flat Bible? Dispensational or ethically Christocentric? Your choice will determine what you think the Bible says is God's will for us today.

The hermeneutical approach to the Scriptures that sees Jesus as the point with which one begins to study and interpret all Scripture was foundational for the 16th-century Anabaptists. The Mennonite Church and other Christians in and beyond the Anabaptist tradition read the Bible Christocentrically both spiritually and ethically for all of life. For them, Jesus is the fullest and most complete revelation of God's will. Therefore, Jesus the Christ becomes the court of last review when there is a difference between and within the Old and New Testaments.

Mennonite social scientist Guy F. Hershberger describes the different ways the two Testaments can relate to each other. In one sense, the Old

Testament prepares for the New Testament. It fulfills or completes it. But more than anything else, the New Testament supersedes the Old Testament, not in a way that makes the Old Testament unimportant but in that Christ is the final authoritative word of God.[6]

Then Why Study the Old Testament?

In light of the revelation of the historic Jesus and the Radical New Creation called the church, we see what God was trying to accomplish during the time of the Old People of God. And we can appreciate God's dynamic, ongoing relationship with a people who were inconsistent in their faithfulness.

It enables us to see the fuller dimensions of Jesus the Messiah and his mission in the New Testament, historic and salvation history contexts.

The Old Testament helps us see that Jesus comes to us through salvation history context, not in a disconnected dropping-out-of-the sky fashion as he is for those who don't know *Heilsgeschichte.*

It's important to be intentional in how we deal with disunity in the Bible. Our strategy in solving this problem leads us to our ethics. Knowing how others address the problem helps us understand and appreciate them better. The assumptions and presuppositions we bring to the Bible determine what the Bible says to us.

---

6   Guy F. Hershberger, *War, Peace and Nonresistance* (Scottdale, PA, Herald, 1969).

Model *Heilsgeschichte*

By Marion Bontrager

Creation and Fall: Problem Defined

In the beginning God created order out of chaos with the spoken word *dabar* and declared the creation very good. But sin enters into the world through the first humans. Sin breaks the relationships with us and God, us and others, us with our self and us with all creation. This is expressed through four fall or sin stories. The first is the garden fall story of Adam and Eve where they want to be equal with God by eating the forbidden fruit resulting in the broken relationships. The second story is about violence where Cain kills his brother Abel. The third story is also about violence where the earth was full of violence. God sends a flood to cleanse the earth but saved Noah and his family and some animals. The fourth story is about pride in which humans try to build a tower that reaches above the dome where God dwelt. The first and last stories are about pride and the middle two are about violence.

The creation and fall stories set the stage for the dynamic salvation history story where God seeks to solve the broken relationships that sin causes by creating a chosen covenant shalom people out of all peoples. Throughout *Heilsgeschichte* we ask three questions: What is the problem? What is God doing to solve the sin problem? How faithfully are God's people cooperating?

Patriarchs and Matriarchs (2000-1700 BCE): Solution Promised

God seeks to solve the sin problem by creating a chosen covenant shalom people where all the relationships are healed. God prepares and promises the solution by choosing the Patriarchs and Matriarchs to begin this mission to all peoples in the world and the creation. The four major Patriarchs and Matriarchs are Abraham and Sarah, Isaac and Rebekah, Jacob, Leah and Rachel and Joseph and Asenath.

There are three main themes in these stories: (1) Chosen, which means chosen for a mission, not God's favorite people. (2) Covenant, which creates a relationship between God and the people. And (3) Providence in which God intervenes in the stories to keep the story going. Two crucial words if misunderstood will warp how one reads the whole Bible including world politics today. Chosen means chosen for a mission, not favorite. "Nation" means "people" the way we refer to native American tribes such as the Cherokee Nation, which does not refer to a geographic nation-state place, but a people.

Joseph, the favorite son of Jacob, is sold into slavery into Egypt by his jealous brothers. He lands in jail in Egypt but God providentially blesses Joseph and he rises to power as an Egyptian ruler who prepares for the coming famine. His brothers, also facing famine, come to Egypt where Joseph forgives them and gives them food. The family moves to Egypt.

Exodus-Sinai—Crisis 1 (1280 BCE): Old Solution Begun

The Israelites (Jacob's name becomes Israel) multiply in Egypt and are enslaved by a Pharaoh who doesn't know the Joseph story. They keep multiplying. The Pharaoh attempts to have all the boy babies killed but Moses is saved by his mother and adopted by a daughter of Pharaoh. He grows up in the palace but he identifies with his oppressed people. One day he kills an Egyptian beating an Israelite slave. So Moses has to flee to the desert. While herding sheep for his father in law he sees a bush that isn't being consumed. A voice tells him to go back to Egypt to lead the slaves to freedom. When Moses asks who is speaking, the voice says "I am that I am," which means that God is actively present in the world. (It is translated YHWH, or Yahweh.) So Moses goes back to Egypt and asks Pharaoh to let the slave people go. But God hardens Pharaoh's heart and he refuses. Then Yahweh sends ten plagues on Egypt, each one worse than the other. Finally Yahweh lets the slaves go after the plague of the first born son's death in all the Egyptian families. These plagues are the "Terror of the Lord" as

Yahweh fights for the slaves. A mixed crowd follows the Israelites out of Egypt to the Red Sea. Then Pharaoh changes his mind and sends his army after them. The people complain to Moses that he brought them to the wilderness to die. Moses tells the people to "stand still and see the salvation (deliverance) of the Lord because the Egyptians they see today they won't see anymore." So the people stand still trusting Yahweh. Yahweh parts the waters and the people cross. When Pharaoh's army tries to go through the sea, Yahweh brings the waters together and the army drowns. This is the "Terror of the Lord" and the original model of Holy War when the people trust Yahweh to fight for them. Miriam leads the people in a song and dance celebrating God's deliverance.

Moses leads the people to Mt. Sinai where he meets Yahweh on the mountain. Yahweh makes a covenant we call the Eleven Words. The first word is the word of Yahweh's prior grace, "I am the Lord who brought you out of the land of Egypt." That is the *haggadah*, followed by ten commands called the *halakhah*. The laws were to teach them how to live together peacefully as the missionary community that reveals God to the whole world.

The Exodus Sinai event is the Old People of God's formative salvation event in which a mixed crowd of ex-slaves are formed into a community (nation) through a common experience. The Sinai covenant creates the chosen covenant shalom community, a priestly people chosen to be God's missionary people to all peoples in the world. This community is the solution to the sin problem. Yahweh becomes their king which is called a theocracy. The Exodus Sinai salvation event is referred to again and again in the Old Testament as Yahweh's miraculous deliverance.

Wilderness Wanderings

Moses leads the people through the wilderness where Yahweh provides manna and water for their survival. God got the people out of Egypt, but now must get "Egypt" out of the people. Some Midianite/Kenite people joined the freed slaves including Moses's father in law, Jethro, who was a Midianite priest. When they get to Kadesh on the edge of Canaan, Moses sends 12 spies into the land. They come back with glowing stories about the fertile land. Ten said they could not go in because there are giants in the land. But Joshua and Caleb said that Yahweh would fight Holy War and give the land to them. The people believed the ten and continued to complain. God said that those who were twenty years old and older would die in the wilderness. Moses is a faithful leader but dies on Mt Pisgah where he could look into the promised land but not enter.

These young in the faith ex-slaves needed to learn four things:

1. They had to learn how to trust God. God provided manna and water for them in the wilderness.
2. They had to learn how to worship. The tabernacle was where the Sinai Covenant was kept in the Ark (box) of the Covenant. Manna was also kept there to remind them what Yahweh had done for them. Their worship was to remember God's grace, give thanks and rededicate themselves to be the chosen covenant shalom community.
3. Even Moses had to learn servant leadership. What they had known in Egypt was brutal leadership. Moses learned how to delegate from his father-in-law Jethro. He learned how to lead the people without coercion.
4. They had to learn how to be a theocratic shalom missionary community. The Eleven Words and the Jubilee system continued to teach them how to be a shalom community devoted to people's needs.

Conquest, Infiltration, Revolution (1240)

Joshua leads the people to the Jordan River. God again parts the water to let them cross. Joshua sets up a monument of twelve stones, one for each tribe so the people will remember to tell the story of what Yahweh had done for them. The third commandment after loving God and neighbor is to tell the story to their children.

In the land the wilderness people (conquest) meet distant relatives who had infiltrated into the southern part of Canaan before the Egyptian enslavement (infiltration). The conquest people were also joined by the Habiru, marginal and enslaved people of Canaan (revolution). Joshua takes the three groups to Shechem where he tells *Heilsgeschichte* up to date and asks them who they will serve. They make in a covenant with Yahweh. The story and covenant is new for the two groups but a re-covenant for the Wilderness tribes.

The people attempt to drive out the Canaanites but were not totally successful. The history reason was because the Canaanites had weapons of iron and the Israelites only bronze. There were two *Geschichte* reasons why they couldn't drive out all the people. Because the people were unfaithful, Yahweh didn't fight Holy War for them, and Yahweh left Canaanites in the land to test them.

Tribal Confederacy and Judges—Crisis 2 Syncretism (1200 BCE)

The second crisis is religious syncretism with Baal worship. Syncretism is the gradual mixing of two religions. Baal was a term for a variety of gods/idols and was responsible for the fertility of land and animals. This religion was attractive because the wilderness tribes had to learn how to farm from the Canaanites. Some of the judges who tried to stop the syncretism were Gideon, Deborah, Jephthah and Samuel.

This part of the story is written in deuteronomistic cycles of six elements. First, the people are unfaithful and combine Baal worship with Yahweh. Second, Yahweh's judgment allows them to be oppressed by their neighboring people. Third, the people cry out to God. Fourth, God raises up a judge to lead them out of their oppression. Fifth, while the judge lives, the people are more faithful. Sixth, when the judge dies the people relapse and the cycle begins again. The solution is not working well!.

The tribal confederacy story ends with moral decline stories about Eli and Samuel's sons and the rape of a Levite's concubine. But nevertheless, the people were still a theocracy with Yahweh as their king, and not a nation-state, an amazing reality.

United Monarchy—Crisis 3 (1020 BCE)

Samuel was the last judge but also a prophet and kind of priest. With the moral decline and the Philistines defeating them, the people asked Samuel to anoint a king who would fight their battles for them. Samuel objected saying that Yahweh was their king. But the people insisted. So Yahweh told Samuel to anoint a king for them but to warn them that a king would tax and oppress them. Yahweh said that when the king oppresses them and they cry out, he will not answer them! Theocracy is God's ultimate will and monarchy is God's remedial will.

Becoming a nation-state with a king established geographical and political boxes around God and the people of God. Yahweh is no longer the God of all the earth but is limited to the political and geographical boundaries of the nation-state Israel. Yahweh's now becomes a national god. The people are being very unfaithful to their chosenness to be God's missionary people to all the peoples of the world.

Samuel anoints Saul, the first king who lives in a humble dwelling, doesn't have a large harem and leads in some battle victories. But he breaks the rules of Holy War and takes on religious leadership by offering a sacrifice. Samuel rejects him. Samuel commits treason and anoints David king while Saul is still king! David is very popular and successful in wars. He moves the capital to Jerusalem and builds a palace. He promotes the arts. But he breaks the rules of Holy War by committing adultery with Bathsheba during wartime and has her husband killed. Nathan the prophet confronts David and he repents.

Solomon is the third king who expands the nation state of Israel to a regional political power. He builds an opulent Temple. But Solomon marries foreign wives with their religions and has a huge harem that requires heavy taxes. He also uses forced labor for his building projects. His misuse of power leads to the division of the kingdom after his death. Each of the kings misused power that led to more injustices. Yahweh had led the people out of slavery in Egypt but by the time of Solomon, they were back into a slavery of their own making. They were hardly a chosen shalom missionary community.

With the rise of kings comes the rise of prophets who try to keep the kings in check. They preach against the oppression of the poor and religious syncretism. The prophets tell the story and keep the theocracy vision alive.

Division of the Kingdom— Crisis 4 (922 BCE)

Jeroboam is in charge of Solomon's forced labor. He makes friends among the workers. The prophet Ahijah wearing a new robe meets Jeroboam and acts out a prophecy by tearing his robe into 12 pieces and gives 10 to Jeroboam, essentially proclaiming he will be king of the Northern tribes. Solomon hears of this and tries to kill Jeroboam who flees to Egypt where Pharaoh Shishak gives him political asylum.

Solomon dies and his son Rehoboam goes to Shechem to be enthroned king. Jeroboam hears of this and returns. He and his supporters ask Rehoboam what kind of a king he is going to be. Will he be like his father or will he lighten the load on the people? Rehoboam's older advisors advise him to lighten the taxes and lessen the people's load. Rehoboam doesn't like that so he goes to his younger advisors who had grown up in the palace. They said to make the people's load heavier.

Rehoboam returns to Jeroboam and the people and says that his father disciplined them with whips but he will discipline them with scorpions. Jeroboam and the northern people answered him with, "What share do we have with David? To your tents, O Israel" (I Kings 12:16). The division between the northern ten tribes and the two tribes in the south couldn't be stopped.

The *Geschichte* reason for the division is Ahijah's prophecy. The history reason is that Rehoboam listened to his young advisors and refused to listen to the request of the northern tribes. The *Geschichte* reason why the division succeeded was because the prophet Shemaiah told Rehoboam not to attack his brothers. The history reason was because Pharaoh Shishak was attacking Judah from the south and Rehoboam couldn't fight a battle on two fronts.

The Northern Kingdom is called Israel or house of Joseph and the Southern Kingdom is called Judah or house of David. The unfaithfulness of kings led to the final division. Now the two kingdoms would sometimes fight each other and other times be allies. This is a long way from being the chosen-for-a- mission, shalom community.

Israel and the Fall to Assyria—Crisis 5 (722 BCE)

Jeroboam had to establish the kingdom in the north. The southern writers accused Israel's kings and kingdom of three things; they didn't have kings in the line of David, didn't have priests in the line of Levi, and didn't have the Temple in Jerusalem. To avoid the people going to Jerusalem Jeroboam set up two worship centers at Dan and Bethel that pictured Yahweh above a bull. But the people began to worship the bulls instead of Yahweh above the bull which led to more syncretism.

There were four dynasties in the north (Jeroboam was the first). Omri starts the next dynasty; he moves the capital to Samaria. His son Ahab is pictured as the most evil king who is influenced by his Phoenician wife Jezebel, a strong promoter of Baal worship. Jehu begins the next dynasty. He kills all of Ahab's family and Baal prophets. The prophets are conflicted about whether this was good or bad. Jeroboam II begins the last dynasty; he brings back prosperity to Israel. But after his reign the kingdom declines ending up falling to Assyrian in 722 BCE.

Kings are not respected in the North as in Judah because there the theocracy vision is still alive. So there are a number of coups in the north and the story of Israel is more about the prophets than the kings. Amos and

Hosea are two writing prophets in the north. Amos thundered against both personal and social injustice sins. Hosea pleaded with the people to come back to God. The non-writing prophet Elijah defeats the prophets of Baal on Mt Carmel when Yahweh sends fire to burn up his offering and altar. The second non-writing prophet, Elisha, roams beyond Israel, even anointing a king in Syria. He led in a nonviolent Holy War when the Assyrians raided Israel.

The Assyrian leader Shalmaneser led the attack on Israel that was finished by Sargon 2 who laid a three- year siege around the capital Samaria. The Assyrians conquered israel in 722 BCE and to weaken Israelite faith and culture, they deporting nearly half of the Israelites and brought in the same number of foreigners. These people intermarried and their children were called Samaritans, a people group despised during the time of Jesus. .

Judah's Fall and Exile to Babyloniaia—Crisis 6 (587 BCE)

Judah interprets the fall of Israel as God's judgment and their survival as a sign that they were more righteous so God spared them. The historic reasons why Judah didn't fall when Israel did are that Judah's King Ahaz paid off the Assyrians and Sargon had to return home to deal with crises there. The *Geschichte* reason was that it was because they had kings in the line of David, priests in the line of Levi and the Temple in Jerusalem.

Judah had both good and evil kings, but they were all in one dynasty in the line of David. Some were just as evil as any Northern king. Manasseh was one of the most evil, placing altars and symbols of Baal and other gods in the Temple. He even sacrificed his own son to a god. Manasseh is seen as the reason Jerusalem was destroyed and exiled. Judah's best king was Josiah who cleansed the Temple of foreign gods when the book of the law was found. He repented for the people and led in a religious reform. During his reign the Egyptian Pharaoh Necho sends his army along the coast northward to battle Assyria. Josiah attempts to cut him off at the Megiddo pass, but is killed in the battle. Now Judah becomes a vassal to Egypt. So now as Egypt goes politically so goes Judah.

The Babyloniaians defeat the Assyrians, so when the Egyptians go northward, they fight Babyloniaia instead of Assyria. They lose to Babyloniaia in the battle of Carchemish. So now Egypt and Judah become a vassal to the Babyloniaians. They both have to pay annual tribute to them.

Judah's kings were puppet kings serving under Babylonia. They had religious freedom but they were not independent. After a while Judah's puppet king Jehoiakim revolted against Babylonia. The Babyloniaian army attacked and Jehoiakim died during the battle. His son Jehoiachin became king and was defeated and taken to Babylonia with 10,000 of the leading citizens. What made these puppet kings revolt against such great odds? They remembered Holy War stories when Yahweh miraculously saved Jerusalem when they were attacked. In addition they trusted in the Davidic unconditional covenant (there will always be a king in the line of David). They felt invincible.

Years later the last king in Judah, Zedekiah, also revolted against Babylonia even though the prophet Jeremiah told him not to. Patience at an end, King Nebuchadnezzar laid siege to Jerusalem. He destroyed the city, Temple and walls, killing thousands. The last thing Zedekiah saw was all his sons being killed and then they blinded him. They took apx. 99% of the population to Babylonia along with their blind king.

The Judah people had lost everything--their land, king and Temple. The city and Temple lay in rubble. Where was Yahweh and his promises? This was the crisis of crises. But the gift of the exile was that Yahweh smashed apart the nation-state and geographic boxes. It was the worst of times but also a new opportunity for the people to be faithful to Yahweh's choosing them to be a missionary people to all people groups in the world.

Exile and Adaptations in Babylonia

We have said that the prophets afflicted the comfortable and comforted the afflicted. With the people's unfaithfulness, suffering, questions and crisis, the prophets Jeremiah and II Isaiah speak comforting and hopeful words to the people.

Will Yahweh faith survive? The crisis raised critical faith questions. "Has Yahweh abandoned us?" The prophets said, "No,.the people have abandoned Yahweh." "Is Marduk greater than Yahweh since he won the battle?" "No," said the prophet, "Yahweh fought with Marduk against his own people." "Does Yahweh keep covenants?" "Yes," said the prophets, "Yahweh keeps both his unconditional and conditional covenants. The people have not kept their covenant with Yahweh." "How can we worship in a foreign country?" The prophet Ezekiel had a vision in which he saw God's throne on a platform with wheels. The wheels went in all four directions meaning that Yahweh is present everywhere. Yahweh is not in a national or geographic box.

To keep their identity alive, leaders gathered and edited stories of salvation history together during the exile. They moved from altar-centered worship to book-centered worship. They moved from Temple-centered worship to worship in synagogues. With book-centered worship, the scribes become the main leaders who copied the scriptures and interpreted them and without altar sacrifices, the role of the priests diminishes. Their name also changed from Israelites to Jews since they came from Judah.

Some theological faith changes also happened. They moved from henotheism to monotheism. Through contact with Zoroastrianism, they were introduced to cosmic dualism in which the world is the battleground between God and Satan. Satan now becomes the source of evil and suffering.

Return From Exile—Crisis 7 Ethnocentrism (538 BCE)

The Persians conquer Babylonia. The Persian King Cyrus changes policies including more religious freedom and allows captured people to return to their homelands if they wished. The biblical writers refer to him as a messiah for allowing them to return to Jerusalem.

About 25% of the Jews return to Jerusalem in four groups. Sheshbazzar leads the first group and lays the Temple foundation. Zerubbabel leads the second group and builds the Temple. Ezra leads in a religious revival and re-covenanting with Yahweh. Nehemiah leads in rebuilding the city walls. Ezra sees that some of the men had married women of the land. Ezra made the men promise to send their wives and children away since they were not of Jewish blood. Ezra dramatically laments these intermarriages by throwing himself down in front of the Temple and pulling out his hair. Nehemiah goes further and beats the men who had married the women of the land.

Ezra had some legitimate concerns about intermarriages. In Israel's history, syncretism came into Israel through intermarriage. But Ezra asks the wrong question. As people chosen to show God's love to all people, they should have asked, "Are you willing to follow Yahweh?" instead of "What is your ethnicity?"

The non-Jewish women could adopt the Yahweh faith, but they could not change their ethnicity. Yahweh had smashed apart the boxes of nation-state and geography, but now Ezra puts up a new box: ethnocentrism. This ethnocentrism was still strong in the time of Jesus.

The book of Jonah can serve as a sermon challenging the ethnocentric box. As an allegory, Jonah is Judah, the big fish is Babylonia, the 3 days inside the fish is the exile, getting spit out is the return from exile and

Nineveh equals all people groups (including enemies) who aren't part of God's people. Jonah is called for a mission to proclaim God's message to the people of Nineveh (Assyrians). But Jonah doesn't want these people to be saved from destruction. So thinking God is a geographic god, he goes to the sea to get away from God.

But surprise, God is present even in the sea. When the storm comes, the sailors sacrifice everything to save the ship and Jonah. Ironically the pagan sailors cared more for one man's life than Jonah did for a whole city of people! Finally at Jonah's instigation they throw him overboard. But in God's grace a fish swallows Jonah. God's compassion for the unfaithful Jonah saves Jonah from his own destruction. Is this beginning to sound like Judah being swallowed by the Babyloniaians because of their unfaithfulness to their chosenness?

Jonah prays in the belly of the fish. And then the fish spits him out giving him another chance to be faithful and go to Nineveh. He does go but reluctantly hopes that the people won't repent and be destroyed! But the people do repent in contrast to Jonah --another irony. And God saves these Assyrian people!

Jonah is angry with God for extending grace to the enemy Ninevehites. He doesn't "love kindness." Judah is similar, when they put up the new box of ethnocentrism.

Intertestamental Times—Crisis 8 Hellenism (333 BCE)

Alexander the Great, a Greek leader, conquers much of the then known world and spreads Greek Hellenistic thought with his armies. But he dies suddenly ten years later. His empire is divided among his generals. Two of his generals deal with the Jews who live in Palestine. The Ptolemies who also rule North Africa are the first rulers of Palestine. They are tolerant of the Jews and their religion.

But the Seleucids who rule Asia Minor gain control over Palestine. They impose Hellenism, which is Greek thought, religion, culture and worldview, on the Jews and outlaw Judaism. The worst of the Seleucid rulers is Antiochus IV who imposes the death penalty for circumcision, keeping the sabbath and carrying a Torah. He arrogantly desecrates the Temple by sacrificing a pig on the Temple altar to the Greek god Zeus. The Jews are outraged which leads to revolts, although some compromised.

Mattathias and his five sons lead a revolt in 167 BCE and are fairly successful with a guerilla war strategy. They are able to gain semi-independence and have control over the Temple. The Temple is cleansed and rededicated in 142 BCE with the feasts of lights which is celebrated today as Hanukkah. This semi-independence lasts until 63 BCE.

Two visions emerge among the Jewish people. The Hasmonean (Maccabean family and descendants) vision is to create a nation-state with the goal of complete political freedom. This group produces the Zealots and Sadducees. In contrast, the Hasidim seek to recreate a separate, holy people who do not compromise. Their only goal is religious freedom. They produce the Pharisees and Essenes.

Two Hasmonean brothers compete for the the Jewish throne. They both appeal to the Roman General Pompey for support. He seizes the opportunity. In 63 BCE he attacks Jerusalem, slaughters 12,000 Jews and begins the 700 years of Roman rule.

Christ-Pentecost—Crisis 9 (30 CE): Solution Accomplished

Jesus is born in 4 BCE in Bethlehem. King Herod is threatened by the word that a new king is born and kills the baby boys in Bethlehem. Mary, Joseph and Jesus escape to Egypt. They return and Jesus grows up in Nazareth of Galilee. Jesus is baptized in the Jordan River by John the Baptist. Here he is ordained as servant-king. At his baptism the Spirit comes on him and a voice says, "This is my beloved son in whom I am well pleased." This was the empowerment for his ministry and mission.

Jesus goes into the desert to reflect on his baptism and how he will do his mission. He is tempted with three alternative ways to establish his kingdom. The first temptation is to turn stones into bread that could feed people who would then follow him because of what they gain from Jesus. Jesus faced this temptation after he fed the 5000 and the people came to make him king. The second temptation was to jump down from the highest point in the Temple and have angels miraculously catch him so he wouldn't be hurt. This would gain him a following also. Jesus faced this temptation when he rode into Jerusalem and entered the Temple with the crowds on his back. The people would follow him as a super human Messiah. The third temptation was to worship Satan and become a military Messiah, establish his kingdom by force and rule the whole world. He faced this temptation in the Garden when he was betrayed. He rebuked Peter to put up his sword. "Don't you know I could call 10,000 angels..." all of these temptations would have help jesus avoid the cross; all of them would have brought shalom in a non-shalom way. But Jesus rejected them all and went about establishing his mission through teaching and healing.

Jesus also faced different expectations about what the Messiah would be and do. The Pharisees wanted a new Moses and lawgiver. The Sadducees wanted a Temple Messiah. The Zealots wanted a military Messiah. And the Essenes wanted an apocalyptic Messiah who would end history and establish the eternal kingdom. Jesus pleased none of them.

Jesus begins his ministry by choosing twelve diverse disciples alluding to the twelve tribes. He would teach these and other disciples. Jesus meets in the synagogue at Nazareth and challenges ethnocentrism by citing two examples when God was gracious to non-Israelites.Because of these two stories, they tried to throw him off a cliff. Why, because Jesus challenges their ethnocentrism and became angry when God showed grace to non-Israelites!

Jesus also quoted from the Old Testament in the synagogue when he described his ministry. He said that the Spirit of the Lord is on him to proclaim good news to the poor, recovery of sight to the blind, proclaim Jubilee. In the Sermon on the Mount Jesus challenges what Moses said before and says to love as God loves, even enemies. Jesus heals many and re-reveals the purpose of the law when he heals people on the Sabbath.

In the last week Jesus rides into Jerusalem on a donkey, enters the Temple where he teaches and throws out the money changers and those selling animals for sacrifice. Jesus keeps Passover (Last Supper) with his disciples and washes his disciples' feet. He goes to the Garden of Gethsemane to pray. Judas betrays him. Peter tries to defend him with the sword. Jesus rebukes him. He is taken to the High Priest and to Pilate. He is beaten and ultimately crucified as a political insurrectionist along with two other men. Why did Judas betray Jesus? A guess is as a former Zealot, he tried to force Jesus to act and come out fighting to establish his kingdom violently since he had the crowds on his side. When he saw that Jesus would not act but be killed, he killed himself in remorse.

Jesus was crucified, buried and resurrected on the third day. But why was Jesus killed?

From a history view it did not take any faith to see that if Jesus went to Jerusalem and challenged the religious and political leaders, he would get killed if he was nonviolent and didn't fight back. Jesus threatened both the Jewish religious leaders and the Roman political leaders who worked together to kill the nonviolent Jesus in order to hold their positions.

From a *Geschichte* interpretation, Jesus exposed the evilness of Satan and the evil powers when they killed an innocent person. And Jesus revealed his Father's love and forgiveness which we can trust because Jesus loved and forgave sins in his last breath on the cross. And in his resurrection he overcame the most feared and powerful power—death. Humans can claim forgiveness of sin and resurrection from the dead through Jesus' life, death and resurrection.

Jesus appeared to the disciples after his resurrection. After three years of intensive training, they still didn't understand the nature of Jesus' kingdom. Just before Jesus ascends, they ask him whether he is now going to restore the nation-state of Israel! This reveals how deep the Jewish nationalism was even among Jesus' followers and how difficult it was to grasp the nature of Jesus' kingdom. Two disciples on the road to Emmaus said, "We hoped that he was the one to redeem Israel."

Pentecost (50 days after Passover)

Jesus told the disciples to wait in Jerusalem for the Spirit to come and then they will be witnesses in Judea, Samaria and to the ends of the earth. 120 disciples waited for the day of Pentecost. When the Holy Spirit came on them, it was like a strong wind and fire. This was the formative event for the Church. Wind parted the Red Sea and a pillar of fire guided the slaves at the formative event for the Old People of God. The 120 speak in different languages.

A crowd gathers. They are diaspora Jews who had come from all over the Middle East for Pentecost. They were all Jews but spoke different languages. When the disciples spoke in tongues, they all understood. The Tower of Babel event was reversed! Peter preached to the crowd from parts of Salvation History and then connected Jesus to it. They were deeply convicted and 3000 were baptized. This was the beginning of the New Creation called the Church.

The religious leaders attempt to stop the Jesus movement but couldn't. Stephen is a deacon in the church and is persecuted. Before he is stoned, he tells *Heilsgeschichte* and includes Jesus the Messiah. The gospel spreads to Samaria. Then Peter sees a vision on a rooftop in which a sheet with many different kinds of animals in it is lowered. A voice says, "Rise, kill and eat." But Peter says he never ate anything unclean. This happened three times. Soon messengers come to Peter from Cornelius, a Roman centurion and Gentile Godfearer, asking Peter to see Cornelius. Peter goes to Cornelius' house and tells the whole household about Jesus. The Spirit falls on all of them and Peter baptizes them. Peter says that he now knows that God shows no partiality but anyone from any race can become a member of God's people. The Gospel has spread from diaspora Jews to Samaritans and now to Gentiles.

Saul, a devout Jewish leader, tried to stop the Jesus movement. He was present when Stephen was stoned. On his way to Damascus to persecute Christians, a great light knocked him off of his horse and a voice said, "Saul, why do you persecute me?" Here Saul meets the resurrected Jesus. Saul is blinded but gets his sight back when Ananias prays for him in the city. His name is changed to Paul. He preaches the gospel, especially to Gentiles, and starts churches. The church spreads among both Jewish and Gentile people.

Jerusalem Conference—Crisis 10 (49 CE): Solution Realized

The church grew because all kinds of people were welcome and baptized; Jews, Gentiles, men, women, slaves, free, educated and uneducated. Conservative Judaizers argued that Gentile men must be circumcised, or in other words become Jewish, to become members of the church. So a conference is called in Jerusalem to deal with this issue.

Peter, Paul and James argue for the new reality that Jesus is Lord of the church and nothing else. The other agree that no circumcision is needed, The Church finally gets it right. Christ-Pentecost creates the New People of God and the Jerusalem Council confirms it.

The sin problem that God has been working to solve throughout *Heilsgeschichte* is now solved because now there truly is a People of God out of all Peoples. The broken relationships are restored in the church. Jews and Gentiles who despised each other are reconciled. God's mission is being realized! The Church is the Radical New Creation where Jesus and nothing else rules. They finally get it right.

Persecution and the Church Grows—Crisis 11 (60-313 CE)

Roman Emperor Nero orders persecution in the 60's. Christians flee to other places, spreading the gospel. The Church continued to grow despite or because of persecution when martyrs shared their testimonies and went to their deaths with joy. The phrase "The blood of the martyrs is the seed of the church" was true. Paul and others write letters and gospels to encourage the church. Jerusalem revolts in 66 CE and is destroyed by the Romans in 70 CE. A more severe persecution comes when Emperor Domitian requires emperor worship. All the Christians needed to do was say, "Caesar is Lord." But they refused to deny Jesus as Lord. Many were martyred for their faith.

In the first 100 years Jewish Christians met with fellow Jews in their synagogues on the Sabbath and then met with Christians on the first day of the week. In the early days of the church Jewish Christians were the majority. But by the end of the first century, there were more Gentile Christians. The Church and the Jewish community gradually drifted apart.

"Marriage" of Church and State—Crisis 12 (313-380 CE)

In 313 Emperor Constantine legalizes Christianity with the Edict of Milan. He favors the Christians.

Church and state, the cross and the sword, begin to merge. Until this time the Christian Church was not a legal religion and Christians were nonviolent, following a nonviolent Jesus and his teachings. But now Christians begin to serve in the Roman military. The church center becomes Rome, as the church and state continued to merge.

And in 380 CE Emperor Theodosius makes the Christianity the only legal state religion, the state church. This redefines what the church is. The formerly persecuted become the persecutors. The emperor, not Jesus, becomes Lord. The nation-state and geography boxes around God and the people of God are recreated. Church membership is no longer voluntary. The church identifies with wealth and power and now uses violence. A form of Christianity is imposed from the top down by military conquest of countries.

The state benefits from this as the church blesses its violence. The church benefits as the state enforces its beliefs and ethics. Even church leaders support persecution for religious heretics!

Medieval Era (400s-1500s CE)

Monasticism, the religious orders of monks and nuns, seeks to bring renewal but it creates two levels of ethics in the church. Mohammed is born in 570 CE. He begins Islam and it spreads into parts of eastern Europe. It spreads westward resulting in the Battle of Tours (France) in which the Christian army defeats the Muslim army keeping Europe Christian.

Church and state struggle for the greater power. In 800 CE, Pope Leo III crowns the Emperor Charlemagne. This means that if the Pope puts the crown on the head of the emperor, he can also take it off! The church becomes increasingly wealthy and corrupt.

In 1054 CE the western Roman Catholic Church and Eastern Orthodox Church divide, a schism that continues to this day. And in 1095 the Crusades begin against the Muslims, Orthodox Christians and Jews of the Middle East. Fueled by greed, their stated goal was to reclaim the Holy Land for the Church. These violent bloody pillaging crusades are still remembered by Muslims today.

Renaissance (1300s-1500s CE)

Muslim scholars bring to the west their genius in science, math and literature, sparking a rebirth of classical learning, art and literature. The invention of the moveable printing press by Gutenberg in about 1400 BCE revolutionized communication, fueling the Renaissance. The Bible and other books became affordable and ideas spread rapidly as literacy increased.

Reformation Era (1500s CE)

- Lutheran Reformation: In 1517 in Wittenberg, Germany, Martin Luther posted his 95 theses against indulgences challenging the Roman Catholic Church and sparking the Protestant Reformation. His church reforms were supported by some German princes and growing German nationalism against Rome. The Lutheran Church retained the church-state union and is still the state church in some European countries today.
- Reformed Reformation: In 1519 Ulrich Zwingli leads the reformation in Switzerland resulting in the Reformed Church that spread throughout western Europe. It was also still a state church.
- Anabaptists (rebaptizers) were more radical in their call to reform the church. Some of Zwingli's followers, unhappy with his compromises, decide to baptize each other on January 21, 1525, creating the first free church. They are free from state control, breaking the thousand-year old union of church and state. Conrad Grebel, Felix Manz, and George Blaurock were three of the early leaders.
- Anabaptist Christian Emphases: They separate church and state. They refuse military service, practicing the nonviolence and peacemaking. Church is a voluntary community, where they baptize only adult believers who freely choose to join. They seek to create a radical new creation where Jesus is Lord separate from the state. Like the early church and some renewal movements throughout

church history, they were persecuted, by both Catholics and Protestants. They were called Swiss Brethren and are the spiritual ancestors of the Amish, Hutterites and Mennonites throughout the world today.

- In 1536 Menno Simons, a Catholic priest in the Netherlands, became an Anabaptist and the leader of Anabaptists in North Germany and the Netherlands. So those Anabaptists were called Mennonites.
- 17th-20th centuries: The European Mennonite Christians emigrated to Poland/Prussia, United States, Russia, Central Asia and then to North and South America after World War I and World War II. Mennonite missions throughout the world have resulted in over two million Anabaptist Christians today. There are many more Anabaptist Christians in the world today in Africa, Asia, and Central and South America than in Europe and North America.

And of course the story is not yet complete. Each generation writes its own chapter. What is your story?

Bibliography

"Interpretation of the Bible." Ronald Youngblood, ed. *Nelson's Illustrated Bible Dictionary.* Nashville: Thomas Nelson, 2014.

"The First Book of Maccabees." *The Apocrypha and Pseudepigrapha of the Old Testament, Vol I.* Oxford: Clarendon Press, 1963.

Adams, Sean A. "The Relationships of Paul and Luke: Luke, Paul's Letters and the 'We' Passages of Acts." Stanley Porter and Christopher Land, ed. *Paul and His Social Relations.* Leiden: Brill, 2013.

Anderson, Bernhard W., et al. *Understanding the Old Testament*, 5th ed. Upper Saddle River, NJ: Pearson Education, Inc., 2007.

Arnold, Bill T. *Introduction to the Old Testament.* New York: Cambridge University Press, 2014.

Augustine, *Quaestiones/ Evangeliorum//, II, 19.* Cited in Dodd, C.H., *The Parables of the Kingdom.* New York: Scribners, 1961.

Bailey, James and Lyle Vander Broek. *Literary Forms in the New Testament: A Handbook.* Louisville: Westminster/John Knox, 1992.

Bailey, Kenneth E. *Jesus through Middle Eastern Eyes: Cultural Studies in the Gospels.* Downers Grove: IVP Academic, 2008.

Barclay, William. *The Letters to the Galatians and Ephesians.* Lousiville: John Knox Press, 1958.

Barth, Karl. *Table Talk*, ed. John Godsey. Richmond: John Knox Press, 1962.

Bauckham, R.J. "Gospels (Apocryphal)." Joel B. Green, ed. *Dictionary of Jesus and the Gospels.* Downers Grove: InterVarsity Press, 1992.

Bausch, William J. *Storytelling: Imagination and Faith.* Princeton, NJ: Clear Face Publishing, LLC, 2015.

Bernard of Clairvaux. "Letter to Eastern France and Bavaria Promoting the Second Crusade, 1146." *Council of Centers on Jewish-Christian Relations*, Accessed June 22, 2016. www.ccjr.us.

Blosser, Don, et al., *Jesus: His Life and Times.* Lincolnwood, IL: Publications International, Ltd.

Boice, James Montgomery. *Foundations of the Christian Faith.* Downers Grove: InterVarsity Press, 1986.

Bonhoeffer, Dietrich. *Cost of Discipleship.* New York: Touchstone, 1995.

Boring, Eugene. *An Introduction to the New Testament: History, Literature, Theology.* Louisville: Westminster John Knox, 2012.

Bracke, John. *Jeremiah 30-52 and Lamentations.* Louisville: Westminster/ John Knox, 2000.

Breuggemann, Walter. *Prophetic Imagination.* Minneapolis: Fortress Press, 1978.

Breuggemann, Walter, *Prophetic Imagination.* Minneapolis: Augsburg Fortress, 1982.

Bruce, F.F. "Canon." Joel B. Green, et al. *Dictionary of Jesus and the Gospels,* edited by Joel B. Downers Grove: InterVarsity Press, 1992.

Burnett, Richard E. *Karl Barth's Theological Exegesis.* Grand Rapids: Eerdmans, 2004.

Chalmers, Aaron. *Exploring the Religion of Ancient Israel: Prophet, Priest, Sage and People.* Downers Grove: InterVaristy Press, 2012.

Charles, Howard H. "Why Study the New Testament." Lecture, Introduction to the New Testament Course, Associated Mennonite Biblical Seminaries, Elkhart, IN. 1962.

Clare, John. "The Crusades." Dr. Tim Dowly, ed. *Introduction to the History of Christianity.* Minneapolis: Fortress Press, 2002.

Cohn, Norman. *Cosmos, Chaos and the World to Come: The Ancient Roots of Apocalyptic Faith,* 2nd ed. New Haven: Yale University Press, 2001.

Driver, John. *Kingdom Citizens.* Scottdale, PA: Herald Press, 1980.

Elias, Jacob W. *Remember the Future: The Pastoral Theology of Paul the Apostle.* Scottdale, PA: Herald Press, 2006.

Fast Facts about American Religion, Hartford Institute for Religious Research, Hartford Seminary, http://hirr.hartsem.edu/research/fastfacts/fast_facts.html#denom. Accessed June 22, 2016.

Fee, Gordon and Douglas Stuart. *How to Read the Bible for All Its Worth.* Grand Rapids: Zondervan, 2003.

Freedman, Noel David, et al. "Corporate Personality." *Eerdmans Dictionary of the Bible.* Grand Rapids: Wm. B. Eerdmans Publishing Company, 2000.

Furcha, Edward J. and Ford Lewis Battles. *Selected Writings of Hans Denck: Edited and Translated from the text as established by Walter Fellmann.* Eugene, OR: Wipf and Stock Publishers, 1976.

Green, William Scott. "Introduction: Messiah in Judaism: Rethinking the Question." Jacob Neusner, ed. *Judaisms and their Messiahs at the Turn of the Christian Era.* Cambridge University Press, 1987).

Grimsrud, Ted. *Triumph of the Lamb.* Scottdale, PA: Herald Press, 1987.

Harris, Stephen L. *Understanding the Bible,* 3rd ed. Norway: Mayfield, 1992.

Hayes, Edward. "A Prayer Rug Introduction," in *Twelve and One-Half Keys.* Leavenworth, KS: Forest of Peace Books, Inc., 1981.

Hayes, John and Carl Holladay. *Biblical Exegesis: A Beginner's Handbook,* rev. ed. Louisville: Westminster John Knox, 1987.

Hengel, Martin. *The Zealots.* Edinburgh: T&T Clark, 1989.

Herezog, William R. II. *Jesus, Justice and the Reign of God: A Ministry of Liberation.* Louisville: Westminster John Knox Press, 2000.

Herodotus, *The Histories,* ii, 141, 5. A.D. Goodly, ed. Perseus Digital Library. Accessed June 22, 2016. http://www.perseus.tufts.edu/hopper/

Hershberger, Guy F. *War, Peace and Nonresistance.* Scottdale, PA, Herald, 1969.

Hoehner, H. W. "Herodian Dynasty." Joel B. Green, ed. *Dictionary of Jesus and the Gospels.* Downers Grove: InterVarsity Press, 1992.

Hurtado, L.W. "Gospel Genre." Joel B. Green, et al. *Dictionary of Jesus and the Gospels,* edited by Joel B. Downers Grove: InterVarsity Press, 1992.

Irenaeus, *Against Heresies* 3.21.2

Johnson, Luke Timothy. *Living Jesus: Learning the Heart of the Gospel.* San Francisco: Harpercollins Publishing, 1999.

Ketola, Kimmo. "A Cognitive Approach to Ritual Systems in First-Century Judaism." Petrii Luomanen, ed. *Explaining Christian Origins and Early Judaism*. Leiden: Brill, 2007.

Klassen, Walter, ed. *Anabaptism in Outline*. Scottdale, Pa.: Herald Press, 1981.

Korb, Scott. *Life in Year One: What the World Was Like in First-Century Palestine*. New York: Riverhead, 2010.

Kraus, Norman C. *Dispensationalism in America: It's Rise and Development*. Richmond: John Knox Press, 1958.

Kraybill, Donald. *The Upside-Down Kingdom*. 25th Anniversary ed. Scottdale, PA: Herald Press, 2003.

Lasor, William Sanford, et al. *Old Testament Survey: The Message, Form, and Background of the Old Testament*. Grand Rapids: William B. Eerdmann Publishing Company, 1996.

C.S. Lewis, "Learning in War-Time," in *The Weight of Glory: And Other Addresses*. New York: HarperCollins, 2001.

Lind, Millard C. *Yahweh is a Warrior: The Theology of Warfare in Ancient Israel*. Scottdale, PA: Herald Press, 1980.

Lowell, James Russell. "The Present Crisis." Bartleby.com. Accessed June 3, 2016. http://www.bartleby.com/42/805.html.

MacArthur, John. *The MacArthur Study Bible, New International Version*. Nashville: Thomas Nelson, 2013.

Metzger, Bruce M. *The Text of the New Testament*. New York & London: Oxford University Press, 1964.

Mounce, Robert H. *The Book of Revelation*, Revelation ed. Grand Rapids: Eerdmans, 1998.

Noll, Mark A. *Turning Points: Decisive Moments in the History of Christianity.* Grand Rapids: Baker Academic, 9th ed. 2008.

Pasachoff, Naomi and Robert Littman. *A Concise History of the Jewish People.* Lanham, MD.: Rowman and Littlefield, 1995.

Pate, C. Marvin, et al. *The Story of Israel: A Biblical Theology.* Downers Grove: InterVarsity Press, 2004.

Perdue, Leo G. *Interpretation: A Bible Commentary for Teaching and Preaching: Proverbs.* Louisville: John Knox Press, 2000.

Pew Research Center. "Religion & Public Life." Accessed June 22, 2016. http://www.pewforum.org/2015/04/02/religious-projections-2010-2050.

Poole, Gary William Poole. "Flavius Josephus," *Encyclopedia Britannica.* Accessed June 1, 2016. www.britannica.com.

Rajak, Tessa. *The Jewish Dialogue with Greece and Rome.* Boston: Leiden: Brill, 2002.

Richardson, Peter Richardson. *Herod: King of the Jews and Friend of the Romans.* Minneapolis: Fortress Press, 1999.

Roop, Eugene F. *Believers Church Commentary: Genesis.* Scottdale, PA: Herald Press, 1987.

Ruether, Rosemary Radford. *Faith and Fratricide: The Theological Roots of Anti-Semitism.* New York: Seabury Press, 1974.

Sacchi, Paolo. *The History of the Second Temple Period.* London & New York: T&T Clark, 2000.

Saldarini, Anthony. *Pharisees, Scribes and Sadducees in Palestinian Society.* Grand Rapids: Eerdmans, 1988.

Schiffman, Lawrence. "Messianism and Apocalypticism in Rabbinic Texts." Steven Katz, ed. *The Cambridge History of Judaism,* v. 4, ed. Cambridge University Press, 2006.

Schroeder, David. "The Scholar of the Bible." *Mennonite Life* 19, no. 2. April 1964.

Shirkov, Peter and Dr. Eli, Lizorkin-Eyzenberg. "Council of Jamnia and Old Testament Canon." *Jewish Studies Blog, Official Forum of Israel Institute of Biblical Studies.* Accessed June 2, 2016. http://jewishstudies.eteacherbiblical.com/jamnia/.

Sire, James W. *The Universe Next Door: A Basic Worldview Catalog,* 3rd ed. Downers Grove: InterVarsity Press, 1997.

Smith, G.V. "Prophet." *The International Standard Bible Encyclopedia,* ed. Geoffrey Bromiley, v. 3. Grand Rapids: Eerdmans, 1986.

Spencer, Aida Besancon. *Paul's Literary Style.* Lanham, MD: University Press, 1998.

Stegemann, Ekkehard and Wolfgang Stegemann. *The Jesus Movement: A Social History of its First Century.* Minneapolis: Fortress Press, 1999.

Steinberg, Rabbi Paul. "Celebrating the Jewish Year." *The Winter Holidays: Hanukkah, Tu B'shevat, Purim.* Philadelphia, PA: 2007.

Sumney, Jerry L. *The Bible: An Introduction.* Minneapolis: Fortress Press, 2010.

Tertullian, *Apology for the Christians. WM Reeve, AM. Trans. and Annotated.* The Ancient & Modern Library of Theological Literature, vol. 31.

Thomas, John Christopher and Frank Macchia, *Revelation.* Grand Rapids: Eerdmans, 2016.

Towner, W. Sibley. *Daniel. Interpretation, A Bible Commentary for Preaching and Teaching.* Atlanta: John Knox, 1984.

Wooten, R.W.F. "Translating the Bible." Dr. Tim Dowly, ed. *Introduction to the History of Christianity.* Minneapolis: Fortress Press, 2002.

Yoder, Perry B. *Shalom: The Bible's Word for Salvation, Justice, and Peace.* Newton KS: Faith and Life Press, 1987.

Yoder, Perry B. *Toward Understanding the Bible: Hermeneutics for Lay People.* Eugene, OR: Wipf and Stock Publishers, 2006.

Acknowledgments

Michele Hershberger

I want to thank Marion Bontrager, John Sharp, and other Bib Lit teachers for seeing the patterns, creating the timeline—finding a way to make the Bible a connected story for so many, including me. I also gained so much from countless faculty members at Hesston College who ministered with students as Bib Lit study group leaders. They cared for students, gave me advice, and helped me laugh at myself when things got crazy in class.

I'm grateful to Hesston College for supporting the unique Introduction to Biblical Literature class, Elaine Schmidt for her behind-the-scenes work, Justin Heinzekehr for help with research, and André Swartley for making this book happen.

My deepest gratitude, however, goes to my husband Del, who reminds me that I am loved, whether the writing's going well or not.

John E. Sharp

The Bible as story became real to me in childhood. Before I could read, my parents read to me the stories of the Bible and from church papers, such as the Youth's Christian Companion. I am grateful for this introduction to the printed page. My thanks also to two of my six siblings, Alta Edwards and Urie Sharp, who entertained me with stories from their creative imaginations. They demonstrated the power of story and instilled in me a passion for storytelling.

I also thank my teachers and mentors at Belleville Mennonite School, Rosedale Bible Institute, Hesston College, Goshen College, and Anabaptist Mennonite Biblical Seminary. The Bible became richer, fuller and deeper through their instruction.

I'm grateful to Marion Bontrager, Elam Peachey, and Mark Yoder who brought me to Hesston College to teach in 2005. A long-time friend, Marion became my teaching colleague. As he retired he relinquished to me Bib Lit and other Bible courses.

In recent years, it's been my privilege to team with Michele Hershberger in teaching Bib Lit. Her serious scholarship and her contagious enthusiasm for the Bible continue to inspire me. I'm grateful also for my students who constantly challenge and stretch me in the classroom and beyond.

My thanks also to the administration for supporting this project, to Justin Heinzekehr for his helpful critique, and to André Swartley, who shepherded this book to its completion.

I also thank my children—Erin and Alex, M.J., Laura and Nick—for their support and for rounding out my worldview. Finally, as always, I thank my wife Michele Miller Sharp, companion in life and learning for her continued affirmation and support.

CPSIA information can be obtained at www.ICGtesting.com
Printed in the USA
LVOW10s0725210916

505329LV00004B/5/P